Distribution of personal wealth
in Britain

A.B. ATKINSON
Professor of Political Economy
University College London

A.J. HARRISON
Assistant Professor of Economics
McMaster University
Hamilton, Ontario

CAMBRIDGE UNIVERSITY PRESS

CAMBRIDGE

LONDON·NEW YORK·MELBOURNE

Published by the Syndics of the Cambridge University Press
The Pitt Building, Trumpington Street, Cambridge CB2 1RP
Bentley House, 200 Euston Road, London NW1 2DB
32 East 57th Street, New York, NY 10022, USA
296 Beaconsfield Parade, Middle Park, Melbourne 3206, Australia

First published 1978

Printed in Great Britain at
the Alden Press Oxford London and Northampton

Library of Congress Cataloguing in Publication Data

Atkinson, Anthony Barnes.
Distribution of personal wealth in Britain.

Includes bibliographical references and index.
1. Wealth–Great Britain. I. Harrison, Alan James,
1947-   joint author. II. Title.
HC260.W4A83   330.1'6   77-2715
ISBN 0 521 21735 0

CONTENTS

*These sections are more technical – see page 16.

LIST OF TABLES

LIST OF FIGURES

SYMBOLS AND NOTATION

The choice of notation posed a number of problems and the authors would like to apologise in advance for the infelicities which remain: for example, that in certain cases the same symbol is used with different meanings in different chapters. The problems stemmed first from our wanting to use more symbols than can be accommodated by the Latin and Greek alphabets, and second from the fact that the book draws on a number of different areas of economics, each with its accustomed notation (for instance, f is the typically preferred choice both for frequencies and for production functions).

We have given below for convenience a list of the main symbols in order of appearance in the text (not the appendices). Those which are used elsewhere with a different meaning are marked with an asterisk at the end of the definition.

Chapter 2

w wealth (w_{ai} is average wealth of person in age class a and size class i, $\bar{w}$ is overall mean wealth)

n number of estates (n_{ai} is the number of persons in age class a and size class i)*

P population (P_a is number in age class a)

N total deaths (N_a is number in age class a)*

m multiplier (m_{ai} is multiplier applied to age class a and size class i)

λ social class differential applied to multiplier (λ_{ai} applies to age class a and size class i)*

W total wealth (W_i is total wealth in size class i)*

$F_j, F(w)$ proportion of population in size classes j and below, with wealth w and below

$f_j, f(w)$ frequency in size class j (as proportion of population), with wealth w

$L_j, L(w)$ share of size classes j and below in total wealth, with wealth w and below

α Pareto exponent

B constant in formula for Pareto distribution[*]

$\underline{w}$ lowest wealth covered by Pareto distribution

E excluded population as a proportion of the total[*]

σ average wealth of excluded population relative to $\underline{w}$ (σ^* is average relative to the included population)[*]

G Gini coefficient

Chapter 3

γ share of 'lower wealth'[*]

R_j ratio of wealth at end of range j to mean wealth in that class and above[*]

W^* exogenous total wealth[*]

W^e estimated total wealth

Φ W^*/W^e

θ proportion of excess wealth allocated to the excluded population[*]

Chapter 4

d_s 'discount' applied to certain settled property

d_p 'discount' applied to occupational pensions

Chapter 5

V coefficient of variation

D relative mean deviation

μ adjustment to estate data for under-recording[*]

N sample size[*]

$F1, F2$ sampling fractions

W_t observed share of top x per cent in year t[*]

W_t^* 'true' value of W_t

$\hat{W}_t$ estimated value of W_t

ϵ_t error term in year t

T time trend

ρ serial correlation parameter[*]

η proportion at upper end of wealth range

Chapter 6

$D1$ dummy variable (0 until 1938, 1 thereafter)

$D2$ dummy variable (0 until 1959, 1 thereafter)

Chapter 7

Y total investment income (Y_j is investment income for asset type j)

A_j amount invested in asset type j[*]

R_j yield on asset type j[*]

B_j, β_j parameters of portfolio composition equation[*]

r_j, ρ_j parameters of return/wealth relationship[*]

Chapter 8

A_i current wealth-holding of dynasty i^*

K_t^i amount inherited by dynasty i born at t

S savings propensity

E_t earnings at time t^*

r_t investment income per unit of wealth at time t^*

θ parameter of savings relationship*

k_t capital per person at time t

y_t output per person at time t

g production function

S^w/S^c,

K^w/K^c savings, capital of workers/capitalists

$(1+n)$ number of children

K_t^* wealth passed on at death at time t

Ω proportion of wealth left to sons

$p(X_2|X_1)$ probability that a man with wealth X_1 marries a woman with wealth X_2

ρ correlation between husbands' and wives' inheritances*

δ share of labour in total income

σ coefficient of variation of earnings*

a, b, d parameters of Shorrocks queuing model*

μ_s, σ_s^2 mean and variance of savings process*

γ parameter of savings process*

δ^* parameter of Pearson Type V distribution

λ proportion of the population dying at any instant*

h parameter of division of estates

τ rate of inheritance tax

Chapter 9

Π index of share prices

PW 'popular' wealth

RR dividend yield after inflation and taxation

ED estate duty paid by top 1 per cent as proportion of capital minus overall rate of estate duty on capital

K, K_1 total capital, capital of top 1 per cent

W_1, W_1^* observed and 'true' share of top 1 per cent

Ψ proportion married for men and women

β proportion of the population married*

PREFACE

Many people have helped us with our work on this book, and we should like to express our gratitude to them.

First, a number of official bodies and their staffs have assisted us. The Social Science Research Council provided a grant (HR1462) for £6,883 over the period October 1971 – September 1974. This allowed one of us (A.J.H.) to work full-time on the project for three years, and without this support, the investigation would never have got off the ground. The Inland Revenue has throughout been a constant source of help and advice. Unpublished tabulations, essential for our work, were readily supplied, and members of staff were always willing to correct our misapprehensions about the official statistics, and – despite the great pressures on their time – comment on earlier drafts. We are most grateful to Stanley James, then Director of Statistics, for making this possible, and to John Astin, Ted Butler, Tony Dunn and Bill Gonzalez, who dealt with us so patiently at various times. They of course bear no responsibility for the use made of the data or for the views expressed, but the book has certainly been greatly improved as a result of their assistance.

The establishment of the Royal Commission on the Distribution of Income and Wealth during the latter stages of our work provided a valuable stimulus to research in this area. We have benefited from the Commission's published reports and from discussions with the staff. In addition we would like to thank Fred Bayliss and Michael Parsonage of the Commission, who sent us detailed comments on the final draft of the book.

Secondly, our work has led us into many different areas of academic research and in each of these we have been very fortunate in obtaining advice and information. At an early stage, when we began using the national balance sheet approach, Jack Revell and Alan Roe made available their working papers and unpublished data, and gave freely of their time to discuss the problems which arose. Tom Stark assisted us with the use of the investment income method in Chapter 7. John Whalley provided helpful comments on the estate method, and went through the draft manuscript with great thoroughness. Discussions with Tony Shorrocks and Richard Vaughan were most helpful in clarifying our thinking on a number of theoretical points; Charles Beach and Peter Phillips provided invaluable econometric advice; and all of them very kindly commented in detail on draft chapters. We drew on Paddy Lyons' work for Ireland in a number of respects, particularly in the treatment of family wealth in Chapter 9. Colin Harbury, Kathleen Langley, Harold Lydall, Cedric Sandford and Christopher Trinder all read parts of the manuscript, and gave us most useful comments.

At the Press, Jo Bradley, Patricia Williams and Colin Day in turn dealt very tolerantly with a book whose gestation period turned out to be more than twice that of the elephant. Francis Brooke was responsible for the subediting and was most helpful.

Lastly, there are those who have shared the task of typing and re-typing the manuscript. Early versions were the responsibility of Jill Adlington and Sheila Ogden at the University of Essex. Phyllis Pattenden managed to fit it in with her other duties as Departmental Secretary at Essex and was most philosophical about the continual revisions. Anne Robinson at University College London produced the final typescript with great care and good humour, and without her hard work the enterprise might never have reached an end.

May 1977
University College London
Queen's University, Kingston

1

INTRODUCTION

1.1 Aim of study

The concentration of wealth in Britain is an important feature of our society, but it is one which has received relatively little attention from economists and other social scientists. At the time this study began in October 1971, statistical information on wealth-holding was far more limited than on, say, the pattern of consumer expenditure or the structure of industrial production, and that which was published had been subject to much less careful scrutiny. Since then, the need for further investigation of the subject has been recognised by the establishment of the Royal Commission on the Distribution of Income and Wealth; but the Commission has to date (May 1977) been mainly concerned to summarise the available evidence and catalogue the many major questions which remain unanswered. If we turn to the explanation of the degree of concentration, and the way wealth-holding has changed over time, then we find again that this has not been a primary concern in the economics literature. There are relatively few theories of the size distribution of wealth, and little effort has been made to test how far they are consistent with the evidence, making it difficult to assess the role played by factors such as accumulation and inheritance in leading to concentration.

It is against this background that we have attempted to provide a new analysis of some of these issues. Lacking the kind of resources available to the Royal Commission, we decided to centre our attention on five main topics:

First, we have presented a detailed critique of the 'official' estimates published by the Inland Revenue. These estimates, which cover the years since 1960, have been widely quoted and are in fact the only figures available for the period. At the same time, they suffer from a number of drawbacks and the starting point of the present analysis is a detailed examination in chapter 2 of the methods used by the Inland Revenue and the sources they employ.

Secondly, we have developed new estimates using the estate method for

1

the years 1966–72. These build on the work not only of the Inland Revenue but also of earlier academic investigators. Our use of the estate approach does, however, differ from that in earlier studies in a number of respects. Most importantly, we have examined in greater detail than previously the properties of the mortality multiplier technique employed, the adjustments which can be made for missing wealth, and the sensitivity of the results to the assumptions made. This occupies a major part of the book (chapters 3–5).

Thirdly, employing the same methods, we have tried to give a series over time covering the period 1923–72 which is constructed as far as possible on consistent assumptions. In our opinion, this provides a firmer basis for discussing trends over time than the figures typically used in public discussion, but there remain a number of serious difficulties (chapter 6).

Fourthly, we have compared the estimates using the estate method with those based on the alternative investment income approach pioneered by Sir Robert Giffen. Although this has been used in the past, no attempt has ever been made to examine the consistency of the estimates made by the two approaches. In chapter 7, we investigate the relationship between the results, and the relative merits of the investment income and estate methods.

Finally, there is the analysis and interpretation of the findings. Since in our view, this can only be approached with the aid of an explicit theoretical framework, we first in chapter 8 survey the various theories of the development of wealth-holdings. This provides the background for chapter 9, which investigates some of the factors underlying the changes in the share of the top 1 per cent, the holding of wealth within families, and the role of life-cycle considerations.

The primary focus of the book is on the distribution of wealth in Britain but it is hoped that the discussion of methodology will be of interest to those concerned with wealth-holding in other countries. Indeed, we have tried thoughout to pay particular attention to the conceptual problems which arise, as illustrated by such questions as the choice of mortality multipliers, the theory of the investment income approach, and the relationship between theories of the distribution of wealth and the observed evidence. The resolution of these problems requires advances in terms of theory and of empirical practice. The present study attempts to make some contribution to both; nonetheless, it will be clear to the reader that a great deal remains to be done, and in chapter 10 we have described briefly some of the possible directions for future research.

The study was initiated some three years before the establishment of the Royal Commission on the Distribution of Income and Wealth in August 1974. Much of the work was completed (and available to the Commission) before the publication of its Initial Report in July 1975, and in particular the report took over (with modifications) the balance sheet method developed in chapter 4 (previously described in Atkinson (1975)). Although the Commission accepted our recommendations in this and other respects, there are a number of points where we do not agree with the Initial Report, and where we feel that the official estimates can be further developed. These are referred to in the text at appropriate points, and the main criticisms are brought together in the final chapter (chapter 10).

1.2 Delimitation of the field

In seeking to provide answers to the questions outlined above within the compass of one book, it is necessary to limit the field covered, and the way in which we have done this is described below.

Two restrictions on the scope of the analysis have already been indicated in the title. First, we deal in the main with wealth-holding in Great Britain (one exception is chapter 7). This reflects the form in which the data were available and a desire to maintain consistency as far as possible with earlier investigators (although the Inland Revenue has recently begun to make estimates for the United Kingdom – see also Lyons (1972)). Secondly, we are concerned with wealth owned by the personal sector, that is wealth owned by persons, unincorporated businesses and personal trusts.[1] The significance of this may be seen from the estimated national balance sheet produced by Revell and Roe (1971). According to this, total national wealth in 1966 was £140 billion (throughout the book we use the term 'billion' to denote thousand million), and this was made up as shown below.[2]

	£ billion
Personal sector	105
Company sector	29
Public sector	6

We are, therefore, dealing with the greater part, but not the whole, of total national wealth.

The reasons for limiting attention to the personal sector should be apparent. Nonetheless, it should be made clear at the outset that it precludes

---

1 The definition follows that of Revell (1967:15) and includes the undistributed estates of deceased persons. It may be noted that it is a narrower definition than that employed in the national income accounts; in particular, the personal sector as defined here excludes all non-profit bodies, as well as life assurance and superannuation institutions.
2 The definition of the personal sector is here rather wider, including elements such as non-profit bodies.

consideration of certain aspects of wealth-holding. If we are concerned with the concentration of wealth on account of inequality in investment income, then a study of the personal distribution may be quite adequate. If, however, we are concerned about the control over the economy which wealth may convey, then we should obviously need to consider the distribution among other sectors. A related problem is the treatment of the net worth of these other sectors. Should the net worth of the public sector be ignored or allocated in some way to persons? More important in quantitative terms according to the estimates of Revell and Roe is the net worth of the company sector (the excess of the net value of assets over the stock exchange valuation). There are a number of possible explanations for this, and potential capital gains tax liabilities need to be taken into account, but if even a part of this were allocated to the shareholders, it would make a substantial difference to the size distribution. These qualifications need to be borne in mind.

The wealth of the personal sector consists of physical assets, such as houses and consumer durables, and of claims on other sectors net of liabilities to other sectors. (The terms 'wealth' and 'net worth' are used interchangeably throughout the book to denote the net value of assets minus liabilities.) This raises the question of the definition of the assets and liabilities to be included. Following the precedent set in the literature on the definition of income (for example Simons 1938), we should ideally define wealth in a comprehensive manner, including all assets which convey command over resources. In practice, empirical estimates of the size distribution of income fall short of that ideal, and in our work on wealth we have from the start excluded two major types of capital. The first of these is 'social property', or the rights to benefits from the state. The item most commonly referred to in this context is the value of state pension rights (Atkinson 1972 and Royal Commission 1975), but it would also include other social security benefits and the right to access to communal assets such as schools and hospitals. This type of wealth has been excluded, not because we believe it to be unimportant, but because it raises serious conceptual problems which we do not feel have been adequately resolved,[3] and because it is typically viewed as being rather different in nature from 'private' wealth. The second category is 'human capital', or the capitalised value of future earning capacity. This is usually seen as arising from investment in education or training, but may also be associated with restricted access to particular jobs resulting from the activity of trade

---

3   For example, previous estimates of the value of state pensions have not paid sufficient attention to the problems raised by imperfections in the capital market, in terms both of differences between borrowing and lending rates and of differences between individuals.

unions or professional associations, or with the advantages conveyed by parental socio-economic status. The estimation of such human capital again raises major problems and the issues are rather different from those which are the main concern of the present book. The book is, therefore, concerned with the distribution of private, 'non-human' wealth.

Closely related to the definition of wealth is the problem of the basis for valuation. In this book, we consider two different bases, which do not exhaust the possibilities but provide some means of assessing the sensitivity of the results to the choice of definition. The first is valuation on a 'realisation' basis, or the value obtained in a sale on the open market at the date in question. The second is valuation on a 'going concern' basis, or the value to a person or household on the assumption that the asset is retained.[4] These valuations can clearly differ, and we can distinguish at least two reasons. To begin with, even in a perfect market, the value of an asset to an intra-marginal holder may exceed the market price, and this may be part of the explanation for the apparent positive net worth of the company sector referred to earlier. However, such 'surplus' is not taken into account in the standard approach to income measurement, and in what follows we concentrate on the second reason for differing valuations — market imperfections. The problems arising in the case of the definition of income have been described by Simons: 'The precise, objective measurement of income implies the existence of perfect markets from which one . . . may obtain the prices necessary for routine valuation of all possible inventories of commodities, services, and property rights. In actuality there are few approximately perfect markets and few collections of goods or properties which can be valued accurately by recourse to market prices' (1938:56). These may be illustrated by the case of furniture, which would typically fetch second-hand considerably less than its value to the household as a going concern. In certain cases, such as occupational pensions, the realisation value may well be zero. Although Simons may have been unduly pessimistic about the possibility of applying market values, there are undoubtedly difficulties, and it is for this reason that we have considered the two alternative bases for valuation.

The distinction between 'realisation' and 'going concern' valuations is related to the concept of 'marketability' employed by the Royal Commission: 'the key idea is that of marketability, and . . . different approaches to the

---

4 For similar definitions in the accounting literature, see, for example, Bedford and McKeown, who define the net realisable value as 'the maximum net amount which can be realised from the disposal of that asset within a short period (not a forced sale situation)' (1972:333), and replacement cost as 'the cost today of purchasing assets, having services equivalent to those now held' (1972:334).

definition of personal wealth hinge essentially on varying degrees of market-ability of assets' (1975:9—10).[5] In particular, the Commission distinguish the category of 'non marketable' assets, or those with zero realisation value (which includes state and occupational pension rights), and construct estimates both excluding and including this category. The relationship may be seen with the aid of the schema below.

	Method of valuation	
Type of market	realisation value	going concern value
perfect market	A	A
imperfect market (gap between buying and selling price, but latter non-zero)	B	C
no market	zero	D

The Commission presents estimates of $(A + C)$, that is marketable assets only, and of $(A + C + D)$; our estimates are of $(A + B)$ and of $(A + C + D)$, although in the latter case we have, as explained earlier, excluded social property.[6] Our choice of $(A + B)$ rather than $(A + C)$ is based on the fact that we can see little case for attaching special significance to a zero realisation value, preferring to treat marketability as varying continuously, and the feeling that our realisation value corresponds more closely 'to everyday usage' (Royal Commission 1976:47) than the Commission's own procedure.

Two further issues of definition concern the unit of analysis and the time period. Most of the published figures relate to wealth holdings by (adult) individuals, reflecting the form in which the basic data are available, and the same applies to the estimates here in chapters 3—6. We have however in chapter 7 derived estimates using the investment income method which relate to the wealth owned by tax units (husbands and wives), and in chapter 9 explored different ways of 'marrying-up' individual holdings. These allow one to form some view of the effect of moving from an individual to a family basis. The question of time period introduces the distinction between the wealth at a point in time and 'lifetime' or 'inherited' wealth (i.e. a measure of the wealth received in gifts, bequests and other capital transfers over the lifetime). The estimates presented here, like those in earlier studies, relate to current wealth, and allow no conclusions to be drawn about inherited wealth. We do, however, consider some of the questions of interpretation in chapter 9.

5 This paragraph has benefited from very helpful comments by the staff of the Commission, who suggested the schema used below.
6 The Commission's coverage of social property is limited to state pensions.

To sum up, we are concerned in our empirical work with the distribution of the current, private, non-human wealth of adult individuals on both realisation and going concern bases for valuation. As we have emphasised, this definition of the field is restrictive and the qualifications need to be borne in mind throughout the analysis. Finally, we have for much of the book concentrated on the position of *top wealth-holders,* taken to be broadly the top 10 per cent, and more particularly the top 1 per cent. Although we are concerned to estimate the wealth of the entire adult population, we have not devoted much attention to the distribution *within* the bottom 90 per cent. This further delimitation of our field of study is in part a reflection of the data employed, which do not allow us to draw any precise conclusions about the shape of the lower part of the distribution (see the next section). It is also the case that the share of the top wealth-holders is the aspect of the distribution which has received most attention in public debate (the estimates given by the Royal Commission, for example, do not go below the top 20 per cent) and which is the most relevant to issues of taxation policy, such as the introduction of the wealth tax. The distribution of property among the majority of the population — for example, between owner-occupiers and tenants — is an important subject, but one for another book.

1.3 Review of earlier studies

Three main methods have been employed in Britain to estimate the size distribution of wealth. The official statistics produced by the Inland Revenue are derived using the *estate method.* Academic authors have also used this method, but in addition have followed two alternative approaches, the *investment income method* and the *sample survey method.* In this section we provide a brief explanation of each and describe the main earlier studies in Britain. At the end of the section, we refer to work on this subject in other countries.

(a) Estate method

Under the present system of taxation (in 1977), the only occasion when a person's total assets and liabilities are revealed to the fiscal authorities is when he dies. Although many people are not sufficiently wealthy for their estates to come to the notice of the Inland Revenue, the returns made for the purpose of estate duty (now capital transfer tax) are an important source of information about the distribution of wealth. (Estate duty was in force during the period covered by our estimates, and it is to this that we refer throughout the book. The introduction of capital transfer tax in 1974 does not, however, affect the basic principle of the method.)

The Inland Revenue has for many years published the details of estates based on a sample drawn from its records. This information, classified by the size of the estate, and by the age and sex of the deceased, provides in turn the foundation for estimates of the distribution of wealth. The basic method is in fact straightforward. Assuming that those of a particular age and sex dying in a given year are representative of the living population, the overall distribution may be obtained by 'blowing up' the estate data by a mortality multiplier equal to the reciprocal of the mortality rate. In other words, if the mortality rate for a particular male age group is 1 in 1,000, we assume that for every man who died at this age in a given year, there are 999 alive in similar circumstances and multiply the numbers and values of estates in this age group by 1,000. In effect the dead are used as a random sample of the living (although the sampling fractions are not under the control of the investigator!), except that the estates of those not liable to estate duty (and which do not require probate) do not come to the notice of the Inland Revenue. The number of such 'missing' people is quite large, and the adjustments necessary are discussed later.

The estate approach has a long history, although it has become more refined over the years. In the earliest studies, a single multiplier was applied to all capital wealth, so that when Baxter (1869) made an estimate of total personal wealth on the basis of the revenue from the Probate Duties, he used a multiplier of thirty, which he took to be 'the cycle for each devolution of property'. Later writers used multipliers ranging from twenty-nine to fifty-five, which led to what Mallet described as 'the most disquieting discrepancies' (1908:66). Mallet was, in fact, the first to employ multipliers related to the age at death,[7] a method which was at once accepted as clearly more accurate, although in the discussion of Mallet's paper it was suggested by Bailey that the mortality rate used 'should not be that of the general mortality of the whole country, but some such table as that of the mortality amongst the families of the peerage; or, perhaps, the mortality tables derived from the life assurance companies' (1908:85). In the subsequent paper by Mallet and Strutt (1915), such social class multipliers were applied, and the method thus amended has been used by nearly all subsequent investigators employing the estate approach, including the Inland Revenue.

The studies by Mallet (1908) and Mallet and Strutt (1915) dealt with aggregate personal wealth, and the first application of the mortality multiplier technique to the size distribution of wealth was that by Clay in 1925. Since that date interest in the subject has followed a cyclical pattern with major studies following at approximately ten-year intervals: Daniels and

7   The idea was suggested by Coghlan in the discussion of Harris and Lake (1906).

Campion (1936) and Campion (1939) in the mid 1930s, Langley (1950 and 1951) at the beginning of the 1950s, and Lydall and Tipping (1961). Table 1.1 summarises these studies, including those where the distribution of wealth was not the primary concern, such as Barna (1945) and Cartter (1953). The main features are discussed in more detail below. The estate method is, of course, used by the Inland Revenue in constructing the official estimates, but consideration of this is postponed to chapter 2.

Rather than describe each study in chronological order, it seems more helpful to consider in turn the main aspects of the estate method. The first question concerns the choice of mortality multipliers. Clay began by applying to estates over £500 a multiplier based on occupations of a 'clerical and professional character', and applying the general multiplier to estates below £500. Wedgwood (1929) followed Clay in using these death rates, which, he argued, were relevant to the bulk of the upper and middle classes. The next writers to adopt the estate method were Daniels and Campion (1936) and Campion (1939). These studies made estimates using both general mortality rates and social class mortality rates, although the authors felt that the latter were more appropriate. The social class multipliers were derived from the Registrar General's report on occupational mortality, and the same source provides the basis for the present day estimates of the Inland Revenue. The data on occupational mortality are a product of the decennial census of population and are only published with considerable delay. In particular, the studies by Langley (1950 and 1951) and Cartter (1953) could draw on no more recent data than 1931 and they applied the same class mortality differentials as Campion. Since the Second World War two further reports have become available and that for 1951 was employed by Lydall and Tipping (1961). Finally, the estimate by Revell (1965) for 1960 was intended to be compared with those of earlier investigators and for this purpose he felt that the general mortality rate was adequate (the 1960 figure being compared with those obtained by Daniels and Campion, and Langley using general mortality rates).

The second way in which the studies have differed has been in their treatment of small wealth-holdings. As explained, the estate data omit a substantial number of deaths, typically those where little property is left. The various ways in which this problem has been treated are set out in the last column of table 1.1. In 1925, Clay made an estimate of the wealth in the hands of people with less than £100 (the estate duty limit at that time) based on the funds of savings banks and other 'working class' savings and the value of household goods etc. In the the following investigations, Wedgwood (1929), Daniels and Campion (1936), Campion (1939) and Langley (1951) all based

Table 1.1 Studies using estate method

Author	Year(s)	Coverage Area	Age	Types of multipliers (see notes)	Treatment of small wealth-holdings
Clay (1925)	1911–13 1920	EW	Over 15 and occupied ('income units')	GMR for estates under £500; over £500 mortality rates of occupations of a clerical and professional nature	Estimated value of furniture, tools, and personal effects of exempt persons plus collective savings of this group
Wedgwood (1929)	1923–4	EW	Over 25	SMR for males, based on Clay. GMR for females	Takes Clay's figure for 1920 as still applicable to 1924
Daniels and Campion (1936)	1911–13 1924–30	EW	25 and over	GMR and SMR based on Registrar-General's data	Follows Clay's technique but estimates adjusted downwards
Campion (1939)	1911–3 1926–8 1936	EW	25 and over	As Daniels and Campion	As Daniels and Campion
Barna (1945)	1937	UK (Merely % adjustment for NI)	No control total population used	GMR	No adjustment
Langley (1950 and 1951)	1936–8 1946–7	EW and GB	25 and over	GMR (and SMR) based on Campion	Extrapolates estimates of Daniels and Campion
Cartter (1953)	1947–9	GB	Over 25	SMR based on Campion	Assumes average holding below £100 of £45
Langley (1954)	1950–1	GB	25 and over	GMR	As earlier study for less than £100; extrapolates ED figure below £2,000
Lydall and Tipping (1961)	1951–6	GB	20 and over	SMR based on Registrar-General's data	Uses results of Oxford Savings Survey, and extrapolates ED figures
Revell (1965)	1960	EW	Over 25	GMR	No adjustment

Notes: GMR General mortality multiplier   SMR Social class adjusted multiplier   GB Great Britain
NI Northern Ireland   ED Estate duty.   EW England and Wales

their estimates on extrapolations of Clay's original figures, although Daniels and Campion adjusted the estimate since they thought it was too high (1936:49). The increase in the estate duty threshold to £2,000 in 1946 meant that the problem of allowing for small wealth-holdings became more serious, but no very satisfactory solution was proposed until the study of Lydall and Tipping (1961) who combined sample survey and estate information to provide coverage of the whole wealth range.

The third aspect of these studies which should be noted is the paucity of adjustments for property which may be missing as a result of estate duty avoidance. Settled property is the only element which has received much attention. Mallet and Strutt (1915:575) suggested that the total exempt settled property might be quite substantial. Daniels and Campion, whilst acknowledging this, argued that its exclusion does not vitiate comparisons of the relative distributions for different years (1936:38). Campion (1939:108) was similarly disposed, and it was left to Barna (1945:260) to make some allowance adding exempt 'settled' property proportionately to other estates. Langley, like others before, made no attempt at distributing an estimated total for settled property (1951:33), utilising Campion's arguments on the insignificance of the effect of its exclusion. Lydall and Tipping (1961) made an allowance for excluded property, including occupational pension rights, and attempted for the first time to allocate this by ranges.

(b) Investment income (Giffen) method
Although the estate method has been that most commonly employed in Britain in the past fifty years, the investment income approach was much used by early writers. It is particularly associated with Giffen, who described it as follows:

> It becomes possible by means of the income tax assessments to apply a certain number of years' purchase, according to the best estimate that can be formed, to the different descriptions of income from property, and by this means an estimate of the capital yielding income can be arrived at. There is, no doubt, some difficulty in establishing what the multiplier in each case should be [but] great masses of the property are in such a form, for instance railway shares and stocks, that anyone with a knowledge of market conditions can easily apply an approximate figure by which the total income may be multiplied so as to show the capital represented at its market value [Giffen 1913:346–7].

The essence of the investment income approach, therefore, is to apply a 'yield multiplier' to work back from the distribution of investment income to the distribution of wealth: if, for example, the yield is thought to be 5 per cent, the multiplier is 20, so that an investment income of £5,000 would be assumed to correspond to wealth of £100,000. The yield multiplier varies with the form in which wealth is held and the normal procedure has been to calculate a weighted average yield based on the composition of wealth indicated by the estate duty statistics. In this calculation it is necessary to allow for the fact that the composition of wealth varies with the size of the holding (for example, cash and bank deposits tend to be held more by those at the lower end of the distribution and company shares more by the rich) and for assets which yield no money income. The coverage of the estimates depends on that of the investment income data, and typically these are restricted to upper income, and hence wealth, ranges.

The investment income method has mainly been employed to prepare estimates of total personal wealth, and only a few authors have used it to estimate the distribution of property among persons. Campion (1939), for example, devotes an entire chapter to the Giffen method but this is concerned only with aggregate wealth and, for this reason, is not considered here. The main studies of interest are Barna (1945), Cartter (1953), and a short article which appeared in the *Economist* (1966). However, even these are not particularly helpful for our purposes.

The studies by Barna and Cartter were directed not at the preparation of estimates of the distribution of wealth but at relating capital holdings to income ranges. Barna (1945) first estimated the distribution of assets left at death for different ranges of estates, and derived the average yield of capital in different estate ranges. The resulting yield curve was used to calculate the capital corresponding to a given investment income; and if Barna had gone further he would have been able to compare the distribution from this source with that derived from the estate duty data. The study by Cartter (1953) similarly did not make any comparison of the results obtained by the two methods, and as far as the derivation of the yield multiplier is concerned, his approach did not deviate from that followed by Barna.[8] The final estimate, that made by the *Economist* for 1959–60, probably most closely approaches the method adopted here, although it is impossible to be more precise since the text of the article only provides the barest details of the method used. The estimates were based on 'the recorded investment income of the living' and estimated yields for different assets were then applied to the breakdown of wealth by asset type. Beyond this, however, there is no indication of the methods.[9]

8 Reference may also be made to the yield curves estimated by Stark (1972) for a similar purpose.

9 Correspondence with the editor of the *Economist* did not throw any further light on the methods employed.

(c) Sample surveys

The estate method and the investment income method are both open to the objections that they provide only indirect evidence about wealth-holding and that they cover only the upper part of the distribution. The attraction of sample surveys is that they provide direct information on wealth among the living population and that they can potentially cover the whole population.

Such surveys have, however, only been carried out rather rarely, and the best known, those carried out by the Oxford Institute of Statistics, are now more than twenty years out of date. These surveys collected data on net worth for the years 1953 and 1954 from a national sample of income units, although the definition of net worth covered only a restrictive class of assets. The results for net worth are described in (*inter alia*) Hill, Klein and Straw (1955), Hill (1955) and Straw (1955). (Further details are given in appendix I.) No surveys of savings on the same scale have been mounted in recent years, although reference should made to the Essex—LSE poverty survey (Townsend 1977) which included questions on net worth, and to market research surveys such as that by the Economists Advisory Group (Morgan 1975) discussed in appendix I.

The main use of sample survey evidence has been as a supplement to estate data, as, for example, in the work of Lydall and Tipping (1961). The Oxford survey was however used on its own in a comparison of the United States and Britain by Lydall and Lansing (1959). For this purpose it suffered from a number of serious shortcomings, particularly those arising from non-response, incomplete response, and incomplete coverage in survey design. The serious-ness of this position was brought out by Lydall and Tipping as follows:

> The 1954 savings survey achieved a response rate of only 67 per cent amongst the 'income units' approached for interviews; and there was almost certainly a substantial amount of under-statement of assets even by those who were 'successfully' interviewed. In the outcome, the estimates of the total amount of personal capital which can be derived from this survey appear to represent only about two-thirds of the true amount [1961:85].

In appendix I, we describe in more detail the problems with the use of the savings surveys which lead us — like Lydall and Tipping — to conclude that they are unlikely to provide by themselves an adequate source of estimates of the extent of concentration among top wealth-holders. It is not just a question of *total* capital being under-stated but one of the *distribution* being mis-represented, particularly as a result of differential non-response. The same conclusion is reached in the Economists Advisory Group study, which states explicitly that 'survey studies can tell nothing about the very rich' (Morgan 1975:60).

It is for this reason that we concentrate here on the estate method and the investment income method. Data for sample surveys may be a valuable supplement, particularly in casting light on the lower part of the distribution, but cannot be expected to replace the indirect methods entirely.

(d) Studies in other countries

The methods employed to estimate the size distribution of wealth in Britain reflect the particular features of the British tax system; in countries, for example, with an annual wealth tax, these records provide a more direct source of evidence about holdings at the top of the scale (this is illustrated by the Scandanavian countries, although the data need to be used with care). In view of this, we concentrate in this short survey of studies in other countries on those whose tax system is in the Anglo-Saxon tradition.

In the United States, the estate data were used by early investigators (see Merwin 1939), but the first systematic application of the mortality multiplier technique — that by Mendershausen (1956) — came relatively late. The method was considerably developed by Lampman (1962), whose use of balance sheet totals has been followed here in Chapter 4. His estimates, together with the recent work of Smith (1974), provide a series for the shares of top wealth-holders covering selected years between 1922 and 1972. 'Top wealth-holders' are taken to be those required to file estate tax returns, and in 1969 they represented some $5\frac{1}{2}$ per cent of the adult population. The coverage is therefore more restricted than that of the British estate duty data. The Americans appear to have made relatively little use in recent years of the investment income method, although this was extensively discussed in the 1930s (Lehmann 1937 and Stewart 1939). They have however a much stronger tradition of survey evidence, dating from the period when the census enumeration included wealth declarations (the 1860 Census records Abraham Lincoln as having a total wealth of $17,000 (Soltow 1975:233)). The major surveys include the Survey of Financial Characteristics of Consumers in 1963–4 (Projector and Weiss 1966) and the 1967 Survey of Economic Opportunity. The limitations of these surveys have however been emphasised: 'The SFCC is far from an ideal source on wealth inequality on several counts' (Taussig 1976:7).

In Canada, 'only limited data have ever existed on estates' (Poduluk 1974: 203) and the federal government no longer levies an estate tax. For this reason the only regular source of data is from household surveys carried out since the 1950s. These surveys were conducted by Statistics Canada in 1956,

1959, 1964 and 1970 and the results are described in Poduluk (1974). (An appendix by Emmerson (1974) discusses the use of balance sheet totals.) In Australia, the picture is similar. Podder and Kakwani (1976) describe the results of the Australian Survey of Consumer Finances and Expenditures carried out on a nation-wide basis in 1966—8. In New Zealand, on the other hand, estate data are available and have been used to estimate the size distribution (Easton 1974 and Crothers 1975). Finally, in Eire, the estate method has been applied by a number of authors, the most recent being Lyons (1974), whose approach to the treatment of family wealth-holding is adopted here in Chapter 9.[10]

This book will be concerned with the distribution in Britain but we hope that the methods applied will be of some interest in countries such as those described above.

1.4 Reader's guide

The structure of the book follows the lines of investigation set out at the beginning of this chapter, and it may be summarised as follows:

Critique of official statistics (chapter 2). Our purpose here is to examine in detail the methods employed in constructing the official estimates, and the objections which have been raised from a variety of sources. Are they as unreliable as some commentators have suggested? Do they tend to exaggerate or to under-state the degree of concentration?

Refinement of estate estimates (chapters 3—5). In this part we seek to develop the estate method, particularly with reference to the choice of mortality multipliers and the use of balance sheet data. On the basis of this work, we provide in chapter 5 estimates for the period 1966—72 which meet some of the criticisms of the official figures.

Trends over time (chapter 6). We investigate the existing evidence about changes in concentration; and construct a series for 1923—72 which is closer to being comparable over time. We discuss how far this allows one to draw conclusions about the decline in the share of top wealth-holders.

Alternative investment income approach (chapter 7). The use of this method and its deficiencies are analysed; and we consider the extent to which the results are consistent with those derived using the estate method.

Analysis of the results (chapters 8 and 9). In chapter 8, we provide a survey of different theories of the generation of wealth-holdings. Chapter 9 then draws on this in exploring the factors underlying the changes in the share of the top 1 per cent, and the roles of marriage and the life-cycle.

10 For recent discussion of his estimates, see Harrison and Nolan (1975), Chesher and McMahon (1976) and Harrison (1976a).

Conclusions (chapter 10). The main findings and our recommendations for future research in this area are summarised.

The reader who wants to skim the results is advised to start with chapter 10 and then read the summaries given in the last section of each of chapters 2–9.

The reader who wishes to avoid some of the more technical material is advised to omit those sections which are starred in the list of contents. (Signposts are provided by footnotes in the text.) We have tried to ease the flow of the text by making extensive use of appendices, but the subject is 'not hammock reading for a lazy summer afternoon' (Samuelson 1973:vii).

Table 2.1 (continued)

Range of net wealth (lower limit £)	1967 Number	Amount	1968 Number	Amount	1969 Number	Amount	1970 Number	Amount	1971 Number	Amount	1972 Number	Amount	1973 Number	Amount
Nil-	5,398	2.8	5,190	2.8	4,705	2.4	3,924	2.0	4,211	2.1	3,567	2.3	3,599	1.6
1,000-	5,273	9.8	5,415	9.7	5,718	9.8	5,423	9.8	5,491	10.1	4,288	8.0	4,804	8.5
3,000-	2,966	11.6	2,918	11.4	3,125	11.7	2,766	10.9	2,912	11.4	2,349	9.2	2,279	9.0
5,000-	2,177	15.3	2,191	15.6	2,930	20.5	3,217	23.4	3,799	27.1	3,675	26.7	4,082	29.8
10,000-	620	7.6	598	7.4	687	7.9	710	8.5	962	11.8	1,500	18.6	2,229	27.7
15,000-	270	4.8	288	5.1	308	5.1	339	5.9	412	6.6	503	8.9	782	13.9
20,000-	157	3.4	148	3.5	188	3.9	206	4.5	232	5.2	303	7.3	415	9.8
25,000-	279	9.9	326	11.2	323	10.5	318	10.9	380	13.0	522	18.9	629	20.9
50,000-	109	7.5	121	8.1	123	7.9	132	8.4	158	10.3	210	13.7	211	13.1
100,000-	37	5.1	40	5.4	41	4.9	40	5.0	49	6.7	70	9.0	79	10.0
200,000-	14	5.8	20	7.8	20	6.8	19	7.7	26	8.4	30	15.8	31	19.4
Total	17,300	83.6	17,255	88.0	18,168	91.4	17,094	96.8	18,632	112.7	17,017	138.4	19,140	163.9

people with net wealth in different ranges together with the total amount of wealth they own. Although the tables do not, unfortunately, give the number of millionaires, one can see that in 1973 there were estimated to be 31,000 people worth more than £200,000. Their average wealth was over £600,000 and their share in the total wealth recorded by the Inland Revenue amounted to some 12 per cent. The top million people in 1973 were broadly those worth more than £25,000, and they accounted for an estimated £63 billion out of a total of £164 billion, or nearly 40 per cent. The numbers in the top wealth groups have increased considerably since 1960: there were only estimated to be some 260,000 worth more than £25,000 at that time. For the lower wealth ranges, the pattern appears rather erratic, and some of the reasons why the numbers have gone up and down from year to year are discussed later.

The distribution of wealth may be summarised in a variety of ways. One of the most common is to calculate the share of total wealth belonging to different percentile groups. In order to make this calculation, it is necessary to determine the base population, and this point has caused a great deal of confusion. In certain presentations, notably that by the Central Statistical Office in past issues of *Social Trends* (for example 1974: table 68), the base population is taken as those wealth-holders appearing in the Inland Revenue estimates. This does not, however, provide a full coverage of the potential wealth-holding population, for reasons set out in more detail below, and as may be seen from the fact that the Inland Revenue estimates in 1973 identify some 19 million wealth-holders, compared with an adult population (aged 18 and over) of 39 million. In view of this, the Inland Revenue have followed the practice of making two assumptions:

> *Series A* Base population equals the total covered by the estimates;
> *Series B* Base population equals the total adult population, and those not covered are assumed to have zero wealth.

These two assumptions have been employed for a number of years in the calculation of the Gini coefficients published by the Inland Revenue, these coefficients being an alternative way of representing the degree of concentration.[3]

The results of summarising the official estimates in this way are illustrated in figure 2.1. The two assumptions about the base population are shown by dashed lines (series A) and solid lines (series B) respectively.[4] The figures are taken from the Initial Report of the Royal Commission on the Distribution

3 The Gini coefficient is one half the mean difference divided by the mean. Geometrically, it is the ratio of the area between the Lorenz curve and the diagonal to the whole area below the diagonal — see Appendix IV.
4 The Series B is based on the population aged 18 and over; the Inland Revenue typically publish figures based on the population aged 15 and over.

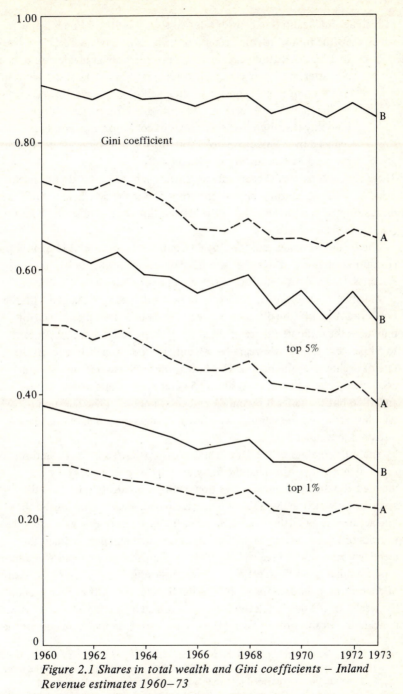

Figure 2.1 Shares in total wealth and Gini coefficients – Inland Revenue estimates 1960–73

Source: Royal Commission (1975): table 45.

of Income and Wealth (henceforth referred to as the 'Royal Commission'), which drew the following conclusions on the basis of series B:

> In 1973, the latest year for which estimates are available, more than a quarter of all personal wealth was owned by the richest 1 per cent of the adult population . . . about a half of all the wealth was owned by the richest 5 per cent . . . While total wealth remains very unevenly distributed, the extremes of concentration have been reduced over time . . . Since 1960, the trend towards greater equality has broadly continued [1975: 139–40].

These conclusions – of substantial concentration but of a steady downward trend in the share of top groups – correspond to the widely held view of the distribution of wealth, and one of the aims of this book is to see how far this is in fact a valid picture.

The Inland Revenue, and the Royal Commission, are careful to qualify the conclusions drawn and to emphasise the deficiencies of the underlying statistics. One indication of the possible scope for disagreement is in fact provided by the substantial difference between the results obtained with the two series A and B (the distance between the dashed and solid lines). Not only does the estimated share of the top 5 per cent range from 39 per cent to 51 per cent for a single year (1973), but also there is a difference in the rate of decline over the period. This latter point is illustrated by the Gini coefficient, where the series A falls by 5 percentage points between 1964 and 1966 but the series B by only 1 percentage point.[5] (The question of sampling error and the significance of such changes in summary measures is discussed in chapter 5.)

The shortcomings of the official statistics have indeed led some authors to reject them totally. Although the essay by Titmuss (1962) was largely directed at data on income distribution, he was also highly critical of the statistics on which the wealth estimates are based. Meacher has argued that 'the accumulation of these deficiencies in the estate duty figures renders the calculations derived from them, frankly, sheer mathematical artifacts increasingly remote from reality' (1972:192). Similarly Polanyi and Wood have suggested that the official estimates give a misleading impression of the degree of concentration and, more generally, that 'Estate Duty Office figures about the wealth of the dead . . . cannot be transformed by statistical devices to indicate the wealth of the living' (1974: back cover). In the remainder of the

---

5 The relationship between the two coefficients, G_A and G_B, may be seen from the equation: $G_B = G_A + (1 - G_A)E$, where E is the proportion of the total population not covered by the Inland Revenue estimates. A fall in G_A may therefore be offset by a rise in E, if the extent of coverage has decreased. (We are grateful to John Astin for pointing out this relationship.)

chapter, we try to assess just how important are the deficiencies of the official estimates.

2.2 The estate method

Before examining the Inland Revenue statistics in detail, it may be helpful to set out the basic estate method more fully and to provide a simple framework within which the effect of different assumptions may be investigated.

For this purpose, it is convenient to employ the following notation. The estate data on individual wealth-holdings at death are assumed to be classified according to:

(i) age, sex and other relevant considerations (such as marital status) — denoted by index $a = 1, \ldots, A$;

(ii) estate size — denoted by index $i = 1, \ldots, t$, where the size class i contains estates with wealth w, where $w_i \leqslant w < w_{i+1}$.

The number of estates in a particular cell is denoted by n_{ai} and their average wealth by w_{ai}. It is in this form that the data have been published for many years by the Inland Revenue and have been used to estimate the distribution of wealth. In order to do this it is assumed that the total number of living people, P_a, in each class a is known from external sources, as is the total number of deaths, N_a, so that $\bar{m}_a = P_a/N_a$ is the overall mortality multiplier for that class (in other words, the total deaths are multiplied by $\bar{m}_a$ to give the total population in class a). Moreover, these multipliers have typically been adjusted for social class differentials in mortality so that the multiplier applied to a particular estate range i in class a is written as

$$m_{ai} = \lambda_{ai}\bar{m}_a$$

where λ_{ai} is the social class differential. It follows that the estimated number of people in the living population with wealth in class i is given by

$$P_i \equiv \sum_a P_a \lambda_{ai} \left(\frac{n_{ai}}{N_a}\right) \tag{1}$$

(where $\sum_a$ denotes summation over the range $a = 1, \ldots, A$), and their estimated total wealth is given by

$$W_i \equiv \sum_a P_a \lambda_{ai} \left(\frac{n_{ai}}{N_a}\right) w_{ai} \tag{2}$$

The total number of wealth-holders identified in these estimates falls short of the total adult population, denoted by P, on account of the incomplete coverage of estates. Similarly, total wealth, denoted by W, exceeds the sum of

W_i over classes $i = 1, \ldots, t$ on account of the wealth owned by the 'excluded population'.

If we now consider the share of total wealth owned by different percentile groups, then the proportion of the total population in wealth classes $i = j + 1, \ldots, t$ (i.e. the top $t - j$ groups) is given by

$$1 - F_j = \sum_a \frac{P_a}{P} \sum_{i=j+1}^{t} \lambda_{ai} \left(\frac{n_{ai}}{N_a} \right) \tag{3}$$

and their share in total wealth is given by

$$1 - L_j = \sum_a \frac{P_a}{P} \sum_{i=j+1}^{t} \lambda_{ai} \left(\frac{n_{ai}}{N_a} \right) \frac{w_{ai}}{\bar{w}} \tag{4}$$

where $\bar{w}$ equals W/P (i.e. average wealth). From these equations we can identify two important sets of considerations, which provide the basis for our critique of the Inland Revenue method below.

The first concerns the 'grossing up' from the estate data, as embodied in equations (1) and (2). Here the choice of the general mortality multipliers (P_a/N_a) and of the social class differentials (λ_{ai}) may be of crucial importance; and we need to consider the sampling and other errors which may arise as a result of the way in which the data become available. The methods used by the Inland Revenue to deal with both of these are discussed in section 2.3. The second set of considerations relates to the extent to which wealth is missing from the estate data or is not recorded in an appropriate manner. This affects equation (4) in two ways. On the one hand, it is necessary to take account of the net worth of the excluded population when estimating the overall average wealth ($\bar{w}$). On the other hand, it may be necessary to adjust the wealth recorded in the estate data (w_{ai}), both because wealth is 'missing' and because the method of valuation may not be appropriate. These problems are considered in section 2.4.

In investigating the consequences of different assumptions or adjustments, it is often valuable to use models of the distribution which, although grossly over-simplified, give some indication of likely orders of magnitude, or at least directions of change. For this purpose we have taken the following simple 'Pareto' model, where differences according to age etc. are ignored:

(i) estates are distributed continuously according to the Pareto distribution with density $f^*(w)$ for $w \geqslant \underline{w}$

$$f^* = B\alpha\, w^{-\alpha-1} \underline{w}^{\alpha}, \text{ where } \alpha > 1 \tag{5}$$

(ii) a constant social class differential is applied to all estates greater than or equal to $\underline{w}$, so that the combined multiplier is $m\lambda$ and the density of wealth-holdings for $w \geqslant \underline{w}$ is

$f = Bm\,\lambda\alpha\,w^{-\alpha-1}\underline{w}^{\alpha}$

and hence the cumulative distribution (expressed as a fraction of the total population)

$$1 - F(w) = Bm\lambda(w/\underline{w})^{-\alpha} \tag{6}$$

(iii) the excluded population expressed as a proportion of the total population is therefore

$$E = 1 - Bm\lambda \tag{7}$$

(evaluating (6) at $w = \underline{w}$) and it is assumed that their average per capita wealth is $\sigma\underline{w}$, where $0 \leqslant \sigma \leqslant 1$.

(iv) it follows that average wealth is given by

$$\bar{w} = \underline{w}\left[E\sigma + (1-E)\frac{\alpha}{\alpha-1}\right] \tag{8}$$

and the shares in total wealth by

$$1 - L(w) = (w/\underline{w})^{-(\alpha-1)}\bigg/\left[1 + \frac{E}{(1-E)}\sigma^*\right] \tag{9}$$

where $\sigma^* = \sigma/(\alpha/(\alpha-1))$ is the average wealth of the excluded population *relative to the included population*.

(v) eliminating $(w/\underline{w})$ from equations (6) and (9), we obtain the Lorenz curve:

$$1 - L = \left(\frac{1-F}{1-E}\right)^{(\alpha-1)/\alpha}\bigg/\left[1 + \frac{E}{(1-E)}\sigma^*\right] \tag{10}$$

It is of course unrealistic to expect that all aspects of the actual distribution of wealth in Britain could be adequately summarised in terms of the three parameters (α, E and σ^*). The model is only intended as a simple laboratory within which we can explore some of the features of the estate method. For this purpose it is sufficient that it provides a broad approximation, and we may note, for example, that where $\sigma^* = 0$ (as in the estimates considered so far) the values $\alpha = 1.5$ and $E = 0.55$, which do not seem unreasonable when the model is applied to Britain in the late 1960s, imply the shares in total wealth shown below.

Pareto model: share in total wealth

	1%	28%
Top	5%	48%
	10%	61%

These, and the Gini coefficient (0.78), are not so dissimilar from the actual estimates shown in figure 2.1 (series B) as to suggest that the model is without value. In what follows, we shall therefore use it to form a preliminary view as to the sensitivity of the results to the methods employed.

2.3   Grossing up from estate data to wealth estimates

(a) Mortality multipliers

The estate method was described in the previous section; we consider now the way in which it is applied by the Inland Revenue. The basic estate data are a more detailed version of those published in *Inland Revenue Statistics*. The cells are classified by the age, sex and country of the deceased to allow for differing mortality experience.[6] Following earlier writers, the Inland Revenue applies different multipliers to different sizes of estate to allow for variation in mortality with economic status. Since no mortality data are available by wealth or income group, it is assumed that wealth is correlated with social class (as defined by the Registrar General's occupational categories), and the following mortality multipliers adopted:

(i) for estates over £5,000 those relating to social classes I and II (broadly the managerial and professional classes),

(ii) for estates under £5,000, rates midway between those for social classes I and II and those for the population as a whole (the division was made at £3,000 before 1970/1).

The social class differentials are derived from the Registrar General's Decennial study of occupational mortality (Registrar General for England and Wales 1971), which in turn is based on matching the deaths registered for a five-year period (most recently 1959–63) to the population at risk as enumerated in the Census of Population (in 1961).

This use of the mortality multiplier technique follows the pattern set by earlier academic investigators (whose work was reviewed briefly in chapter 1); there are, however, a number of aspects which warrant closer attention than they have received in the past. We discuss first those relating to the general mortality multiplier (P_a/N_a) and then those affecting the social class adjustment (λ_{ai}).

6   The age ranges are 'under 25', '25 to 34', ... '75 to 84', '85 and upwards'. In a certain number of cases (1.4% males, 1.8% females in 1970–1) the age is not stated, and they are apportioned over the older age groups on the basis of a special sample carried out in 1963/4.

The general mortality multiplier depends on the accuracy with which N_a (deaths during the year) and P_a (midyear population) are recorded.[7] In the latter case, the Registrar General's midyear estimates of the population are recognised to be subject to error and are typically revised when later population data become available. Although errors of estimation apply particularly to the age/sex composition, they may also affect the total population estimate (P). In 1975 the Registrar General for England and Wales reported that 'when the results from the 1971 Census of Population were analysed it was discovered that the estimate of population for 1971, carried forward from 1961, was some 350,000 higher than that based on the 1971 Census' (1975:3). The significance of such revisions for the estate estimates is discussed in chapter 5.

The general mortality multipliers are in effect averages for age groups, and it can be objected that they are weighted according to the age distribution of the total population and not according to the age distribution of persons possessing estates in each group. If wealth tends to increase with age, then the average age of people appearing in the estate statistics in each age group is higher than the average age of the population in the same age group; and this causes the multiplier to be too high. The work of Mallet (1908) showed clearly that if the whole population were regarded as an age group then the error involved would be considerable. With the ten-year age groups used by the Inland Revenue, the error is undoubtedly much smaller, and Daniels and Campion, referring to the calculations by Snow in the discussion of Mallet and Strutt (1915), concluded 'that the error introduced by age grouping is not likely to be very considerable' (1936:13). Its precise effect on the Inland Revenue estimates has not however been thoroughly investigated.

The social class adjustments have been subjected to close examination by a number of authors, particularly Revell (1967), and this has suggested that they suffer from a number of drawbacks:

(i) The mortality rates are obtained by combining information from two different sources and there are serious discrepancies between the occupational statements at death registration and those at the Census. This is reflected first in the numbers recorded as 'unoccupied' because of lack of information. Although the Census schedule asks retired respondents to record their previous occupations, many fail to follow this instruction. This problem may also

7 The variables N_a and P_a relate to different dimensions, the former being a flow and the latter a stock. It can, however, be seen from equations (3) and (4) that F_j and L_j are pure numbers. The distribution should be seen therefore as pertaining to a particular date, rather than as covering all those alive at some point or other during a given year.

arise at death registration but the evidence shows that it is much less prevalent. As a result, the size of the occupied population is relatively under-stated, and hence their mortality rate over-stated.

(ii) These discrepancies also arise between occupational categories and 'there is a tendency for the death registrations to give a somewhat more rosy view of the social class distribution of the deceased than the Census' (Lydall and Tipping 1961:99). This has been demonstrated at successive Censuses by special matching exercises carried out by the Registrar General for England and Wales who concluded that 'for males aged 20—64, there is evidence of a strong tendency to report occupations assignable to Social Classes I and II more often at death registration than on the Census Schedules' (1958:7).

(iii) The Registrar General's analysis of female mortality does not include widows. More generally, no allowance has so far been made for differing mortality experience by marital status, which the American data suggest to be of some considerable importance, see Smith (1974).

(iv) The Inland Revenue's use of a cut-off level (applying the average multiplier for class I and II combined above this level, and lower multipliers below) makes inadequate allowance for the social class gradient. The £5,000 plus group ranges 'from the man of 45 who has just finished paying off the mortgage on his house and has few other possessions at one end to the man whose total wealth is £3 million or more at the other' (Revell 1967:114). There are therefore good reasons for graduating the multiplier with wealth above this level. More generally, the assumption that wealth is correlated with social class as measured in the Census of Population is open to question. As is pointed out by Revell (1967:116), it is probably a better approximation to a hierarchy of earned income than to a hierarchy of wealth.

(v) The Inland Revenue makes inadequate allowance for differential trends in mortality over time. The social class mortality rates are assumed to remain the same percentage of the general mortality rate for long periods, whereas mortality in the upper social classes may improve, or worsen, relative to that for the remainder of the population. The only adjustment made has been the switch to use of results based on the 1961 Census. In the 110th Annual Report of the Inland Revenue, estimates were presented for the first time on this basis (from 1964 on). Comparing the estimates for two overlapping years (1964 and 1965) in the 109th Report, table 166, and the 110th Report, table 185, it appears that this adjustment led to a discrete jump in the series, increasing the total numbers and amounts of wealth by about 5 per cent.

The first of these problems (i) is dealt with by the Inland Revenue in the same way as Lydall and Tipping (1961), who simply allocate the unoccupied proportionately over all social classes at the Census and at death registration. This assumption is described by the Registrar General as one 'which is almost certainly untenable in fact; but which allows a clearer indication of the main tendencies' (1958:7). Lydall and Tipping also made an adjustment for the problem (ii). They estimated from the matching study of the 1951 Census of Population, 'it would appear that the "upper class" mortality rates for males are over-estimated by 8.3 per cent' (1961:99), and therefore adjusted by this amount the rates for men. (This argument was assumed also to hold for males in Scotland.) The Inland Revenue made the same adjustment for multipliers based on the results of the 1951 Census, but has not made any adjustment to more recent data. The third problem (iii) is under consideration by the Inland Revenue, although no analysis has yet been published. Problems (iv) and (v) remain.

There has been very little detailed investigation of the effect of these deficiencies or indeed of the properties of the mortality technique in general. In qualitative terms, there has been little analysis of the direction of the effects of changes in the multipliers. Would the adoption of a larger social class differential raise or lower the estimated shares? What would happen if the multipliers were graduated more evenly with estate size? Quantitatively there have been few attempts to compare the results with different multipliers or to assess the importance of the various shortcomings of the Inland Revenue multipliers. For example, Polanyi and Wood claim that 'estimates of the distribution of wealth are highly sensitive to whichever assumption is made about the appropriate mortality rate to be used' (1974:25), but provide no calculations to support this position.

A first indication of the answers to some of these questions may be obtained from the simple 'Pareto' model outlined in the previous section. The assumptions that the social class multiplier applies to the entire Pareto distribution, and that this covers all recorded estates, mean that an increase in the social class differential decreases E (via equation (7)) but otherwise leaves the model unchanged. From equation (10) it may be shown (by differentiating with respect to E) that a rise in λ, and hence a fall in E, reduces the share of a given percentage group if

$$\alpha > \frac{1 + \sigma^* E/(1 - E)}{1 - \sigma^*} \tag{11}$$

If, as in the estimates described in section 2.1, $\sigma^* = 0$, then this condition will always be satisfied. An increase in the social class multiplier will lead to an inward movement of the Lorenz curve. On the other hand, where the excluded population are assumed to have wealth ($\sigma^* > 0$), then the effect may go the other way, as is illustrated by the case $\alpha = 1.5, E = 0.5$ and $\sigma^* = 0.25$. Quantitatively, we may note that where $\sigma^* = 0, \alpha = 1.5$, a rise in the social class multiplier which reduces E from 0.55 to 0.5 has the effect of lowering the share of the top 1 per cent by 1 percentage point. This suggests that the estimates of the shares would not be unduly sensitive, but that the effect is not sufficiently small that it can be neglected.

In Chapter 3 we examine both the theory of mortality multipliers (to see whether the conclusions reached using the simplified Pareto model apply more generally) and the particular features of the Inland Revenue approach. In the latter case we concentrate on the following three main areas:

> errors in occupational statements (i and ii),
> marital status (iii),
> graduation of multipliers with estate size (iv).

(The problem of differential trends (v) is taken up in chapter 6.)

(b) Sampling problems

There are four main types of problem which arise from the use by the Inland Revenue of the estate statistics as a sample of wealth-holding. Firstly, there are the problems which arise from the employment of sample data in any form. Suppose for the moment that we view the estate data as a random sample, stratified by age, sex and country, of living persons with dutiable wealth, the overall sampling fraction being some $1\frac{1}{2}$ per cent. This process of sampling, even leaving aside the method by which the sample is selected, introduces the possibility of sampling error. Moreover, there is a further stage of sampling from estates to compile the data made available by the Inland Revenue. They do not make a complete analysis of all estates (except for certain summary tables). Instead the procedure followed is to include all insolvent estates and all those over a specified limit (varying with age), and to sample a percentage of the remainder. In 1972–3, for example, the sampling fraction was only 1 per cent for estates in the range nil to £3,000 where the person was aged 45 or over at death, and for estates in the range £5,000 to £10,000 it was 5 per cent.[8]

8 Where the sampling fraction is less than 100%, there may be some variation from the desired random sample in view of the temptation to pass over bulky, and therefore probably 'difficult' files, but this is likely to be relatively unimportant, since 'difficult' cases tend to involve large estates, where the sampling fractions are higher.

Even with the complete coverage of the largest estates and the youngest age groups, the number of cases in each cell may be extremely small: in 1969–70, for example, only one man died between the ages of 35 and 45 leaving an estate of over £200,000. The Inland Revenue attempt to reduce the error involved by:

(i) combining the observations partly across age groups and partly across estate classes and applying a combined multiplier,

(ii) in the case of the largest wealth groups, averaging the multiplied-up data over a number of years.[9]

The first of these adjustments means that in particular estate classes the multiplier applied is not that appropriate to the particular age group but is instead a weighted average of a number of different age groups' multipliers. In our view, this procedure is not entirely satisfactory, and we depart in what follows from the Inland Revenue practice of combining observations across age groups. The reason for concern is not that errors may be introduced through variation in the total number of deaths in a particular age group, since this would be reflected in an exactly offsetting variation in the mortality multipliers. The problem arises with the distribution of estates among wealth classes. This suggests that any combination of observations before applying the multipliers should be not between age groups, which would introduce errors arising from variation in the overall mortality rate for each group, but solely between estate classes. It should however be borne in mind that when estate classes are combined this reduces the detail of the final results. If ranges i and j are combined, even if only for a single age group, then the ranges cannot be distinguished in the final estimates. As noted earlier, the Inland Revenue does not provide any figure for the number of millionaires. The most obvious alternative is to average the multiplied-up data over a number of years. This procedure has been employed by a number of authors, but it too suffers from several drawbacks. In chapter 5 we examine the consequences of aggregating estate classes and aggregating over years, as well as the more general issue of the magnitude of sampling errors.

The second set of problems concerns the method by which the estate sample is drawn. The fundamental assumption underlying the estate method is that those in a particular age/sex/country group dying in a given year may be regarded as a representative sample of the living population in that age group, but this is naturally open to question. Those dying in a particular age group are likely to have had below-average health and this may well have

9 It may be noted that a further, exceptional adjustment was made to the data for 1972–3 'owing to the co-incidental occurrence of the deaths of several millionaires in the younger age-groups' (*Inland Revenue Statistics* 1974: 175).

affected their wealth. Those with poor health may have retired earlier and hence been less able to accumulate savings; they may have had nursing and other medical expenses which have caused them to draw on their savings.[10] Perhaps more importantly, those with a shorter life expectancy are more likely to have taken steps to avoid estate duty. The effect of such action depends on the form which avoidance takes. In certain situations, such as the deathbed purchase of agricultural property, the full value is still reported; in others the wealth may disappear completely. In the case of gifts *inter vivos*, which were under estate duty probably the single most important form of avoidance, the effect is less straightforward.

The implications of gifts *inter vivos* for the estate duty method have long been the subject of controversy, it being argued that such gifts render the approach invalid.[11] As pointed out by Mallet and Strutt (1915) the recipients are subject to the same laws of mortality and the wealth appears in the estates of those in this group who die in a given period. If a person aged 65 transfers part of his wealth to his son aged 40, this wealth is still represented in the estate duty estimates, since some of those aged 40 will die and the lower mortality rate will be offset by the higher multiplier. The gift will have changed the distribution of wealth, but the post-gift distribution is correctly represented.

If both donors and recipients had the same life expectancy as others in their age/sex groups, this refutation of the criticism appears correct. There are, however, reasons to doubt whether this condition holds:

> the death toll in any age group is taken from two sections – those who have been in failing health and almost expect the event and those who are cut off by accident, or otherwise, unexpectedly in health. Now if, as it is quite reasonable to suppose, the habit of giving *inter vivos* is mainly confined to those who are failing, and they give generally to those in the lower age group who are not failing, then . . . the fundamental assumption is not absolutely sound, and more fortune is going out of the multiplier computation at one stage than is coming into it at the other [Stamp 1916:413].

The same point has been made more recently by Lampman: 'it might seem reasonable to assume that persons, particularly at older ages, with shorter

---

10 An obvious example is funeral expenses! These are added back by the Inland Revenue in their estimates, as is the capital gains tax liability arising from the realisation deemed to have taken place at death (where this applied).

11 Under estate duty if the donor lived for a specified period after the gift was made, it was not counted as part of his estate. The time limit was initially one year (Finance Act, 1894), was increased to three years in 1909, five years in 1946 and to seven years in 1968.

than average life expectancy for their age group, would be more likely to be donors than those with longer expectancies' (1962:68n). There is no firm evidence to support these views but they have some plausibility. If they are correct, and if gifts are made largely by the wealthy (to avoid duty), then the degree of concentration is under-stated. At the same time, a factor working in the opposite direction is that where the donor dies within seven years, the gift is included both in his estate and (applying the Mallet/Strutt argument) in the wealth of the recipient.[12] This double-counting is likely to have the reverse effect, causing the degree of concentration to be over-stated. The net likely bias introduced by these two factors is therefore uncertain.

The third group of problems is of a rather technical nature and concerns the form in which the estate duty statistics are collected. The statistics published, and used by the Inland Revenue, relate to the financial year ending on 31 March and cover estates on which duty was first paid or for which the grant of representation came to the notice of the Estate Duty Office first in that year.[13] In view of the fact that the average delay between death and first payment of duty is estimated by the Inland Revenue to be between three and four months, it is commonly assumed that the statistics may be taken as representing those of the preceding calendar year, and the Inland Revenue estimates of wealth-holding in 1970, for example, are based on the estate duty returns for 1970–1. To the extent that the delay is longer or shorter, this means that the estimates are not fully representative of the period; and there may be a differential effect by estate class.

The position is complicated by the treatment of corrections to the original returns. Corrective returns are reported in the year in which they are received, with (to date) no attempt being made to adjust the statistics for earlier years. This has the effect that:

Numbers. No addition is made to the total number of estates. On the other hand, if as a consequence of a change in the net value of an estate in a subsequent year the estate is transferred to another range, the number of estates in the new range is increased by one in this subsequent year and the number in the original range diminished by one.

Value. The adjustments to the value are reported in the year in which they are notified. Where the addition, or subtraction, leaves the estate within the same capital range, the amount of the change is simply included in this range

12 As pointed out by Lampman (1962:69) this does not all represent double-counting since gifts made in the year of death are unlikely to show up fully in the estates of the recipients.

13 A change recorded in *Inland Revenue Statistics* 1974 is that since 'April 1972 in England and Wales, estates have been counted when duty is first assessed, unless some duty has already been paid, and in some cases this will bring them into the year preceding first payment of duty' (p. 102).

for the later year. Where the change moves an estate between classes, the total capital is added to the new range, and the previous total is subtracted from the old range, both applying to the later year.

To illustrate the way in which this works, suppose an estate of £11,500 is reported in 1969–70, and a further £2,000 is reported in 1970–1. No change would be made to the 1969–70 figures, but for 1970–1 the numbers in the range £10,000 – £12,500 would be reduced by 1 (and the amount reduced by £11,500), whereas the numbers in the range £12,500 – £15,000 would be increased by 1 (and the amount increased by £13,500). As is noted by the Inland Revenue, this procedure leads to 'some blurring of the figures'. It may on occasion lead to negative totals appearing in the upper estate classes, and to the average estate size lying outside the class interval. For example, the estate returns for 1966–7 show minus 2 for the number of estates in the range £100,000 – £200,000 owned by men aged 25–34, and the average size of estates in the range £50,000 – £100,000 owned by women of the same age was £177,000 (*Inland Revenue Statistics* 1970: table 114).

The importance of these problems depends on the stability over time of the mortality multipliers and the changes taking place in asset prices. If there is an upward trend in the mortality multipliers, the number of current deaths is smaller than those appearing, with a delay, in the estate duty figures, and the number of wealth-holdings is over-stated.[14] Similarly, the adjustments made relating to earlier estates over-state those likely to be made on current estates. On the other hand, an upward trend in asset prices causes the adjustments to be under-stated, and in a time of substantial capital gains this might be an important factor. It is difficult, however, to make any adequate estimate of its quantitative importance without data on estates by length of delay, by size, and by asset composition (since this is likely to affect the delay).[15]

Finally, there is the problem of errors in the recording of wealth on the estate duty returns for estates below the estate duty exemption limit. As is explained by the Inland Revenue, 'the figures obtained from estates below the exemption limit for estate duty . . . are less reliable than those from estates paying duty because in general they do not have to be examined so thoroughly' (*Inland Revenue Statistics* 1972:155). The fact that small estates are checked less thoroughly may lead one to expect that the average wealth is

14 This aspect is set out clearly by Langley, who suggests that 'a very considerable error may be introduced' (1954:2). It is not, however, obvious that there will be a large error in the *distribution* (percentage shares) as opposed to absolute amounts of wealth.

15 A further problem prior to 1965 was that large estates where duty was payable in instalments were recorded on a 'payment' basis, that is only capital on which duty was actually paid was recorded.

under-stated; however, it has been suggested to us by the Inland Revenue that, for estates below the threshold where there is personal application, assets, particularly chattels, tend to be over-valued. Moreover, liabilities may be under-stated: 'when an estate is clearly not liable to duty, nobody has any incentive to do elaborate sums to compute the debts owing by the deceased and they will almost certainly be under-stated' (Revell 1967: 158–9). This is taken up when we come to the balance sheet estimates in chapter 4, but for the present the net effect is unclear.

2.4 'Missing' wealth and problems of valuation

(a) 'Missing' people

The estate data do not cover all individuals dying in a given year but only those coming to the notice of the Estate Duty Offices. The estates covered are therefore those where there is a grant of representation (grant of confirmation in Scotland), and in addition any cases where there is no grant but the estate is liable to duty. It should be emphasised that the data are not limited to dutiable estates, so that in 1970, for example, when the exemption level was £10,000 there were more than 200,000 estates below that level shown in the statistics.[16] Nonetheless, over half the estates in any year are missing from the statistics: in 1970, for example, there was a total of 290,000 estates included in the Inland Revenue statistics compared with a total of 639,000 deaths (*Inland Revenue Statistics* 1972:156). The omission of these estates from the estate duty returns means that when the mortality multipliers are applied, the number of wealth-holders falls considerably short of the total adult population. In 1970, for example, the estimated number of wealth-holders was 17 million compared with the population figures below.

Population aged:

21 and over	37 million
18 and over	39 million
15 and over	41 million

16 For future reference, the estate duty exemption levels are shown below:

Deaths occurring on or after	Exemption level
10 April 1946	£2,000
30 July 1954	£3,000
10 April 1962	£4,000
4 April 1963	£5,000
16 April 1969	£10,000
31 March 1971	£12,500
22 March 1972	£15,000

(Prior to 1946 the exemption level was £100.)

The excluded population was therefore of the order of 55–60 per cent of the total adult population (the precise figure depending on the definition adopted).

The estates not covered by the statistics are basically those which are neither subject to duty nor for which a grant of representation (probate) is obtained. A grant is in general sought in order to establish the right to recover or reserve any part of the personal estate of a deceased person (Tristram and Coote 1970:7). There are a number of exceptions (apart from the estate of a deceased British sovereign) including:

   (i) property to which title can pass by delivery (e.g. cash or household goods),

   (ii) property where the owner can nominate a person (or persons) to whom the asset should be transferred (e.g. industrial life assurance policies),

   (iii) jointly owned property (such as a house or a joint bank account) passing by survivorship to the other joint tenant,

   (iv) property covered by the Administration of Estates (Small Payments) Act, 1965.

The last of these allows sums up to a specified limit held in certain forms to be transferred without a grant of representation. Prior to 1965, the limit was £100 for most types of asset covered by these provisions. In 1965, the limit was made the same for all types of asset covered and raised to £500. (From August 1975 it was further increased to £1,500). The main assets affected are National Savings Certificates, building society deposits, National Savings Bank and Trustee Savings Bank deposits, and Premium Bonds. From this is appears that estates missing from the statistics are likely to involve relatively small amounts. There are, no doubt, cases where the missing estate exceeds the average wealth (while below the exemption level): for example, where the only substantial asset is a jointly owned house valued (in 1970) at, say, £9,500.[17] It is possible to imagine situations where there is non-aggregable property (see below) which takes the total value of the missing estate above the exemption level. The whole of the missing estate might consist of non-dutiable property, such as a surviving spouse settlement or growing timber, although it should be emphasised that the whole of the estate has to be in a form which can be transferred without probate in order for it to be missing from the statistics. The joint ownership of houses is probably a more

---

17 In this respect it is important to note the introduction in the Finance Act 1972 of the additional exemption for transfers to surviving spouses, allowing up to £30,000 to be transferred to the spouse without the estate being dutiable.

important source of exceptions, but this can only affect a minority of the missing estates.

If it may be assumed that the bulk of the wealth-holders missing from the official estimates belongs to the lowest ranges, then it follows that ignoring the existence of these wealth-holders, as in the Inland Revenue Series A, causes the degree of concentration to be under-stated. Moreover, the degree of under-statement varies over time with changes in the estate duty provisions. In this context, the Administration of Estates (Small Payments) Act 1965 is important since it increased the limit below which small amounts could be transferred without probate. As a result the coverage of small estates was less complete after 1965 than before; and it may be seen from table 2.1 that the number of wealth-holders indicated by the Inland Revenue statistics fell from 19.5m. in 1964 to 17.4m. in 1966. Estimates which ignore those not covered by the estate duty statistics may, therefore, give a misleading impression of the downward trend.[18,19] Moreover, the fact that the fall in the number of wealth-holders over this period can be accounted for almost entirely by the range £0–1,000 (table 2.1) provides some support for the view that the missing wealth-holders belong largely to the lowest wealth ranges.

The alternative Series B, on the other hand, is based on the extreme assumption that the excluded population have zero wealth, and this errs in the opposite direction. The effect may be illustrated using our simple Pareto model, where $\alpha = 1.5$. The table below has $\sigma^* = 0$ (excluded population has zero wealth) and different values of E.

	E		
	0.0	0.55	0.6
Share of top 1%	22%	28%	29%
Share of top 5%	37%	48%	50%

On this basis, the move from Series A to Series B raises the share of the top 1 per cent from 22 per cent to 28–9 per cent, which is close to that actually observed in figure 2.1. The last two columns give some indication of the effect of different definitions of the adult population. In general, taking a lower age limit tends to raise the estimated shares. For example, taking the

18 In effect a number of small wealth-holdings were simply removed from the estimates. The Inland Revenue's notes on this point were incorrect until *Inland Revenue Statistics* 1972.

19 Another factor contributing to the variation over time in the Inland Revenue estimates is the changing estate duty exemption limit (to the extent that the estates do not require probate). This may, for example, be partly responsible for the apparent decline in numbers below £5,000 in 1963 (table 2.1).

population 15 and over rather than 21 and over, so that in broad terms E is 0.60 rather than 0.55, tends to increase the share of the top 5 per cent by two percentage points. (This assumes of course that no estates are in the age range 15–20.)

Clearly neither of the assumptions A or B is adequate for our purposes. To ignore the existence of half the adult population is obviously wrong. At the same time it is not reasonable to suppose that they own no wealth at all, and it is necessary to investigate in more detail the likely wealth of those who do not appear in the Inland Revenue tables. This has been done in a number of earlier studies by academic investigators. For example, Lydall and Tipping based their estimates of the wealth of those below the estate duty exemption level on three main sources and techniques: '(1) extrapolation of cumulative frequency curves, (2) evidence gleaned from the 1954 savings survey about the relative holdings of particular assets by those above and below this level, and (3) information about total assets of persons (e.g. life funds) available from independent sources' (1961:86). The approach here employs the third of these techniques, and in Chapter 4 estimates are presented using independent evidence about the total holdings of particular assets by the personal sector, there being much more extensive information available now than at the time of the Lydall and Tipping study.

Before leaving the subject of missing estates, it is interesting to see from the Pareto model how the estimates would be likely to be affected by different assumptions about the wealth of the excluded population. From equation (10), it may be seen that as σ^* rises, the estimated shares fall. Since in 1970 the mean wealth for the Inland Revenue estimates was £5,660 per person, we can calculate the effect on the shares of different assumptions about the wealth of the excluded popualtion (in 1970 terms, and with

Percentage share of:	top 1%	top 5%
Series B ($\sigma^* = 0$)	28%	48%
Average wealth £500 ($\sigma^* = 0.09$)	25%	44%
Average wealth £1000 ($\sigma^* = 0.18$)	23%	40%
Series A ($E = 0$)	22%	37%

$\alpha = 1.5, E = 0.55$). Even, therefore, quite substantial allowance for the wealth of the excluded population (in 1970 terms) leaves the estimates above those based on Series A.[20]

20 With the values of E and α used in this calculation, the shares only fall below those for Series A if σ^* is greater than 0.25. In 1973 that would have implied an average wealth of £2,150 per person for the excluded population.

(b) Missing wealth

So far we have been concerned with estates which are totally missing from the returns. Reliance on statistics derived from the estate data is also open to criticism on the grounds that even for those covered the returns provide an incomplete picture of wealth-holding. This arises on account of the provisions in the estate duty law which allow wealth to be transferred without duty being paid or at a reduced rate of duty. While it is not true that all these provisions lead to wealth not appearing in the returns,[21] there can be little doubt that substantial amounts are 'missing' from the estate duty statistics, or, as it is expressed by the Inland Revenue, 'certain elements are omitted because no duty is payable on them either because of special exemptions or because they fall outside the scope of estate duty law' (*Inland Revenue Statistics* 1974:175).

The missing property is best considered under two broad headings:

(I) Exclusions with no limit, including:

(i) property settled on a surviving spouse (with no power to dispose of the capital) which bore estate duty, or would have borne it but for the exemption limit, and which is exempt on the death of this spouse,

(ii) property held under discretionary trusts (before the 1969 Finance Act),[22]

(iii) objects of national, scientific, historic or artistic interest which are exempt from duty,

(iv) growing timber, which is not aggregated with the rest of the estate and on which duty is not paid unless and until the timber is sold,

(v) annuities for life and rights to occupational pensions,

(vi) death benefits under certain pension schemes.

(II) Exclusions subject to specified limits, including:

(i) joint property and property settled by the deceased where their total value together with the free estate does not exceed the point at which duty becomes payable,

21 A person may, for example, purchase agricultural property; because of the lower rates of duty, this reduces his estate duty liability, but the full value of the assets is still shown in the return. (The existence of the provisions may well, of course, affect the demand for such property and hence its market price.)

22 Under the Finance Act 1969 estate duty was, in broad terms, payable on the death of a beneficiary under a discretionary trust on the same proportion of the trust property as the proportion of trust income received by the deceased in the preceding seven years. Depending on the policy followed by the trustees, it was still possible for property held in this form not to appear in the statistics.

(ii) items treated as estates by themselves which do not appear if they do not exceed the exemption limit: for example, certain life policies and property settled otherwise than by the deceased when the rest of the property does not exceed a certain level.

In the case of group (II), both the size of the excluded property and the size of the total estate is limited. In the case of (I), the missing property and the estate to which it belongs could in theory be of any size. The incentive to avoid estate duty means however that the occurrence of such property, and its size, probably increase as we move up the wealth scale.[23] Although surviving spouse settlements may be relatively small, discretionary trusts are only likely to be established by those with substantial wealth. The same applies to categories (iii) and (iv). Pensions and annuities are, of course, an exception since other considerations are relevant.

The Inland Revenue make no attempt to adjust their annual estimates for missing wealth but this has been done by a number of academic investigators.[24] In their estimates for 1954, Lydall and Tipping made some very approximate adjustments and added to their total of £40,000 million for personal wealth, a further £2,000 million for pension funds, £3,000 million for property settled on a surviving spouse and £1,000 million for discretionary trusts. In the case of settled property, they assumed that it belonged entirely to the top 10 per cent in the wealth distribution: 'very little such property is likely to find its way into the hands of persons below the top ten per cent of property owners, since the top ten per cent in 1951–6 included everyone with more than £1,700 of capital' (1961:92). They assumed that half the pension funds belonged to the top 10 per cent. With these assumptions, the addition of missing property makes little difference to the estimates, the effect of the two components on the percentage shares tending to net out. On the other hand, if the whole of the settled property belonged to the top 1 per cent, then their share would be increased on this account from 43 per cent to 46 per cent; whereas if none of the occupational pension funds belonged to this group, their share would be reduced by 2 per cent. Individual items may therefore have a noticeable effect, and in chapter 4 we try to

23 Reference should also be made to the problem of evasion of estate duty, which clearly leads to property being missing. However, as is pointed out by Revell, 'most people would probably agree that this is at a low level in Britain – if only because the legal methods of avoidance are so many' (1967:112). How far this has changed as a result of the introduction of the Capital Transfer Tax is yet to be seen.

24 It should however be noted that the Inland Revenue have given estimates of certain types of missing property in the Appendix to the Wealth Tax Green Paper and in evidence to the Select Committee on the Wealth Tax. These are referred to in chapter 4.

provide more accurate, and more recent, estimates for the effects of missing property.

Further blurring of the estate statistics is caused by the non-aggregation provisions and by the fact that, for technical reasons, settled property is usually reported separately from the free estate.[25] These may cause an estate with total capital W to appear in the statistics as two (or more) estates with capital W_1 and W_2 where $W_1 + W_2 = W$. In other words, the numbers, but not the amounts are counted twice. This is illustrated by the two examples below:

> Mr A whose estate is   £50,000 free
>   £10,000 settled
> Mr B whose estate is   £5,000 free
>   £10,000 settled

In the case of Mr A the statistics show two estates, of £50,000 and £10,000 respectively, rather than a single estate of £60,000. This causes the degree of concentration to be under-stated. In the case of Mr B, only one estate of £5,000 is reported, and the £10,000 is missing as explained earlier.

(c) Method of valuation and geographical coverage

The valuation of assets in the estate data was discussed by Revell in the context of national balance sheets, and he concluded that 'in general the valuation of items for estate duty is just what we need — a valuation at market prices' (1967:112). However, as we have seen in chapter 1, market value may be an ambiguous concept in the light of the fact that many markets are characterised by imperfections, such as transaction costs, etc. A contrast was drawn there between the value obtainable on realisation (a 'sell-up' value) and the value to the person or household as a 'going concern'. The Inland

---

25 The non-aggregation provisions have varied over the years, but the most important for the period covered here are:

(i) prior to the Finance Act 1969, property in which the deceased never had an interest was not aggregated with any other property but was treated as an estate by itself. This was abolished by the 1969 legislation with the exception of certain life policies effected before 20 March 1968;

(ii) where the value of the deceased's own property, including settled property derived from the deceased and certain other items, is below a specified level, then this property is not aggregated with other settled property;

(iii) growing timber (see I(iv) on p. 39).

The limit for (ii) was £10,000 for deaths before 31 March 1971, £12,500 between 31 March 1971 and 21 March 1972, and £15,000 (plus any surviving spouse relief or relief for bequests to charities and national heritage bodies due) after 21 March 1972.

Revenue method of valuation is in certain respects closer to the former. In the case of household goods, for example, the valuation is based on second-hand market prices, and, as Revell points out, with the exception of cars, these values 'are usually derisory' and would not be applicable if the household was viewed as a going concern. Nonetheless, whichever basis for valuation is adopted, adjustments need to be made to the Inland Revenue estimates, as is brought out by the examples below:

(i) *Life policies.* For this class of assets the estate duty valuation is clearly inappropriate on both approaches. In the estate duty statistics, life assurance policies on the deceased's own life are valued at the sum assured (plus any bonus), whereas in the hands of the living they are worth less than this amount. Campion (1939) felt in fact that wealth should be estimated without any additions due to death and therefore excluded life policies altogether. However, as Langley has noted, 'the possession of a policy puts a person in a similar position to a man of capital in many ways. He may, for example, assume risks and obligations which he would otherwise hesitate to assume and may raise a loan on the policy' (1951:34). She goes on to suggest that the policies have a surrender value which could be employed. This, or the market sale price of a policy, might be appropriate for valuation on a 'sell-up' basis. On the other hand, in the case of the going concern valuation Revell has argued that 'surrender value is always computed so as to impose a penalty on surrender, and it is therefore inappropriate for the holder viewed as a "going concern" . . . For this there is no alternative but the present value of the income stream or capital payment' (1967:31). He assumes that this latter value is equal to the actuarial reserves or fund held against the policy and uses this as the basis for his estimates.

(ii) *Pension rights.* This class of assets brings out very clearly the difference between the two different methods of valuation. On a 'sell-up' basis, no value would in general be attached to these assets, since the holder cannot realise the asset or borrow on the strength of it (even in the case of insured pension schemes it is not usually possible to pledge them against a loan). The Inland Revenue treatment may therefore be appropriate in this case. On the other hand, these rights are worth something to the holder as a going concern, and on this alternative basis allowance would be made for their value.

(iii) *Settled property.* It has been argued that the estate duty valuation of settled property may be inappropriate in certain circumstances. For example, the formula introduced in the Finance Act 1969 to allocate the capital held in discretionary trusts based on income received may not correspond at all accurately to the value of the deceased's interest. Settled property is again an example where different bases for valuation are likely to lead to rather different results. It also illustrates the fact that the sum of separate interests in a property may fall short of the value of the property as a whole.

(iv) *Consumer durables and trade assets.* We referred earlier to the low valuation placed on household goods in the Inland Revenue estimates. This aspect has been emphasised by Polanyi and Wood (1974) who suggest that the figures are 'impossibly low' and that this leads to an important bias in the official estimates. It should be remembered, however, that the same applies in the case of the assets of unincorporated businesses. If valued for estate duty purposes on a second-hand basis, this may be quite different from that to the owner on the assumption that he continues in business. According to Revell (1967) the difference in the case of plant and equipment could be substantial. He goes on to point out that part of the difference may appear under the headings of 'goodwill' or 'unallocated share of partnership', but these fall considerably short of the whole discrepancy. On a going concern basis adjustments are therefore necessary for trade assets, which are likely to be less widely distributed than assets such as consumer durables.

(v) *Houses.* It has been suggested that the value of houses may be understated in the Inland Revenue estimates. Polanyi and Wood state that 'in 1970 the value of homes owned may have exceeded the Inland Revenue estimate by more than 50 per cent' (1974:29). The difference between the estimated total and that derived from independent sources may be explained in part by factors such as the exclusion of certain joint property and that the independent totals make inadequate allowance for the separation of interests (again the sum of individual interests may be less than the value of the property in its entirety).

In chapter 4 we consider the adjustments that may be made under these headings and the implications of different bases for valuation.

Finally, we should refer to the related issue of geographical coverage. In broad terms, the estate data cover:

    (i) all property situated anywhere in the world which is owned by persons domiciled in Great Britain (prior to the Finance Act 1962 immovable property situated overseas was exempt),

    (ii) all property situated in Great Britain owned by persons domiciled elsewhere, apart from certain UK government securities which carry exemption from estate duty when the deceased holder was neither domiciled nor ordinarily resident.

In the case of (ii), double taxation relief normally applies, but the full value of the asset still appears.

The Inland Revenue make no adjustment to the estate data but two aspects warrant consideration. Firstly, if domicile is accepted as the appropriate definition, then wealth in category (ii) should be excluded. The evidence from Revell (1967:131) indicated that these estates constituted between 1.4 per cent and 2.1 per cent of the gross capital value of estates of £3,000 and over in 1959–61 and about 1 per cent below this level. The assumption made here is that in 1968, 1 per cent of estates below £5,000 (in 1972, £10,000) and 2 per cent above this level should be deducted. No great confidence can be attached to these adjustments, but we lacked the resources to explore this further. It should be noted that the total deducted in 1972 (£2,300 million) is close to the £2,000 million used by the Royal Commission (1975:85), whose approach was similar to that adopted here.

The second aspect is possibly more important but is certainly more debatable. This concerns the definition of residence and whether the tax law concept of domicile is really appropriate. As Meacher has argued 'given the increasing rapidity of travel and communications today, a foreign domicile is not incompatible with wide business and social interests in this country' (1972:192). Where one would like to draw the line is obviously open to dispute but there must certainly be people who are not legally domiciled but who have continued to participate in British society and whose families are likely to maintain roots in this country. In what follows we have made no attempt to adjust for this factor,[26] but we agree with Whalley that the extension of the estimates to include such people would raise the degree of concentration: 'as the tax incentives to migrate to a tax haven increase sharply with wealth a "proper accounting" must be expected to make things more unequal' (1974).

2.5 The Inland Revenue statistics – a summing up
The first point to be made in any assessment of the official estimates is that they do not set out to measure the extent of inequality in wealth-holding viewed in a normative sense. What they set out to measure is the distribution of current personal wealth-holding by individuals in a particular year. From this pattern it may be possible to make judgements about the justice or otherwise of the distribution, but this presupposes a standard of equity and may involve the interpretation of the evidence to allow for factors such as variation in asset-holding over the life-cycle or the holding of wealth within families.

Our concern here, therefore, is with how accurately the Inland Revenue estimates reflect what they set out to measure. As we have seen, some authors feel that – even within this limited context – the figures are of no value. Our

26 Any such adjustment might, of course, involve adding back part of the wealth deducted under the adjustment described in the previous paragraph.

own assessment is that this extreme view is unwarranted, and indeed those espousing it have produced little convincing evidence that (say) the share of the top 1 per cent in currently held personal wealth would be drastically modified by changes in the method of estimation or that alternative methods would lead to unrecognisably different results. To take one example, Polanyi and Wood (1974) lay great stress on the omission of the wealth of those not covered by the estate statistics. However, we have seen (page 38 above) that even a quite substantial allowance for the wealth of the excluded population leaves the shares of the top wealth groups higher than those based on the Inland Revenue Series A. For example, the analysis earlier suggested that if the average wealth of the excluded population were £1,000 (in 1970 terms), this would reduce the share of the top 1 per cent from 28 per cent to 23 per cent. This is important (and reflects the very considerable addition to total wealth − over £20 billion) but not large enough to mean that the original figure was totally misleading.

Nor is it correct to suggest that the official estimates are systematically biased in one direction. In table 2.2 we have summarised the principal problems reviewed in this chapter, and in the third column we give an approximate indication of the direction in which the degree of concentration, as measured by the shares of the top wealth groups (the top 1−10 per cent), is likely to be biased. Certain aspects, such as the assumption of zero wealth for the excluded population (in Series B) and the omission of occupational pension rights, may cause the shares of the top wealth groups to be over-stated in the official estimates. On the other hand, there are factors, such as the exemption of certain settled and other property, which work in the opposite direction.

At the same time, it is fair to say that the official Inland Revenue estimates suffer from a number of deficiencies and are in need of further development. Inevitably, the Inland Revenue's work is linked to the admini-stration of capital taxation, and it does not make any attempt to cover the entire distribution of wealth or to make full-scale adjustments for factors such as missing wealth. The main corrections necessary are summarised in table 2.2, which also shows where they are discussed in the present book.

In a number of cases, the need for adjustments has been clearly recognised in earlier studies (many of them are discussed, for example, in Langley (1950 and 1951) and Revell (1967)). The quantitative importance of the various effects, or indeed the direction in which they operate, has however been much less fully investigated. This is demonstrated by the large number of question marks in table 2.2. The consequences of changes in the social class multipliers for the estimated size distribution of wealth have not been

Table 2.2 The Inland Revenue method of estimation – a summary

	Method applied by Inland Revenue	Possible sources of error	Likely bias in degree of concentration*	Treated below in
Section 2.3				
(a) General mortality multipliers (P_a/N_a)	Registrar General's data on mortality and midyear population	Errors in population estimates	?	ch. 5
		Grouped by 10 year age groups	?	ch. 3
Social class adjustments (λ_{ai})	Registrar General's data on occupational mortality with adjustment for the unoccupied	Bias in occupational statements	?	ch. 3
		No allowance for marital status	?	ch. 3
		Multipliers not smoothly graduated	?	ch. 3
		Inadequate allowance for differential trends over time	?	ch. 6
(b) Sampling problems	Combining observations	Sampling error	?	ch. 5
		Estates unrepresentative	– ?	} not treated
		Double counting of gifts	+ ?	
		Delays and corrections to returns	?	
		Less thorough checking of small estates	?	ch. 4
Section 2.4				
(a) 'Missing' people	Series A: omission of estates not coming to notice of estate duty office Series B: inclusion on assumption that the missing estates have zero wealth	Neither satisfactory	– ?	ch. 4
Definition of adult	15 and over (18 and over in Royal Commission 1975)	Share of top x% higher with lower age limit	+	ch. 5

Table 2.2 The Inland Revenue method of estimation — a summary

			Sell-up basis	Going-concern basis	
(b) 'Missing' wealth	No adjustment to annual estimates	Exclusions with no limit	—		⎫
		Exclusions subject to specified limits	?		⎬ ch. 4
Double-counting	No adjustment	Non-aggregation	—		⎭ not treated
(c) Method of valuation	No adjustment				
		Life policies	?	?	⎫
		Pension rights	None	+	⎪
		Settled property	?	?	⎬ ch. 4
		Consumer durables and trade assets	None	+?	⎪
		Houses	?	?	⎭
Geographical coverage	No adjustment	Property of overseas residents	?		
		Non-domiciled 'participants in British society'	—?		adjustment described above
					not treated

Note* + denotes shares of the top wealth groups likely to be over-stated; — denotes likely under-statement.

adequately treated (Revell (1967) considers the effect on *total* holdings but not on the *size distribution*). Little is known about the direction, let alone the magnitude, of the effect of adjusting the basis of valuation of life policies. It is this kind of question which is addressed in later chapters. Although the answers provided are far from fully comprehensive (and some problems are not treated at all), it is hoped that they demonstrate that the Inland Revenue estimates can be considerably refined.

In sum, we feel that the Inland Revenue estimates are in need of adjustment, but that they provide a valuable foundation. Indeed, when we bear in mind the very considerable problems which arise with alternative approaches (such as the investment income method discussed in chapter 7), the estate data must form the essential nucleus of any estimate of the upper part of the wealth distribution. It is for this reason that we have devoted a major part of the book to a detailed investigation of the mortality multiplier method and to the preparation of revised estate-based estimates.

3

MORTALITY MULTIPLIERS

Despite the central importance of the choice of multipliers to be applied to the estate duty data, there has been little systematic analysis of the sensitivity of the size distribution to the assumptions made. It is surprising, for example, that there has been so little theoretical discussion of the likely effects of employing social class multipliers (see Shorrocks 1973, for one rare instance). In the first section of this chapter, therefore, we present a more rigorous treatment of mortality multipliers than has been given in the past. Although this discussion is far from comprehensive, we hope that it provides a framework for examining the consequence of different assumptions. The various sources of data, and the multipliers which may be derived, are described in section 3.2. In section 3.3 we give estimates for the distribution of wealth in 1968 based on a range of multipliers, and examine the sensitivity of the results to changes in the multipliers. The main conclusions are summarised in section 3.4.

3.1 The theory of mortality multipliers*

The starting point for our analysis is the formal statement of the estate method given in section 2.2 of the previous chapter, and in particular the expressions (3) and (4) on page 24 for the shares of total population and the shares of total wealth. For convenience, these are reproduced below. The proportion of the population in wealth classes $i = j + 1, \ldots, t$ is given by

$$1 - F_j = \sum_a \left(\frac{P_a}{P} \sum_{i=j+1}^{t} \lambda_{ai} \frac{n_{ai}}{N_a} \right) \tag{1}$$

and their share in total wealth is given by

$$1 - L_j = \sum_a \left(\frac{P_a}{P} \sum_{i=j+1}^{t} \lambda_{ai} \frac{n_{ai}}{N_a} \frac{w_{ai}}{\bar{w}} \right) \tag{2}$$

* This first section is more technical. Some readers may prefer to go straight to the summary on page 60.

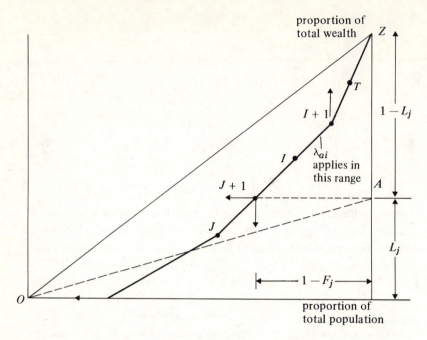

Figure 3.1 Effect of increase in multiplier λ_{ai} (where $w_0 = 0$)

(where $\sum\limits_{a}$ denotes summation over the age/sex classes $a = 1, \ldots, A$). This gives us the point $J + 1$ on the Lorenz curve shown in figure 3.1.

We are interested in the effect of changes in the multipliers as represented by changes in λ_{ai}. For example, $\lambda_{ai} = 1$ corresponds to the assumption of a general mortality multiplier for all estate classes; whereas social class multipliers are represented by $\lambda_{ai} > 1$ for the higher estate classes. It may be noted that since the overall multiplier for class a is

$$\bar{m}_a = \sum_{i=0}^{t} m_{ai} \frac{n_{ai}}{N_a} = \sum_{i=0}^{t} \lambda_{ai} \bar{m}_a \frac{n_{ai}}{N_a}$$

(where the size class $i = 0$ is that containing the excluded population) we have the restriction that

$$\sum_{i=0}^{t} \lambda_{ai} \frac{n_{ai}}{N_a} = 1 \text{ for all } a \tag{3}$$

This means that in considering changes in λ_{ai}, it is necessary to specify the offsetting variation which must take place to ensure (3) is satisfied. Here the asymmetric role played by λ_{a0} (that applied to the excluded population) suggests that the natural variation to consider is an increase in λ_{ai} (for $i \geqslant 1$) combined with a balancing reduction in λ_{a0}. (In empirical applications λ_{a0} is typically treated as a residual.)

The effect of increasing λ_{ai} in this way may be seen by differentiating equations (1) and (2):

$$\frac{\partial(1-F_j)}{\partial \lambda_{ai}} = \frac{P_a}{P} \frac{n_{ai}}{N_a} \quad \text{for } j < i \tag{4a}$$

$$= 0 \qquad \text{for } j \geqslant i \tag{4b}$$

$$\frac{\partial(1-L_j)}{\partial \lambda_{ai}} = \frac{P_a}{P} \frac{n_{ai}}{N_a} \frac{w_{ai}}{\bar{w}} - \frac{(1-L_j)}{\bar{w}} \frac{\partial(\bar{w})}{\partial \lambda_{ai}} \quad \text{for } j < i \tag{5a}$$

$$= -\frac{(1-L_j)}{\bar{w}} \frac{\partial(\bar{w})}{\partial \lambda_{ai}} \qquad \text{for } j \geqslant i \tag{5b}$$

The change in per capita wealth depends on the treatment of the wealth of the excluded population. In the first part of the analysis it is assumed that all those in size class 0 have per capita wealth w_0 (where $0 \leqslant w_0 < w_1$); at a later stage this is replaced by the alternative assumption that the total of personal wealth is known. It follows that we can write

$$\bar{w} = \sum_a \frac{P_a}{P} \left[w_0 + \sum_{i=1}^{t} \lambda_{ai} \frac{n_{ai}}{N_a} (w_{ai} - w_0) \right] \tag{6}$$

and hence

$$\frac{\partial(\bar{w})}{\partial \lambda_{ai}} = \frac{P_a}{P} \frac{n_{ai}}{N_a} (w_{ai} - w_0) \tag{7}$$

Substituting into (5a)

$$\frac{\partial(1-L_j)}{\partial \lambda_{ai}} = \frac{P_a}{P} \frac{n_{ai}}{N_a} \left[L_j \frac{w_{ai}}{\bar{w}} + (1-L_j) \frac{w_0}{\bar{w}} \right] \quad \text{for } j < i \tag{8}$$

In considering the shift in the Lorenz curve arising from the increase in λ_{ai}, it is helpful to consider separately points above the range affected (i.e. $j \geqslant i$, or points $I+1$ to T in figure 3.1) and points in that range and below $(j < i)$. In the former case, the results are straightforward. The population share $(1 - F_j)$ is unaffected (from equation 4b), and the wealth share is reduced as a result of increasing average per capita wealth (from equation 5b). The share in total wealth of the top $(1 - F_j)$ of the population is therefore reduced, and the Lorenz curve shifts up towards the diagonal, as indicated for point $I+1$ in figure 3.1. We have, therefore, demonstrated:

Proposition 1. In response to an increase in λ_{ai} the Lorenz curve shifts inward at all points $I + 1, I + 2, \ldots T$ (where $I + 1$ denotes the end of the ith range): i.e. at all points above the range where the increased multiplier is applied.

The movement in the lower part of the Lorenz curve is not quite so straightforward. From (4a) and (8), it is clear that both $(1 - F_j)$ and $(1 - L_j)$ are increased, so that the point $J + 1$ moves in the way indicated in figure 3.1. In fact the direction of movement is given by:

$$\frac{d(1 - L_j)}{d(1 - F_j)} = L_j \frac{w_{ai}}{\bar{w}} + (1 - L_j) \frac{w_0}{\bar{w}} \tag{9}$$

The Lorenz curve shifts outward or inward at $J + 1$ depending on whether this direction of movement is more or less steep than the slope of the Lorenz curve at $J + 1$. In the case of a smoothly differentiable Lorenz curve, the slope would be the wealth level corresponding to that point (expressed as a proportion of the mean). In the present case of grouped data, the slope depends on the method of interpolation; it is however assumed that this ensures that the slope is equal to $(w_{j+1}/\bar{w})$, which is the end point of range j expressed relative to the mean. The increase in λ_{ai} causes the Lorenz curve to shift, therefore, outward or inward at point $J + 1$ (the end of range j) according as (using (9))

$$L_j w_{ai} + (1 - L_j) w_0 \gtreqless w_{j+1} \tag{10}$$

It follows that if $w_0 = 0$, as is assumed for example in the Inland Revenue Series B, then condition (10) reduces to

$$\frac{w_{ai}}{\bar{w}} \gtreqless \frac{w_{j+1}}{\bar{w}} \frac{1}{L_j} \tag{10a}$$

Since the right-hand side is greater than unity,[1] this shows that a sufficient condition for the Lorenz curve to shift inwards at all points is that $w_{ai} \leqslant \bar{w}$. We have, therefore, demonstrated:

Proposition 2. A sufficient condition for the Lorenz curve to shift inwards at all points in response to an increase in λ_{ai} is that $w_0 = 0$ and $w_{ai} \leqslant \bar{w}$: i.e. the average wealth for the estate class concerned is less than the mean wealth.

---

1 This can be seen from figure 3.1 where L_j is the slope of OA and $(w_{j+1}/\bar{w})$ (the slope at $J + 1$) is necessarily greater given the concavity of the Lorenz curve.

It may be noted that the lowest group (the excluded population) have a zero share so that the Lorenz curve meets the horizontal axis and that this point moves to the left in response to any increase in λ_{ai} for $i = 1, \ldots, T$.

Where $w_0 > 0$ or $w_{ai} > \bar{w}$ it is quite possible that the Lorenz curve shifts outwards at some points. The case where $w_0 > 0$ is illustrated by the lowest section of the curve, which — under the assumption that all the excluded population have wealth equal to w_0 — is a straight line with slope $w_0/\bar{w}$. The effect of an increase in the multiplier applied to any class (with $w_{ai} > w_0$) is to raise $\bar{w}$ (see equation (7)) and hence reduce the slope, so that at the bottom the Lorenz curve lies outside its previous position. The case where $w_{ai} > \bar{w}$ is illustrated by a hypothetical example in Atkinson and Harrison (1975:17).

Social class multipliers

So far we have examined changes in individual multipliers; we now turn to a special case of particular importance — social class multipliers. (This is the case considered by Shorrocks (1973)). This involves an increase in the multipliers applied to all estate classes of size k and above (and all age groups) again with an offsetting reduction in λ_{a0}. In particular let us write (for all a)

$$\lambda_{ai} = \lambda \text{ for } i \geqslant k$$
$$= 1 \text{ for } 1 \leqslant i < k$$

and define

$$1 - F_j(\lambda) = \sum_a \frac{P_a}{P} \left\{ \sum_{j+1}^{t} \lambda \frac{n_{ai}}{N_a} \right\} \quad \text{for } j \geqslant k - 1 \tag{11a}$$

$$= \sum_a \frac{P_a}{P} \left\{ \sum_{k}^{t} \lambda \frac{n_{ai}}{N_a} + \sum_{j+1}^{k-1} \frac{n_{ai}}{N_a} \right\} \quad \text{for } j < k - 1 \tag{11b}$$

$$1 - L_j(\lambda) = \sum_a \frac{P_a}{P} \left\{ \sum_{j+1}^{t} \lambda \frac{n_{ai}}{N_a} \frac{w_{ai}}{\bar{w}} \right\} \quad \text{for } j \geqslant k - 1 \tag{12a}$$

$$= \sum_a \frac{P_a}{P} \left\{ \sum_{k}^{t} \lambda \frac{n_{ai}}{N_a} \frac{w_{ai}}{\bar{w}} + \sum_{j+1}^{k-1} \frac{n_{ai}}{N_a} \frac{w_{ai}}{\bar{w}} \right\} \quad \text{for } j < k - 1 \tag{12b}$$

(where $\bar{w}$ is a function of λ).

The implications of employing social class multipliers ($\lambda > 1$) have not in the past been very fully analysed. It is believed by some investigators that their use leads to a greater degree of concentration than general mortality multipliers ($\lambda = 1$): see, for example, Lampman (1962:212n). That this is not true in general was demonstrated in the previous chapter using the simple 'Pareto' model, where it was shown that an increase in λ could lead to a fall in the share of the top 1 per cent.

In order to examine more generally the effect of an increase in λ, we differentiate equations (11) and (12) with respect to λ:

$$\frac{\partial(1-F_j)}{\partial\lambda} = \frac{1}{\lambda}(1-F_j(\lambda)) \quad \text{for } j \geqslant k-1 \qquad (13a)$$

$$= \frac{1}{\lambda}(1-F_{k-1}(\lambda)) \quad \text{for } j < k-1 \qquad (13b)$$

$$\frac{\partial(1-L_j)}{\partial\lambda} = \frac{1}{\lambda}(1-L_j(\lambda)) - \frac{(1-L_j(\lambda))}{\bar{w}(\lambda)}\frac{\partial\bar{w}}{\partial\lambda} \quad \text{for } j \geqslant k-1 \qquad (14a)$$

$$= \frac{1}{\lambda}(1-L_{k-1}(\lambda)) - \frac{(1-L_j(\lambda))}{\bar{w}(\lambda)}\frac{\partial\bar{w}}{\partial\lambda} \quad \text{for } j < k-1 \qquad (14b)$$

and

$$\frac{\partial\bar{w}}{\partial\lambda} = (1-L_{k-1}(1))\,\bar{w}(1) - w_0(1-F_{k-1}(1)) \qquad (15)$$

For the lower wealth ranges $(j < k-1)$, the results are the same as if we treated the top k classes as a single group. In particular, we have the analogue of (10) that the Lorenz curve shifts outward or inward at the end of range j according as

$$L_j(\lambda)\left[\frac{(1-L_{k-1}(\lambda))\,\bar{w}(\lambda)}{1-F_{k-1}(\lambda)}\right] + w_0(1-L_j(\lambda)) \gtrless w_{j+1} \qquad (16)$$

where the term in square brackets is the average per capita wealth of classes k and above. Since this is greater than the mean, the sufficient conditions of proposition 2 are no longer helpful, although $w_0 > 0$ still implies that the lowest part of the Lorenz curve shifts outward.[2]

Our interest is particularly in the effect on the top wealth classes $(j \geqslant k-1)$. In examining this, it is convenient to define

$$\gamma = L_{k-1}(1) + (1-F_{k-1}(1))\frac{w_0}{\bar{w}(1)} \qquad (17)$$

This quantity, referred to here as 'the share of lower wealth', may be seen as a measure of the relative importance of the wealth not affected by the introduction of social class multipliers.[3] This interpretation is illustrated by the fact that (from equation (6)):

---

2 Since the average per capita wealth of classes k and above is greater than w_0, $\bar{w}$ rises with λ and hence the slope of the lowest section of the Lorenz curve declines.

3 The second term appears because a rise in λ reduces the size of the excluded population, so that the first w_0 of the wealth of the estate population is offset against the amount subtracted from the wealth of the excluded population.

or

$$\frac{\overline{w}(\lambda)}{\overline{w}(1)} = 1 + (\lambda - 1)\left[1 - L_{k-1}(1) - (1 - F_{k-1}(1))\frac{w_0}{\overline{w}(1)}\right]$$

$$\overline{w}(\lambda) = \overline{w}(1)\left[\gamma + \lambda(1 - \gamma)\right] \tag{18}$$

Combining equations (13a), (14a) and (15), and using (17) and (18), the direction of movement in the Lorenz curve at $J + 1$ is given by

$$\frac{d(1 - L_j)}{d(1 - F_j)} = \left(\frac{1 - L_j(\lambda)}{1 - F_j(\lambda)}\right)\left(1 - \frac{\lambda(1 - \gamma)}{\gamma + \lambda(1 - \gamma)}\right) \tag{19}$$

As before we need to compare this with the slope of the Lorenz curve at this point $(w_{j+1}/\overline{w}(\lambda))$, and the curve shifts outward or inward at point $J + 1$ according as

$$1 - \frac{\lambda(1 - \gamma)}{\gamma + \lambda(1 - \gamma)} \gtrless \frac{w_{j+1}/\overline{w}(\lambda)}{(1 - L_j(\lambda))/(1 - F_j(\lambda))} = R_j \tag{20}$$

where the right-hand side is the ratio of wealth at the end of range j to the mean wealth in that class and above. (R_j is less than unity and is independent of λ for $j \geqslant k - 1$.) Rearranging, the Lorenz curve then shifts outward or inward at the end of range j according as

$$\lambda \lessgtr \frac{\gamma}{1 - \gamma}\frac{1 - R_j}{R_j} \tag{21}$$

In particular we have:

Proposition 3. If the share of lower wealth (γ) is less than or equal to R_j, then an increase in social class multipliers ($\lambda > 1$) shifts the Lorenz curve inwards at the end of range j (where $j \geqslant k - 1$).

This has the implication that:

Corollary. If social class multipliers are applied to all estate classes and $w_0 = 0$, then the Lorenz curve shifts inwards.

The condition (21) can be interpreted as follows. R_j may be taken as an indicator of the degree of concentration of wealth-holding in ranges $j + 1$ and upwards; a low value means that there is a large gap between those just entering class $(j + 1)$ and the average above that point. The use of social class multipliers may therefore shift the Lorenz curve outwards where there is a high degree of concentration of wealth-holding or where the share of lower wealth is large. Returning to the Pareto model of the previous chapter, R_j is then a constant (equal to $(\alpha - 1)/\alpha$) and $\alpha = 1.5$ would imply that the use of social class multipliers shifts the Lorenz curve inwards if the share of lower wealth is less than a third.[4] If γ were as high as a half, then in this case the Lorenz curve would be shifted outwards until $\lambda = 2$.

Independent wealth total

The analysis so far has been based on the assumption that the wealth of those not covered by the estate statistics is known. In certain cases we may not know w_0 but instead have independent information about total personal wealth. It is therefore interesting to examine the results obtained where total wealth is given exogenously $(= W^*)$.

For any given multipliers λ_{ai}, there will be an estimate W^e of total wealth covered by the estate returns (classes $1 \leqslant i \leqslant t$). The implications of changes in λ_{ai} depend on how the shortfall from the known total $(W^* - W^e)$ is allocated. The simplest case is that where all the excess is allocated to those not covered by the estate returns. Since the mean wealth $W^*/P(= w^*)$ is given, the effects of an increase in λ_{ai}, with an offsetting reduction in λ_{a0}, is given by

$$\frac{d(1 - L_j)}{d(1 - F_j)} = \frac{w_{ai}}{w^*} \quad \text{for } j < i$$

$$= 0 \quad \text{for } j \geqslant i \tag{22}$$

It follows from this that the Lorenz curve at $J + 1$ is unaffected by changes in the multipliers applied to lower estate classes but is shifted outwards by changes applied to higher estate classes. Correspondingly, the adoption of social class multipliers definitely shifts the Lorenz curve outwards.

The results just given are based on the assumption that all the adjustment is made by varying w_0; on the other hand, if the excess were to be allocated to all wealth classes in proportion to w_{ai}, then we would obtain the same results as in the previous sections (with $w_0 = 0$). In practice, there are likely to be a variety of reasons for the discrepancy between the estate estimate of total wealth and the independent total. In part, the discrepancy may arise from the unknown holdings w_0, but it may in part reflect deviations of the estate wealth w_{ai} from its true value. As an intermediate case, therefore, let us assume that a proportion θ of the excess is allocated to the lowest group (w_0) and that the remainder is allocated proportionately to all

---

4 The relationship to condition (11) on p. 29 in chapter 2 may be seen from the fact that $\gamma = \sigma^*/(\sigma^* + (1 - E_1)(1 - \sigma^*))$, where E_1 denotes E evaluated at $\lambda = 1$, and that $1 - E = \lambda(1 - E_1)$. The values $E_1 = 0.5$ and $\sigma^* = 0.25$ imply $\gamma = 0.4$, so that with $\alpha = 1.5$ the Lorenz curve shifts outwards for $\lambda \leqslant 1.33$. (At that value of λ, $E = \frac{1}{3}$ and the right-hand side of condition (11) in chapter 2 is equal to 1.5.)

estate holdings by classes $i = 1, \dots, t$. If we take the case where social class multipliers λ are applied to all estates (that is $k = 1$) and the initial value of w_0 is zero, the estimated wealth derived from the estate data is (as a function of λ)

$$W^e(\lambda) = \sum_a P_a \sum_{i=1}^{t} \lambda \frac{n_{ai}}{N_a} w_{ai} \quad \text{(where it is assumed that } W^e(\lambda) < W^*)$$

If $(1 - \theta)$ of the excess of the exogenous total capital W^* over W^e is allocated proportionately to all holdings, then

$$1 - L_j = \sum_a \frac{P_a}{P} \left(\sum_{j+1}^{I} \lambda \frac{n_{ai}}{N_a} \frac{w_{ai}}{w^*} \right) [\theta + (1 - \theta) W^* / W^e]$$

and

$$\frac{d(1 - L_j)}{d(1 - F_j)} = \left[\frac{1 - L_j(\lambda)}{1 - F_j(\lambda)} \right] \left[\frac{\theta}{\theta + (1 - \theta) W^* / W^e(\lambda)} \right] \tag{23}$$

If $\theta = 1$, the second bracket is unity and the Lorenz curve shifts outward.[5] If $\theta = 0$, then the second bracket is zero and the curve shifts inwards (since $1 - F_j$ increases). For the case $0 < \theta < 1$, it is more likely that the Lorenz curve shifts outward the larger is θ and the smaller is the proportion of unallocated wealth (W^*/W^e). Defining $\Phi = W^*/W^e(1)$, and rearranging (23) we have

> *Proposition 4.* If social class multipliers are applied to all estate classes, total wealth is given exogenously, and a proportion θ of the excess wealth is allocated to those not covered in the estate statistics, then the Lorenz curve shifts outwards or inwards at $J + 1$ according as
>
> $$\frac{\theta}{\theta + (1 - \theta)\Phi/\lambda} \gtrless R_j \tag{24}$$

To give some idea of what this condition means, let us take $\Phi = 1.4$: i.e. an extra 40 per cent has to be added to total wealth estimated from the estate returns when $\lambda = 1$. The figures below show the value of the left-hand side of (24) for different λ and θ. In the example of the Pareto distribution where

$\lambda =$	1.0	1.2	1.4	1.6
$\theta = 0.25$	0.19	0.22	0.25	0.28
0.5	0.42	0.46	0.5	0.53
0.75	0.68	0.72	0.75	0.77

---

5 Since $(1 - L_j)/(1 - F_j)$ is greater than (w_{j+1}/w^*) – see figure 3.1.

R_j is a third, the use of social class multipliers would shift the Lorenz curve outwards where θ is of the order of 40 per cent and above.

Marital status and aggregation of age groups[6]

The final aspect of the multipliers considered here is the error introduced by aggregation over groups with different mortality experience. In chapter 2 we drew attention to two aspects of this: (i) the failure to use multipliers differentiated according to marital status and (ii) the aggregation into ten year age groups.

In order to obtain some measure of the possible error introduced, we consider the (highly simplified) example where there are two categories a and b with different mortality experience. The 'true' values are given by:

$$1 - F_j^* = \sum_{i=j+1}^{t} \left[\frac{n_{ai}}{N_a} \frac{P_a}{P} + \frac{n_{bi}}{N_b} \frac{P_b}{P} \right] \tag{25a}$$

$$1 - L_j^* = \sum_{i=i+1}^{t} \left[\frac{n_{ai}}{N_a} \frac{w_{ai}}{\bar{w}} \frac{P_a}{P} + \frac{n_{bi}}{N_b} \frac{w_{bi}}{\bar{w}} \frac{P_b}{P} \right] \tag{25b}$$

where for convenience we take the case of general mortality multipliers ($\lambda_{ai} = 1$), and assume $\bar{w}$ is fixed exogenously. On the other hand, the values estimated ignoring differences between a and b are given by:

$$1 - F_j = \sum_{i=j+1}^{t} \left[\frac{n_{ai} + n_{bi}}{N} \right] \tag{26a}$$

$$1 - L_j = \sum_{i=j+1}^{t} \left[\frac{n_{ai}w_{ai} + n_{bi}w_{bi}}{N\bar{w}} \right] \tag{26b}$$

(where $N = N_a + N_b$). Rearranging gives

$$F_j - F_j^* = (1 - F_j^a)\left(\frac{m_a}{\bar{m}} - 1\right)\frac{N_a}{N} + (1 - F_j^b)\left(\frac{m_b}{\bar{m}} - 1\right)\frac{N_b}{N} \tag{27a}$$

where F_j^a, F_j^b denote the shares of the population in groups a and b respectively in class j and below. Since from the definition of the overall multiplier $\bar{m}$ ($= P/N$) the coefficients of $1 - F_j^a$ and $1 - F_j^b$ sum to zero, we can see that bias in the estimate of F_j arises where (i) the multipliers m_a and m_b are different, and (ii) F_j^a is different from F_j^b. The presence of bias depends, therefore, on the aggregated groups having both different mortality experience and a different distribution of estates by size classes. An alternative expression for the bias is:

---

6 In revising this section, we have benefited from reading the unpublished paper by Buse (1976); he is, however, primarily concerned with the effect on total wealth rather than its distribution.

$$F_j - F_j^* = (F_j^b - F_j^a) \left(\frac{m_a}{\overline{m}} - 1\right) \frac{N_a}{N} \tag{28a}$$

If the group with the lower mortality (higher m) has fewer people in class $j + 1$ and above (higher F_j) then the share in total population F_j is understated, or equivalently $1 - F_j$ is over-stated. In the case of the shares of total wealth we may derive a similar expression:

$$L_j - L_j^* = (1 - L_j^a)\left(\frac{m_a}{\overline{m}} - 1\right)\frac{N_a \overline{w}_a}{N\overline{w}} + (1 - L_j^b)\left(\frac{m_b}{\overline{m}} - 1\right)\frac{N_b \overline{w}_b}{N\overline{w}} \tag{27b}$$

$$= (L_j^b - L_j^a)\left(\frac{m_a}{\overline{m}} - 1\right)\frac{N_a \overline{w}_a}{N\overline{w}} \tag{28b}$$

The application of these formulae may be illustrated by reference first to aggregation across age groups and then to marital status. Suppose that we are interested in the distribution within a ten-year age group (e.g. 45–54) and that we wish to calculate the bias involved in using the whole group rather than two sub-groups (e.g. 45–49, 50–54). If a denotes the younger group, so that $m_a > \overline{m}$, then we should expect $F_j^a > F_j^b$ (i.e. a higher proportion of the younger age group are in estate class j and below). This would mean that $(1 - F_j^*)$ is over-stated, or equivalently that the multiplier applied in the aggregated case is too high. This accords with what Mallet (1908) found to be the case when the population as a whole was treated as a single age group. From inspection of the mortality data for 1968 (see table 3.3 below) and of population data, it does not seem unreasonable to take $m_a/\overline{m} = 1.3$ and $N_a/N = 0.55$ (it should be emphasised that these are intended purely to be illustrative). In this case the bias in F_j^* would be 0.165 per cent for each percentage point difference between F_j^a and F_j^b. If therefore $F_j^a = 4.8$ per cent and $F_j^b = 5.2$ per cent, the population share would be biased up by some 0.07 per cent. The small size of this correction seems relatively reassuring, but more extensive calculations are necessary, making use of actual data (unavailable to us) on finer age groupings.[7]

The application to marital status may be shown making the simplifying assumption that there are no age and sex differences, so that only two categories (a = married and b = single) are considered. If married persons have a lower mortality, and if $F_j^b < F_j^a$, as one might expect in the case of women (that is single women are more likely to own property than married)

---

7 One approach would be to interpolate within age groups, as suggested by Snow (see the discussion of Mallet and Strutt (1915 : 594)).

then $1 - F_j^*$ is again over-stated — the multiplier applied is too high. On the other hand, if $F_j^b > F_j^a$, as may be the case with men, then the multiplier applied is too low. If these suppositions about F_j^a and F_j^b are correct, then the bias for men will tend to cancel that for women. In order to form some idea of the quantitative importance we may take a mortality advantage for the married such that $\bar{m}_a = 1.15\,\bar{m}$ (see page 66 below) and suppose that they constitute two thirds of the population. The bias is therefore 0.1 per cent for each percentage point difference between F_j^a and F_j^b. The figure of 0.1 per cent is smaller than that with the age calculation; the differences in the distribution of estates may, however, be rather larger. Again more extensive calculations, using data on the marital composition of estates, are needed.

Summary

This analysis of the theory of mortality multipliers has shown that the effect of different multipliers is less straightforward than is sometimes supposed. Indeed, the reader may have been persuaded that little can be said *a priori*; however, we have tried to argue that some qualitative conclusions can be reached and these are summarised below.

The first case considered is that where the wealth of each range is known and where an individual multiplier, that applied to range i, is increased. The results (Propositions 1 and 2) show that the Lorenz curve is shifted inwards at all points above this range and at all points below if average wealth in range i is less than the mean and the wealth of the excluded population is zero. Where these latter conditions are not satisfied, then the Lorenz curve may shift outwards at some points.

The second set of findings concerned the use of social class multipliers. Proposition 3 showed that the effect of this on the Lorenz curve depends on the 'share of lower wealth' and the degree of concentration among those covered by the social class differential. It is however the case that where the social class multipliers are applied to all estate classes and the wealth of the excluded population is zero, then the Lorenz curve shifts inwards.

Thirdly, we may have independent information on total wealth-holding. Proposition 4 shows that in this case the use of social class multipliers depends on the difference between the exogenous total and the estate esti-mate, on how this excess is allocated and on the extent of concentration among those covered by the social class differential. The application of the propositions described above is illustrated in section 3.3, but before that we need to examine the sources of mortality data.

3.2 The derivation of mortality multipliers

In this section we examine the two main sources of social class mortality multipliers: the Registrar General's Decennial Supplement on occupational mortality, and the life offices' Continuous Mortality Investigation. The former, referred to here as the Registrar General's data, form the basis for the Inland Revenue estimates discussed in the previous chapter; the latter, referred to as the life office data, have been used by Revell (1967), on whose work we have drawn extensively.

In the previous chapter we identified three major problems with the use of the Registrar General's data, which are here discussed in turn.

(a) Errors in occupational statements

The way in which errors in occupational data arise is described clearly by Revell:

> In many mortality studies the population is known with almost complete certainty, and the problem is merely to mark off those known members of the population who die year by year. In the Registrar General's analysis of occupational mortality the procedure is necessarily different. The population is classified to social classes on the basis of occupational statements on the census schedules, while deaths are allocated to social classes on the basis of occupational statements recorded in the death registers. It is only because of these two quite different acts of classification that a person can be allocated to one social class when alive and to another on his death. These discrepancies arise mainly because in the great majority of cases the informants on the two occasions are different persons. At the census the informant is the head of the household, and many men (but far fewer women) will thus provide information on their own occupations. On death the informant can never be describing his own occupation, and in a significant proportion of cases the informants are not even close relatives of the deceased [1967:118].

The first way in which discrepancies arise is through the use of the 'unoccupied' category. Although there are certain people who have never had paid employment to whom this classification does apply, there are many who are described as 'unoccupied' when in fact they have retired. In the census, a retired individual is asked to record his occupation prior to retirement, but a substantial number fail to follow this instruction. As a result, the number of men enumerated at the 1951 census classified as unoccupied (excluding students) were, as a percentage, as shown below.

Age:	16–	20–	25–	35–	45–	55–	65–	70–
	0.88	0.78	0.69	0.66	0.84	1.78	6.73	12.96

(Registrar General for England and Wales 1958:6)

The rise for age 65 and over is unnatural, and must be largely explained by failure to follow the instructions. The Registrar General concluded that the true proportion of men aged 20 and over never gainfully employed was no higher than 0.7 per cent, so that the number of genuinely 'unoccupied' is considerably over-stated in the older age groups.

The over-statement of the 'unoccupied' in the Census affects the mortality rates, since it is much less common at the death registration (Revell 1967: 120). This means that the mortality of the occupied tends to be over-stated and hence the social class differential (social classes I and II in relation to all persons) under-stated. The quantitative significance of this has been investi- in chapter 2. The results of this exercise for 1951 indicate that the re- asignment of the excess over 0.7 per cent from the unoccupied group to all occupied and retired males would reduce the apparent mortality by 2 per cent for those aged 55–64 rising to 13 per cent at ages 70 and over (Registrar General for England and Wales 1958:6).

In what follows we adopt the procedure, similar to that of Lydall and Tipping (1961), and the Inland Revenue, of allocating the excess unoccupied proportionately to all social classes. This involves the arbitrary assumptions that (i) the 'reassigned' unoccupied can be distributed *pro rata*, and (ii) the mortality rate for the 'genuine' 0.7 per cent unoccupied is the same as that for the population as a whole. The effect is relatively small for most age groups. The resulting social class differentials (λ_{ai}) in 1961 are shown in column 1 of table 3.1.

The second difficulty is that, among the occupied, the occupational classifications may differ at the two stages. This may arise through minor variation in description, or as a result of a change in occupation: one actual example was a person who was a fitter at the census and a master photo- grapher at death registration. There is however a systematic bias in the direction of a more flattering (higher social class) description being given at death. This was demonstrated by the 1951 matching exercise, which showed that for males aged 20–64 'there is evidence of a strong tendency to report occupations assignable to Social Classes I and II more often at death registration than on the census schedules, with a compensatory under- reporting of occupations classifiable to Social Classes IV and V' (Registrar General for England and Wales 1958:7). In the case of married women, classified according to their husband's occupation, there was no relationship for those aged 16–64, but for those aged 65 and over there was a clear excess of deaths assigned to classes I and II. The sample contained only a small number of single women, and the report concluded that no clear pattern of social class discrepancies can be discerned. The results of a rather smaller matching exercise for the 1961 Census were not published in such detail, and it is not easy to assess the extent to which the social class mortality rates are biased upwards. There is some reason to believe that the errors were somewhat less serious: the proportion of men where the classification of social class differed at death from that at the census was 17 per cent compared with 25 per cent in 1951 (Registrar General for England and Wales 1971:17).[8]

The 1951 data were used by Lydall and Tipping in making their estimates of the distribution of wealth in 1954 and they attempted to correct for errors in occupational statements. They observed that from the matching study 'it would appear that the "upper class" mortality rates for males are over-estimated by 8.3 per cent' (1961:99), and therefore adjusted by this amount the rates for men (but not women).[9] (This correction was assumed also to hold for males in Scotland.) The source of this adjustment may be seen from the following figures from the matching study (Registrar General for England and Wales 1958:7), where the 'not allocated' category has been distributed *pro rata*.

	(Number of people)
Males 20–64	
Social class I and II at Census	219
Social class I and II on death	261
	(1.19)
Males 65 and over	
Social class I and II at Census	564
Social class I and II on death	583
	(1.03)
Total	
Social class I and II at Census	783
Social class I and II on death	844
	(1.08)

8 Also the 10% sample used to give occupational data in 1961 was reported to have a slight overstatement of certain occupations, affecting social classes I and II, and hence causing mortality differentials to be over-stated. The overstatement of Socio-Economic Groups 1–4 (employers, managers and professionals) was some $2\frac{1}{2}\%$, compared with 1% for all economically active men (Registrar General for England and Wales 1966, p. xx).

9 The same adjustment was made by the Inland Revenue when using multipliers based on the 1951 Census; for later estimates (1964 and after) no adjustment is made.

(The figures in brackets are the adjustments required to the multi-pliers.) Given the variation with age, and the indication that under-statement was less in the 1961 data, we have increased social class differentials for 1961 by the following amounts:

Males   : 64 and under   1.05
            : 65 and over   1.02
Females : no adjustment

The effect is shown in the second set of social class differentials in table 3.1.

These corrections for the discrepancies in occupational statements are only very approximate, and it is clearly necessary to consider what checks can be made on their accuracy. One possible test is suggested by William Farr's observation in the Registrar General's Supplement of 1861, that despite 'the uncertainty in the naming of trades' there are certain occupations which are well defined. Errors of classification are likely to be less important for occupations such as teachers, clergymen and doctors. (Although clergymen may become teachers, dons may become politicians, so that even here a person may belong to two or more occupational groups.) Although data for individual occupations are obviously not sufficient to give reliable multi-pliers, they may provide a lower bound to the relative mortality rate. Table 3.2 shows the relative mortality rates for certain occupations included in social classes I and II. In so far as these occupational rates are relevant to the upper wealth groups (a point discussed below), they suggest that if anything the social class differential could be rather larger than the range 1.26 to 1.43 (for men 25–64) in table 3.1, particularly when we allow for the fact that no adjustment has been made to the figures for individual occupations. At the same time, they indicate that (apart from university teachers!) the mort-ality rate is unlikely to fall much below 60 per cent of the general rate, so that a social class multiplier of 1.67 would be at the upper end of the likely range.

(b) Female mortality and marital status

The procedure adopted by Lydall and Tipping (1961) and followed by the Inland Revenue, was to base the female social class mortality rates on the average for married women (classified by husband's occupation) and single women (classified by their own occupation). This would, however, only be satisfactory if the social class distribution were independent of marital status, and this is the second main problem with the mortality data.

The role of marital status has been examined in the work of Smith (1974) for the United States. As he points out, most studies show that

Table 3.1 Social class differentials applied to mortality multipliers

Age group	Column 1 (adjusted for unoccupied)		Column 2 (adjusted for occupational statements)	Column 3 £1,000–£3,000		Column 4 £10,000–£15,000 Graduated multipliers		Column 5 £25,000–		Column 6 Life office data
	Male	Female	Male†	Male	Female	Male	Female	Male	Female	(Male and female)
England and Wales										
Under 25	1.12	1.05	1.18	1.15	1.05	1.20	1.06	1.20	1.06	1.01
25–34	1.33	1.29	1.40	1.21	1.30	1.44	1.33	1.46	1.34	1.37
35–44	1.36	1.27	1.43	1.21	1.26	1.47	1.32	1.50	1.32	1.45
45–54	1.29	1.20	1.35	1.20	1.18	1.39	1.24	1.41	1.24	1.43
55–64	1.20	1.16	1.26	1.13	1.13	1.29	1.18	1.30	1.19	1.50
65–74	1.09	1.05	1.11	1.06	1.03	1.12	1.06	1.13	1.06	1.39
75–84	1.05	1.02	1.07	1.03	1.01	1.07	1.02	1.08	1.02	1.29
85 and over	1.02	1.01	1.04	1.0	1.0	1.0	1.0	1.0	1.0	1.18
age not stated*	1.25	1.21	1.28	1.14	1.13	1.30	1.23	1.33	1.25	1.36
Scotland										
Under 25	0.85	0.81	0.89	1.0	1.0	1.0	1.0	1.0	1.0	1.01
25–34	1.21	1.25	1.27	1.14	1.25	1.30	1.29	1.31	1.29	1.37
35–44	1.23	1.34	1.29	1.14	1.33	1.32	1.40	1.34	1.41	1.46
45–54	1.19	1.27	1.25	1.14	1.24	1.25	1.32	1.29	1.33	1.43
55–64	1.16	1.20	1.22	1.11	1.16	1.24	1.23	1.26	1.24	1.50
65–74	1.10	1.15	1.12	1.06	1.10	1.13	1.17	1.14	1.19	1.39
75–84	1.04	1.10	1.06	1.03	1.06	1.06	1.11	1.07	1.12	1.29
85 and over	1.01	1.03	1.03	1.0	1.0	1.0	1.0	1.0	1.0	1.18
age not stated*	1.09	1.12	1.12	1.06	1.07	1.13	1.13	1.14	1.14	1.37

Notes: †Female as in previous column. *A weighted average of those aged 45 and over.
The figures for columns 1–5 relate to 1961; those in column 6 to 1953–8.

married men and women at every age have a considerably lower mortality rate than single, widowed or divorced persons of the same sex. Klebba (1970) for example, found that for white males the mortality rate for single and widowed was 50 per cent higher than for married and the rate for divorced men was double. For women the differentials were rather smaller. Smith then showed that the marital composition of estates was such that the number of women top wealth-holders was reduced as a result of using marital specific

Table 3.2 Mortality rates relative to all males – selected occupations, England and Wales 1961

Occupation Unit	Age				
	25–34	35–44	45–54	55–64	15–64
270 Ministers of the Crown, MPs and senior government officials	(71)	70	58	80	75
271 Local authority senior officers	(21)	(44)	64	65	62
280 Doctors	92	84	92	89	89
281 Dentists	(66)	(55)	65	64	64
286 University teachers	(49)	(50)	(50)	62	56
287 Teachers	65	56	59	60	60
292 Chemists and other scientists	85	71	87	92	88
296 Accountants	78	77	72	79	76
298 Clergy	(38)	(45)	58	66	62
299 Lawyers	(77)	(66)	74	78	76
Column (2) in table 3.1 (implied mortality rates)*	71	70	74	79	

Source: Registrar General for England and Wales 1971: table 3A.
Notes: Figures in brackets are based on fewer than 50 deaths.
* adjusted for the unoccupied and for discrepancies in occupational statements. No adjustments have been made to the figures for individual occupations.

multipliers, and that the number of men top wealth-holders was increased. This is in line with the argument of the previous section.

In Britain, it is possible from the Registrar General's data on mortality to obtain the differences by marital status for women, and the results for 1961 show mortality differences for married and single women ranging from 18 per cent to 100 per cent (Registrar General for England and Wales 1971: tables 3B and 3C). The latter figure is not, however, typical and it should be noted that these figures are not standardised for social class. If husbands in social class I households on average live longer, then a disproportionate number of women in this class would be married rather than widowed. The more favourable mortality experience of married women may therefore reflect their social class composition rather than a genuine effect associated with marital status. Conversely, if there is a higher level of divorce in social class I, then this would cause the marital status effect to be under-stated.

As we have seen, the significance of these differences depends on the extent to which the marital composition of estates differs from that in the population as a whole. The Inland Revenue collect data on marital status on the estate returns, but at the time of writing no information has been pub-lished. (For this purpose we require data on the status classified by age, as well as by estate, so that the earlier analysis by the Inland Revenue (e.g. for 1926–7) is not sufficient, since marital status varies systematically with age.)

In view of this, we have not attempted to construct marital status-specific multipliers. It is an area where further research is undoubtedly necessary.

(c) Graduation of multipliers with estate size

The last main group of problems concerns the social class gradient and its relationship with estate size. As pointed out in chapter 2, the use by the Inland Revenue of a single differential based on social classes I and II for all those above £5,000 (£3,000 before 1970) involves a sharp jump in the multiplier and a smoother graduation might be desirable. Moreover, there are arguments for varying the cut off with age and adjusting it more smoothly over time (the Inland Revenue used £3,000 throughout the 1960s).

In order to examine the way in which the results might be affected, we explored the approach of linking the multiplier to the percentage ranking of the estate. (This retains the assumption – discussed below – that social class is a reasonable proxy for wealth.) The procedure followed was to:

    (i) smooth the multiplier by a straight line fitted to 1.0 at the midpoint of the population and to the adjusted class I and II differential at the midpoint of the joint class interval,[10]

   (ii) divide estates into six class ranges and apply the appropriate multi-plier given by the straight line for the midpoint of the range. The ranges are: £1,000–, £3,000–, £5,000–, £10,000–, £15,000–, £25,000–. For those below £1,000 the multiplier applied is that for the general population.

This means that the social class differential applied, for example, to the estates of men aged 45–54 in England and Wales in the range £3,000–£5,000 is calculated as follows. The adjusted social class differential from column 2 of table 3.1 is 1.35 and the midpoint of the class interval 8.35 per cent. The

10 In view of the rather small numbers in class I we did not use the separate class observations. The differentials for the age groups 'under 25' in Scotland and '85 and over' in both countries were set at 1.0.

gradient is therefore 0.0084 per 1 per cent of the population. The midpoint of the estate range is 15.0 per cent of the population so that the graduated differential is 1.29.[11] The results for three illustrative ranges are shown in columns 3–5 of table 3.1.

Underlying the use of the census data is the assumption that wealth and social class are highly correlated; however, as emphasised earlier, this assumption is open to question. This is brought out by the occupations listed in table 3.2, which include many unlikely in themselves to offer the opportunity to acquire substantial wealth (e.g. clergy) and at the same time exclude those with no occupation (living on private means). In order to explore this question further, it would be interesting to obtain the occupational distribution of a sample of estates by linking probate records with death certificates, but our resources did not allow us to pursue this. Some idea of the possible results of such an examination is provided by the small sample taken by Wedgwood in 1924, which showed that 93 estates in the range £10,000–£200,000 were distributed as shown below.

Landed gentry and titled	4
Professions	26
Unclassified gentlemen of means	5
Bankers, stockbrokers, large-scale manufacturers and traders	39
Shop-keepers and small-scale manufacturers	17
Farmers	2

Source: Wedgwood 1929:174.

Similarly, Daniels and Campion report that an analysis, using the published reports of wills, of estates over £1,000 gave some justification for assuming that the majority belonged to social classes I and II (1936:15).

A second line of approach is to consider alternative sources of information about the mortality of the wealthy. One which naturally suggests itself is that of investigating the mortality of the aristocracy. Although titled persons only accounted for a small percentage of the estates examined by Wedgwood in the range of £10,000–£200,000, they are probably more important among the largest estates. A major study of the demography of the peerage has been undertaken by Hollingsworth, who reached the general conclusion that 'male members of the nobility had little advantage (in terms of mortality experience) over the general population at adult ages during the period after 1841. The female members, on the other hand, had lower mortality rates than the general population at all ages' (1957:53). These results are based

---

11 In these calculations the estate intervals relate to Great Britain and the social class intervals to England and Wales, but it was felt that no appreciable error was introduced.

on a relatively small number of deaths but are nonetheless of considerable interest and suggest that the social class multipliers might, in fact, be too high in the case of men.

Life office multipliers

The deficiencies of the Registrar General's data were regarded by Revell (1967) as so serious as to render it 'quite useless' for the purpose of deriving mortality multipliers, and he accordingly rejected it in favour of data derived from the Continuous Mortality Investigation. This latter source is based on the mortality experience of life offices in the United Kingdom and covers those accepted for ordinary life and endowment policies at standard rates of premium. As Revell points out, one major attraction of this source is that the population is known throughout, so that there are none of the problems of incorrect classification discussed above. There are, however, a number of difficulties:

(i) there is the problem of 'selection' by health,
(ii) the relationship between the lives covered and the estate duty statistics is not clear,
(iii) the coverage of female lives is inadequate.

The first of these problems stems from the fact that acceptance for life assurance at a standard premium depends on evidence of health. As a result the data do not cover those who are excluded because of ill health (they may either be accepted at an above-standard premium, or be rejected, or not apply). As a result, the mortality rates are under-stated in the life office data. To correct for this, Revell adjusted the rates by amounts (based on actuarial advice) ranging from 15 per cent for the youngest age group to zero for those aged 75 and over.

The second problem concerns the relationship between the lives studied and the estate data. Revell argues that:

> Basically the reason for regarding the mortality of assured lives as an analogue of the mortality of those with wealth of £3,000 or more is that the 'class' selection of this population is in terms of an object of wealth. A life policy is itself a dutiable asset, which figures at an exaggerated value . . . in the estate duty statistics; a man who does not possess a policy has that much less chance of appearing in the estate duty statistics when he dies [1967:124].

Revell's comparison of the assured lives population with the general male population showed that in 1956 it ranged from 6 per cent for the age group 15—24, rising to 30 per cent for those aged 45—54, and then falling to some 5—7 per cent above 65. The coverage did not coincide very closely with that of estates in excess of £3,000, and in particular the assured lives provide a very much more restricted coverage at older ages. Moreover, there have been noticeable changes over time in the extent of assurance: fifty years ago life assurance was effected by a smaller and probably rather different section of the population. One difficulty therefore with using the life office data is that their coverage of different age groups is uneven. Moreover, it could be argued that they give too much weight to certain groups (e.g. professional and clerical workers) with relatively low mortality.

The link between the holding of life policies and wealth may be investigated using the data on the asset composition of estates. At first sight, the relationship does not appear particularly strong. In 1968 under half the estates were recorded as containing policies of assurance (including industrial policies, which are not covered by the life office data); and if we take estates in excess of £20,000, the proportion is in fact rather lower (30 per cent). One explanation is that many life policies are missing from the estate duty statistics. This was considered by Revell in some detail in the context of the balance sheet totals (see below), but it seems unlikely that it can entirely explain the high proportion with no apparent holdings of life policies. This reinforces the doubts concerning the appropriateness of the life office evidence.

The third problem with the life office data concerns the exclusion of female lives. On the basis of the life office experience with female life annuitants, Revell suggests that the ratio of female to male mortality is the same as in the general population. He therefore applies the same social class differential as for men. Revell describes this procedure as 'definitely *faute de mieux*', but points out that there are similar difficulties with the Registrar General's data.

The resulting social class differentials are those shown in column 6 of table 3.1, and we have taken these to illustrate this approach in the next section.[12] The life office multipliers are in general higher than those based on the Registrar General's data. It should be noted that in applying the life office data, Revell took the same dividing line as the Inland Revenue (£3,000), but that he did not follow them in applying to estates below £3,000 a multiplier midway between that for the general population and that for estates

12 The differentials relate to 1953–8. From evidence on the trends in mortality for assured lives relative to the general population published from time to time in the *Journal of the Institute of Actuaries*, it appears that there has been a slight relative improvement for assured lives in the younger age groups, so that the differentials should be somewhat higher for these age groups when applied to data for the 1960s. This would tend to increase the differences between the life office multipliers and those based on the Registrar General's data.

over £3,000. Instead he applied the general mortality multiplier to all estates below £3,000, quoting in support of this procedure the fact that the mortality of lives assured on industrial policies is very close to that of the general population.

Summary

In this section we have described four main sets of social class differentials, and in what follows they will be referred to as:

> *Assumption A1.* Social class multipliers based on the Registrar General's data as used by the Inland Revenue (with adjustments for the unoccupied). The multipliers to be applied to estates over £3,000 (in 1968), and below this level multipliers based on mortality rates halfway between these and the rates for the general population.[13]
>
> *Assumption A2.* Social class multipliers as under A1 but adjusted for errors in occupational statements (as in column 2 in table 3.1).
>
> *Assumption A3.* Social class multipliers as under A2 but graduated by estate size as described on pages 67–8.
>
> *Assumption A4.* Social class multipliers based on life office data (as in column 6 in table 3.1) for estates of £3,000 and over. General mortality multipliers below this level.

In the next section we examine the differences in the results obtained with these assumptions, drawing on the theoretical analysis of section 3.1.

3.3 Comparison of estimates for 1968

In this section we compare the estimates obtained applying the different multipliers A1–A4 to the basic estate data for 1968–9. The Inland Revenue kindly made available their 'Unity Runs' giving estates classified by 32 size categories, by age and sex of the deceased, and by country. These clearly provide no information about those not covered by the estate returns, and for the first part of the section we assume that the wealth of this group (w_0) is zero. The multipliers for the general population, referred to here as Assumption A0, are set out in table 3.3, and the other multipliers are obtained by applying the appropriate social class differential from table 3.1 (or using the procedure indicated in the text).

The first aspect we consider is the move from the general mortality multiplier to the social class multiplier (A1), which is similar to that employed

---

13 The results for these multipliers differ from those published by the Inland Revenue in that we have not combined age groups before applying the multipliers, nor have we smoothed the multiplied-up figures across years (see the discussion in section 2.2).

by the Inland Revenue. In terms of the analysis of section 3.1, this may be seen as consisting of two steps: (i) the application of the social class differential ($\lambda > 1$) to all estate classes, and (ii) a reduction in the multiplier for estates below £3,000.[14] From the Corollary to Proposition 3, it can then be seen that the first step causes the Lorenz curve to shift inwards. The effect of the second step can be seen from Proposition 2. The ranges affected (£3,000 and below) are close to or below the mean wealth, so that the Lorenz curve is likely to shift outward as a result of a reduction in the multiplier applied.

Table 3.3 General mortality multipliers 1968

Age group	England and Wales		Scotland	
	Male	Female	Male	Female
Under 25	1102.18	2581.16	979.00	2943.94
25−34	1050.33	1565.19	766.15	1317.09
35−44	429.76	605.93	319.57	471.06
45−54	142.72	233.51	111.89	182.43
55−64	47.32	96.52	41.49	79.03
65−74	18.62	35.51	17.10	30.59
75−84	8.11	12.47	8.04	11.39
85 and over	3.74	4.67	3.88	4.29
age not stated*	30.27	37.50	27.99	35.30

Source: *Annual Abstract of Statistics 1969:* tables 10, 30 and 31.
Note *A weighted average of those aged 45 and over (see p.26, n.6).

The net effect of the change from a general mortality multiplier to the social class multiplier (A1) is shown by the results in table 3.4 and figure 3.2 (which covers the top part of the distribution). In each case the share of total wealth for a given wealth range is greater under the social class multiplier but the share of the population is also increased and the net effect is for the Lorenz curve to shift inwards. If we use a log—linear interpolation of the Lorenz curve to estimate the share of the top 1 per cent in total personal wealth, the results are:[15]

    A0   General multiplier   36.6%
    A1   Social class multiplier   34.7%

Given the substantial differences in the multipliers, these figures are surprisingly close. The move from general to social class multipliers leads to a con-

14 The effect of the differences in social class multipliers by age may be taken into account by an extension of the earlier analysis.
15 This method of interpolation is used throughout this section (apart from Figure 3.2). The question of interpolation is discussed more fully below in chapter 5.

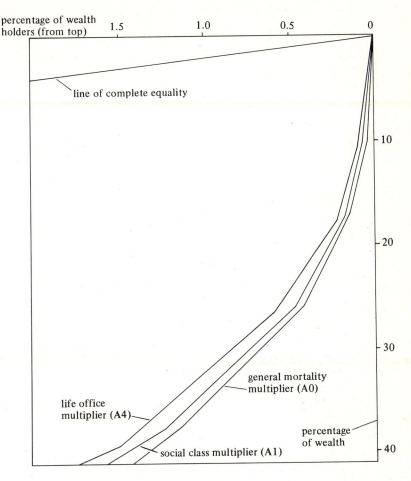

Figure 3.2 Effect of different multipliers on Lorenz curve 1968

siderable increase in estimated total personal wealth: from £76 billion to £90 billion. Similarly, the estimate of the proportion of the population covered by the estate returns rises from 38 per cent on assumption A0 to 44 per cent with the A1 multiplier. In comparison with these large changes in the absolute magnitudes, the distribution at the top shows a relatively limited response to the higher multipliers.

The effect of the move from the general multiplier to the social class multiplier may also be viewed as an increase in an overall social class multiplier plus a further increase restricted to those above £3,000. From Proposi-

Table 3.4 Estimates of the distribution of wealth using different multipliers – Great Britain 1968*

	General mortality multipliers (assumption A0)		Registrar General multipliers as used by Inland Revenue (assumption A1)		Adjusted for errors in occupation (assumption A2)		Graduated for estate size (assumption A3)		Life office multipliers (assumption A4)	
	% Population	% Wealth	% Population	% Wealth	% Population	% Wealth	% Population	% Wealth	% Population	% Wealth
Not covered by estate duty returns	61.5	0	56.2	0	55.3	0	56.4	0	55.9	0
Cumulative % above: £										
1,000	26.1	96.3	30.2	96.6	30.9	96.6	31.2	97.0	33.9	97.2
3,000	14.0	84.6	16.8	85.7	17.3	85.8	17.2	85.8	19.6	88.6
5,000	7.9	72.5	9.5	73.2	9.8	73.2	9.9	74.0	11.2	75.9
10,000	3.4	55.7	4.0	56.1	4.1	56.1	4.2	57.0	4.7	58.4
15,000	2.0	47.5	2.4	47.8	2.5	47.8	2.5	48.6	2.9	49.8
20,000	1.4	41.5	1.6	41.8	1.7	41.7	1.7	42.4	2.0	43.6
25,000	1.1	37.7	1.3	38.0	1.3	38.0	1.4	38.6	1.5	39.6
50,000	0.40	25.5	0.47	25.8	0.48	25.7	0.49	26.2	0.56	26.7
100,000	0.13	16.2	0.15	16.5	0.16	16.5	0.16	16.8	0.18	17.0
200,000	0.04	10.2	0.05	10.5	0.05	10.5	0.05	10.7	0.06	10.7
Total wealth (£ billion)		76.4		90.2		92.5		94.2		102.6

*Population aged 18 and over.

tion 3 we can then see that the effect on the shares of groups owning more than this amount depends on the share of lower wealth (γ) and the value of R_j. From the data for 1968 it may be calculated that the latter lies broadly in the range 0.3−0.45, whereas the share of lower wealth (those below £3,000) is approximately 15 per cent. We should therefore expect, from Proposition 3, that the Lorenz curve would be shifted inwards for the top wealth groups − as is borne out by the numerical results.

The same method of analysis may be applied to the change from A1 to A2 involving as it does an increase in all multipliers but a larger increase above £3,000. We should again expect the Lorenz curve to shift inwards, and this is borne out by the results in table 3.4. Thus in both cases 96.6 per cent of wealth is held by those above £1,000 but in the case of A1 the population involved is 30.2 per cent of the total compared with 30.9 per cent for A2. This shows that the Lorenz curve has shifted in towards the diagonal, albeit by a very small amount.

The graduated multipliers may also be seen as a sequence of social class multipliers applied to progressively smaller classes of estates, and again Proposition 3 may be applied. From the shares of lower wealth (γ) indicated by the general mortality multiplier results in table 3.4, it appears that increases in the multipliers applied to ranges above approximately £10,000 are likely to shift the Lorenz curve outwards. Table 3.4 shows that this is in fact the case: for example, the share of the top $2\frac{1}{2}$ per cent rises from 47.8 per cent (with A2) to 48.6 per cent (with A3). The effect is again small, and the net result is to leave the results with A3 close to those with A1. The interpolated share of the top 1 per cent is 34.5 per cent with A3, compared with 34.7 per cent with A1.

The final column in table 3.4 shows the effect of applying the life office multipliers (A4). Revell argued that the social class differential should be rather wider, which would in itself tend to shift the Lorenz curve inwards; on the other hand, he also suggested that the multipliers applied below £3,000 should be lower (advocating the use of general multipliers (GM) in this range). This has the opposite effect on the Lorenz curve, so that the results given in table 3.4 reflect the netting out of two opposing changes. The end result is in fact such that the curve shifts inwards. The effect of making the changes individually is illustrated by the figures below.

	Interpolated share of top 1 per cent
A1 multipliers and Inland Revenue treatment estates under £3,000	34.7%
A1 multipliers and GM applied to estates under £3,000	35.2%
Life office A4 multipliers and GM applied to estates under £3,000	33.7%

Overall, the effect is relatively small, especially given the increase (14 per cent) in estimated total wealth.

The results so far relate to the case where $w_0 = 0$. Some idea of the implications of $w_0 > 0$ may be obtained from Proposition 3. As noted above 0.3 is broadly the lowest value taken by R_j in 1968, and for the wealth of £3,000 and above we have (in round terms) $L_{k-1} = 15$ per cent, and $F_{k-1} = 85$ per cent. From the expression for

$$\gamma = L_{k-1} + (1 - F_{k-1}) \frac{w_0}{\bar{w}(1)}$$

we can see that $\gamma \leqslant 0.3$ for $w_0 \leqslant \bar{w}(1)$, which is likely to be satisfied in any application. It remains the case, therefore, that increased multipliers above £3,000 tend to shift the Lorenz curve inwards. The results may, however, be different where there is independent information about the total wealth of the population and a fraction ($\theta > 0$) of the excess over that estimated from the estate data is allocated to those not covered by the estate statistics. Whether in such a case the adoption of social class multipliers shifts the Lorenz curve inwards depends from Proposition 4 on the values of θ and Φ (the extent of wealth not covered by the estate estimates). The determinants of Φ are discussed in the next chapter but for present purposes it does not seem unreasonable to take the value of 1.4 used earlier. The figures given on page 57 show the value of the left-hand side of equation (24) where $\Phi = 1.4$, and comparing them with the observed values of R_j, it does indeed appear possible that the Lorenz curve may shift outwards as a result of applying social class multipliers where θ is greater than 0.5.

To this point, we have confined our attention to the five main sets of multipliers (A0–A4). In order to form some assessment of the consequences of further variation in the multipliers, we now investigate the sensitivity of the estimates to changes in individual multipliers. Table 3.5 takes as its starting point the estimates reached by applying the general mortality multipliers ($\lambda_{ai} = 1$) and shows the effect on the share of the top 1 per cent (calculated by log–linear interpolation) of increasing each individual λ_{ai} by 10 per cent. The share of the top 1 per cent extends to approximately £25,000. From Proposition 1, we know that an increase in the multiplier applied to lower estate classes tends to decrease the share of a given group. This is borne out for the top 1 per cent and the results show that the reduction ranges from 0.086 per cent to less than 0.001 per cent. Above £50,000, increases in the multipliers shift the curve outwards, and it was for this reason that graduation of the multipliers (A3) tended to shift the Lorenz curve outwards.

These results suggest one way of estimating the possible range of variation in the share of the top 1 per cent. Suppose that we could choose any social class differentials λ_{ai} subject only to the constraints that they do not decrease as the estate size rises and that $1 \leqslant \lambda_{ai} \leqslant \lambda^*$. If we want to maximise the share of the top 1 per cent, then a first-round solution[16] involves setting (for a given a) $\lambda_{ai} = 1$ until the first positive entry in table 3.5 and then $\lambda_{ai} = \lambda^*$. This typically means social class differentials being

Table 3.5 Sensitivity of share of top 1% – increase in share from 10% increase in multiplier (percentage points)

Estate class	Age group								
	Under 25	25–34	35–44	45–54	55–64	65–74	75–84	85over	Total
Male									
0–1000	−0.018	−0.014	−0.011	−0.010	−0.008	−0.004	−0.002	*	−0.067
1,000–	−0.022	−0.025	−0.025	−0.021	−0.019	−0.010	−0.003	*	−0.125
2,000–	−0.015	−0.031	−0.026	−0.023	−0.023	−0.011	−0.005	*	−0.134
3,000–	−0.020	−0.062	−0.067	−0.054	−0.054	−0.028	−0.011	−0.002	−0.298
5,000–	−0.018	−0.070	−0.080	−0.071	−0.078	−0.045	−0.018	−0.003	−0.383
10,000–	−0.010	−0.058	−0.075	−0.075	−0.086	−0.053	−0.025	−0.005	−0.387
25,000–	−0.001	−0.008	−0.015	−0.025	−0.029	−0.018	−0.009	−0.002	−0.107
50,000–	*	0.018	0.013	0.020	0.033	0.019	0.011	0.003	0.117
100,000–	*	0.017	0.018	0.025	0.037	0.022	0.013	0.004	0.136
200,000–	*	0.008	0.082	0.101	0.056	0.065	0.022	0.006	0.340
Female									
0–1000	−0.018	−0.007	−0.008	−0.009	−0.008	−0.008	−0.004	−0.001	−0.063
1,000–	−0.011	−0.011	−0.009	−0.016	−0.015	−0.014	−0.007	−0.002	−0.085
2,000–	−0.006	−0.005	−0.012	−0.018	−0.013	−0.015	−0.009	−0.002	−0.080
3,000–	−0.004	−0.008	−0.018	−0.026	−0.032	−0.029	−0.020	−0.004	−0.141
5,000	−0.005	−0.011	−0.019	−0.035	−0.056	−0.055	−0.032	−0.007	−0.220
10,000–	−0.009	−0.017	−0.025	−0.028	−0.072	−0.069	−0.037	−0.010	−0.267
25,000–	*	0.004	−0.007	−0.016	−0.020	−0.016	−0.010	−0.003	−0.068
50,000–	*	0.008	0.008	0.020	0.021	0.021	0.014	0.005	0.097
100,000–	*	0.003	0.017	0.021	0.022	0.030	0.016	0.005	0.114
200,000–	*	0.120	0.026	0.015	0.032	0.029	0.015	0.005	0.242
Total	−0.157	−0.149	−0.233	−0.225	−0.312	−0.189	−0.101	−0.013	−1.379

*less than ± 0.001.

applied only at £50,000 and above. Conversely, to minimise the share of the top 1 per cent, a first-round solution is to apply $\lambda_{ai} = \lambda^*$ for all estate classes. For $\lambda^* = 1.1$, this gives a range for the share of the top 1 per cent of 35–8 per cent. For this relatively modest differential it implies therefore a range around the general mortality multiplier of about ± $1\frac{1}{2}$ per cent. In the previous section we suggested that a social class differential of 1.67 would be a

16 A complete solution requires an iterative procedure, since the entry for λ_{ai} in table 3.5 depends on the value of the other multipliers.

reasonable upper limit. With this value of λ^*, the range about the general mortality multiplier is around ± 5 per cent.

It should be emphasised that the range just given relates to extreme situations, in terms both of the value of λ^* and of the graduation of the multipliers with estate size. In reality the extent of variation will probably be closer to that indicated by the assumptions considered earlier in this section. In particular, it does not seem unreasonable to take the figures below as representing the likely range for the shares of the top wealth-holders.

			share of top 1 per cent
'Upper' figure	:	A0 General mortality multiplier	36.6%
'Central' figure	:	A3 Graduated multiplier	34.5%
		(or A1)	(34.7%)
'Lower' figure	:	A4 Life office multiplier	33.7%

3.4 Summary

In this chapter we have examined in detail the properties of the mortality multiplier method, the different sources of multipliers, and the results obtained under different assumptions. In certain respects the results are reassuring, since they indicate that the different multipliers considered do not – despite the substantial changes in the estimates of total wealth – lead to widely differing estimates of the share of top wealth-holders. The two adjustments suggested to the multipliers employed by the Inland Revenue (those for errors in occupational statements and for graduation with estate size) tend to work in opposite directions, with the net result close to that given by the official method. At the same time, the differences are not sufficiently small that they can be neglected; and when, for example, comparing trends over time, it is important to ensure that the multipliers are derived on a consistent basis. Additionally, there are features, such as the role of marital status, which warrant further study.

The main assumption employed in the estimates presented in later chapters is that referred to here as A3, or the Registrar General's data adjusted for errors in occupational statements and graduated with estate size. In our view this corrects for some of the deficiencies of the multipliers used by the Inland Revenue without introducing the problems attendant on the use of the life office data. The reader who feels that this assumption is inappropriate will, we hope, be able to see the effect of alternative approaches from the theoretical analysis of section 3.1 and from the actual estimates in section 3.3. In particular, some indication of the range of results for different social class multipliers is provided by assumption A0 (higher) and A4 (lower); and these are the two assumptions employed when discussing the overall sensitivity of the results in chapter 5.

4

RECONCILIATION WITH NATIONAL BALANCE SHEET DATA

In chapter 2, we saw that there are three major reasons why the estate method, even with the appropriate mortality multipliers, is likely to lead to an estimate of total personal wealth different from that reached using independent information about the total holdings of particular assets:

    (i) the omission of the property of wealth-holders excluded from the estate data,

   (ii) certain assets are not valued on an appropriate basis,

  (iii) certain types of property may be missing from estates recorded in the statistics.

In this chapter, we examine the adjustments for these factors which can be made to the estimates of the size distribution derived from the estate returns. The adjustments involve two main stages. First, it is necessary to assess how far one can obtain independent information about total holdings; and in this we draw heavily on the work of Revell (1967) and Roe (1971) on the construction of national balance sheet data. The second stage is one not undertaken by Revell and Roe and concerns the adjustment of wealth by ranges.

Section 4.1 discusses the relationship between the estate estimates of total personal wealth and the balance sheet data, examining the main sources of the discrepancy between the figures. Section 4.2 describes the adjustments to individual assets and the methods of allocating the missing wealth by ranges. The results of applying this procedure to the data for 1968 and 1972 are presented in section 4.3, where we investigate the sensitivity of the results to the precise assumptions made. Finally, section 4.4 summarises briefly the main findings and their relation to the criticisms which have been levelled against the official estimates.

4.1   'Missing' wealth and the balance sheet totals

The starting point for our analysis is the work on the balance sheet totals pioneered in this country by Revell and continued by Roe.[1] Revell's main interest was in preparing a full set of balance sheet totals for all sectors, but for our purposes the important point is that he was able to prepare more reliable totals for the holding of certain assets by the personal sector than those produced using estate data. In some cases he was not able to do this, and had to use the estate estimate. Where, however, he drew on independent information about total holdings, this allows us to assess the extent of wealth missing from the size distribution derived from estate returns. To take one example, we know that, as a result of the Administration of Estates (Small Payments) Act 1965, many small holdings in the National Savings Bank are missing from the estate estimates. Using information from the issuing source, Revell estimated the true total held, and hence we can determine the likely magnitude of the omitted wealth.

At the same time, the differences between the aims of this study and those of Revell mean that the balance sheet data should not be used uncritically. We should not simply in all cases replace our estate estimate totals by the corresponding balance sheet item, and we do not agree with the Royal Commission that the discrepancies can entirely 'be attributed to the errors introduced by the various deficiencies in coverage and valuation of the estate multiplier approach' (Royal Commission 1975:85). For some types of asset, the estimates by Revell for the personal sector totals are derived as residuals from the estimates for other sectors, and the divergence from the estate estimates may at least in part reflect errors in these other estimates. The Royal Commission's approach runs the risk of replacing the admittedly incomplete estate estimates by a series which might be at least as inaccurate and possibly more so.

In view of this, we have tried to base our adjustments on the following general principles:

(a) adjustments should only be made where there is an *a priori* reason to expect that the divergence corresponds to a source of wealth which is missing from the estate returns (because of the excluded population, or missing property) or which is incorrectly valued,

(b) note should be taken of Revell's assessment of the reliability of his estimates (see table 4.1 below) and as far as possible balance sheet totals only employed where they are rated by him as A (very reliable) or B (fairly reliable),

(c) since our concern is primarily with the total size of wealth-holdings rather than with their asset composition, adjustments are not made

---

1 The primary reference is Revell (1967), but the reader is also referred to Roe (1971) and Revell and Tomkins (1974). The authors would like to reiterate their gratitude to Professor Revell and Mr Roe for the assistance given.

Table 4.1 Discrepancy between estate duty estimates and national balance sheet totals 1961*

| | £ billion (UK) | | | |
	Estate estimate	Balance sheet	Our adjustment (number)	Revell's assessment of accuracy‡
Assets				
(i) *Unadjusted estate estimates used*				
Quoted UK government, UK local authority and overseas government	3.0	3.0	–	B/C
Overseas company	1.1	1.1	–	–
Non-trade debtors	3.2	3.2	–	B
(ii) *Estate estimates used in smoothed form*				
Unquoted UK shares (including debentures and preference)	3.2	5.4	7	D
House mortgages (as assets)	0.6	0.6	–	C
Cash at bank	6.1	5.5	2	B
Quoted UK debenture and preference	0.7	0.8	–	C
(iii) *Independent information*				
Unquoted UK government	3.4	4.2	1	A
Savings bank deposits	2.9	3.2	1	A/B
Building society deposits	3.6	3.1	3	A/B
Quoted UK ordinary shares	11.5	12.2	7	B
Household goods	2.1	4.0	4	–
Life policies and pension rights	7.2	13.5	8	A/B
Notes and coin	0.2	0.3	2	D
Trade assets	2.2	4.4	5	–
Land and buildings	13.1	20.1	9	C
Expectant interests and cessers of annuities	2.5	0.0	6	–
Other†	1.5	1.3	–	–
Liabilities				
Debts in UK	2.9	4.9	10	B
House mortgages	1.2	4.9	10	B
Other	0.1	0.0	–	–
Net worth	63.9	76.1	–	–

Source: Revell (1967), table 7.1, rounded.

Notes

* No allowance has been made for exempt settled property. This means that in both cases this item has been subtracted from the last columns in Revell's table.

† Includes unquoted UK local authority, loans to persons, deposits with co-operative societies, friendly societies etc. (Inland Revenue category 'money on bonds').

‡ Accuracy

A = a very reliable figure

B = a figure involving some estimation, but fairly reliable

C = a figure involving considerable estimation and not very reliable

D = a very unreliable figure

(Assessment of the accuracy is not always given).

where there are likely to be offsetting adjustments under other headings.

In considering the application of the principles, it may be helpful to begin with the estimates made by Revell for 1961, and these are set out in table 4.1. In that year the estimate of total personal wealth in the United Kingdom made by him from estate duty statistics using the life office multiplier was £63.9 billion,[2] compared with the final national balance sheet total of £76.1 billion, or some twenty per cent higher. The main sources of this shortfall are shown in table 4.1, where we have classified the items according to the relationship between the balance sheet totals and the estate estimates, and have indicated in column 3 the cases in which we have made adjustments. In the first group, Revell simply takes the estate estimate and no adjustments are made here. In the second group, the estate series was 'smoothed' by Revell over the period 1957–61 to reduce sampling fluctuations. Unlike Revell we are not primarily concerned with the asset composition of wealth-holdings and for this reason we have made only limited adjustments under this heading, preferring to treat the problem of sampling error in relation to *total* wealth-holdings in chapter 5. The third group are those for which independent information was employed, and these are the main items for which adjustments are made. For convenience of reference, they are listed below, together with the category numbers (in brackets) corresponding to those in *Inland Revenue Statistics* 1971: table 115:

1. Unquoted UK government securities and savings bank deposits (1, 2, 28)
2. Cash and bank deposits (27, 29, 30)
3. Building society deposits (21)
4. Household goods (25)
5. Trade assets (31–37)
6. Settled property (38, 40)
7. UK company shares (11–16)
8. Life policies and pension rights (26)
9. Land and buildings (49–57)
10. Liabilities (43, 46, 59, 60)

For the more recent years with which we are concerned in this chapter (1968 and 1972), we have constructed the balance sheet totals for these ten categories shown in column 1 of table 4.2. The derivation of these totals is described in detail in appendix II, but in general it follows the same methods as employed by Revell and Roe. In particular we have made

---

2 Excluding wealth held by overseas residents, and with an allowance for Northern Ireland.

considerable use of unpublished estimates by Roe, extending the data in
Roe (1971), and of the figures for 1969 and 1970 given by Revell and
Tomkins (1974). [3]

The totals have been adjusted in three respects to bring them into line with
the basis for the estimates here, which are for Great Britain, relate to the
adult population (defined at this point as 18 and over) and are averaged over
the year (the weights being those implicit in the estate method). In the first
case, the balance sheet totals have been approximately adjusted to cover
Great Britain rather than the United Kingdom applying the percentage
reduction indicated by Revell's estimates of wealth for Northern Ireland in
1961; the adjustment is only approximate in that it may not make adequate
allowance for double-counting (see Revell 1967:132). Similarly, we have
excluded those elements of property likely to be held by children, although
again the correction is only very approximate. The date of valuation is more
complicated. The estate estimates relate to dates throughout the year, with
the winter months receiving more weight on account of the higher mortality
in that period; whereas the balance sheet estimates relate to 31 December (or,
in some cases, 30 June). If the level of wealth is rising, this difference in
timing may account, in part, for the balance sheet totals being higher. From
information about the pattern of deaths corresponding to the estates
recorded in the tax year 1967—8 supplied by the Inland Revenue, we estimated that the total amounts of capital could be allocated approximately as
shown below. On the assumption that this is broadly representative, we have

Date of death	Percentage
Before March 1967	36
April—June 1967	20
July—September 1967	18
October 1967—March 1968	26

taken weighted averages of the balance sheet figures for December of the
preceding year, June and December (with weights of 36 per cent, 38 per cent
and 26 per cent respectively). Where the June figure is not available, we have
taken a weighted average of the figures for December of the preceding year
(weight 56 per cent) and December (weight 44 per cent).

The balance sheet totals for each asset category are to be compared with
those derived from the estate data. For this purpose, it is necessary to disaggregate the estate estimates by asset type. The Inland Revenue publish
estimates of total personal wealth by asset type, but these are derived using

3 An earlier set of estimates for 1968 alone was given in Atkinson (1975); these
  have been corrected and adjusted in certain respects. Subsequently, the Royal
  Commission has made adjustments for 1972 using balance sheet data.

one particular set of multipliers. In order to obtain estimates using the different multipliers discussed in the previous chapter, it is necessary to have the estate returns classified by age/estate range/sex/asset type, but this information was unfortunately not available. In view of this we have had to apply the estimated asset composition by ranges derived using the Inland Revenue multipliers to the size distribution estimates obtained in chapter 3. This procedure is not completely satisfactory in that it makes allowance neither for the way in which the multipliers differ across age groups nor for the Inland Revenue's practice of combining age groups, but it was the best which could be done with the information at our disposal. A selection from the asset composition data for 1968 and 1972 is shown in table 4.3. As is to be expected, the importance of the different asset categories considered here varies considerably with the size of wealth-holding. Of particular significance is the decline over the ranges covered (broadly average wealth and above) in the proportion held in life policies and houses. The estate data are also adjusted for property owned by overseas residents (see chapter 2) and for non-distributed estates.[4]

The estate estimates for different asset categories (based on multipliers A1) are shown in the second column of table 4.2. In many cases the figures are substantially different from the balance sheet totals, and such large sums clearly could have a significant effect on the size distribution of wealth. Whether they will in fact do so depends on how far it is appropriate to include in the distribution the excess of the balance sheet totals over the estate figures and on the allocation of such wealth by ranges. The answers to these questions depend in turn on the reasons for wealth not appearing in the estate statistics, and on the view one takes of the reliability of the balance sheet totals.

In the present state of knowledge it is obviously difficult to provide precise answers to these questions, and any allocation of the excess wealth is bound to be open to debate. We have, therefore, followed the approach of giving results based on a range of assumptions. We feel that this procedure, in contrast to that adopted by the Royal Commission in its Initial Report (1975), allows the reader to form a clearer idea of the sensitivity of the results. These assumptions may be summarised in terms of the three factors identified at the beginning of this chapter:

4 These are estates of deceased persons which have not yet been distributed to beneficiaries. Revell (1967: 156–7) argues that these should be counted as part of personal property and suggests that an approximate adjustment may be made by increasing the value of all assets as estimated by the estate method by 1%, and this is the procedure we have followed. It allocates all the amount to the included population, but given the type of property affected and likely length of delays, this does not seem unreasonable.

Table 4.2 Balance sheet and estate method totals 1968 and 1972 (£ million)

Category	1968 1. Balance sheet	2. Estate method (A1)
1. Unquoted government securities and savings bank deposits	8,330	6,090
2. Cash and bank deposits	8,610	6,370
3. Building society deposits	7,120	6,530
4. Household goods	9,290	2,930
5. Trade assets	5,170	2,560
6. Settled property	(see text)	
7. UK company shares	(see text)	
8. Life policies and occupational pension rights	22,750	13,010
9. Land and buildings – dwellings – other	42,700	27,250
10. Liabilities – debts	7,290	3,925
– house mortgages	(see text)	
	1972	
1. Unquoted government securities and savings bank deposits	9,430	6,010
2. Cash and bank deposits	11,920	7,640
3. Building society deposits	12,830	9,680
4. Household goods	13,660	4,600
5. Trade assets	5,590	3,120
6. Settled property	(see text)	
7. UK company shares	(see text)	
8. Life policies and occupational pension rights	32,250	20,560
9. Land and buildings – dwellings – other	77,700	56,350
10. Liabilities – debts	10,100	6,030
– house mortgages	(see text)	

Source: See text and appendix II. All figures have been rounded (to the nearest £10 million in the case of the estate estimates).

(i) Property of wealth-holders excluded from the estate data (the 'excluded population'). From the fact that these are likely to be predominantly small wealth-holdings, and from the circumstances in which wealth is transferred without probate, we can form a reasonable idea of the types of asset likely to be affected, and adjustments are made for categories 1–4, 8–10. The allocation by ranges is based on four assumptions:

B1: No adjustment – as Inland Revenue,

B2: Lower bound to concentration – where wealth is allocated as far as reasonable to excluded population, and to lower wealth ranges among the included population,

B3: Central estimate — based on best available information,

B4: Upper bound to concentration — where wealth is allocated as far as reasonable to included population (and within that group to those above the exemption level).

(ii) Inappropriate valuation in the estate statistics. In chapter 2 we described some of the assets affected by this problem, and in the light of this we make adjustments for categories 4—6, 8 and 9, employing the two main assumptions described earlier:

C1: Realisation valuation — valued at current market selling price,

C2: Going-concern valuation — value to household on assumption that the asset is retained.

(The Inland Revenue basis is referred to as CO.)

(iii) Property 'missing' from estate returns. There are a number of ways in which wealth-holdings which appear in the statistics are nonetheless incomplete. On the basis of the analysis in chapter 2, we make adjustments to categories 1—3, 6, 8—10, and the results are denoted by:

D1: No adjustment — as Inland Revenue,

D2: Adjusted — details given in section 4.2.

It should be noted that these assumptions are inter-dependent, so that the adjustments under D2, for example, may depend on which of assumptions B1—B4 is selected.

It is an essential feature of the method adopted here that one needs to consider each asset type separately, and this is the subject of the next section. This inevitably involves discussion of the special factors surrounding particular assets, such as savings bank deposits, but we feel that such detailed analysis is necessary if effective use is to be made of the balance sheet totals. Without it, only the very broadest of ranges can be derived for the shares of different wealth groups.

4.2   Adjustments to individual asset categories*

In this section we consider each of the ten asset categories in turn, outlining the adjustments and explaining the reasons underlying them. Table 4.4 summarises the adjustments made under the different assumptions.

1. Unquoted government securities and savings bank deposits

There are three main explanations of the substantial shortfall for this item:

(i) omission of small wealth-holdings,

---

* This section is more technical. Some readers may like to consult table 4.4, which summarises the assumptions made, and then continue with the discussion of the results in section 4.3 (page 100).

Table 4.3 Asset composition: percentage of net capital value held in asset type 1968 and 1972

1968

Range of net wealth £	3,000–20,000	20,000–25,000	25,000–50,000	50,000–60,000	60,000–100,000	100,000–200,000	>200,000	Total
Asset type								
1. Unquoted government securities and savings bank deposits	8.4	5.3	2.7	1.8	1.4	1.2	1.2	6.8
2. Cash and bank deposits	7.5	6.3	6.3	7.1	5.7	5.9	5.2	7.1
3. Building society deposits	9.7	12.4	9.0	5.2	4.0	2.9	0.7	7.3
4. Household goods	3.4	1.9	2.1	1.9	1.8	2.0	2.1	3.3
5. Trade assets	3.0	6.0	4.8	4.1	3.7	2.1	1.4	2.9
8. Life policies	20.4	9.8	6.7	4.7	3.1	1.7	0.8	14.4
9a Dwellings	38.7	28.1	15.6	11.7	8.9	6.7	6.9	26.4
9b Other realty	1.7	4.7	7.5	8.7	6.3	7.7	8.4	3.9
10. Debts (items 43 and 46)	−3.6	−4.5	−4.5	−5.2	−5.1	−5.0	−5.6	−4.3

1972

Range of net wealth £	3,000–5,000	5,000–10,000	10,000–15,000	15,000–20,000	20,000–50,000	50,000–100,000	100,000–200,000	>200,000	Total
Asset type									
1. Unquoted government securities and savings bank deposits	8.3	5.3	4.8	3.7	2.8	1.5	1.2	1.0	4.3
2. Cash and bank deposits	6.9	5.1	5.0	4.4	5.0	5.8	5.2	3.9	5.4
3. Building society deposits	7.9	6.9	9.0	9.0	9.6	6.3	3.9	1.0	6.9
4. Household goods	4.6	3.6	2.9	2.5	2.2	2.0	2.1	3.3	3.2
5. Trade assets	1.9	2.0	1.8	3.3	3.4	2.1	2.0	1.0	2.2
8. Life policies	23.6	22.0	19.0	18.0	11.9	4.6	2.6	1.6	14.7
9a Dwellings	46.7	53.4	52.2	47.3	32.6	16.9	11.3	12.7	35.2
9b Other realty	0.5	1.4	1.6	3.1	7.1	8.1	10.4	10.7	4.9
10. Debts (items 43 and 46)	−2.6	−1.8	−1.2	−2.4	−1.4	−0.3	−1.6	−17.6	−3.9

Sources: 1968 supplied by Inland Revenue
1972 *Inland Revenue Statistics 1974*: table 106.

Table 4.4 Summary of assumptions about allocation of excess wealth by ranges

	B2	B3	B4	Adjustment for Valuation
1. Unquoted government securities and savings bank deposits	90% allocated to EP (B2); 10% not allocated.	65% allocated to EP (B3); 25% allocated equally to those below exemption level (D2); 10% not allocated	40% allocated to EP (B4); 50% allocated proportionately to holdings in estate estimates (D2); 10% not allocated	No
2. Cash and bank deposits	65% to EP (B2); 35% to included population proportionately to holdings (D2).	30% to EP (B3); 20% to included population proportionately to holdings (D2); 50% not allocated.	10% to EP (B4); 10% to included population proportionately to holdings (D2); 80% not allocated.	No
3. Building society deposits	75% allocated to EP (B2); 20% allocated equally to those below exemption level (D2); 5% not allocated	50% allocated to EP (B3); 45% proportional to holdings below exemption level (D2); 5% not allocated	25% allocated to EP (B4); 70% proportional to holdings in estate estimates (D2); 5% not allocated	No
4. Household goods	All allocated to EP (or average holding per head if less) (B2).	EP allocated holding equal to that in range £0–3,000 (£5,000 in 1972) (B3).	EP allocated holding equal to three quarters of that in range £0–3,000 (£5,000 in 1972) (B4).	Yes on C2

Table 4.4 continued

5. Trade assets	No adjustment			Yes on C2
6. Settled property	See text			Discount d_s
7. Shares	No adjustment			
8. Life policies	Industrial branch policies allocated to EP (B2−B4); non-aggregable policies allocated proportionately to total estate duty wealth (D2)			See text
Occupational pension rights (D2)	Distributed to top 10½ m. men and 4½ m. women Equally (B2)	In proportion to life policies (B3)	In proportion to total estate duty wealth (B4)	
9. Land and buildings	See text			
10. Liabilities	25% allocated to EP (B2) and those below exemption level (D2); remainder proportionately to estate duty estimates (D2)	50% allocated to EP (B3) and those below exemption level (D2); remainder proportionately to estate duty estimates (D2)	All debts allocated to EP (B4) and those below exemption level (D2)	No

Note: EP denotes excluded population (those not covered by the estate returns).

(ii) under-statement of holdings of those covered by the estate returns (particularly those below the exemption limit),

(iii) errors in the balance sheet totals (e.g. those arising from dormant accounts or from errors in estimating non-personal holdings).

The first of these is important, particularly in view of the Administration of Estates (Small Payments) Act 1965. The assets in question include those typically held by small savers, such as savings certificates, Premium Bonds and deposits in the National Savings Bank. The obvious assumption for the lower bound (B2) is that all the excess wealth (less 10 per cent not allocated — see below) be attributed to the excluded population. This would allocate an amount per head of the excluded population (on assumption A1) of £108 in 1968. This appears rather high,[5] and when we bear in mind that certain of the assets included in this category are unlikely to be held by small savers (such as tax reserve certificates), it seems probable that it does indeed provide an over-estimate of the amount which should be allocated to the excluded population. Turning to the other assumptions, Revell (1967: 168—9) estimated on the basis of a special analysis of death claims for 1960 that 40 per cent of the excess wealth in that year was attributable to the excluded population. In 1965, the limit for probate was increased from £100 to £500 and it is reasonable to suppose that the proportion in the period 1966—72 was higher. The figure of 40 per cent may therefore represent a reasonable basis for the lower assumption B4; and for assumption B3 we take the 'central' figure of 65 per cent.

There remains the problem of explaining the remainder of the excess wealth. It is possible that the balance sheet figure is too high on account of errors in non-personal holdings, money held in dormant accounts (i.e. those where there has ceased to be any active ownership, either because the holder has died or because the holder has forgotten its existence), and amounts held by children. In view of the low level of non-personal holdings, it does not seem reasonable to attribute more than 5 per cent of the excess to this source of error (see appendix II); and the limited evidence about dormant accounts does not suggest that they are likely to exceed 5 per cent of the excess.[6] This leaves 25 per cent of the excess wealth under assumption B3 and 50 per cent under B4 which is assumed to represent under-statement in the estate data, as may occur, for example, if accrued interest is not credited to an account

---

5 The estimates in the Page Report suggested, for example, that the median *account* in the National Savings Bank was £6 in 1968 (Page 1973:112) and that 70% of Premium Bond holders had £10 or less in 1971 (Page 1973:160).

6 In 1971 the National Savings Bank had 28.7 million inactive accounts (defined as not having been used for five years or more) and the total balances were £61.3 million — or less than 2 per cent of the excess in 1972 (Page 1973:130).

where the estate is clearly not dutiable. In view of this, assumption B3/D2 allocates the remaining 25 per cent equally to those below the exemption level; whereas B4/D2 allocates the 50 per cent proportionately to holdings shown in the estate data (which seems reasonable for an upper bound).

2. Cash and bank deposits

This item consists of two components: notes and coin, and bank deposits. The estate estimate of the former is clearly of dubious value, because of evasion, because the dying have less need of cash, and because it will typically be most important in estates for which probate is not necessary. There should therefore be an allowance for the excluded population and for the under-statement of holdings.

Notes and coin are, however, only a relatively small part of the total. In the case of bank deposits, Revell suggests that in theory there should be no shortfall: 'the figures shown in the estate duty statistics for bank deposits ought to be both complete and accurate. The affidavit requires the detailing of each bank account separately . . . Moreover, we can take it that there will be very few persons with bank accounts but no other asset needing probate' (Revell 1967:151). The situation seems, however, to be rather different today. Not only is there a substantial discrepancy between the balance sheet and estate duty estimates of the total holdings (see table 4.2) but also the number of holders appears to be seriously under-stated. Sample survey evidence (e.g. Morgan 1975:17) suggests that in 1974 there were over 13 million people with bank current accounts, whereas the Inland Revenue esti-mates indicate fewer than 10 million. This evidence needs to be treated with care. The sample survey figures are subject to considerable error, and if there are missing accounts it may be because they are overdrawn. The discrepancy may arise in part because of joint accounts passing by survivorship to the other joint holder. In view of these considerations, and the uncertainty surrounding this category of assets, we have made a wide range of assumptions:

> B2: Allocate 65 per cent of difference to excluded population, 35 per cent on D2 to included population proportionately to holdings;
> B3: Allocate 30 per cent of difference to excluded population, 20 per cent on D2 to included population proportionately to holdings;
> B4: Allocate 10 per cent of difference to excluded population, 10 per cent on D2 to included population proportionately to holdings (to adjust for cash element only).

In the case of B3 and B4, the remaining percentage is attributed to errors in the balance sheet data (and B4 is equivalent to making no adjustment at all for bank deposits).

3. Building society deposits

The considerations underlying the treatment of this category are rather similar to those for category (1), although there are sufficient differences to make alternative percentage allocations necessary. In particular, the proportion attributable to the excluded population is probably smaller than for National Savings (Revell 1967:168–9). Moreover, dormant accounts, those held by children, and errors in non-personal holdings are likely to be less important. In view of these considerations, the proportion allocated to the excluded population is smaller in all cases, and only 5 per cent is not allocated – see table 4.4.

4. Household goods

The difference between the balance sheet and estate duty estimates arises in this case because of:

   (i) omission of small wealth-holdings,
   (ii) the adoption of a going-concern basis for valuation (this is not relevant for assumption C1).

The former suggests that the natural assumption under B2 is to allocate the entire excess wealth to the excluded population. (In certain situations, this would mean that the amount allocated per head would exceed that for those covered by the estate statistics, and in this event the excluded population are allocated an amount equal to the average holding.) For assumption B3, we make the assumption that the average holding of the excluded population equals the average for the range £0–3,000 in the estate statistics (£0–5,000 in 1972), a figure which is approximately half the average for estates as a whole. At the upper extreme (B4) we assume that the figure for the excluded population equals three quarters of the average for those in the range £0–3,000.

The adjustment for the basis of valuation is of major importance, since the realisation value in effect used by the Inland Revenue is typically considerably less than the value to a household as a going concern. On the going-concern assumption C2, the remaining excess of the balance sheet figure over the estate figure (after the allowance for the excluded population has been made) is allocated proportionately to all holdings. For 1968 this gives, on assumption B3, a factor of 1.7, so that the holdings are increased by 70 per cent when a going-concern basis is adopted.

5. Trade assets

The reasons for the substantial discrepancy between the estate duty estimates and the balance sheet figure for this item (they differ by a factor of two) are discussed by Revell (1967:140–5) and stem primarily from differences in the method of valuation. In view of this the adjustments made are:

C1 (realisation) – no adjustment,

C2 (going concern) – increase all holdings proportionately to give balance sheet total.

6. Settled property

The starting point for estimating the extent of exempt settled property is provided by the figures below derived from Revell (1967:137). These

	£ million
Property settled on a surviving spouse	1,250
Discretionary trusts	200

(Property held in accumulating trusts for minors is not taken into account.)

estimates may be on the low side. In the case of discretionary trusts, Revell himself comments that 'many people who have practical experiences of settled property would claim that the figure . . . is far too low', and he goes on to say that 'undoubtedly an enquiry on similar lines taken today (1967) would yield a much larger figure because corporate trustees all report a great increase in this form of trust' (1967:138). The estimates made by earlier investigators were in fact considerably higher. Campion's figure for the settled property missing from the estate duty estimates in 1936 was between £750 million and £1,300 million (1939:21). In 1954 Lydall and Tipping assumed that discretionary trusts accounted for £1,000 million and 'settled property' (presumably that covered by the surviving spouse exemption) for £3,000 million.

In view of this we have broadly taken the Revell total as a lower bound (B2) and the higher estimate by Campion as an upper bound (B4), in each case extrapolated in line with total wealth. The assumption B3 is taken as midway between these. The split between surviving spouse and other trusts takes account of the trends over the period, and in particular the rapid growth in the number of discretionary and accumulating trusts. The resulting figures for missing settled property are shown below (in £ million). These

	1968			1972		
	B2	B3	B4	B2	B3	B4
Surviving spouse trusts	1,250	2,000	3,000	1,250	2,000	3,000
Other non-dutiable trusts	1,250	3,250	5,000	1,750	5,000	8,000
Total	2,500	5,250	8,000	3,000	7,000	11,000

estimates are inevitably based on a considerable element of guesswork, but it was reassuring to us that the Inland Revenue, making use of special enquiries carried out in 1963–4 and 1974, arrived at a total of £8,500 (split £2,500/ £6,000) for 1972, which is not too different from the figures above (Royal Commission 1975:237).[7]

It seems reasonable to assume that much of this missing property should be allocated to the higher wealth ranges, and the investigations by Revell (1961 and 1967) provide some guide in this respect. It is assumed that all wealth in 'other non-dutiable' trusts belongs to those with wealth of over £50,000, and that this should be allocated in proportion to wealth in excess of this amount as indicated by the estate duty estimates. Property settled on a surviving spouse may be held lower down the scale and is allocated in proportion to wealth in excess of £5,000 (£10,000 in 1972).

There are further problems concerning settled property. First, the inclusion of 'expectant interests' involves double-counting (Revell 1967: 113) and this item is excluded. Second, the adjustments described in the previous two paragraphs may involve double-counting if, at the same time, we are using the national balance sheet estimates to correct for missing wealth. In order to avoid this, it is assumed that the net addition of settled property (allowing for the exclusion of expectant interests) is distributed among different assets in the way shown below (which is based on the estimates in Revell 1967: table 6.2):

	(per cent)
Land and buildings	10
Quoted UK government securities	15
Quoted UK ordinary shares	70
Life policies	5

Thirdly, there is the question touched on in chapter 2 of the appropriate valuation of settled property, and whether in the case of the 'missing' settled property, particularly discretionary trusts, the sum of individual prospective interests may fall short of the value of the trust as a whole. In view of this, we later consider the effect of applying a 'discount' factor (d_s) to the discretionary trust element of the settled property adjustment, with $d_s = 0.5$ replacing the value of 1.0 used in the main calculations.

7 The publication of this estimate in the Initial Report of the Royal Commission led us to make a modest upward revision in our totals for 1968, so that the figure for B3 is higher than that of £4,700 million used in Atkinson (1975). It also convinced us that the split between the two categories should be altered. The basis for the Inland Revenue estimates is described in their evidence to the Select Committee on a Wealth Tax (1975: col. IV, 1523).

7. UK company shares

The coverage of quoted ordinary shares is discussed by Revell (1967:153–5), who argues that 'the estate duty statistics ought to give a complete coverage of all personal holdings since it is virtually impossible to transfer holdings of a deceased person without probate'. If this is correct, then the problem becomes largely one of valuation. There are obviously differences in the prices used for this purpose, and Revell's analysis (1967: table 7.3) suggests that the estate estimates were rather lower than those derived from register surveys. He goes on to say that 'the reasons for the apparent errors in these particular estate duty estimates are by no means clear', and in view of this we have, following the principles outlined in the previous section, decided to make no adjustment.

This leaves the question of the year-to-year fluctuations in share prices – as opposed to their general level – and this is a problem which affects unquoted shares even more than quoted shares. Revell himself used a smoothed series for the latter to overcome the sampling errors which caused the estimates to fluctuate 'wildly' from one year to the next. As noted earlier, unlike Revell, we are not primarily concerned with the asset composition of wealth holdings, and as a consequence we are less worried about sampling errors which cause wealth to appear in one form rather than another (the total value being unaltered). We have therefore not made explicit adjustments for the holding of particular assets but have treated the problem in the context of sampling errors in total wealth-holding (see chapter 5).

8. Life policies

In chapter 2 we saw that there were three main problems with the Inland Revenue treatment of this item:

(a) the method of valuation – sums assured – is inappropriate. In what follows we have based the going-concern valuation C2 on the value of the underlying funds or, in the case of unfunded pensions, on their actuarial value. The realisation value C1 is assumed to be a constant proportion of the going-concern valuation (so that the treatment is described mainly in terms of C2).

(b) the estate estimates of sums assured under life policies may exclude a number of items, among them:

certain claims paid without production of probate (including many industrial branch policies),

death benefit at discretion of trustees of occupational pension schemes,

non-aggregable policies (where applicable).

(c) no allowance is made for the value of rights to occupational pensions, apart from certain death benefits.

Appendix II describes the method by which balance sheet totals have been estimated for:

Life policies (value of funds)

Funded pension rights (value of funds)

Unfunded pension rights (actuarial value)

The last two are treated as a combined item 'pension rights' in what follows.

In the case of life policies, we consider first the allocation of the missing sums assured (item (b) above) and then the conversion from a sums assured to a fund basis. We have independent information on the total sums assured under ordinary and industrial branches (see appendix II); and we follow the same procedure as Revell (1967:173) in allocating the missing sums assured between the two branches.[8] The whole of the missing industrial branch policies are attributed to the excluded population. This accounts for a substantial part of the sums assured but there is still a major unexplained shortfall. Revell (1967:172) attributes this to the netting out of policies securing loans, especially for house purchase. According to the Estate Duty Office, such netting out would not be correct practice in the administration of estates, but it is striking that the estate estimate of house mortgages is considerably lower than that indicated by independent information (Revell 1967:173). Such netting out would affect the asset composition but not total wealth-holding, and for our purposes it would be best to leave both life policies and mortgage liabilities unadjusted. This is the practice followed, although it obviously warrants further investigation. Finally, an approximate allowance of 5 per cent is made for non-aggregable policies (on the basis of the evidence in Revell (1967:173)). This is allocated proportionately to the wealth indicated by the estate statistics, since a large part was intended (prior to 1968) to avoid duty.

---

8 Revell sets up a pair of simultaneous equations in X_O and X_I (the number of ordinary and industrial policies, respectively, included in the estate figures):

$$\frac{X_O}{1.25} + \frac{X_I}{2.5} = X$$

where X is the number of estates including life policies and the numbers of policies per person are assumed to be 1.25 and 2.5 respectively. The total value of policies (sums assured) in the estate data is assumed to be

$$A_O X_O + 1.5 A_I X_I$$

where A_O and A_I are the respective average sums assured per policy (see appendix II), and 1.5 is the factor used by Revell to adjust for the higher value for industrial branch policies included in the estate duty statistics. Having solved the equations, an amount $(1.5 A_I N_I)$ is then subtracted from the sums assured under the industrial branch to give the amount missing.

The second stage is to convert from a sums assured to a fund basis. Here our procedure was simply to reduce the estate estimates, the value of industrial policies, and the non-aggregable policies by an adjustment factor equal to the ratio of life funds to total sums assured. More sophisticated adjustments could clearly be devised, and in particular allowance should be made for the variation with age. This requires more refined data than we had available, but it should be borne in mind that the wealth of younger persons will tend on this account to be relatively over-stated and that of the elderly relatively under-stated, a point to which we return in chapter 9.

To give some idea of the amounts involved, this procedure led to the total value of life policies being reduced from £21 billion (estate estimate) to £11 billion (assumption C2) in 1972. Of this, around £1.5 billion was allocated to the excluded population. (Unlike the Royal Commission (1975:239) we do not allocate the *whole* of industrial policies to the excluded population, since some part appears in the estate statistics.)

The allocation of the value of pension rights can, in the present state of knowledge, only be approximate. Some guidance is provided by the surveys of occupational pensions carried out periodically by the Government Actuary. The 1967 survey (Government Actuary 1968) indicated that some $9\frac{1}{2}$ million male and $2\frac{1}{2}$ million female employees were covered by occupational schemes and in 1971 the corresponding figures were 8.7 million and 2.4 million (Government Actuary 1972: table 1). Moreover, the survey of financial circumstances of pensioners in 1965 showed that about 2 million were receiving occupational pensions at that time, a figure which had increased to 3 million by 1971, of which $2\frac{1}{2}$ million were former employees, and $\frac{1}{2}$ million were widows and dependants (Government Actuary 1972: table 7). Making some allowance for wives with a prospective title to a widow's pension, these figures suggest that in the late 1960s about 15 million people held rights to occupational pensions, of which $10\frac{1}{2}$ million were men and $4\frac{1}{2}$ million women. There is good reason to expect those holding such rights to be among the better paid and support for this is provided by the evidence of the 1970 New Earnings Survey. The percentage covered by occupational schemes was 75 per cent for non-manual full-time men, compared with 47 per cent for manual. Within each group, the coverage rose with earnings: for example, in the case of non-manual workers it increased from 21 per cent to 88 per cent over the range £12–£60 a week (Department of Employment Gazette, August 1971: table 5). Although earnings and wealth are not perfectly correlated, it may not be too unreasonable to assume that those employees with rights to occupational pensions correspond to the top 15 million in the wealth distribution. Such an assumption would not, of course, apply to cases such as the person with substantial wealth who has never been employed, but it seems a not-unrealistic first approximation.[9]

This top 15 million is taken as relating to all men covered by the estate returns (approximately $10\frac{1}{2}$ million in both 1968 and 1972) and to all women with wealth in excess of £1,000 (which gives broadly $4\frac{1}{2}$ million). The allocation of the rights between ranges is based on the following assumptions. At one extreme, it is assumed that the rights are held equally by all — assumption B2 — although this clearly makes inadequate allowance for the expected variation with age. At the other extreme is the assumption B4 that the rights are distributed proportionately to estate duty wealth. The intermediate, and more appealing, assumption B3 is that pension rights are distributed in the same way as life policies in the estate data. For individuals there may well be a negative correlation between life insurance and pension rights, but for broad ranges of wealth it seems highly probable that they are positively correlated.[10]

Finally, there is the question of the proportion of the balance sheet total which should be allocated, which will vary with the basis for valuation. On assumption C1 (realisation) we make no allowance for pension rights, and in the case of life policies we have taken 50 per cent of the fund as corresponding to the (very approximate) cash value.[11] On assumption C2 we have taken the full value of life funds, but felt that there were a number of reasons why a discount factor should be applied to the value of pension rights. Membership of an occupational scheme is not subject to the same degree of choice as with other forms of saving; the value of such rights was, until the recent legislation, reduced by non-transferability; and in many schemes there is considerable uncertainty (to the individual) surrounding the value of the

9 Subsequent to our adopting this approach, the Royal Commission (1975) made a similar assumption, except that they confined it to a smaller group (the top 12 million).

10 As noted earlier, the life policy holdings of younger persons are relatively over-stated; however, in view of the trend towards more extensive occupational pensions it may be correct to tilt the balance of pension rights towards younger age groups.

11 This ratio may be compared with that used in the US studies by Lampman and the Internal Revenue Service. Lampman (1962:55—6) estimated the ratio of 'equity or cash surrender value' to face value to be 23.9% for all age groups (it increased from 4.5% at age 20 to 78.1% at age 85 and over). Smith (1974: 169) reported that 'face value ranges between six and seven times cash surrender', giving a ratio of 0.14—0.17. The combination of our adjustment to a funds basis and the 50 per cent discount factor has the effect of applying a ratio of some 0.15—0.20, so that it is broadly in line with the American studies (except that we had to use an average figure for all age groups).

benefit. In view of this we have under C2 taken a proportion d_p of the value, with a 'central' figure of $d_p = 0.7$, but a range about this being used in the results of the next section. This range, together with $d_p = 0$ in the case of C1, may help the reader to assess the sensitivity of the results.

9 Land and buildings

The shortfall for this item is very substantial. Moreover, it could be attributed to any number of different factors, including the following:

(a) the omission of wealth-holdings including houses from the estate duty estimates: for example, where there is jointly-held property and the rest of the estate consists of assets for which probate is not obtained,

(b) the omission of cases of ownership from the estate duty estimates: for example, where there is jointly-held property and the rest of the estate is below the exemption limit (although probate is obtained),

(c) the under-valuation of houses in the estate estimates: for example because valuers err on the side of generosity[12] or because the delay in estates appearing in the statistics means that they do not keep up with rising house prices,

(d) the over-valuation of property in the balance sheet estimates: for example, because they do not allow adequately for the separation of interests or because of errors in the method of estimation,

(e) the inclusion of settled property.

The last of these has been allowed for in our estimates in the way described above, but only accounts for a small part of the discrepancy.

In appendix III we describe in detail two possible approaches to this problem, and the assumptions implicit in the adjustments which have been made by others. From this it is clear that there are considerable difficulties surrounding this item, and in view of this we have not incorporated the adjustments into assumptions B–D. Instead, we have made the following special assumptions (details are given in appendix III).

> *Assumption E1.* The whole of the discrepancy arises from differences in valuation and all estate holdings are adjusted proportionately.
>
> *Assumption E2.* Half of the discrepancy for dwellings is allocated to the excluded population. The remainder for dwellings, and the whole of the discrepancy for 'other land and buildings', is allocated proportionately to estate holdings.

(The 'no adjustment' case is denoted by assumption E0.)

12 In the 1950s, there was an administrative concession which had this effect – see chapter 6.

10 Liabilities

The discrepancy in the case of mortgage liabilities was referred to earlier, and for the reasons explained no adjustment is made. In the case of other liabilities, the discrepancy may be attributed to, among other items:

    (i) inadequate coverage of unincorporated businesses (trade creditors),

    (ii) estates below the exemption level, since, as noted earlier, those administering the estate are unlikely to do elaborate sums to compute the debts owing by the deceased and the amounts are almost certain to be under-stated, and

    (iii) the liabilities of the excluded population.

The first of these is probably relatively small. (Revell's figures suggest that in 1961 trade credit extended to unincorporated businesses accounted for a small fraction of the total item (Revell 1967:159).) In view of this, a relatively large part is allocated to estates below the exemption level and to the excluded population, the proportion being highest in the case of B4 and lowest for B2.

4.3   Results for 1968 and 1972

In this section we examine the effect of the various adjustments on the estimated size distribution of wealth in 1968 and 1972. The results are here presented primarily in terms of the share of total wealth received by different groups, and it is important to emphasise at the outset one major limitation. In allocating wealth to ranges covered by the estate statistics, the adjustments have been made in terms of the average wealth in each range. This means that the wealth intervals no longer have any meaning (those given in the first column of table 4.5 relate only to the unadjusted estimates), since holdings previously near the top of one interval may be moved up into the next. For this reason we refer to wealth ranges 1–10 rather than the absolute figures. More seriously, this approach assumes that the ranking by size of holding is the same before and after the allocation, which need not necessarily be the case. This aspect needs to be looked at more closely.

Initially we consider the results obtained using the multipliers A1, assuming a realisation basis for valuation (C1), and allowing for incomplete coverage (D2). These are set out in table 4.5. They do not include any adjustment for land and buildings, and the discount factor for settled property is set at $d_s = 1.0$. The first point to note is the range of results obtained, particularly at the bottom of the scale. The 1968 share of the bottom group goes from 3.7 per cent under B4 to 11.6 per cent under B2, and in 1972 there was a similar spread. Higher up the wealth scale, the variation is proportionately smaller. The share of the upper five groups in

Table 4.5a Sensitivity to assumptions B2–B4 1968 (assumptions A1/C1/D2/E0)
Percentage of total wealth

Range of wealth[†]	Range no.	No adjust-ment[*]	Assump-tion B2	Assump-tion B3	Assump-tion B4
Below £1,000	1	3.4	11.6	7.2	3.7
Cumulative % above £					
1,000	2 and above	96.6	88.4	92.8	96.3
5,000	3 and above	73.0	69.4	73.3	77.3
10,000	4 and above	56.0	55.0	58.8	62.3
15,000	5 and above	47.7	48.0	51.5	54.8
20,000	6 and above	41.7	42.8	46.2	49.3
25,000	7 and above	37.9	39.3	42.6	45.5
50,000	8 and above	25.7	27.4	30.4	33.0
100,000	9 and above	16.5	17.9	20.4	22.4
200,000	10 and above	10.5	11.5	13.3	14.7

Notes [*] The 'no adjustment' estimates differ from those in chapter 3 in that allowance
has been made for non-distributed estates and the holdings of overseas residents.
[†] The ranges relate to wealth *before* adjustment.

Table 4.5b Sensitivity to assumptions B2–B4 1972 (Assumptions A1/C1/D2/E0)
Percentage of total wealth

Range of wealth	No adjustment	Assumption B2	Assumption B3	Assumption B4
1	1.8	11.4	6.3	3.0
2 and above	98.2	88.6	93.7	97.0
3 and above	86.2	79.3	84.0	87.5
4 and above	67.1	63.5	67.7	71.5
5 and above	54.1	52.4	56.3	60.0
6 and above	47.9	47.1	50.9	54.4
7 and above	43.0	42.5	46.3	49.7
8 and above	29.7	30.2	33.6	36.7
9 and above	19.7	20.4	23.9	27.1
10 and above	13.1	13.4	16.3	18.9

Note: See notes to table 4.5a.

1972 lay between 47.1 per cent and 54.4 per cent. Secondly we may note
that the effect of the adjustments is to shift the Lorenz curve outwards at the
top and inwards at the bottom. On assumption B2 the outward shift is
confined to the higher wealth classes (above £50,000 in terms of unadjusted
wealth in 1972); on assumption B4 it applies to most of those covered by the
estate data.

The effect of a move from a realisation to a going-concern basis (C2) is
shown for 1968 in table 4.6, where we have taken the 'central' discount
factor for occupational pensions $d_p = 0.7$ (and $d_s = 1.0$ again). The effect is
to reduce the shares of all those above £1,000, with the absolute reduction
being most marked in the middle ranges. This adjustment interacts with that

made under B2–B4 (e.g. in the case of life policies and household goods), and the net outcome varies both with B2–B4 and with the level of wealth. Taking the central assumption B3, the effect is quite large for range 8 and above (their share falls by over 4 percentage points), whereas for range 3 and above, the adjustment is relatively less important.

The estimates presented in tables 4.5 and 4.6 suggest that the variation of the results in response to the assumptions made can be quite substantial, indicating the critical nature of the allocation of missing wealth by ranges and the need for further research to narrow the bounds placed on the allocation. At the same time, the analysis of the previous section has allowed us to make some progress in this direction. In figure 4.1 we have shown the Lorenz curves (linearly interpolated) for 1968 under the three 'crude' assumptions (the total to be allocated was derived on assumptions B3/C2/D2/E0):

    – all difference between balance sheet total and estate duty allocated to excluded population,

    – difference allocated proportionately to included population (i.e. 'no change'),

    – all difference allocated to those above £100,000,

together with those from our assumptions. The range with the assumptions made here (dashed lines) is clearly a lot smaller than with these crude assumptions, so that although there still remains a considerable gap, the consideration of individual asset categories has permitted us to narrow the spread of results quite noticeably.

The distributions shown above are the product of adjusting eight separate asset categories, and it is interesting to see the individual contribution each makes. Table 4.7 shows the effect of the different adjustments on the share of total wealth of different groups in 1968 in the case of the central assumption B3. It appears from this that the main adjustments reducing the share of the upper wealth groups are those for unquoted government securities and savings bank deposits, household goods, and life policies, which together reduce the share of the top groups by approximately 2–5 per cent (on assumption C2). The main adjustment which increases the share of the wealthy is – as might be expected – that for settled property, with the life policy adjustment (but not that for occupational pensions) working in the same direction on assumption C1.

From this we can see the importance of the categories of settled property and of occupational pensions, and hence of the discount factors d_s and d_p. To see how the shares depended on these, we calculated the results below for the share of ranges 4 and above in 1968. In the central B3 case, it appears that different assumptions about occupational pensions would lead to variation of

Table 4.6 Basis of valuation C2 compared with C1 1968 (assumptions A1/D2/E0)

Percentage of total wealth

Range	Assumptions B2/C1	Assumptions B2/C2	Assumptions B3/C1	Assumptions B3/C2	Assumptions B4/C1	Assumptions B4/C2
1	11.6	14.4	7.2	8.9	3.7	5.7
2 and above	88.4	85.9	92.8	91.1	96.3	94.3
3 and above	69.4	63.4	73.3	69.5	77.3	74.4
4 and above	55.0	49.1	58.8	54.0	62.3	59.2
5 and above	48.0	42.3	51.5	46.3	54.8	51.7
6 and above	42.8	37.5	46.2	40.7	49.3	46.1
7 and above	39.3	34.2	42.6	37.3	45.5	42.5
8 and above	27.4	23.5	30.4	26.0	33.0	30.3
9 and above	17.9	15.2	20.4	17.1	22.4	20.3
10 and above	11.5	9.8	13.3	11.1	14.7	13.2

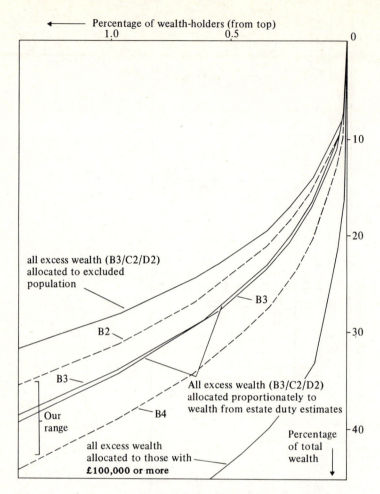

Figure 4.1 Range of results under 'crude' and refined assumptions

about 2 per cent in the share, whereas the effect of the 50 per cent discount applied to missing settled property is to reduce the share by about 1 per cent.

	B2	B3	B4
Settled property (C2) ($d_p = 0.7$)			
$d_s = 0.5$	48.8	53.2	58.3
$d_s = 1.0$	49.1	54.0	59.2
Occupational pensions (C2) ($d_s = 1.0$)			
$d_p = 0.4$	50.9	54.9	59.3
$d_p = 0.7$	49.1	54.0	59.2
$d_p = 1.0$	47.5	53.1	59.1

The contribution of the different asset categories to the wealth of the excluded population may be seen from the fact that our central adjustments imply that the wealth of the average 'small saver' was made up as shown below in 1968 (assumptions A1/B3/D2/E0). These figures are considerably

	Realisation value	Going concern
	£	£
Government securities etc.	66.10	66.10
Cash and bank deposits	30.50	30.50
Building society	13.40	13.40
Household goods	82.60	161.70
Life policies	33.50	67.10
Liabilities	−47.90	−47.90
Total	178.20	290.90

below the £500 and £1,000 taken illustratively in chapter 2 for the average wealth of the excluded population (although the latter related to 1970); they do not however include any allowance for home ownership, to which we now turn.

So far we have made no adjustment for land and buildings. Taking the estimates based on A1/B3/C2/D2 as a starting point, we can see from table 4.8 the effect of the two assumptions described in the previous section. The first point to be noted is that assumption E1 leads to a fall in the share of range 1, whereas assumption E2 leads to the reverse effect. This reflects the allocation under E2 of part of the excess wealth to the excluded population. In 1968 the average amount allocated was £111.70 per person, which raised average wealth to just short of £300 on a realisation basis and on a going concern basis to over £400. For the top wealth groups, the effects of the different adjustments are rather similar, and tend to move the Lorenz curve slightly inwards. Overall, it appears that, despite the magnitude of the sums being added to total wealth, the effect on the distribution − as least on these assumptions − is relatively small.

Finally, there is the effect of different mortality multipliers. As we have seen in the previous chapter, the implications of adjustments based on balance sheet totals depend on the multipliers used in deriving the estate duty estimates, since with lower multipliers a greater excess wealth remains to be allocated. The results obtained with assumptions B3/C2/D2/E0 and different multipliers are set out in table 4.9. As expected, the adjustments required in the case of the life office multipliers are smaller, and the general effect is to shift the Lorenz curve closer to that derived under A1. In the case of the

Table 4.7 Effect of different adjustments 1968 (assumptions A1/B3/D2/E0)

Adjustment	Adjustment to share of							
	Range 9 and above		Range 8 and above		Range 4 and above		Range 3 and above	
	C1	C2	C1	C2	C1	C2	C1	C2
(1) Unquoted government securities, etc.	−0.36		−0.57		−1.23		−1.61	
(2) Cash and bank deposits	−0.13		−0.21		−0.42		−0.54	
(3) Building society	−0.10		−0.15		−0.33		−0.43	
(4) Household goods	−0.31	−0.72	−0.49	−1.15	−1.06	−2.32	−1.38	−2.87
(5) Trade assets	0	−0.15	0	−0.05	0	+0.33	0	+0.37
(6) Settled property	+2.51	+2.37	+2.90	+2.74	+2.26	+2.16	+1.62	+1.57
(8) Life policies and pension rights	+1.91	−0.45	+2.67	−0.65	+2.42	−0.94	+1.28	−0.97
(10) Liabilities	+0.38	+0.21	+0.56	+0.32	+1.09	+0.74	+1.37	+1.00
Overall	+3.90	+0.68	+4.73	+0.30	+2.75	−2.01	+0.35	−3.48

Note: Columns do not necessarily add to overall total due to rounding.

Table 4.8 Different adjustments for land and buildings 1968 and 1972 (assumptions A1/B3/C2/D2)

Range	% of total wealth 1968			% of total wealth 1972		
	No adjust-ment E0	adjust-ment E1	adjust-ment E2	No adjust-ment E0	adjust-ment E1	adjust-ment E2
1	8.9	8.2	10.1	7.4	6.7	7.7
2 and above	91.1	91.8	89.9	92.6	93.3	92.3
3 and above	69.5	69.7	68.4	81.4	82.3	81.5
4 and above	54.0	53.6	52.8	63.8	64.3	63.7
5 and above	46.3	45.6	45.1	52.0	52.1	51.8
6 and above	40.7	39.8	39.5	46.5	46.4	46.1
7 and above	37.3	36.3	36.0	41.9	41.8	41.6
8 and above	26.0	25.0	24.9	29.7	29.3	29.1
9 and above	17.1	16.5	16.4	20.9	20.5	20.5
10 and above	11.1	10.7	10.6	14.2	13.9	13.9

graduated multiplier A3, the adjustments tend again to be smaller, at least in the lower wealth ranges.

4.4 Summary

One of the main criticisms of the official estimates has been that they omit certain types of wealth. Some authors have emphasised the wealth of those excluded from the statistics, the wealth owned by 'small savers', whereas others have drawn attention to wealth missing on account of estate duty avoidance by the rich. In the analysis presented in this chapter we have looked at both types of 'missing wealth', and tried to investigate their quantitative importance.

Our main tools in doing this have been the personal balance sheet estimates, and the independent information about total holdings which they embody. These estimates are not themselves without error, and a number of items are described as 'involving considerable estimation'. For this reason we have not slavishly adjusted the estate-based totals to the balance sheet figures. In this respect our procedure differs from that of the Royal Commission, who, in our view, were too uncritical in their use of the balance sheet evidence. What we have done is to allocate wealth only where there is an *a priori* reason for expecting it to be missing and, as far as possible, to make adjustments only where the balance sheet totals are thought to be reliable.

On this basis we have in the case of 1968 (taking assumptions A1/B3/D2/E2):

> – added £12 billion to the estate estimates on a realisation basis, and £33 billion on a going concern basis,

Table 4.9 Adjusted estimates – different multipliers 1968

| | Percentage of total wealth | | | | | | | | |
| | Assumption A1 | | | Assumption A3 Graduated multipliers | | | Assumption A4 Life office multipliers | | |
Cumulative % above £	Population	No adjustment	Adjustments B3/C2/D2/E0	Population	No adjustment	Adjustments B3/C2/D2/E0	Population	No adjustment	Adjustments B3/C2/D2/E0
1,000	29.79	96.6	91.1	30.80	97.0	91.8	31.28	97.2	93.0
5,000	9.30	73.0	69.5	9.69	73.8	70.6	10.94	75.8	73.2
10,000	3.91	56.0	54.0	4.11	56.8	55.0	4.64	58.3	57.0
15,000	2.37	47.7	46.3	2.49	48.4	47.2	2.82	49.7	48.9
20,000	1.61	41.7	40.7	1.69	42.3	41.5	1.93	43.5	43.1
25,000	1.26	37.9	37.3	1.32	38.5	38.0	1.50	39.5	39.4
50,000	0.46	25.7	26.0	0.48	26.1	26.5	0.55	26.7	27.3
100,000	0.15	16.5	17.1	0.16	16.8	17.5	0.18	16.9	17.8
200,000	0.05	10.5	11.1	0.05	10.7	11.3	0.06	10.7	11.4

– allocated £6½ billion (£290 per head) to the excluded population on a realisation basis and £9 billion (£400 per head) on a going concern basis,

– the remaining £5½ billion (£24 billion on a going concern basis) is allocated to the included population to allow for wealth missing from the estate data or for differences in the method of valuation.

Our assumptions are in certain cases rather arbitrary, but we feel that by examining individual assets we have in most cases been able to arrive at an allocation of the missing wealth which is not unreasonable as a first approximation.

The estimates must undoubtedly be qualified, but we hope that they will nonetheless be of value. At the very least they should rule out of court the most extreme views about the extent of missing wealth. Thus the suggestion by Meacher (1972) that the true total of personal wealth was *over three times* the estate estimate clearly cannot be reconciled with the independent evidence: his figure for 1969 is £276 billion compared with a balance sheet estimate for that year of £134 billion (for the UK). Equally unlikely is the suggestion made by Polanyi and Wood that the average wealth of the excluded population might be as high as £5,000 (in 1970) (1974:39). If one were to allocate the whole of the difference between the balance sheet and estate estimates in that year to the excluded population, it would only give some £1,700 a person. The value of the balance sheet data may also be seen if we go back to the assumptions A and B made by the Inland Revenue. These two methods of treating the excluded population led to a wide range of estimates for the share of the top 1 per cent in 1972 (22.1–29.9 per cent). Our assumptions B2–B4 (interpolating from table 4.5b) give a range of estimates of 26.7–29.2 per cent (with assumptions A1/C1/D2/E0). We have therefore gone a considerable way towards narrowing the gap.

5

NEW ESTATE METHOD ESTIMATES

The previous chapters investigated in detail two important aspects of the estate method: the selection of multipliers and the adjustment for 'missing wealth'. In both cases we suggested that the Inland Revenue procedure is not fully satisfactory, and have examined a range of alternative adjustments. In this chapter we assemble the results of this analysis, present a new 'adjusted' series of estimates, and consider some of the major remaining problems outlined in chapter 2. The first section summarises the basic approach to the construction of the new series and compares it with that underlying the official estimates. It also contrasts the methods with those adopted by the Royal Commission (1975). Section 5.3 is concerned with the robustness of the results and the problems of interpolation. Section 5.4 brings together the main conclusions.

5.1   A new approach

In the 'adjusted' series of estimates presented below, we make rather different assumptions from those employed by the Inland Revenue, and these are described below. At the same time, our work is in some respects closer to that of the Inland Revenue than that of some other researchers. We have not — for the reasons described in chapter 3 — followed Revell (1967) in totally rejecting the social class multipliers derived from the Census of Population. We have not, in contrast to the Royal Commission (1975), assumed that in all cases the balance sheet totals are superior to those obtained using the estate method.

The main differences between our assumptions and those of the Inland Revenue may be summarised under the following headings:

A; *Multipliers*
We have used social class multipliers based on the Registrar General's data with adjustments for the unoccupied but differing from the current Inland Revenue treatment in that:

   (i) adjustments are made for errors in occupational statements,
  (ii) the multipliers are graduated by estate size as described in chapter 3,
 (iii) no 'smoothing' correction has been applied (i.e. we have not combined estates across age groups as is done by the Inland Revenue).

The reasons for the differences in method have been discussed at some length in chapter 3. Although we stressed that further developments are necessary (e.g. to allow for variation with marital status and to examine in greater depth the relationship of mortality to wealth), we feel that our multipliers have definite advantages over those employed to construct the official statistics.

B: *Wealth of the excluded population*

The estimates presented below are based on the assumption B3 described in the previous chapter, and obtained from a consideration of individual asset categories. This 'central' assumption inevitably involves a substantial element of judgement, but it seems clearly preferable to the assumption that the excluded population have no wealth (B1), and the sensitivity of the results may be assessed by looking at the extreme assumptions B2 (lower bound to share of top wealth ranges) or B4 (upper bound to share of top wealth ranges).

C: *Method of valuation*

We have argued that there is no single basis of valuation which is appropriate for all purposes, and to illustrate the range of results have taken two different bases:

        C1: realisation value
        C2: going concern value

(The Inland Revenue treatment is denoted by C0.) In the case of two particular asset types, we apply discount factors: for discretionary trusts there is a discount factor d_s (central value 0.75) to allow for possible over-valuation; and for occupational pensions on a C2 basis there is a discount d_p (central value 0.7).

D: *Incomplete coverage of wealth*

The Inland Revenue make no adjustment for wealth which is, for a variety of reasons, missing from the estates covered by its statistics. We have made a correction for this item on the basis of the assumption D2 described in the previous chapter, and again this is based on the consideration of individual asset categories. We also make an allowance for nondistributed estates and for overseas holdings (see chapter 4).

E: *Land and buildings*

The difficulties with this class of assets have been described in detail, and we have discussed two different approaches. In the estimates presented in this chapter, we have followed the Royal Commission (assumption E2), not because we felt that this method was inherently superior but because it typically allocated some part of the missing wealth to the excluded population (in contrast to the Revell assumption E1, which allocates none to the excluded population). This element of the adjustments needs to be treated with especial caution,[1] and in presenting the result we have, in a number of cases, taken it separately. The Inland Revenue make no adjustment for this item (assumption E0).

Before turning to the estimates for the whole period 1966–72, it may be useful to summarise the effects of the various adjustments on the wealth shares for 1968, which was one of the two years discussed in detail in the previous two chapters. In table 5.1 we have shown the effect on the estimated shares of the top 1 per cent and top 5 per cent of the adult population (defined as 18 and over), as we change the assumptions step by step. It should be noted that the shares are obtained by log–linear interpolation of the Lorenz curves, a method which has certain shortcomings discussed below in section 5.3.

Table 5.1 Effect of different adjustments on shares of top 1% and top 5%

Line	Assumptions					Estimated share of top	
						1%	5%
1	Inland Revenue*					32.7	59.0
	Our estimates						
2	A3	B1	C0	D1	E0†	34.7	60.5
3	A3	B3	C0	D1	E0	33.6	58.6
4	A3	B3	C1	D1	E0	36.8	60.9
5	A3	B3	C1	D2	E0	39.0	62.6
6	A3	B3	C2	D2	E0	34.0	58.1
7	A3	B3	C2	D2	E2	32.9	57.0

Notes *From Royal Commission (1975), table 45.
†These figures differ from those given in chapter 3 because allowance has been made for non-distributed estates and overseas holdings.

The first step in the adjustments involves the use of A3 multipliers, and in 1968 this had the effect of raising the shares of top wealth groups (the fact that we did not use the Inland Revenue smoothing procedure is important here). The subsequent steps may be set out schematically as shown below.

1 One reservation about assumption E2 is that the amounts allocated to the excluded population vary considerably from year to year. For two of the years considered (1969 and 1971) the amount allocated for land and buildings would have been negative, and it was therefore set to zero.

	Approximate effect on share of top 5% (percentage points)
Allowance for wealth of excluded population (B3) (line 2 to line 3)	-2%
Conversion to a realisation basis (C1) (line 3 to line 4)	$+2\frac{1}{4}\%$
Allowance for missing wealth (D2) (line 4 to line 5)	$+1\frac{3}{4}\%$
Change from realisation to going concern basis (C2) (line 5 to line 6)	$-4\frac{1}{2}\%$
Adjustment for land and buildings (E2) (line 6 to line 7)	-1%

It should be noted that the adjustments are interdependent and that their marginal contribution depends on the other assumptions made. Also the impact of the adjustments varies with the composition of wealth-holdings, so that, for example, the effect of changes in valuation is proportionately greater for the top 1 per cent than for the top 5 per cent.

The fact that these adjustments are relatively small, and tend to cancel each other out, may lead the reader to think that the analysis was unnecessary; this would however be wrong. Without a detailed investigation of the various deficiencies, it would not have been possible to reach any conclusion regarding their quantitative significance. Moreover, the small size of the adjustments is, in some respects, reassuring. That our estimate for the share of the top 5% in 1968 is only some 2 per cent different from that published by the Inland Revenue suggests that — for this year at least — the official figures may not be as misleading as some writers have argued. On the other hand, the year 1968 may have been atypical, and indeed there are certain grounds for supposing that it was (in particular there appear to have been an unusually large number of estates in the top ranges). For this reason the examination of the results for a more extended period is necessary, and we turn to this in the next section.

5.2   Adjusted estimates 1966–72

In the preparation of the adjusted estimates, the availability of data is of crucial importance, and it may be useful at this stage to review the main sources. As will be clear, extension of the estimates to years other than the benchmarks of 1968 and 1972 involves a number of difficulties. On the basis of the assumptions described below, we have made adjustments A3/B3/C1/C2/D2/E2 for the years 1966–72. (For earlier years it did not seem possible, with the data available, to follow the same pattern; and the longer time series presented in the next chapter for 1923–72 is consequently based on a more restricted range of adjustments.)

Adjustment A3

To apply this correction, we need estates classified by age, sex and size of estate. For this purpose, we have employed in this chapter unpublished data ('Unity Runs') made available by the Inland Revenue. These give a considerably more detailed break-down by estate ranges than the published tables (e.g. table 100 in *Inland Revenue Statistics 1974*), and provide separate figures for England and Wales, and for Scotland. They have also been adjusted for funeral expenses and capital gains tax paid at death, these being added back to the estate.[2]

Adjustment B3

In general we require the estimated total holdings of particular assets, obtained by applying appropriate multipliers, which can then be compared with the balance sheet totals.[3] Ideally, we should have liked to have obtained these estimated total holdings by applying the A3 multipliers to the estate data classified by asset composition. Unfortunately, we did not have this information, and had to make a number of approximations.[4] It does not seem likely that any substantial error was introduced, but this is an area

---

2 In using the estate data we assumed that all those in the '24 and under' age category were 18 or over. The Inland Revenue assured us that no significant error was introduced by this assumption.

3 For certain assets (e.g. life policies) we also require the total number of cases; and for one category (household goods) we need the average holding in the range £0–3,000.

4 The problem may be seen as follows: Let K_i denote the total holding of asset type i and A_{ij} the proportion of wealth held in this asset in wealth class j, and W_j the total wealth in this class:

$$K_i = \sum_j A_{ij} W_j \tag{i}$$

If λ denotes the social class differential relative to that employed by the Inland Revenue, then all these variables are functions of λ, and $K_i(\lambda)$ may be written as:

$$K_i(\lambda) = K_i(1) + \sum_j [\Delta A_{ij} W_j(\lambda) + A_{ij}(1) \Delta W_j] \tag{ii}$$

where Δ denotes the difference between the values at λ and at 1. For the years 1968 and 1972 we used data on $A_{ij}(1)$, and calculated $K_i(\lambda)$ from (ii) neglecting the terms in ΔA_{ij}. It seems likely that the error involved would not be too large to invalidate our use of the estimates, but one cannot be any more confident than this. For other years, our procedure was even more approximate, since we had no data on $A_{ij}(1)$. What we did was to take for each year the total estimated using the Inland Revenue multipliers and to apply the adjustment $K_i(\lambda)/K_i(1)$ from the nearer benchmark year (1968 for 1966–70, 1972 for 1971–2).

where more disaggregated data ('Unity Runs' classified by asset composition) would have been valuable.

Adjustments C1, C2, D2 and E2

In order to make these adjustments we cannot avoid an attempt to estimate the asset composition by wealth ranges, since this is essential for the allocation of missing wealth and the revaluation procedures. As described in the previous chapter, we had to assume that the asset proportions are unaffected by changes in the multiplier, and use the asset composition as estimated by the Inland Revenue. Since the Inland Revenue asset composition estimates were only available for 1968 and 1972, we were forced to extrapolate for other years. The only guide that we have in making this extrapolation is that the totals for the asset categories should (with the wealth levels calculated using Inland Revenue multipliers) equal those published in the Inland Revenue tables, and, if we accept the approach described above under B3, that they should equal (with wealth levels based on A3 multipliers) the totals projected on that basis. This still leaves a large number of degrees of freedom, and the procedure adopted to adjust the asset composition is to a considerable extent arbitrary,[5] although again we do not feel that any substantial error was introduced.

This 'hierarchy' of adjustments clearly involves an increasing element of judgement, and without the asset composition data for 1968 and 1972 the last set of adjustments would have been impossible. This means that when considering the long-run trends in the next chapter, our estimates are, as noted above, based on a more restricted range of adjustments. In particular, we have made no adjustment to a going concern valuation (C2), no allowance for missing wealth in estates covered by the returns (D2), or for land and buildings (E2). In view of this we have presented the estimates here in two stages. Firstly, we compare the official published figures with the 'first stage' estimates obtained on assumptions A3 and B3, but no other adjustments (i.e. C0/D1/E0). Secondly, we compare the official figures with the 'final' estimates (A3/B3/C1/C2/D2/E2).

The first set of results are presented in table 5.2 for the run of years 1966–72. We would expect the adjustment B3 to lead to an inward shift of the Lorenz curve, and that, on the basis of the results of chapter 3, the change in multipliers would shift it outwards, at least at the very top. To

---

5 The method used was the simplest possible (adjusting the asset proportions A_{ij} proportionately for a given i) with it being assumed that the adjustment would be absorbed by asset categories other than those considered here.

some extent, therefore, the adjustments tend to cancel. Overall, the adjusted estimates indicate that the difference between the Lorenz curve derived from our estimates and that derived from the Inland Revenue figures is smaller than one might have expected. We have allowed an average amount per head of excluded population ranging from, on a realisation basis, some £250 in 1966 to nearly £400 in 1972, or totals of £5.3 billion and £8.4 billion respectively. Yet the share of the top 1 per cent is changed in most years by less than 1 percentage point. The effect is rather larger for the top 10 per cent and there are some years in which the difference is more marked. Nonetheless, the results suggest that, with an allowance for the wealth of the excluded population on a realisation basis, the effect is not large, and that there are other factors (in this case the graduation of the multipliers) working in the opposite direction.

The second stage, or 'final', estimates are given in table 5.3. As pointed out in the preceding chapter, the effect of the adjustments under the assumptions C, D and E is that the wealth ranges no longer have any meaning. The estimates are therefore shown simply in terms of points on the Lorenz curve. As may be seen, there is a general tendency for the adjusted Lorenz curve to lie inside that derived from the official estimates at the bottom of the scale (the share of the bottom 65–70 per cent being larger) but to lie outside at the upper end. The point of intersection of the Lorenz curves depends on the basis for valuation, coming at around the top 5–10 per cent for a realisation basis (C1) and at around the top 1 per cent for the going concern assumption (C2). There is also a tendency for the point of intersection to move down over the period, suggesting that the relationship between the two sets of estimates (the official and our final adjusted) may have changed.

The broad conclusions described above take no account of the fact that the points on the two Lorenz curves are not strictly comparable (for example, the fourth point in 1968 corresponds to 2.4 per cent of the population in one case and 2.5 per cent in the other). The standard way of proceeding to more precise conclusions is to standardise the population groups under consideration, taking for example the top 1 per cent, 5 per cent and 10 per cent, and calculate their shares in total wealth by interpolation. For this purpose, the typical method employed is that of log–linear interpolation, and the results of applying this to the estimates are set out in table 5.4. This gives a picture of the size distribution which is much easier to interpret, although the procedure of interpolation introduces a further possible source of error, which is discussed in section 5.3.

The official estimates appear from table 5.4 to give, for most years, figures which are slightly lower than ours for the top 1 per cent, within our

Table 5.2 Estimates of distribution of wealth for 1966−72 − first stage

1966 Wealth range	Official estimates* Cumulative share (%) of		First stage estimates (A3/B3) Cumulative share (%) of	
	Population	Wealth	Population	Wealth
£1,000−	30.07	95.4	29.85	92.8
£5,000−	8.50	68.2	8.44	66.7
£10,000−	3.45	50.5	3.49	49.9
£15,000−	2.05	41.7	2.09	41.4
£25,000−	1.02	31.8	1.03	31.6
£50,000−	0.37	20.6	0.37	20.8
£100,000−	0.11	11.8	0.10	11.6
£200,000−	0.04	6.6	0.04	7.0
Total[†]	38.5	76.8	38.5	81.6
1967 Wealth range	Official estimates* Cumulative share (%) of		First stage estimates (A3/B3) Cumulative share (%) of	
	Population	Wealth	Population	Wealth
£1,000−	30.71	96.7	30.79	94.0
£5,000−	9.45	71.1	9.38	69.2
£10,000−	3.83	52.8	3.86	51.7
£15,000−	2.23	43.7	2.26	42.9
£25,000−	1.13	33.9	1.14	33.3
£50,000−	0.41	22.0	0.42	21.8
£100,000−	0.13	13.0	0.14	12.8
£200,000−	0.04	6.9	0.03	6.7
Total[†]	38.8	83.6	38.8	88.2
1968 Wealth range	Official estimates* Cumulative share (%) of		First stage estimates (A3/B3) Cumulative share (%) of	
	Population	Wealth	Population	Wealth
£1,000−	31.06	96.8	30.80	93.9
£5,000−	9.61	72.8	9.69	71.5
£10,000−	3.97	55.1	4.11	55.1
£15,000−	2.43	46.7	2.49	46.9
£25,000−	1.31	36.9	1.32	37.3
£50,000−	0.47	24.2	0.48	25.3
£100,000−	0.15	15.0	0.16	16.2
£200,000−	0.05	8.9	0.05	10.4
Total[†]	38.8	88.0	38.8	95.9

Table 5.2 (Contd.)

1969 Wealth range	Official estimates* Cumulative share (%) of		First stage estimates (A3/B3) Cumulative share (%) of	
	Population	Wealth	Population	Wealth
£1,000–	34.56	97.4	34.11	93.1
£5,000–	11.86	73.9	11.89	69.4
£10,000–	4.34	51.4	4.42	52.6
£15,000–	2.57	42.8	2.63	43.8
£25,000–	1.30	32.9	1.30	33.4
£50,000–	0.47	21.4	0.46	21.6
£100,000–	0.16	12.8	0.16	13.0
£200,000–	0.05	7.4	0.04	7.0
Total[†]	39.0	91.4	39.0	97.6

1970 Wealth range	Official estimates* Cumulative share (%) of		First stage estimates (A3/B3) Cumulative share (%) of	
	Population	Wealth	Population	Wealth
£1,000–	33.73	97.9	34.15	93.8
£5,000–	12.76	76.6	12.81	73.0
£10,000–	4.52	52.5	4.53	50.4
£15,000–	2.70	43.7	2.70	42.2
£25,000–	1.30	33.0	1.30	32.1
£50,000–	0.49	21.8	0.50	21.6
£100,000–	0.15	13.1	0.15	13.4
£200,000–	0.05	7.9	0.05	8.2
Total[†]	39.0	96.8	39.0	106.3

1971 Wealth range	Official estimates* Cumulative share (%) of		First stage estimates (A3/B3) Cumulative share (%) of	
	Population	Wealth	Population	Wealth
£1,000–	36.92	98.0	37.56	94.9
£5,000–	15.41	79.1	15.64	76.1
£10,000–	5.68	55.0	5.82	53.3
£15,000–	3.22	44.5	3.34	43.4
£25,000–	1.57	34.1	1.65	33.4
£50,000–	0.60	22.5	0.61	22.0
£100,000–	0.19	13.3	0.20	13.1
£200,000–	0.07	7.5	0.08	7.2
Total[†]	39.0	112.7	39.0	122.3

Table 5.2 (Contd.)

1972 Wealth range	Official estimates* Cumulative share (%) of		First stage estimates (A3/B3) Cumulative share (%) of	
	Population	Wealth	Population	Wealth
£1,000–	34.48	98.3	34.99	94.8
£5,000–	17.47	85.9	18.02	83.0
£10,000–	8.05	66.6	8.30	64.9
£15,000–	4.20	53.2	4.32	52.3
£25,000–	2.13	41.5	2.21	41.6
£50,000–	0.79	27.8	0.82	28.7
£100,000–	0.26	17.9	0.26	19.1
£200,000–	0.08	11.4	0.08	12.8
Total[†]	39.0	138.4	39.0	155.3

Source: Official estimates from *Inland Revenue Statistics* 1973, Table 92 and
1974, table 104.
Notes: [†]The ranges correspond to those in the published tables; the figures
for the share of the top 1 per cent etc. referred to below are calculated
from unpublished tables with a finer classification of wealth ranges.
*Population (aged 18 and over) in millions; wealth in £ billion.

range C1–C2 for the top 5 per cent, and slightly higher than ours for the
top 10 per cent. This is in line with the statements about the Lorenz curve
made earlier. The differences are in each case small, and overall the conclusions that can be drawn are rather similar. Using our estimates and averaging over 1969–72 to give a figure for the distribution at the beginning of
the 1970s, we have:

	Realisation valuation	Going concern valuation
Top 1%	33%	30%
Top 5%	57%	53%
Top 10%	69%	66%

On this basis, it does seem broadly true that – at that date – the top 1 per
cent owned around a third, and the top 5 per cent more than a half of
total private wealth currently owned by individuals. The robustness of this
conclusion is discussed further in the next section.

As explained in chapter 1, our concern here is primarily with the share of
top wealth-holders: the top 1, 5 and 10 per cent shown in table 5.4. The
earlier tables do, however, give some indication of the form of the distribution lower down the scale. According to the official estimates, those with
£1,000 or less in 1970 – broadly the bottom two thirds of the adult population – owned 2.1 per cent of total wealth. This figure is obviously artificially
low on account of the omission of the wealth of the excluded population,

Table 5.3 Final estimates of distribution of wealth for 1966–72

1966 Cumulative shares (%)	Official estimates		Final estimates†		
	Population	Wealth	Population	Wealth C1	Wealth C2
	30.07	95.4	29.85	90.8	89.5
	8.50	68.2	8.44	68.1	65.1
	3.45	50.5	3.49	52.7	49.1
	2.05	41.7	2.09	44.7	40.9
	1.02	31.8	1.03	35.2	31.4
	0.37	20.6	0.37	23.9	20.9
	0.11	11.8	0.10	13.9	12.0
	0.04	6.6	0.04	8.5	7.3
Total*	38.5	76.8	38.5	89.5	107.6

1967 Cumulative shares (%)	Official estimates		Final estimates†		
	Population	Wealth	Population	Wealth C1	Wealth C2
	30.71	96.7	30.79	91.7	90.5
	9.45	71.1	9.38	70.2	67.4
	3.83	52.8	3.86	54.3	50.8
	2.23	43.7	2.26	46.2	42.3
	1.13	33.9	1.14	36.9	33.0
	0.41	22.0	0.42	25.0	21.9
	0.13	13.0	0.14	15.2	13.2
	0.04	6.9	0.03	8.2	7.0
Total*	38.8	83.6	38.8	95.0	114.0

1968 Cumulative shares (%)	Official estimates		Final estimates†		
	Population	Wealth	Population	Wealth C1	Wealth C2
	31.06	96.8	30.80	91.6	90.4
	9.61	72.8	9.69	72.2	69.2
	3.97	55.1	4.11	57.3	53.5
	2.43	46.7	2.49	49.8	45.7
	1.31	36.9	1.32	40.6	36.4
	0.47	24.2	0.48	28.4	24.9
	0.15	15.0	0.16	18.8	16.3
	0.05	8.9	0.05	12.2	10.6
Total*	38.8	88.0	38.8	103.0	123.5

1969 Cumulative shares (%)	Official estimates		Final estimates†		
	Population	Wealth	Population	Wealth C1	Wealth C2
	34.56	97.4	34.11	93.1	91.8
	11.86	73.9	11.89	71.9	68.8
	4.34	51.4	4.42	56.3	52.5
	2.57	42.8	2.63	47.9	43.7
	1.30	32.9	1.30	37.6	33.4
	0.47	21.4	0.46	25.3	22.0
	0.16	12.8	0.16	15.8	13.6
	0.05	7.4	0.04	8.8	7.5
Total*	39.0	91.4	39.0	105.0	127.3

Table 5.3 (Contd.)

1970 Cumulative shares (%)	Official estimates		Final estimates†		
	Population	Wealth	Population	Wealth C1	Wealth C2
	33.73	97.9	34.15	93.0	91.8
	12.76	76.6	12.81	74.7	71.9
	4.52	52.5	4.53	53.9	50.1
	2.70	43.7	2.70	46.3	42.1
	1.30	33.0	1.30	36.5	32.3
	0.49	21.8	0.50	25.6	22.3
	0.15	13.1	0.15	16.6	14.2
	0.05	7.9	0.05	10.4	8.9
Total*	39.0	96.8	39.0	112.2	135.0

1972 Cumulative shares (%)	Official estimates		Final estimates†		
	Population	Wealth	Population	Wealth C1	Wealth C2
	34.48	98.3	34.99	93.7	92.9
	17.47	85.9	18.02	83.8	81.7
	8.05	66.6	8.30	67.4	64.2
	4.20	53.2	4.32	55.8	52.2
	2.13	41.5	2.21	45.4	41.8
	0.79	27.8	0.82	32.5	29.2
	0.26	17.9	0.26	22.7	20.3
	0.08	11.4	0.08	15.4	13.7
Total*	39.0	138.4	39.0	161.0	188.7

1971 Cumulative shares (%)	Official estimates		Final estimates†		
	Population	Wealth	Population	Wealth C1	Wealth C2
	36.92	98.0	37.56	94.8	93.6
	15.41	79.1	15.64	78.8	75.8
	5.68	55.0	5.82	57.5	53.6
	3.22	44.5	3.34	47.9	43.9
	1.57	34.1	1.65	38.0	34.2
	0.60	22.5	0.61	26.2	22.9
	0.19	13.3	0.20	16.2	14.0
	0.07	7.5	0.08	8.8	7.6
Total*	39.0	112.7	39.0	121.1	146.0

Source: Official estimates as given in table 5.2.
Notes: *Population in millions; wealth in £ billion.
   † Adjusted estimates on assumptions A3/B3/D2/E2.

and the first stage estimates show that the estimated share on assumptions A3/B3 is 6.2 per cent. The final estimates are similar on a realisation basis, but rise to 8.2 per cent on a going concern valuation. As we should expect, the adjustments we have made lead to substantial changes in the share of the bottom two thirds. For them an increase of 2 percentage points is a major difference. This should be borne in mind in the rest of our analysis, relating as it does to the shares of the few top wealth-holders.

Turning to the changes between 1966—72, the estimates suggest that there has been a decline in the shares of the top groups. This does however need to be viewed with caution. First, this conclusion may depend on the end-year chosen. The results for 1972, for example, appear rather different from those of earlier years, and the Inland Revenue have tended to base conclusions about trends on the period up to 1971. Secondly, there is a noticeable year-to-year variation, which may reflect sampling or other errors in the estimates, or the influence of systematic factors such as changes in asset prices. The Inland Revenue suggest that the difference for 1972 was 'probably because of the very big upsurge in the price of Stock Exchange Securities' (*Inland Revenue Statistics 1974*: 176), which was undoubtedly important (see chapter 9). In the next section we consider the magnitude of sampling errors and the significance of changes such as the 3 per cent fall in the share of the top 1 per cent between 1966 and 1971 in the light of possible errors in the data.

Finally, we can use the adjusted estimates to calculate summary measures of concentration. Although we have reservations about such summary measures, we felt that, in view of their widespread use by other authors, it would be interesting to examine some of their properties. We have therefore calculated the values of three of the indices considered by the Royal Commission (1975): the coefficient of variation (V), the relative mean deviation (D), and the Gini coefficient (G). The last is, of course, that typically applied to the distribution of wealth. The calculation of these indices raises again the problems of the interpolation of grouped data. We have followed the common practice of assuming that all wealth-holdings in an interval are located at the group mean. This clearly represents a lower bound on the measures of concentration considered, since it ignores any within-group variation. It is equivalent to using straight line interpolation of the Lorenz curve, which — given the convexity of the Lorenz curve — represents a lower bound on the shares of top wealth groups. (It should be noted that the Inland Revenue when calculating the Gini coefficient do not make this assumption, and make a correction for grouping — see the discussion of interpolation in the next section.)

Table 5.4 Shares of top wealth groups 1966–72

	1966	1967	1968	1969	1970	1971	1972
% Share of top 1%							
Official estimates	31.8	32.1	32.7	29.0	29.0	27.6	29.9
Adjusted (final) estimates:							
C1	34.8	35.1	36.9	34.2	33.3	31.6	34.7
C2	31.1	31.3	32.9	30.2	29.4	28.1	31.4
% Share of top 5%							
Official estimates	56.7	57.2	59.0	54.0	56.3	52.1	56.3
Adjusted (final) estimates:							
C1	58.7	58.6	60.6	58.0	55.6	54.5	58.2
C2	55.4	55.2	57.0	54.2	51.9	50.5	54.7
% Share of top 10%							
Official estimates	71.8	72.3	73.8	69.4	70.1	67.4	71.9
Adjusted (final) estimates:							
C1	71.3	71.5	72.8	69.0	69.2	68.3	71.2
C2	68.5	68.6	69.8	65.7	66.1	64.8	68.2

Sources: Official estimates from the Royal Commission (1975), table 45. (It should be noted that these are based on a finer classification by ranges than that shown in table 5.2.)
Adjusted estimates obtained by log–linear interpolation from a more detailed version of table 5.3.

Table 5.5 Summary measures of concentration of wealth 1966–72

	1966	1967	1968	1969	1970	1971	1972
(V) Coefficient of variation	5.93	7.28	7.58	5.26	7.16	4.42	9.85
(D) Relative mean deviation	1.255	1.260	1.269	1.230	1.246	1.240	1.273
(G) Gini coefficient	0.767	0.773	0.775	0.776	0.765	0.768	0.780

Source: Calculated from a more detailed version of table 5.3 (assumption C2).
Note: The Gini coefficients shown here cannot be compared with those calculated by the Inland Revenue (and discussed in chapter 2), since the latter include a correction for grouping.

As is well known, different summary measures reflect different features of the distribution. Thus the study by Champernowne (1974) using a theoretical distribution function suggested that the Gini coefficient was most sensitive to the 'spread of the less extreme incomes', in contrast to the coefficient of variation which was most sensitive to inequality associated with the exceptionally rich. His study was primarily directed at the distri-

bution of income; and for our purposes it may be more illuminating to
return briefly to the 'Pareto' model described in chapter 2. In particular,
in that model the Gini coefficient is given by (see appendix IV):

$$G = \frac{(1-E)}{2\alpha - 1} + E\left[1 - \frac{E\sigma^*}{E\sigma^* + (1-E)}\right] \tag{1}$$

where E is the extent of the excluded population and σ^* is their average
wealth relative to that of the included population. Where $\sigma^* = 0$, we have
an especially simple result, and we can see that G depends sensitively
on α and E. The value of G with $E = 0.5$ may be seen to fall from 0.75 to
0.67 as α (the Pareto exponent) increases from 1.5 to 2.0, and from 0.75 to
0.70 as E falls from 0.5 to 0.4 (with $\alpha = 1.5$). The effect of σ^* is relatively
small; e.g. taking the value $\sigma^* = 0.05$ causes G to fall from 0.75 to 0.73
(with $\alpha = 1.5$ and $E = 0.5$). (This value of σ^* would allocate over £400 per
head to the excluded population in 1972.) A fuller treatment together with
discussion of the coefficient of variation and the relative mean deviation,
is given in appendix IV.

The performance of the three summary measures over the period 1966–
72 is shown in table 5.5. The coefficient of variation, not surprisingly, is
sensitive to the top of the distribution, and tends to behave rather erratically.
The Gini coefficient, on the other hand, exhibits relatively slight changes,
its lowest value being 0.763 and its highest 0.780. In some cases the indices
move in different directions. Thus between 1969 and 1970 both V and D
increased, indicating more concentration, but G fell. Comparing 1966 and
1970, D fell, V rose, and G changed only by 0.002. These differences are due
to the fact that the measures give differing weight to different parts of the
distribution, and mean in effect that one has to examine the underlying
Lorenz curves in order to understand what is going on. To this extent the
value of using summary measures is diminished. Moreover, inspection of the
Gini coefficients calculated by the Inland Revenue for the longer period
1960–73 indicates that much of the variation over time could be explained
by movements in E and in the share of the top 1 per cent. (This specification,
which was suggested by equation (1) above, and the estimated relationship
are discussed in appendix IV.) In what follows we shall concentrate mainly
on the shares of top wealth groups, and not make extensive use of summary
measures when presenting the results.

5.3 Reliability of the results*

In the previous section we described the results obtained for 1966–72; we now turn to three questions which are important when assessing the weight which can be attached to these new estimates. First, there is the issue of sensitivity with which we have already been concerned in earlier chapters. Do the methods employed lead to results which are systematically biased in one direction or another? Second, how much are the estimates affected by sampling error and other sources of random variation? Finally, how far does the presentation in terms of the shares of the top 1 per cent, 5 per cent, etc. introduce errors of interpolation? These questions are taken up in turn.

(a) Sensitivity

In considering the sensitivity of the results to the assumptions made, it may be helpful to make use of the formal statement of the estate method given in chapter 2. Starting from the number of estates in range i belonging to people of type a (n_{ai}) and their average wealth (w_{ai}), we estimate the points on the Lorenz curve as follows:

$$1 - F_j = \sum_a \left[\left(\frac{P_a}{N_a} \right) \sum_{i=j+1}^{t} \lambda_{ai} n_{ai} \right] \Big/ P \qquad (2)$$

Proportion of	General	Social	Total
population in	mortality	class	population
($j + 1$) and	multiplier	differential	
above			

$$1 - L_j = \sum_a \left(\frac{P_a}{N_a} \sum_{i=j+1}^{t} \lambda_{ai} n_{ai} w_{ai} \mu_{ai} \right) \Big/ W \qquad (3)$$

Proportion of	Adjustment to	Total wealth
total wealth	estate data for	including that of
	under-recording	excluded population

(We have introduced a factor μ_{ai} to allow for wealth 'missing' from the estate returns.) Each of the factors identified in these schema may lead to systematic bias in the results, and in a number of cases alternative assumptions may be made.

General mortality multiplier. As noted in chapter 2, the general multiplier may be affected by errors in the Registrar General's mid-year estimates of the population. These are likely to become successively more serious between censuses and may have a systematic influence on the conclusions drawn about trends over time.[6] Comparison of the results based on the revised

---

* Parts of this section are more technical and some readers may prefer to go straight to section 5.4 (on page 136) which summarises the main conclusions.

6 Thus, for example, the estimates for 1971 and 1972 above are based on revised population figures derived from the 1971 Census.

and unrevised figures for England and Wales in 1970 (a year when the revisions were relatively large) suggests, however, that the effect would not be sufficiently great to be a matter for concern.

Social class differential. This aspect has been investigated in chapter 3, where we concluded that alternative multipliers did not lead to widely different estimates of the share of top wealth-holders. At the same time, the differences are not sufficiently small that they can be totally rejected; and some indication of the range of variation is provided by assumption A0 (general multipliers) which gives a higher figure for the shares of the top 1 per cent and 5 per cent, and assumption A4 (life office multipliers) which gives a lower figure.

Total population. The estimates presented so far relate to the population aged 18 and over. The principles underlying the definition of the 'adult' population for our purposes are considered further in the next chapter but here we should point out the consequences of using the alternatives of 25 (as in earlier studies) or 15 (as in the Inland Revenue statistics). The results for England and Wales in 1970 are shown below.

	Share of top 1%	5%	10%
Population aged 25 and over	28.8	52.5	67.4
aged 18 and over	29.7	53.7	68.9
aged 15 and over	30.4	54.8	70.1

(Note: estimates constructed on assumptions A2/B3/C0/D1/E0.)

Since we have assumed that all those appearing in the estate returns are aged 18 and over, the only difference between the second and third lines is in the total population P; for the first line, however, the lowest age class in the estate returns is excluded. As may be seen, the change in definition can lead to noticeable differences in the wealth shares, with a range of over two percentage points in the share of the top 5 per cent.

Adjustment for missing wealth. The allocation of missing wealth to the excluded population and to under-recording in the estate returns was discussed extensively in chapter 4. The range of assumptions B2—B4 was designed to test the sensitivity of the results. If one further adds the possibility of different bases for valuation, and adjustments for land and buildings, then a lower estimate for the shares of the top 1 per cent and 5 per cent can be obtained by taking C2/E2 and a higher figure by taking C1/E0.

Drawing together the different elements, one can obtain some indication of the range of estimates by taking the following combinations of assumptions:

'lower': A4 multipliers (general mortality below the cut-off/population aged 25 and over/assumptions B2/C2/D2/E2 for missing wealth. 'higher': A0 multipliers/population aged 15 and over/assumptions B4/C1/D2/E0 for missing wealth.

The results for 1970, together with the estimates from table 5.4, are given below (rounded to the nearest 1%).

	Share of top	
	1%	5%
Lower	24%	45%
Table 5.4, C1/C2	33%/29%	56%/52%
Higher	37%	62%

The implications of this test of the sensitivity of the results for the conclusions drawn earlier may be summarised as follows. It is possible that the share of the top 1 per cent, at the start of the 1970s, was somewhat less than the figure of a third often quoted; on the other hand, it was of the order of at least a quarter even on the lower estimate. Similarly, the range of variation for the share of the top 5 per cent in 1970 makes it at least 45 per cent and possibly over 60 per cent.

(b) Sampling error

The problem of sampling error in the estate method has received little systematic treatment in the literature. The discussion below does not provide such a treatment, but we felt that it might be useful to set out some of the issues, drawing in particular on one of the few discussions of the problem – that by Lampman (1962:36–41). As he points out, the estate data may be viewed as a random sample stratified by age and sex of living persons with dutiable wealth. In the case of Britain, the process of sampling applied to the estate records has two stages: (1) the 'sampling' by death which is intrinsic to the method, and (2) the sampling from estates to compile the data made available by the Inland Revenue. The sampling fractions at the two stages, together with the resulting absolute numbers, are shown for a representative selection of age groups in 1972 in table 5.6. The table also shows the sampling errors for the mean estate in each age/sex class.[7] As is to be expected, these are largest for the youngest age groups, and are larger for women than for men at younger ages.

7 These calculations use the ranges shown in table 5.6, rather than the more detailed ranges available in the unpublished data. Since the sample is a stratified one, calculation of the standard deviation of the sample, which is used in the estimation of the standard error of the mean, should take account of both within-class and between-class dispersion. We have no information on the former, so assume that all those in an estate class are clustered at the mean estate for that class. The estimation of the standard error of the mean remains useful, however, for the purposes of relative comparisons between age groups.

The implications of sampling error may be assessed in a number of different ways. One approach is to consider the standard errors associated with summary measures of concentration, such as those presented in the previous section. This may be illustrated by reference to the relative mean deviation, drawing on the work by Gastwirth (1974) on the large sample theory of measures of inequality. He shows that the estimate $\hat{D}$ obtained from a sample of N observations is asymptotically normally distributed with variance v^2/N, where v^2 depends on D, the variance of the distribution, and other terms.[8] Substituting the sample estimates into this expression, one can obtain (using a more detailed version of table 5.3) an estimated standard error for $\hat{D}$ in 1972 of 0.017.[9] Viewed in relation to the absolute level of concentration ($\hat{D} = 1.273$) this error does not seem particularly serious. The 95 per cent confidence interval, for example, is 1.240–1.306. We can therefore be fairly confident in asserting that the concentration of wealth is greater than that for income, for which the Royal Commission (1975 : 178) give a value of D equal to 0.454 in 1971/2. Viewed, however, in relation to changes over time, the sampling error is more important. In only two cases in table 5.5 does the year-to-year change exceed 0.017, and all observations except that for 1969 lie within the 95 per cent confidence interval for 1972.

In our presentation of the results we have not made much use of summary measures, but have concentrated on the shares of top wealth groups. In other words, we have tried to describe the (upper part) Lorenz curve rather than confine ourselves to a single summary statistic. Sampling error is, however, relatively more important when one considers smaller groups of the population; and there is a trade-off between the 'richness' with which the results are presented and the extent to which they are subject to sampling error. This may be illustrated by the following approximate calculations of the standard error of different quantiles in 1972.[10] For the top 1 per cent (broadly £40,000 and above in 1972), the calculated standard error is some $3\frac{1}{2}$ per cent, so that if we estimate that the top 1 per cent commences at £40,000, the standard error is around £1,400. For the top 0.1 per cent (broadly £175,000 and above in 1972), the calculated standard

8 See Gastwirth (1974), equation 14. It should be noted that he denotes by V^2 the variance of the mean deviation ($D\mu$) where μ is the mean, and that his D is $D/2$ in our notation.

9 This was based on the same assumptions as those made when calculating the summary measures, and involved interpolation to calculate $F(\bar{w})$. For these reasons the figure is only approximate.

10 The calculation is based on the formula given by Kendall and Stuart (1969 : 237), assuming that the frequency can be approximated by a Pareto distribution, and expressing the standard errors as a percentage of the estimated quantiles.

Table 5.6 Sampling fractions and standard errors 1972

Estate range (lower limit)	Males 25–34			45–54			65–74			85 and over		
	N	F1 %	F2	N	F1 %	F2	N	F1 %	F2	N	F1 %	F2
0–*	71	(20)	0.1	117	(5)	0.7	225	(5)	5.4	110	(5)	24
1,000–	54	10	0.1	18	1	0.6	93	1	5.1	33	1	24
3,000–	290	100	0.1	36	2	0.6	107	2	4.9	43	2	24
5,000–	465	100	0.1	147	5	0.5	486	5	4.8	168	5	24
10,000–	259	100	0.1	1,834	100	0.5	1,008	(15)	4.8	384	(15)	24
25,000–	31	100	0.1	345	100	0.5	1,058	50	4.8	516	50	24
50,000–	12	100	0.1	135	100	0.5	1,001	100	4.8	540	100	24
100,000–	2	100	0.1	41	100	0.5	311	100	4.8	228	100	24
200,000–	2	100	0.1	17	100	0.5	114	100	4.8	92	100	24
Relative standard error of mean†	0.14			0.06			0.04			0.05		

	Females 25–34			45–54			65–74			85 and over		
	N	F1 %	F2	N	F1 %	F2	N	F1 %	F2	N	F1 %	F2
0–*	27	(20)	0.1	11	(5)	0.5	253	(5)	2.8	348	(5)	19
1,000–	10	10	0.1	8	1	0.4	78	1	2.7	73	1	19
3,000–	56	100	0.1	13	2	0.4	99	2	2.6	74	2	19
5,000–	51	100	0.1	38	5	0.4	368	5	2.6	299	5	19
10,000–	20	100	0.1	506	100	0.4	294	(15)	2.6	320	(15)	19
25,000–	9	100	0.1	102	100	0.4	565	50	2.6	801	50	19
50,000–	1	100	0.1	44	100	0.4	545	100	2.6	900	100	19
100,000–	0	100	0.1	21	100	0.4	135	100	2.6	292	100	19
200,000–	2	100	0.1	10	100	0.4	52	100	2.6	82	100	19
Relative standard error of mean†	0.30			0.12			0.04			0.04		

Sources: N = sample size from *Inland Revenue Statistics* 1974, table 100. The figures reported there have been multiplied by (1/F1) (the inverse of the Inland Revenue sampling fraction) and we reversed this procedure to obtain the absolute numbers. Because of variation in F1 (see below) these resulting figures are only approximate. F1 = sampling fraction selected by Inland Revenue (*Inland Revenue Statistics*, 1974 : 102). The figures in brackets are approximate averages for two combined classes. F2 = reciprocal of mortality multiplier, expressed as a percentage and rounded to the nearest 0.1%.

Note: *Includes insolvent estates.

†Standard error divided by mean.

error is some 11 per cent; and for the top 0.004 per cent (broadly all million-aires in 1972), it is over 50 per cent. It is for this reason that the Inland Revenue distributions are published with ten ranges rather than the thirty-two available in the basic estate tables (twenty-five in 1972), and that the top range is £200,000 plus. (We have used the same ranges in earlier tables.) The calculations for the quantiles suggest that for these ranges sampling errors are not going to dominate the results, but that they warrant more careful investigation than they have been given so far.[11]

A rather different approach to the problem is to consider the estimates for a run of different years as observations of the same underlying distribu-tion and to take the variation in these estimates as an indication of the sampling fluctuations. This of course assumes that the underlying distribu-tion is unchanged over the years in question. The same assumption is in effect made by those authors who have averaged the estimates over a number of years. Thus Daniels and Campion (1936) combine 1924–30; Lydall and Tipping average the estimates for 1951–6 to obtain a figure for 'the situa-tion existing at the beginning of 1954' (1961:86); and the Inland Revenue average observations for the largest estates. The rationale for such averaging is not always made explicit, but Lydall and Tipping see it as a method of reducing errors due both to sampling fluctuations and to delays in recording estates (since estates relating to one year may appear in the statistics for subsequent years).

For certain periods it may be reasonable to assume that the distribution is unchanged over time, and Lydall and Tipping argue that this was the case in the early 1950s: 'there was no obvious trend in aggregate capital values between 1951 and 1956' (1961:86). For the 1960s it is not immediately obvious that this is true, and averaging of the data involves, at best, throwing away information about the distribution. In view of this, we feel that it is preferable to consider the data in unaveraged form, and to use the regression approach outlined below.

In order to illustrate this, let us suppose that the observed share in year t of the top x per cent, denoted by W_t, is related to the 'true' value W_t^* by

$$W_t = W_t^* + \epsilon_t \tag{4}$$

where

$$\epsilon_t = U_t + \rho \epsilon_{t-1} \tag{5}$$

and

$$W_t^* = a + bT \tag{6}$$

11 After this chapter was drafted, we were allowed to see an unpublished paper by R.N. Vaughan, in which he sets out more thoroughly the framework for investigating sampling errors in the estate method.

It is assumed that U_t is a normally and independently distributed random variable with mean zero and constant variance, and that it is independent of ϵ_{t-1}. The last equation (6) means that we are assuming, for simplicity, that the true value is determined by a linear trend. The equations (4) and (5) mean that it is measured with an error ϵ_t, where this may exhibit serial correlation: for example there will be negative serial correlation ($\rho < 0$) if a 'bunching' of estates in one year is associated with an error in the opposite direction in the next. These assumptions do not capture the full complexity of the problem. The specification of W_t^* clearly needs more development, and it is possible that a moving average error specification would be more appropriate. These are discussed in chapter 9. The model should however be sufficient here to illustrate the general nature of the approach.

Combining (4) and (6),

$$W_t = a + bT + \epsilon_t \tag{7}$$

The correct procedure for estimating this equation depends on the extent of serial correlation (ρ). If $\rho = -1$, then the formation of a two-year moving average would indeed be an appropriate procedure, but we have no reason to believe that ρ necessarily takes this value. As a first stage in the estimation procedure, let us therefore apply ordinary least squares to equation (7). For this purpose, we take the data for the share of the top 1 per cent over 1966–72 given in table 5.4 and obtain the following estimates:

Official estimates

$$\hat{W}_{1,t} = 32.9 - 0.66T \quad R^2 = 0.55 \quad S.E. = 1.41 \quad D.W. = 2.15$$
$$(27.6) \ (2.5)$$

Adjusted estimates C1

$$\hat{W}_{1,t} = 35.9 - 0.39T \quad R^2 = 0.26 \quad S.E. = 1.54 \quad D.W. = 2.09$$
$$(27.6) \ (1.3)$$

Adjusted estimates C2

$$\hat{W}_{1,t} = 31.9 - 0.32T \quad R^2 = 0.20 \quad S.E. = 1.53 \quad D.W. = 2.06$$
$$(24.8) \ (1.1)$$

where the figures in brackets are t-statistics, $S.E.$ denotes the standard error of the regression, and $D.W.$ the Durbin–Watson statistic. From the last of these we can examine the presence of serial correlation. The small number of observations in our illustrative example means that a formal test has little meaning; however, the values of $D.W.$ are sufficiently close to 2.0 to suggest that there is not in fact serious negative serial correlation.

Accepting for the present the hypothesis that there is no serial correlation ($\rho = 0$), we can see that the results for the official estimates differ from our adjusted estimates. In the former case the downward trend is significantly different from zero at the 10 per cent level, but this is not true of our adjusted estimates. However, even in the case of the official estimates the standard error of the regression is quite large; and if we take this as a measure of the extent of sampling fluctuations, then it gives some grounds for concern. The 95 per cent confidence interval for the predicted value of the official estimate at the midpoint of the period (1969) is 30.3 ± 3.6, which is quite wide (all the observations for 1966–72 lie within this interval). Against this must be set the other factors besides sampling fluctuations which may lead to year-to-year variation. The omission of, for example, changes in asset prices may mean that the equation is mis-specified, and that we are incorrectly attributing to sampling error variation which has a systematic cause.

In this section, we have looked at several different ways of assessing the implications of sampling error. Consideration of the standard errors associated with summary measures of concentration, and with quantiles, suggested that results of the kind presented earlier in this chapter for the *level of concentration* are not likely to be seriously affected by sampling error. Consideration of the year-to-year fluctuations over 1966–72 indicated that the effect might be more important; however, there are good reasons to suspect that it is wrong to attribute all the variation to sampling error. If we turn to the significance of *changes* in the distribution over time, then the analysis suggests that sampling error might be more important – a point which needs to be borne in mind in the next chapter. Finally, we should reiterate that our treatment is inadequate in a number of respects, and that the whole question of sampling error in the estate method warrants much closer attention.

(c) Interpolation

Finally, we consider the variation in the results which may arise, not from the process of construction of the estimates, but from the way in which they are presented. As we have seen, the results are typically summarised in terms either of the shares of different percentiles (top 1 per cent, 5 per cent, etc.) or of summary measures of concentration. In both cases there arises the problem of interpolation from the underlying grouped data. The need for this is perhaps obvious, but the interpolation is frequently made without any comment on the possible error or indeed without any indication of the method employed. For example, formulae for the calculation of the Gini coefficient from grouped data embody a method of interpolation, but this is rarely made explicit.

The possible error introduced by interpolation clearly depends on the width of the underlying wealth ranges. For the present we assume that the data are only available in rather broad groups, and for purposes of illustration take the 1968 'first stage' estimates set out in table 5.2. These involve broader ranges, for example £25,000 to £50,000, than are available in the 'raw' estate statistics. However, it is in this form that the official wealth estimates are published and have typically been used in the past by private researchers. Moreover, the estate data for earlier years are only available for a small number of ranges, and for the 1950s the problems of interpolation are, if anything, more serious than with the data taken for purposes of illustration.[12]

The nature of the problem may be seen from figure 5.1, which shows the upper part of the Lorenz curve drawn from these estimates. The observed points are marked by large dots; and neither the top 1 per cent nor the top 5 per cent correspond closely to one of the observed points. We need therefore to join them up. The diagram shows one way in which this can be done — by linear segments — and from the fact that the Lorenz curve is convex, we know that this is a *lower bound* on the share of the top x per cent. The bound could be attained only where the distribution of wealth within the group was equal: i.e. everyone in the range £10,000–£15,000 has wealth equal to average for that range. The 'true' value of the shares of top wealth groups is therefore in general higher than that obtained by linear interpolation.

The fact that the linear segments provide a lower bound suggests that we could similarly derive an upper bound. This upper bound involves the opposite extreme assumption: that everyone in the range is located at either the upper or the lower limit (with numbers being adjusted so as to give the correct average wealth for the range). This implies that for range i with mean $\bar{w}_i$ the proportion of the population in the range (f_i) is divided into:

$(1-\eta)f_i$ with w_i (the lower limit of the wealth range)

ηf_i with w_{i+1} (the upper limit of the wealth range)

where $\eta(w_{i+1} - w_i) = \bar{w}_i - w_i$. Geometrically, it corresponds to drawing a line upwards through I with slope equal to $w_i/\bar{w}$, and a line downwards through $I + 1$ with slope $w_{i+1}/\bar{w}$ where $\bar{w}$ is the overall mean. The upper

---

12 Estimates for the United States have sometimes involved a 'heroic' amount of interpolation. For example, Lampman's study of the changes over time is based for some years on observing only one point on the Lorenz curve (1962:197–208).

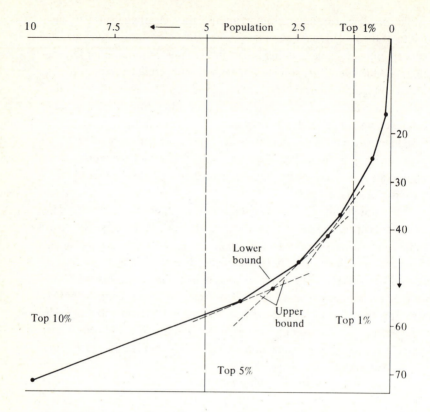

Figure 5.1 Interpolation: 1968 first stage estimates

bound is then given by the smaller of the two values: i.e. proceeding from *I*, we take the line through *I* until we reach the intersection — as shown by the dashed lines in figure 5.1. As may be seen, the resulting Lorenz curve is piece-wise linear and convex.[13]

The results of applying these upper and lower bounds to the estimates for 1968 are shown in table 5.7 — see line 1 where they are referred to as 'linear' bounds. The difference for the share of the top 1 per cent is 1.4 percentage points; that for the top 5 per cent is slightly less, since it is closer to the end of the relevant wealth range, but is still sufficiently large to be of concern.

13 This method can only be applied where the lower and upper limits to the range are known. If they are not known (as in table 5.3), then an alternative would be to use the mean value of the range above, and below, respectively. This procedure will typically give noticeably 'looser' bounds, and will not ensure convexity of the Lorenz curve.

The possibility of such a margin of error has led to attempts to narrow the bounds which can be placed on the estimates. Gastwirth (1972), in particular, has examined the way in which the bounds can be refined if we are willing to impose restrictions on the underlying frequency distribution. A natural restriction in the present context is that the frequency be non-increasing. This rules out the linear bounds described above since in both cases the frequency is assumed to be first zero for some range of wealth and then strictly positive. As Gastwirth (1972) has shown, the 'refined' upper and lower bounds with this restriction are given by:

refined lower bound a uniform distribution over the range

$$[w_i, \hat{w}] \quad \text{where} \quad \hat{w} = 2\bar{w}_i - w_i$$

refined upper bound where ηf_i have wealth w_i and the remainder are distributed uniformly on $[w_i, w_{i+1}]$

$$\eta = \frac{w_i + w_{i+1} - 2\bar{w}_i}{w_{i+1} - w_i}$$

(The fact that the frequency is non-increasing ensures that in the case of the lower bound $\hat{w} \leqslant w_{i+1}$ and that for the upper bound $\eta \geqslant 0$.) These bounds can only be applied where the upper and lower limits of the range are known.

The results obtained by applying these 'refined' bounds to the data are contained in line 2 of table 5.7. They do reduce the range quite considerably. The figures for the top 1 per cent mean that the variation is 0.3 percentage points rather than 1.4 with the linear bounds. In using data with only a small number of broad intervals (nine in this case) application of Gastwirth's refined bounds may therefore be well worthwhile.

The table also shows the results obtained by log–linear or 'Pareto' interpolation. This interpolation procedure was pioneered by the Inland Revenue, and is probably that most widely employed. The underlying assumption is that the distribution is Pareto in form, and if it departs from the Pareto curve, then problems may well arise. In appendix V we show that the interpolated Lorenz curve may be non-convex, and that the interpolation procedure may lead to results outside the linear bounds described above. Although the results given above for 1968 indicate that the log–linear interpolation lies between the linear upper and lower bounds, this is not necessarily the case. For example, in the next chapter, the estimates for 1925 (on a B4 basis) when log–linearly interpolated give a figure of 61.9 per cent for the share of the top 1 per cent, compared with a linear upper bound of 61.7 per cent. This is an unsatisfactory feature of this method, and suggests that it should only be used in conjunction with calculations of the bounds.

Table 5.7 Upper and lower bounds on interpolation – 1968
first stage estimates

	Top 1%		Top 5%	
	lower	upper	lower	upper
Estimates based on ranges in Table 5.2				
1. 'Linear' bounds	32.7	34.1	57.7	58.7
2. 'Refined' bounds	33.55	33.85	58.40	58.55
3. Log–linear interpolation	33.53		58.49	
Estimates based on full set of 32 ranges				
4. 'Linear' bounds	33.63	33.67	58.58	58.60

Source: Calculated from table 5.2 (lines 1–3) and a more
detailed version of that table (line 4).

Our discussion of this problem has concentrated so far on the case where
the data are grouped in relatively broad intervals. Where a more detailed
breakdown is available, then the range of results is much narrower. Indeed
the bounds given in line 4 of table 5.7, based on the full set of 32 ranges,
indicate that in this case the problems of interpolation may be relatively
unimportant, the variation being a lot less than a tenth of a percentage
point. For this reason, the problem of interpolation is probably not of
great significance for the analysis in this chapter. Caution does, however,
need to be exercised when working with data grouped in broad ranges,
and this applies in particular to interpolation from the distributions
published by the Inland Revenue and to estimates for earlier years based
on a small number of estate classes (see Chapter 6). Different methods of
interpolation may in these circumstances lead to estimates of the shares
of the top 1 per cent and 5 per cent which vary by 1–2 percentage points.
Moreover, we have seen that the conventional log–linear interpolation is
open to criticism, and that it should only be used in conjunction with
the bounds described in this section.

5.4 Summary

In this chapter we have presented a revised series of estimates for
1966–72, which differ from those of the Inland Revenue in that we have
used different multipliers, have adjusted for the wealth of the excluded
population, have adopted consistent bases for valuation, and have allowed for
wealth missing from the estate returns. As a result, the revised *totals* of
personal wealth are much higher: in 1970, for example, total wealth on a
going concern valuation was 40 per cent larger than in the official figures.
Despite the addition of such large amounts, however, the *distribution*, as
measured by the shares of top wealth-holders, is not greatly different. Our

estimates of the share of the top 1 per cent are typically slightly higher, and those of the share of the top 10 per cent typically slightly lower, than the official estimates, but the differences are in most cases relatively small (4 percentage points or less). The results indicate therefore that the official figures for the shares at the beginning of the 1970s of the top 1 per cent (around 30 per cent) and the top 5 per cent (around 55 per cent) are not substantially altered by the adjustments we have made, a conclusion which reflects not so much the insignificance of individual corrections as a tendency for them to work in opposite directions. (As explained at the beginning of the book, we are concerned with the upper tail of the distribution; the effect for the rest of the population is more marked.)

The robustness of these conclusions has been examined in section 5.3. This showed first that by taking in each case the assumptions designed to give a low (respectively high) share for top wealth holders, one could generate for 1970 a range of estimates of 24–37 per cent of total wealth for the top 1 per cent, and 45–62 per cent for the top 5 per cent. This indicates that our 'central' figures of 29/33 per cent and 52/56 per cent may be too high or too low by some 5–7 percentage points (for a given basis of valuation). The discussion of sampling error suggested that its effect would probably be rather smaller than that of the systematic factors just discussed, although this is a topic which needs more thorough investigation. Similarly, the problem of interpolation is not likely to affect the results quoted in this chapter, although it may be important when using data grouped in broad ranges.

6

TRENDS OVER TIME

The changes in the distribution of wealth over time have been one of the most widely studied aspects of the subject. As described in chapter 1, a series of investigators have used the estate method to measure the trends in the shares of top wealth-holders, and their conclusions have been widely quoted, a recent example being the *Initial Report* of the Royal Commission (1975). In view of this, we devote the present chapter to a detailed examination of the historical record. The earlier studies, and the conclusions derived from them, are reviewed in section 6.1, where we also draw attention to some of the difficulties involved in making comparisons over time. The data available for different periods are discussed in detail in section 6.2, which relates the estimates by Daniels and Campion, Langley, Lydall and Tipping, among others, to the assumptions made here in earlier chapters. In section 6.3, we present the results of an attempt to produce a consistent series for the period 1923–72, and these are analysed in section 6.4. The main conclusions are summarised in section 6.5.

6.1 Introduction

One of the central problems in examining the trends in the distribution is that of securing a series which is consistent over time. This is recognised by the Royal Commission who begin their discussion by saying that 'in examining trends in the distribution of wealth, it is important that judgments should be based on a consistent series' (1975:97). Since the official Inland Revenue estimates dating from 1960 are constructed on a rather different basis from earlier academic studies, they therefore proceed by considering first the trends up to 1960 and then the trends over the years 1960–73.

The estimates for the period before 1960 employed by the Royal Commission are shown in the left hand part of table 6.1; the right-hand part gives the Inland Revenue series B estimates since 1960. (The whole run of years 1960–73 has not been included; we have simply taken 4-year intervals

Table 6.1 Estimates published by the Royal Commission 1911–13 to 1960 and 1960–73

Percentages of adult population	Percentage of total personal wealth								
	1911–13	1924–30	1936–8	1954	1960	1960	1965	1970	1973
	(Population aged 25 and over, England and Wales)					(Population aged 18 and over, Great Britain)			
Top 1%	69	62	56	43	42	38	33	29	28
Top 5%	87	84	79	71	75	64	59	56	51
Top 10%	92	91	88	79	83	77	73	70	67
Top 20%	–	–	–	–	–	90	89	89	86
Top 1%	69	62	56	43	42	38	33	29	28
2–5%	18	22	23	28	33	26	26	27	23
6–10%	5	7	9	8	8	13	14	14	16
11–20%	}8	}9	}12	}21	}17	13	16	19	19
Remainder						10	11	11	14
Total Population (million)	18.7	22.3	25.6	–	–	37.0	38.3	39.0	39.2
Wealth (£ billion)	6.0	13.7	15.2	–	–	51.6	74.3	96.8	163.9

Source: Royal Commission (1975), tables 41 and 45 (rounded to the nearest 1 per cent) except for the total wealth and population figures, which are taken where available from the original sources (see below).

Note: The source referred to by the Royal Commission for 1911–13 to 1960 is Revell (1965). He took his pre-Second World War figures from Langley (1951: table XVB), who in turn drew on Daniels and Campion (1936: table 23).

and the most recent year available when the *Initial Report* was published). Although many commentators treated this as a continuous series (see, for example, the *Sunday Times*, 3 August 1975), the Royal Commission underline the fact that the earlier estimates differ from those of the Inland Revenue in that they are based on general mortality rates, relate to the population aged 25 and over, and cover only England and Wales. In previous chapters we have shown that the first of these differences is likely to raise the shares of top wealth-holders, whereas the more restricted definition of the adult population tends to reduce the shares. The different factors may therefore tend to cancel out. However, there is no reason to suppose that they will exactly balance. Moreover, there are further inconsistencies between the estimates not mentioned by the Royal Commission, in particular in relation to the wealth of the excluded population (it is not correct that 'the estimates assume that all members of the population not covered in the estate duty returns have zero wealth' (Royal Commission 1975:98)). These are discussed further below.

A second series which has been widely quoted is that shown in table 6.2, where the original sources are those indicated. Once more there is a break in the table at 1960, with the figures in the right-hand part being based on the Inland Revenue estimates (which make no allowance for the wealth of the excluded population). The differences between the estimates for earlier years and those in table 6.1 arise on account of different sources (e.g. Campion (1939) rather than Langley (1951)) and of the estimates being based on social class multipliers. The differences for 1960–70 reflect the coverage of population *15 and over* and the method of interpolation (Polanyi and Wood used the published ranges in *Inland Revenue Statistics* and, as we have seen in the previous chapter, the results may in this case be sensitive to the procedure employed).

The estimates presented in tables 6.1 and 6.2 provide clear indication of a downward trend in the share of top wealth-holders. Both before and after 1960 the share of the top 1 per cent appears to have fallen substantially. There are however certain points on which there has not been complete agreement in the literature.

The first of these concerns the speed of decline. Some authors have been impressed by the very rapid rate of redistribution. Sir Henry Clay found the change between 1911–13 and 1920 'striking and unexpected' (1925:75). Langley, writing in 1951, concluded 'that a very important social development is proceeding and that a *levelling up* process is taking place in the distribution of private wealth' (1951:48). Recently, Polanyi and Wood have stated that wealth has 'become much more evenly spread in the last 50 years'

Table 6.2 Estimates published by Polanyi and Wood 1911−13 to 1951−6 and 1960−70

Percentages of adult population	England and Wales				Great Britain		
	Population aged 25 and over				Population aged 15 and over		
	1911−13	1924−30	1936	1951−4	1960	1965	1970
Top 1%	66	60	56	42	39	34	31
Top 5%	86	83	81	ʼ 68	64	62	56
Top 10%	90	90	88	79	76	75	70
Top 20%	−	96	94	89	91	89	87
Bottom 80%	−	4	6	11	9	11	13
Original source	Daniels and Campion			Campion (1939)	Lydall and Tipping (1961)	Polanyi and Wood (1974)	

Sources: Polanyi and Wood (1974), tables 3 and 4.

(1974: back cover). Other writers, however, have been more cautious. The final conclusion of Daniels and Campion was that:

> Although the scale of wealth is probably higher than before the war, and although there has been some reduction in the inequality of the distribution of private capital, it cannot be said there has been any marked change in the distribution of capital in individual hands in England and Wales during the last twenty-five years (1936:62).

Similarly, Lydall and Tipping, writing in 1961, were more guarded than Langley: 'it is fairly safe to conclude that here has been *some* reduction in the inequality of wealth in the past twenty years. But the extent of this change should not be exaggerated' (1961:93). One of the purposes of the subsequent analysis is, therefore, to assess the extent of the trend on the basis of a consistent series of estimates.

The second point at issue is whether there has been an *acceleration* in the downward trend. Lydall and Tipping suggested that in the final part of the period considered by them from 1936 to 1951−6, 'the distribution of capital appears to have altered much more radically' (1961:92). This was taken up by Polanyi and Wood, who argued that the shift in favour of the majority 'has become most marked since the middle 1930s' (1974:19). The support provided by table 6.2 for this view may be seen from the calculations below of the arithmetic trend in the share of the top 10 per cent. However, it is dangerous to draw firm conclusions from such a limited number of observations, and a relatively small variation in the estimates for one year could have a substantial impact. If, for example, the estimate for 1911−13 were too low by 2 per cent and that for 1924−30 too high by 2 per cent, the trend

	% per annum
1911–13 to 1924–30	0
1924–30 to 1936	−0.22
1936 to 1951–6	−0.51
1960 to 1970	−0.60

(Note: where the estimates relate to more than 1 year, we have taken the midpoint of the period.)

would be not zero but − 0.27 percentage points per annum. In section 6.4, we examine how far the 'accelerationist' argument remains valid with a wider range of evidence.

The third point concerns the extent to which the redistribution has applied generally to all top wealth groups. From the figures in the left hand part of table 6.1, Revell noted that the decline over the period before 1960 had been confined to the top 1 per cent of the population, and that the share of the next 9 per cent *rose* quite considerably. As he observed, 'this is redistribution of a rather special sort, and not quite what we have in mind when we talk of redistribution from rich to poor' (1965:382). Some of the possible explanations for this are discussed by Revell (1965) and Atkinson (1972). Since then, Polanyi and Wood have argued that the changes after 1960 reflect 'a *general* process of "redistribution" *not* confined to the wealthy' (1974:19). In section 6.4, the nature of the redistribution, and the way in which it has changed over time, are investigated in more detail.

In answering the type of question described above, the need for a consistent series of estimates is obvious. There are however a number of serious problems in the construction of such a series, and these have perhaps received too little emphasis in earlier studies. The difficulties arise first in the *source statistics*. The basic estate data have been published for many years, but their form and coverage have changed on a number of occasions. These changes come about because of new estate duty legislation, through changes in estate duty practice, or through variation in the methods by which the statistics are collected or tabulated. The second source of difficulty is in the application of consistent *mortality multipliers*. The evidence about occupational mortality is only available at infrequent intervals, and has been employed in different ways. Our analysis of multipliers in chapter 3 suggested that differences would not lead to dramatic changes in the results, but that the estimates could change by one or two percentage points. This sort of variation may be significant when measuring trends over time, and even more so when considering whether or not they have accelerated. Thirdly, there are problems regarding the *adjustments to the estate data*. Not only has the need for such adjustments varied with changes in the coverage of the estate figures, but also the raw data necessary to make the adjustments are available with varying degrees of accuracy. In the next section, we describe the data available to overcome these three problems and the methods which have employed in earlier studies.

6.2 Historical record

The main studies using the estate method were reviewed in chapter 1, and the reader may find it useful at this juncture to consult table 1.1 (p.10). It should however be noted that these studies have not made use of estate data for all the years for which they are available in a suitable form. The full list of estate data classified by range of estate and age – the minimum requirements – is given in table 6.3. In what follows, we consider in turn the five sub-periods: pre-First World War, 1920s, 1930s, 1950s, 1960 and after.

(a) Pre-First World War

Source statistics. The first years for which data are available classified according to the age of the deceased are 1911–12, 1912–13, 1913–14 and 1914–15. Those for the first three years were used by Clay (1925), and subsequently by Daniels and Campion (1936) and Campion (1939), to arrive at an estimate for the distribution of wealth for the period immediately prior to the First World War (1911–13)[1] covering the population aged 25 and over in England and Wales. There are a number of difficulties with the data for these years. First, in 1911–15 (and 1920–1) they are not classified by sex. Mallet and Strutt (1915:596) gave an overall figure for female deaths (one quarter of the number of estates) and Daniels and Campion used this and the higher proportion indicated by the first available figures (1921, 1923 and 1924) as alternative assumptions. The resulting estimates are necessarily less reliable than those for later years, when the estates are classified by sex.[2] Secondly, the coverage of wealth in the estate statistics at that date differed from subsequent years in that the Settlement Estate Duty was then in force. Settled property on which duty had once been paid was not liable a second time, and as a result a substantial amount of settled property was missing from the statistics. According to Daniels and Campion (1936:38) the amount involved for England and Wales was some £40–£45 million in 1911–13. If we apply an average multiplier of 27.5 and assume that all of this property belonged to the top 10 per cent, then the estimated share would rise by some

---

1 Throughout this chapter, we follow the practice of assuming that data for the tax year ending 31 March relate to the previous calendar year.
2 Clay (1925) did not distinguish between male and female estates. The bias introduced can be estimated according to formulae similar to those given in chapter 3.

Table 6.3 Availability of published estate data classified by range of estate and age

Financial year	Country	Classified by sex	Published in*
1911–2	E W	No	AR 55
1912–3	E W	No	AR 56
1913–4	E W	No	AR 57
1914–5	E W	No	AR 58
1920–1	E W	No	AR 64
1923–4‡	E W	Yes	AR 67
1924–5	E W	Yes	AR 68
1925–6	E W	Yes	AR 69
1926–7	E W	Yes	AR 70
1927–8	E W	Yes	AR 71
1928–9	E W	Yes	AR 72
1929–30	E W	Yes	AR 73
1930–1	E W	Yes	AR 74
1936–7	E W	Yes	AR 80
1938–9	E W and S	Yes	AR 82
1950–1	E W and S		AR 94
1951–2	E W and S		AR 95
1952–3	E W and S		AR 96
1953–4	E W and S		AR 97
1954–5	E W and S		AR 98
1955–6	E W and S		AR 99
1956–7§	E W and S		AR 100
1957–8§	E W and S		AR 101
1958–9§	E W and S		AR 102
1959–60	E W and S	Yes	AR 103
1960–1	E W and S		AR 104
1961–2	E W and S		AR 105
1962–3	E W and S		AR 106
1963–4	G B		AR 107
1964–5	G B†		AR 108, IRS 1970
1965–6	G B		AR 109, IRS 1970, 1971
1966–7	G B		AR 110, IRS 1970, 1971
1967–8	G B		AR 111, IRS 1970, 1971
1968–9	G B		IRS 1970, 1971
1969–70	G B		IRS 1971
1970–1	G B		IRS 1972
1971–2	G B		IRS 1973
1972–3	G B		IRS 1974

Notes * AR denotes Annual Report of the Inland Revenue and IRS denotes Inland Revenue Statistics. EW denotes England and Wales, S denotes Scotland, and GB denotes Great Britain.

† The Inland Revenue have made available on request data for recent years broken down between EW and S, and with a finer classification by ranges than in the published tables.

‡ The data for this year are published in the form of percentages.

§ Figures given separately for Wales.

$1\frac{1}{2}$ per cent, which would make a noticeable difference. This particular relief for settled property was repealed in the Finance Act 1914. Thirdly, the coverage differed from that in later years in that a single estate duty was then in force throughout Great Britain and Ireland. The capital values of movable property were shown in the country in which duty was paid, whereas after the establishment of Northern Ireland (from 22 November 1921) and Eire (from 1 April 1923) as separate taxing jurisdictions, movable property forming part of an Irish estate but situated in England and Wales would be included in the England and Wales estate statistics. However, according to the 63rd Annual Report of the Inland Revenue this only slightly affected the comparability of statistics for Great Britain, and Daniels and Campion suggest that 'the effect on the figures is small' (1936:36).[3]

Mortality multipliers. Daniels and Campion used both general mortality multipliers and social class multipliers, the latter being based on the Decennial Supplement to the 1911 Census. At that date, the occupational classification was in part an industrial classification, and the social class rates are not comparable with those in more recent years. They assumed that the differential mortality rates would lie between those of the top two of the eight classes and derived the differentials shown in the first column of table 6.4a. For reasons discussed more fully below, the social class differentials appear rather too low, particularly when compared with those for the 1950s and 1960s, and there are grounds for believing that comparability would require the application of higher multipliers in 1911–13.

Adjustments to estate data. The main adjustment made by Daniels and Campion is for the wealth of those below the estate duty exemption level (£100). This is based on Clay (1925), who estimated that for the population aged 15 and over the value of furniture, tools and personal effects was £75 million, and that 'working class' savings amounted to £470 million. Daniels and Campion took, for the population aged 25 and over, the range £400–700 million, or £25–45 per person. They do not however give any full explanation of their reasons for choosing this range, and in particular for taking an upper figure some 50 per cent higher than that of Clay. The basis for estimating the wealth of the excluded population is discussed further below. In addition, Daniels and Campion made adjustments (for both 1911–13 and 1924–30) for funeral expenses, and for gifts for national and charitable purposes. The former were assumed to be the same at each age and

3 A further difference between 1911–14 and the post-First World
    War period is in the treatment of estates where duty is paid in
    instalments. According to the 63rd Annual Report, the basis for the
    compilation of the statistics was changed from 'capital brought to
    our notice' to 'capital on which duty is paid in the year'.

sex but to vary from £6 to £45 according to the size of the estate (1936:42). The latter were assumed to have been made solely by men aged 55 and over possessing more than £5,000 and to have been proportional to the value of their estates. (The former brings the data in line with those for the 1960s, and the same adjustment is made in our estimates below.)

(b) 1920s

Source statistics. The estate data for these years (apart from 1920–1) were published in a form similar to that used in recent years, except that they related only to England and Wales and covered only estates above the estate duty exemption level (£100 throughout the period).

Mortality multipliers. The social class multipliers applied by Daniels and Campion are reproduced in table 6.4a. They were based on the 1921 Decennial Supplement and on preliminary results of the 1931 Decennial Supplement. The same source is employed for more recent years in earlier chapters, but it should be noted that the differentials applied by Daniels and Campion are considerably smaller for nearly all age groups than those for 1951 and 1961. For men, in particular, the differentials are around 10–15 per cent less than those obtained on assumption A2 for 1951. This is rather surprising, since it seems unlikely that the social class mortality gradient would be widening over time at such a rapid rate. Daniels and Campion themselves assumed that the reverse had been happening (1936:16), and this was taken into account by them in deriving the differentials for 1924–30. From successive Decennial Supplements, we do in fact get conflicting conclusions about the trend in the social class mortality gradient. The 1931 report drew attention to the diminution in social class contrasts during the decade, whereas by 1961 the Registrar General was of the view that 'the social class gradient increases with successive censuses' (Registrar General 1971:22). In both cases, these need to be qualified,[4] and having examined the evidence, we have formed the view that, although the social gradient may have steepened, it has not done so to the extent indicated by the figures in table 6.4a. In particular, it appears that the procedure of Daniels and Campion differed from that described above under assumption A2 in that (i) they adjusted the differentials downward for the perceived trend in relative mortality, (ii) they made no allowance for errors in occupational statements, and (iii) they made a number of rather *ad hoc* assumptions about the social class mortality rates

4 In 1931 the evidence for the younger age groups in social class II (the single most important for our purpose) showed signs of an improvement in their relative position. In 1961 the increased gradient was particularly attributable to the movements in social classes I and V. For social class II the average relative mortality rate (for men aged 20–64) changed only from 94% in 1931 to 92% in 1951 and then to 81% in 1961.

Table 6.4a Social class differentials used in different studies (England and Wales)

| Age range | Daniels and Campion† (1936) | | | Lydall and Tipping (1961) | | Table 3.1 (column 2) 1961 (A2) | |
| | 1911–13* | 1924–30 | | 1951 (A2) | | | |
	Male	Male	Female	Male	Female	Male	Female
Under 25	1.27	1.21	1.21	1.04	1.50	1.18	1.05
25–34	1.13	1.16	1.17	1.32	1.38	1.40	1.29
35–44	1.11	1.16	1.15	1.35	1.18	1.43	1.27
45–54	1.10	1.08	1.10	1.24	1.12	1.35	1.20
55–64	1.08	1.03	1.06	1.19	1.08	1.26	1.16
65–74	1.05	1.02	1.04	1.14	1.09	1.11	1.05
75–84	1.01	1.01	1.01	1.09 }	1.08 }	1.07	1.02
85 and over	1.0	1.0	1.0			1.04	1.01

Notes * The female rate is the same as for 1924–30.
† We have taken the harmonic mean of the range of relative mortality rates given, following the original authors (1936:19).

Table 6.4b Social class differentials used here (England and Wales) – assumption A2

Age range	1921		1931		1951		1961	
	Male	Female	Male	Female	Male	Female	Male	Female
20–24	1.21	—	1.12	1.37	1.04	1.50	1.18	1.05
25–34	1.25	—	1.33	1.34	1.32	1.38	1.40	1.29
35–44	1.25	—	1.31	1.24	1.35	1.18	1.43	1.27
45–54	1.18	—	1.19	1.18	1.24	1.12	1.35	1.20
55–64	1.13	—	1.10	1.13	1.19	1.08	1.26	1.16
65–74	1.11	—	1.05	1.10	1.14	1.09	1.11	1.05
75–84	1.07	—	1.00	1.08	1.10	1.09	1.07	1.02
85 and over	1.04	—	1.00	1.04	1.04	1.05	1.04	1.01

Source: See text.

for women. In deriving the revised set of differentials set out in table 6.4b we have used data on trends not available at the time Daniels and Campion wrote, we have adjusted for errors in occupational statements, and have used evidence on female mortality by social class contained in the 1931 Decennial Supplement. The results need to be treated with care, and the method as a whole is subject to well-recognised limitations, but we feel that the revised figures in table 6.4b provide a firmer basis for constructing a consistent series. (More details are given in appendix VI.)

Adjustments to estate data. The main adjustment made by Daniels and Campion is again for the wealth of those below the exemption level. As a starting point, they take the estimates by Clay (1925) for 1920—1 covering the population aged 15 and over, which came to a total of £912 million, or about £45 per person. Daniels and Campion argue, however, that this figure, extrapolated to 1924—30, is likely to be too high, because those concerned 'include at least $5\frac{1}{2}$ million married women, many of whom may have little or no property in their own name and will probably include the majority of the 3—4 million persons suffering from unemployment' (1936:49). The source of the over-statement they trace to Clay's allocation of 75—80 per cent of the funds of friendly societies and other saving institutions to those excluded from the estate data, a proportion which they consider too high. It is true that Clay included items (for example the National Health Insurance Fund) which would not be counted on the bases of valuation considered earlier in this book and it is possible that he may have allocated too high a proportion of savings bank deposits etc. to the excluded population. However, taking only one half of savings bank deposits, one third of building society deposits, and an allowance for cash and life assurance, gives a total of some £550 million for 1924—30. This suggests that the figure of £500 million taken by Daniels and Campion as the lower end of the range is too low, and that £600 million plus might be more appropriate.[5] Further support is provided by an examination of the changes between 1911—13 and 1924—30 (taking the results based on social class multipliers). This shows that the average wealth below £100 increased by only 19—22 per cent. Although this is not necessarily inconsistent with the overall average increase of 80 per cent (the average wealth below £100 having been kept down as the richer persons crossed the boundary), it suggests that their estimate of the increase between 1911—13 and 1924— 30 in the wealth of the excluded population is only likely to be correct if the bulk of the small savers saw a decline in the real value of their assets (over the period 1912—27 retail prices rose by some

5 The total includes 5/6 of the realisation value of industrial life insurance and an approximate allowance for cash and bank deposits — see appendix VI.

60 per cent).[6] In view of these questions surrounding the adjustments of Daniels and Campion, we have made our own estimates of the wealth of the excluded population, applying as far as possible the same balance sheet method as in earlier chapters. Details are given in appendix VI.

(c) 1930s

Source statistics. The estate data were only published in the required form for two years: 1936–7 and 1938–9. (It is interesting to note that their reappearance after a six year gap was the result of a petition submitted by the Royal Statistical Society and the Manchester Statistical Society.) There was however a major departure in that for the first time statistics were published covering Scotland. The data were used by Langley (1950, 1951) in her estimates, to which we make particular reference below, and by Campion (1939).

Mortality multipliers. No Decennial Supplement was published between 1931 and 1951, so that Langley based her main results on general mortality multipliers. She did give some estimates using social class differentials, taken from Campion (1939), but she argued that the use of general multipliers 'may not affect the comparability [of the estimates with earlier results] as general mortality rates declined throughout the 1930s' (1950:349). As we have seen, although general mortality rates fell, there was a similar or faster decline in the mortality of the upper social classes, and the social class differential may have widened, or at least remained unchanged, so that this procedure does not seem satisfactory.

Adjustments to estate data. To obtain estimates of the wealth held by those below the exemption level (£100), Langley derives upper and lower bounds of £60 and £35, respectively, per person excluded. The former figure is based on the average for estates less than £100 valued by the Inland Revenue, since, as she argues, 'it is likely . . . that these estates were among the more prosperous estates of less than £100' (1951:38). The lower bound is derived from the Daniels/Campion figure for 1924–30, allowing for an increase in the value of estates since that date. Langley then takes an average of the two figures, or £47.50 per person, to arrive at a total of £911 million. This is relatively close to the figure we obtained using the balance sheet approach (see appendix VI).

6 The change in 'working class savings' was discussed by the Colwyn Committee in 1927. They stressed the difficulty of obtaining firm evidence, but argued that that from National Savings 'does not suggest any failure of per head savings to keep pace with the cost of living' (Committee on National Debt and Taxation 1927:11).

(d) 1950s

Source statistics. The format of the estate statistics remained the same as in 1938, giving figures both for England and Wales and for Scotland, but its comparability with earlier years was affected by the raising of the estate duty threshold to £2,000 (in 1946) and £3,000 (in 1954). Since estates below the threshold were typically not included, this greatly reduced the coverage of the estate data, and made more difficult the problem of estimating the wealth of those not covered. The seriousness of this difficulty is brought out by the estimates of Lydall and Tipping (1961, table 1) which show the multiplied-up estate returns as covering only 8.6 per cent of the population aged 20 and over in 1951—6.

Mortality multipliers. The multipliers applied to data in the early 1950s in the study by Lydall and Tipping (1961) have been described in chapter 3. They correspond to assumption A2 here.

Adjustments to estate data. In their work using the estate data for this period,[7] Lydall and Tipping make a number of adjustments. The most important concern wealth-holdings below £2,000, for which they used a variety of sources including the Oxford savings surveys. The resulting estimates are discussed more fully in appendix VI. Lydall and Tipping also adjusted the valuation of two particular classes of asset. In the case of houses they took account of the administrative concession in force in the early 1950s, under which the Inland Revenue valued an owner-occupied house at less than its market value where occupied by a near relative of the deceased who remained resident in the house (Lydall and Tipping 1961:102). They assumed that this led to the value being under-stated by 10 per cent, and raised holdings by this amount. In the case of life insurance, they noted that the value of policies recorded in the estate returns appeared far too low and replaced it by an estimate of the life funds (excluding pension schemes).

(e) 1960s

A number of the features of the data for the 1960s and 1970s have been described in earlier chapters; here we draw attention to some of the factors affecting their comparability with earlier years.

Source statistics. Since 1960 the estate data have given details of estates below the exemption level which come to the notice of the Inland Revenue, thus extending their coverage considerably. This coincided with the decision to prepare official estimates of wealth-holding and may well have led to the

---

7 Estimates for 1950—1 were also made by Langley (1954), but these were only preliminary in nature, and did not include a figure for total wealth.

estate statistics being collected with more care than in the past.[8] For these reasons there may be a break in comparability between 1959 and 1960.

Mortality multipliers. These have been discussed in chapter 3. The multipliers most comparable with those applied in earlier studies are assumption A2, which was based on the procedure of Lydall and Tipping (1961).

Adjustments to estate data. These have been discussed in chapters 4 and 5. The estimates presented there go beyond those in earlier studies in the adjustments C1 and C2 for valuation and adjustments D and E for missing wealth.

A summing-up

It should be clear from this review of different studies that there are substantial problems in trying to measure changes in the distribution over time. Some of the principal implications for the subsequent analysis are summarised below.

First, there are a number of special problems surrounding the period before the First World War. The estate data were not classified by sex; the occupational mortality data were collected in a different form; there were major changes in the estate duty treatment of settled property in 1913; and the estate returns then covered Eire. All of these mean that there is a greater degree of uncertainty surrounding the estimates for the pre-First World War period, and on account of this we feel that it would be wiser to begin an analysis of the trends in 1923, which is the first year in which the estate data were classified by sex.

Secondly, there have been changes over the period 1923–72 in the form and coverage of the estate statistics, which may well have affected their comparability. The most serious of these possible breaks in the series are between 1938 and 1950, when the substantial increase in the estate duty threshold reduced the coverage of the data, and between 1959 and 1960, when data on estates below the threshold were first published. In view of this, we consider three sub-periods. This follows the practice of the Royal Commission in separating the periods before and after 1960, but also considers the inter-war years (1923–38) separately from 1950–9.

Thirdly, the earlier estimates did not employ comparable social class multipliers, nor did they make the same adjustments for the wealth of the excluded population or other deficiencies of the estate data. In the next

8 It is interesting to note that the ratio of estates over £3,000 to all deaths in the population aged 20 and over rose from 13.2% to 14.6% for men between 1959–60 and 1960–61. Some increase would have been expected in the light of rising average wealth-holdings, but it warrants further investigation.

section we describe some of the steps which can be taken towards a more consistent set of estimates.

6.3 Towards a consistent series

The first step is to choose a consistent *geographical coverage*. The main focus of the book is on the distribution of wealth in Great Britain, but we have seen that no data are available for Scotland before 1938. We therefore present two series: one for England and Wales, and one for Great Britain, the latter dating from 1938. This allows us to examine the differences in the two series during the period of overlap, an aspect which has not been studied at all closely before.

The second stage is the choice of *mortality multipliers*. Those employed here are constructed on the basis of assumption A2, that is the adjusted Decennial Supplement data (but not graduated with estate size), and the social class differentials are those given in table 6.4b. In order to smooth the changes in social class differentials over time, we in each case take a linear interpolation between the Census years (1921, 1931, 1951 and 1961).[9] The multipliers are applied to all estates in excess of the exemption level; in the case of non-dutiable estates which appear after 1960, the general mortality multiplier is used (on the basis of the argument put forward by Revell (1967)) below a specified cut-off level.[10]

By applying the multipliers to the estate data we obtain estimates of the numbers and amounts of wealth in different ranges. In order to put these results in the same form as those of earlier investigators, we need to determine the *total adult population* and *total wealth*. Both aggregates have been discussed at length in connection with the estimates for recent years given in the previous chapter. It was pointed out, for example, that taking the definition of adult as 21 rather than 15 could lead to the share of the top 1 per cent being reduced by some 2 per cent. When considering trends over time, such differences are important. Moreover, it is not simply a matter of securing a standard definition, since social changes over the period may mean that the definition should vary over time. The population aged 25 and over may have been appropriate in 1920, but, with increased economic independence of young people, the relevant population today may be 18 and over.

The customary practice of taking the population aged 25 and over was justified by Daniels and Campion as follows:

9 In the case of women, we take the 1931 differentials for the period 1923–30.
10 The cut-off was taken as £3,000 in 1960 (the exemption level) and increased by stages to £10,000 in 1972 (so as to keep broadly constant the proportion of estates above the cut-off).

> The number of persons aged 15 and over . . . together with boys and girls less than 15 who have inherited estates, includes all those who may possess capital. But it also includes students still at school and universities, juveniles just embarking on their industrial careers, dependents of occupied persons, and married women with no property in their own right. It seems reasonable, therefore, to take the total of adult males and females 25 and over as approximately the total number of persons possessing capital [1936:26].

However, since we are here concerned with the distribution among individuals (the question of family versus individual wealth is discussed in chapter 9), the quantitatively most important point – that about married women – is not relevant. This suggests that the population under consideration should be larger than the total aged 25 and over. Certainly a number of authors were unhappy about the Daniels and Campion argument. Clay stated that 'I do not think we should exclude persons between 15 and 25' (1925:61). Langley (1950) adopted the same assumption as Daniels and Campion for purposes of comparability, but doubted if it were legitimate in 1936–8. Later writers lowered the age threshold, reflecting a feeling both that it had initially been set too high and that it had become even less realistic over time. Lydall and Tipping took the population aged 20 and over; and more recently the *Social Trends* figures are based on the population aged 15 and over (the same assumption is made by Polanyi and Wood – see table 6.2).

What basically is required is a definition of economic independence, allowing us to exclude those young people who are still financially dependent on their parents. For this purpose 25 seems too high in the 1920s, and 15 too low in the 1970s. At the same time, there has definitely been a downward trend in the average age of economic independence. Although some factors may have worked in the opposite direction, such as the expansion of higher education, this has surely been more than offset by the trend to earlier marriage and the acquisition of wealth by young earners. It may be noted, for instance, that the proportion of the age group 20–4 married rose between 1931 and 1971 from 14 per cent to 36 per cent for men and from 25 per cent to 58 per cent for women (*Social Trends* 1972: table 6). In view of this we take the age of majority (18) as the basis in 1973, and the age of 20, following Lydall and Tipping, as appropriate in 1953. Extrapolating linearly gives 23 as the cut off in 1923 (the beginning of the period considered), with in-between years obtained by graduation at the rate of 1/10th per annum. The precise procedure adopted is clearly arbitrary, but it seems a reasonable approximation to the general trend over the period.

Turning now to the aggregate of capital, this depends on the allowance made for the wealth of the excluded population. Our aim here has been to provide estimates on the pattern of assumptions B2–B4, with B3 a central figure, as in chapters 4 and 5. The details of the construction of this series are set out in appendix VI, but in principle the method followed that in chapter 4. The adjustment is based on the balance sheet totals and the resulting estimate of the wealth 'missing' from the estate estimates. The availability of the necessary data varies from period to period, and generally speaking the estimates for the more recent years are more reliable. Thus for the 1960s we could use well-established balance sheet figures and the methods of allocation described earlier. For the 1950s the balance sheet data are only available for the last years of the decade, and we have had to extend the series back; moreover, our estimates of the asset composition of wealth-holding included in the estate data are less firmly based. Going back before the Second World War involves even greater difficulties, and the estimates are in a number of ways more tentative.

The resulting series for the total wealth of the excluded population is shown in table VI.I of appendix VI. In each case we have compared our estimates with those of earlier investigators. The central estimates for the 1920s, following our earlier critique of Daniels and Campion (1936), are somewhat higher than their figures. For the 1930s, our estimates are again higher than those of Campion (1939) but are in line with those of Langley (1951) and with other evidence available about 'working class savings'. A comparison with the estimates of Lydall and Tipping (1961) for the 1950s shows that there are differences for particular asset categories. These can be explained in part by the fact that they used the asset composition of estates (rather than wealth holdings), and by differences in the method of valuation, although it is possible that our allowance for the wealth of the excluded population is too low. For this, and other reasons explained in Appendix VI, the estimates must be treated with due circumspection.

In brief, the series presented here is specified as follows:

— Geographical coverage — separate estimates for England and Wales, for Scotland and for Great Britain as a whole.

— Period: 1923–72 for England and Wales
             1938–72 for Scotland and Great Britain.

— Mortality multipliers based on social class differentials obtained from the Registrar General's Decennial Supplement adjusted for errors in occupational statements and for the unoccupied.

—Total population equals those economically independent, taken as those above an age threshold reduced linearly from 23 in 1923 to 18 in 1973.

—Total wealth equals unadjusted wealth as estimated from the estate
statistics plus the wealth of the excluded population. The latter is
based on a range of assumptions (B2—B4) with a central figure (B3).
(Further details of the assumptions are given in appendix VI.)

The estimates obtained on the basis of these assumptions are set out in
tables 6.5 and 6.6. The former shows estimates using the central figure (B3)
for the wealth of the excluded population, covering both England and Wales
and Great Britain. The latter shows the estimates for England and Wales only,
with the range of variation resulting from assumptions B2 and B4. The former
allocates missing wealth as far as possible to the excluded population; the
latter allocates the minimum wealth to the excluded population consistent
with the evidence available. The range of variation B2—B4 changes over time,
depending on the accuracy of the underlying data. In particular, it is
considerably greater in the 1950s. Thus, the range for 1959 of 60—74 per
cent for the share of the top 5 per cent is sufficiently wide for us to be
considerably less sure about the central B3 figure than for 1969 when the
range is 54—8 per cent. Finally, in figure 6.1 we have plotted the shares of the
top 1 per cent and 5 per cent for England and Wales and for Scotland.

It should be noted that, following the standard practice, we have obtained
the shares by log—linear interpolation. This does, however, introduce a source
of error, as we have shown in chapter 5, particularly where, as in many of the
earlier years, the data are grouped in broad ranges (in 1950, for example, the
share of the top 5 per cent is interpolated from a range 3.5 per cent to 8.7 per
cent). Moreover, unlike some earlier authors, we have not attempted to interpolate outside the range of the estate data. The difficulties in doing this may
be illustrated by 1956, when the estate data cover 5.6 per cent of the
population. Applying the linear bounds described in chapter 5 gives a range
for the share of the top 10 per cent of 74.5 per cent to 85.5 per cent, that is
11 percentage points. Put another way, the figure obtained by log—linear
extrapolation of the lowest estate range (85.2 per cent) could be over ten
percentage points too high.

We believe that the series presented here are closer to being consistent over
time than the estimates usually quoted. At the same time, we should like to
emphasise that they fall short of being ideal in a number of important
respects. First, we have drawn attention to the changes which took place over
the period in the form and coverage of the estate statistics, which may have
affected their comparability, and the most serious of these possible breaks in
the series – between 1938 and 1950, and between 1959 and 1960 – have
been indicated in the tables by dashed lines. Secondly, we have made no
adjustments to the series for the problems of valuation or of wealth missing

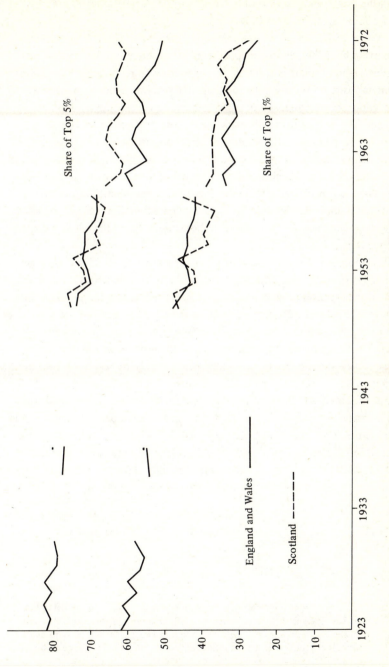

Figure 6.1 Share of top 1% and 5% in England and Wales and Scotland 1923–72

from the estate returns. In terms of the analysis in previous chapters, there are no adjustments of type C, D or E.

Taking first the question of valuation, the series is closest to being on a realisation basis, but there remains the major problem of life policies. This was discussed by Daniels and Campion (1936), who recognised that the estate estimates were on this account too high. They did not however make any correction since they lacked detailed information about the holdings of policies. The first adjustments made were those by Lydall and Tipping (1961), but their estimates were on a going concern basis (taking the life fund). From the analysis in chapter 4, it appears that the adjustment from the estate duty value to a realisation value would tend to increase the relative shares of the top groups. (It may be noted that the amounts allowed for industrial branch policies held by the excluded population have been valued on a realisation basis, in contrast to earlier studies where the whole fund was included).

The adoption of a going concern basis for valuation would involve many more adjustments, most importantly those to household goods, trade assets, occupational pension rights, and to land and buildings. In chapter 4, it was suggested that these adjustments (moving from C1 to C2) would tend to reduce the shares of top wealth-holders. Given the increase in the ownership of consumer durables, and – particularly – the growth of occupational pensions, the significance of this adjustment is likely to have risen over the period. If this is correct it leads to a systematic bias in the measurement of the trend. Some indication of its possible magnitude may be obtained from the estimates of the effect of allowing for occupational pension rights on the share of the top 10 per cent given by Lydall and Tipping (1961), combined with our estimates for 1972 in chapter 4. Taking as a base the estimates without allowing for pension rights, and then allocating them (in full) according to the assumptions made in these studies, we obtain[11]

	Base (no allowance for pension rights)	Adjusted for occupational pension rights
1936	88.0	87.5
1954	79.0	76.4
1972	71.1	67.1

11 Since the Lydall and Tipping figures appear to relate only to funded rights, we have increased their amounts by 100%, an approximate adjustment based on the evidence in Revell (1967:374) that in 1957 unfunded pension rights were, if anything, larger than funded rights. As we have noted, their estimate for the 1950s needs to be viewed with caution, because it is based on an extrapolation beyond the coverage of the estate data. The estimate for 1972 is based on assumptions A3/B3/C2/D2/E2.

Table 6.5 Shares in total wealth 1923−72 (assumption B3)

	England and Wales				Great Britain			
	Top 1%	Top 5%	Top 10%	Top 20%	Top 1%	Top 5%	Top 10%	Top 20%
1923	60.9	82.0	89.1	94.2				
1924	59.9	81.5	88.1	93.8				
1925	61.0	82.1	88.4	93.8				
1926	57.3	79.9	87.4	93.2				
1927	59.8	81.3	88.3	93.8	not available			
1928	57.0	79.6	87.2	93.1				
1929	55.5	78.9	86.3	92.6				
1930	57.9	79.2	86.6	92.6				
1936	54.2	77.4	85.7	92.0				
1938	55.0	76.9	85.0	91.2	55.0	77.2	85.4	91.6
1950	47.2	74.3	−	−	47.2	74.4	−	−
1951	45.8	73.6	−	−	45.9	73.8	−	−
1952	43.0	70.2	−	−	42.9	70.3	−	−
1953	43.6	71.1	−	−	43.5	71.2	−	−
1954	45.3	71.8	−	−	45.3	72.0	−	−
1955	44.5	71.1	−	−	43.8	70.8	−	−
1956	44.5	71.3	−	−	44.0	71.1	−	−
1957	43.4	68.7	−	−	42.9	68.6	−	−
1958	41.4	67.8	−	−	40.9	67.7	−	−
1959	41.4	67.6	−	−	41.8	67.9	−	−
1960	33.9	59.4	71.5	83.1	34.4	60.0	72.1	83.6
1961	36.5	60.6	71.7	83.3	36.5	60.8	72.1	83.6
1962	31.4	54.8	67.3	80.2	31.9	55.4	67.9	80.7
1963	not available[*]				not available[*]			
1964	34.5	58.6	71.4	84.3	34.7	59.2	72.0	85.2
1965	33.0	58.1	71.7	85.5	33.3	58.7	72.3	85.8
1966	30.6	55.5	69.2	83.8	31.0	56.1	69.9	84.2
1967	31.4	56.0	70.0	84.5	31.5	56.4	70.5	84.9
1968	33.6	58.3	71.6	85.1	33.6	58.6	72.0	85.4
1969	31.1	56.1	67.7	83.3	31.3	56.6	68.6	84.1
1970	29.7	53.6	68.7	84.5	30.1	54.3	69.4	84.9
1971	28.4	52.3	67.6	84.2	28.8	53.0	68.3	84.8
1972	31.7	56.0	70.4	84.9	32.0	57.2	71.7	85.3

Notes: − denotes outside the range of estate duty statistics.
[*] The estate data were not available by country for 1963; this means that we could not calculate a figure for Great Britain comparable with those for other years.

Treating the estimates for the moment as comparable (which they are not, as explained earlier), the adjustment for occupational pension rights would increase the annual downward (arithmetic) trend for 1936−72 from 0.47 per cent to 0.57 per cent. The bias in the trend (0.1 per cent) appears rather smaller than might have been expected given the large increase in the relative importance of occupational pension rights (from 4 per cent of total wealth in 1936 to 12 per cent in 1972).

The question of missing property is obviously important. The estimates in Tables 6.5 and 6.6 have not been adjusted for wealth which is missing on

Table 6.6 Sensitivity of shares to assumptions about wealth of excluded
population — England and Wales 1923—72

| | Top 1% | | Top 5% | | Top 10% | | Top 20% | |
	B2	B4	B2	B4	B2	B4	B2	B4
1923	60.1	61.7	80.9	83.0	88.0	90.3	93.0	95.4
1924	59.1	60.8	80.4	82.7	86.9	89.4	92.6	95.2
1925	60.2	61.9	81.0	83.2	87.3	89.7	92.6	95.1
1926	56.6	58.1	78.8	81.0	86.2	88.6	92.0	94.5
1927	59.0	60.6	80.3	82.4	87.2	89.5	92.6	95.0
1928	56.2	57.7	78.5	80.7	85.9	88.3	91.8	94.4
1929	54.7	56.4	77.7	80.1	85.0	87.6	91.2	94.0
1930	57.1	58.7	78.0	80.3	85.4	87.8	91.3	93.8
1936	53.5	54.9	76.3	78.4	84.6	86.9	90.7	93.2
1938	54.3	55.6	75.9	77.8	84.0	86.1	90.1	92.3
1950	43.7	50.0	68.8	78.7	—	—	—	—
1951	42.1	48.8	67.6	78.5	—	—	—	—
1952	39.6	45.7	64.7	74.6	—	—	—	—
1953	39.7	46.9	64.6	76.4	—	—	—	—
1954	41.3	48.5	65.5	76.9	—	—	—	—
1955	39.1	49.2	62.5	78.6	—	—	—	—
1956	39.0	49.3	62.4	79.0	—	—	—	—
1957	38.2	48.0	60.4	75.9	—	—	—	—
1958	36.7	45.4	60.1	74.5	—	—	—	—
1959	36.6	45.4	59.9	74.3	—	—	—	—
1960	32.8	34.6	57.5	60.7	69.3	73.1	80.6	84.9
1961	35.3	37.3	58.7	61.9	69.6	73.4	80.8	85.2
1962	30.6	32.0	53.4	56.0	65.5	68.7	78.0	81.8
1963				not available*				
1964	33.5	35.2	56.8	59.9	69.3	73.0	82.3	86.7
1965	31.9	33.8	56.2	59.6	69.3	73.4	82.7	87.6
1966	29.6	31.3	53.6	56.8	67.0	70.9	81.1	85.8
1967	30.3	32.1	54.0	57.3	67.5	71.7	81.5	86.5
1968	32.2	34.6	55.8	60.0	68.6	73.7	81.5	87.6
1969	29.8	32.1	53.8	57.9	64.9	69.9	79.8	86.0
1970	28.2	30.6	51.0	55.3	65.4	70.9	80.4	87.2
1971	27.2	29.2	50.2	53.7	64.8	69.4	80.8	86.5
1972	30.2	32.7	53.3	57.7	62.7	72.6	80.8	87.5

See Notes to table 6.5.

account of estate duty law avoidance (e.g. settled property). As we have seen
in chapter 4, allowance for these items may significantly influence the results
for the degree of concentration at a point in time. It may however also affect
the trends over time, and in particular we need to take account of the changes
which have taken place in estate duty over the course of this century and of
the changing pattern of response of those who wish to avoid duty.

It is not possible for us to discuss in any detail the modifications to
estate duty legislation over the fifty years, of which there were a large

number (Wheatcroft (1972) records thirty-nine Finance Acts which altered the provisions in that period). Those possibly important for the estimates of the distribution of wealth include (in broadly chronological order):

(i) 1930 exemption of objects of national, etc. interest. The Finance Act 1930 provided for the exemption of objects of national, scientific, historic or artistic interest, subject to specified conditions. This would have reduced the scope of property covered.

(ii) 1940 extension of property covered. The Finance Act (No. 1) 1940 extended the definition of property deemed to pass on death (e.g. certain life interests), and introduced a charge on the benefits received by the deceased from a controlled company. This would have brought in some property previously missing.

(iii) Period of charge for gifts. This was extended from 3 to 5 years under the Finance Act 1946, and from 5 to 7 years under the Finance Act 1968. Any double-counting would therefore tend to be increased.

(iv) Non-aggregation provisions. The Finance Act 1954 made changes in the non-aggregation provisions, which may have affected the number of items appearing as separate estates. The Finance Act 1968 modified the provisions for the non-aggregation of insurance policies.

(v) Immovable property abroad. This was brought within the scope of estate duty under the Finance Act 1962, a change which led to property being included in the estate statistics which had previously been missing.

(vi) Settled property. The Finance Act 1969 imposed a charge on the death of beneficiaries from discretionary trusts. This brought some property into the statistics, although it is still possible for a major part to be missing, depending on the policy pursued by trustees.

(No reference is made to Capital Transfer Tax which came into effect after the period under consideration.)

A number of these legislative changes extended the scope of wealth covered by the statistics, and insofar as much of this property would have been owned by those in the higher wealth ranges the changes would have led to an apparent increase in concentration. To this extent, therefore, the downward trend in the top shares would be under-stated. Working in the opposite direction has been the growth of certain forms of estate duty avoidance. Not all forms of avoidance lead to wealth being missing from the statistics, but where it does, this is likely to cause an under-statement of the degree of concentration. For example, the effect of rising rates of duty, and the closing of other loopholes undoubtedly led to a growth in non-dutiable trusts. To quote from the evidence of the Inland Revenue to the Select Committee on Wealth Tax: 'the figures . . . taken alone, would suggest that there has been a considerable reduction in the concentration of wealth over the past sixty years. However, this apparent reduction has to some extent been counterbalanced by a substantial growth in the value and numbers of non-dutiable trusts' (Select Committee on Wealth Tax 1975:1522). They go on to say that 'there is firm evidence that the numbers of discretionary and accumulating trusts have increased very substantially in the period from 1960 to 1972' (Select Committee on Wealth Tax 1975:1523).

Some indication of the possible effect of settled property may be obtained by taking our estimates in this chapter for 1961 and 1972 as a base and then adjusting for the estimates of non-dutiable settled property given by Revell (1967) and the Inland Revenue (Select Committee on Wealth Tax 1975: appendix 118). Allocating the property according to the assumptions described in chapter 4, the share of the top 5 per cent is as shown below.[12]

	Base	Adjusted for settled property
1961	60.8	61.9
1972	57.2	59.3

The annual (arithmetic) downward trend is now 0.24 per cent rather than 0.33 per cent, so that once again adjustments to the estimates may have a noticeable effect on the estimated trend.

In view of the shortcomings of our estimates described above, they need to be regarded with due caution; and it should be clear to the reader that they could — if necessary data were available — be refined considerably. It is of course possible that when all adjustments were made, the results would be the same as those in table 6.5; however to assume that this will in fact happen would at the present time be nothing more than an act of faith, since we have seen that corrections such as those for occupational pensions or settled property could have a noticeable effect on the measured trend. This should perhaps be emphasised, since there is a school of thought which argues that estate estimates are not dependable as a guide to the degree of concentration at a particular date, but *are* a reliable indicator of the trends over time. This position is adopted by Polanyi and Wood (1974) and appears to be held by the Inland Revenue: 'Because of the deficiencies in the data, the wealth estimates should probably not be used to derive a measure of the absolute

12 The total estimated from Revell (1967) for 1961 is £1,250m. surviving spouse settlements and £350m. other non-dutiable settled property (where we have, in contrast to chapter 4, included accumulating trusts). The Inland Revenue estimates for 1972 are £2,500m. and £6,000m. respectively, reflecting the much greater growth in the latter.

level of the concentration of the wealth of individuals *but they can be used to show the direction in which the level is changing'* (*Inland Revenue Statistics* 1974:176, our italics). The italicised part of this sentence is, however, only correct under certain assumptions about the nature of the errors. If the deficiencies affect all years equally, then it would obviously be right; if the observations are subject to sampling errors which are uncorrelated with the time variable, then again this position is correct. But if, as seems quite possible, there are trends in the extent of missing wealth, or other sources of error, then the changes over time may not be accurately measured by the observed data. In statistical terms, we are in effect omitting an explanatory variable and, if it is correlated with T, the estimated time trend will be biased. Although in practice the Inland Revenue may be right in saying that the *direction* is correctly indicated, the *magnitude* of the trend may be under- or over-stated.

6.4 Trends over time

In this section we examine the answers which may be derived from the data presented in tables 6.5 and 6.6 to the questions posed at the beginning of this chapter. In doing so we need to have regard both to the qualifications set out in the preceding section and to the limited scope of the estimates. In particular, we are concerned in this chapter only with estimates of the distribution of private property among the adult population as a whole, whereas when examining trends in the distribution, it is obviously important to take account of changes in age composition and life-cycle factors. Similarly, in interpreting the findings, we need to bear in mind the major social changes which have taken place over the past sixty years (such as the growth in owner-occupation); and in the shorter-term, the distribution of wealth may be substantially affected by movements in asset prices. These factors are considered in chapter 9.

First, it is interesting to compare our estimates with those given in earlier studies. To this end we have in table 6.7 presented our figures in the same form as in table 6.2. This covers the same periods, with the estimates being averaged over a number of years, except for 1911–13 which is excluded for the reasons described earlier. The only major differences are that our estimates relate to the economically independent population rather than those 25 and over (15 and over from 1960), and that we have not given estimates which involve extrapolation outside the range of the estate data.

The estimates for 1970 are relatively close, our figures being some 1–2 percentage points lower than those in table 6.2 (reflecting the fact that we have made an allowance for the wealth of the excluded population). For certain other years, however, the differences are more marked: for example, our estimate for 1960 shows the share of the top 1 per cent as 5 percentage points lower and that of the top 20 per cent as 7 points lower.[13] Such differences may not seem especially important, but again this illustrates the fact that the measurement of the trends may be more problematic than determining the degree of concentration at a point in time. Both sets of estimates could be said, for example, to be consistent with the view that the share of the top 5 per cent was 80 per cent in the 1920s and 70 per cent in the 1950s. However, in one case the estimated annual downward (arithmetic) trend is 0.6 per cent, whereas in the other it is 0.3 per cent. In the same way, the estimates agree that the share of the top 20 per cent in the 1960s was 85–90 per cent, but in one case the share fell at a rate of 0.4 per cent per annum and in the other the share rose very slightly.

If we turn now to the questions raised at the outset, the first step in answering them is to secure a standard geographical coverage. From figure 6.1, it appears that the distribution of wealth in Scotland has followed a rather different pattern from that in England and Wales.[14] Not only are the shares rather higher, but also the downward trend has been less marked for the top 5 per cent. Indeed the share of the top 10 per cent (not shown) in Scotland appears hardly to have declined at all over the 1960s (Harrison 1975).[15] At the same time, it is clear that the figures for England and Wales dominate the series for Great Britain, as one would expect from the relative sizes of the populations. From table 6.5 it may be seen that the series move closely in line. There appears to be a slight shift in the relationship between

13   It may be noted that the England and Wales figure for 1960 in table 6.1 is quite different from that given by our method (the share of the top 1% is 42% rather than 34% in table 6.5). It is possible that the 1960 figure in table 6.1 really relates to 1959, which would be closer in line with our estimates, but even then a discrepancy would remain. In our view the 1960 figure in table 6.1, even though it has been widely used by others apart from the Royal Commission, including one of the present authors, should not be regarded as very accurate.

14   The division between country is based on the domicile of the owner not the location of the property, so that property in Scotland owned by those living in England is included with the figures for England and Wales.

15   One possible explanation of this pattern is the difference in the extent of owner-occupation. As was noted by Wright in his comparison of personal wealth in Scotland and England, traditionally home-ownership in Scotland has been 'the exception rather than the rule' (1968:26). In 1961, 25% of the housing stock was owner-occupied, compared with a figure for England and Wales of 44%. Moreover, the growth of owner-occupation has been slower, rising only to 30% in 1971, compared with 52% for England and Wales. This slower growth, coupled with the lesser impact of rising house prices (because the owner-occupied sector is smaller), may be one of the explanations for the apparently divergent movements.

Table 6.7 Comparison of our estimates with those of earlier studies

	England and Wales			Great Britain		
	1924−30	1936	1951−6	1960	1965	1970
Earlier studies						
(table 6.2) ⋅						
Top 1%	60	56	42	39	34	31
5%	83	81	68	64	62	56
10%	90	88	79	76	75	70
20%	96	94	89	91	89	87
Our estimates (B3)						
Top 1%	58	54	44	34	33	30
5%	80	77	72	60	59	54
10%	87	86	−	72	72	69
20%	93	92	−	84	86	85

Sources: Tables 6.2 and 6.5.
Note: − denotes outside the range covered by the estate data.

the 1950s and the 1960s, but apart from that the differences are very small. The coefficient of correlation between the two series is in fact 0.99 for the top 1 per cent. In view of this we base most of the subsequent discussion on the longer series for England and Wales. This does not necessarily provide a reliable guide to what has happened in Scotland, but closely approximates the position for Great Britain as a whole. Moreover, the series for England and Wales is less likely to be subject to sampling fluctuations than that for Scotland.

The second step is to consider the sub-periods for which the estimates may be regarded as comparable. Our earlier discussion of the possible discontinuities, marked by dashed lines in the tables, suggests that it may be best to consider three sub-periods. This, however, seriously limits the conclusions which can be drawn from table 6.7, since we have only three observations on the trends over time: 1924−30 to 1936, 1960 to 1965, and 1965 to 1970. In fact, this approach to the measurement of the trends − via estimates averaged over a number of years − involves a significant loss of information. As we saw in the previous chapter, the main justification given for averaging the data over several years has been the presence of sampling errors and delays in recording, but where the underlying distribution has been changing over time it seems preferable to use a regression approach. For this reason we have not averaged the data, and have considered explicitly the determinants of $W_{x,t}^*$, the 'true' value of the share of the top x per cent. To this end, we have elaborated the model described in chapter 5 to allow for the possible discontinuities:

$$W_t^* = a + bT + cD_1 + dD_2 \qquad (1)$$

where T is a time trend, D_1 is a dummy variable (0 until 1938, 1 thereafter) to account for the once-for-all shift between 1938 and 1950, and D_2 is a dummy variable (0 until 1959, 1 thereafter) to account for the shift between 1959 and 1960.

In order to estimate this relationship, we assume that the errors follow the autoregressive process discussed in chapter 5, and proceed by first applying ordinary least squares and testing for serial correlation. Using the full set of observations for England and Wales (data based on assumption B3 and similar to those in table 6.5, but given to 2 decimal places), we obtained the following estimates for the share of the top 1 per cent, $\hat{W}_{1,t}$, and the top 5 per cent, $\hat{W}_{5,t}$, measured in percentage points:

$$\hat{W}_{1,t} = 60.6 - 0.42T - 2.19D_1 - 6.90D_2 \quad \bar{R}^2 = 0.98$$
$$\quad (6.5) \quad (1.6) \quad (7.1) \quad D.W. = 2.26 \tag{2}$$
$$\text{(corrected for 4 gaps)}$$

where the figures in brackets are t-statistics. The corresponding ordinary least squares equation for the top 5 per cent is:

$$\hat{W}_{5,t} = 82.7 - 0.42T + 1.88D_1 - 9.16D_2 \quad \bar{R}^2 = 0.98$$
$$\quad (6.6) \quad (1.1) \quad (9.5) \quad D.W. = 1.96 \tag{3}$$
$$\text{(corrected for 4 gaps)}$$

The Durbin–Watson statistic indicates that in both cases we cannot reject the hypothesis of zero first-order correlation at the 5 per cent level. In the case of the top 1 per cent, the statistic exceeds 2.0, indicating $p < 0$, but it is less than the critical value $(4 - d_u = 2.35)$. As noted in the previous chapter, a moving average error process may be more appropriate. Moreover, we have not considered in any detail the specification of the regression model (1), and the omission of relevant explanatory variables or the incorrect choice of functional form may lead to biased estimates of the coefficients. These considerations, discussed more fully in chapter 9, mean that the results should be regarded as preliminary.

Bearing these qualifications in mind, we now examine the implications of equations (2) and (3). First, they suggest that there was indeed a discrete shift between 1959 and 1960, and that it was quite substantial (some 7 per cent for the top 1 per cent). Such a shift clearly makes a lot of difference to the measurement of the trends and confirms that the Royal Commission were right to sub-divide the period. (The shift variable 1938/1950 is not significant at the 5 per cent level.) When allowance has been made for the structural shift, the trend in the share of the top 1 per cent turns out to be around 0.4 per cent per annum. Extrapolating this trend into the future, a share for the top 1 per cent of 30 per cent in 1970 would fall to 18 per cent by the year 2000. This clearly represents a major decline. At the same time, the annual (arithmetic) trend rate of decline for the top 5 per cent is also 0.4 per cent, so that decline is confined to the top 1 per cent – a point to which we return.

As we have seen earlier in the chapter, the discontinuity between 1959 and 1960 is associated with the much more restricted coverage of the estate data in the 1950s, and the shift may in part be explained by our making too small an allowance for the wealth of the excluded population during that period.[16] It would however require a very substantial addition to the wealth of the excluded population in 1959 to reduce the share of the top 1 per cent by 7 percentage points. In 1959 the total wealth of the excluded population was taken as £12.4 billion. Supposing that this figure was raised by £5 billion, this would reduce the share by 3.3 percentage points. To lower it by 7 per cent would need an additional £10 billion or more. The same point may be illustrated by taking the Lydall and Tipping estimate for 1954, which is larger than our B3 figure. As explained in appendix VI, there are reasons for believing this to be too high, but even so it would only reduce the share of the top 1 per cent by some 3 percentage points. It is possible therefore that some half of the shift between the 1950s and the 1960s could be explained by our allowance for the wealth of the excluded population being too low, but it seems unlikely that this factor can explain the whole of the apparent shift.[17]

The second hypothesis we wish to examine is that the trend has been accelerating over time. As it was put by the Sunday Times, 'the erosion of the share of personal wealth held by the richest [has been] gradual during the first half of the 20th century, but gathering momentum since the Second World War' (3 August 1975). This view was argued by Polanyi and Wood (1974) on the basis of the estimates in table 6.2, and, as noted at the beginning of the chapter, the trend for the top 10 per cent appears from these estimates to have changed from zero (1911–13 to 1924–30) to −0.6 per cent per annum over the 1960s. However, we have seen that there are a number of difficulties with this argument. For example, the estimates for 1911–13 are not comparable with those for later years. In particular, the shares in 1911–13 are likely to be biased downwards relative to those for 1924–30 on account of the greater omission of settled property, and this

16 This paragraph has benefited from very helpful comments by Michael Parsonage of the Royal Commission.
17 To the extent that the estimates for the 1950s are too high (on account of the allowance for the excluded population being too low), there will have been a faster rate of decline between 1938 and 1950 than indicated by the trend – see chapter 9.

Table 6.8 Regression results for time trends 1923–72

Dependent variable	Constant	Time	Time squared	Dummy variables D_1	D_2	$\bar{R}^2$	D.W.
(a) W_1	60.6	−0.42 (6.5)	–	−2.91 (1.6)	−6.90 (7.1)	0.98	2.26
(b) W_1	60.8	−0.45 (3.7)	0.0006 (0.3)	−2.72 (1.4)	−7.1 (6.0)	0.98	2.28
(c) W_1	60.5	−0.33 (3.3)	−0.0065 (3.3)	–	–	0.96	1.26
(d) W_{s-1}	22.0	−0.003 (0.1)	–	4.79 (5.1)	−2.26 (4.5)	0.87	1.68

may obscure the downward trend in the early part of the period. Similarly, Polanyi and Wood attach considerable weight to the movements in the share of the bottom 80 per cent (1974:19) but this is likely to be subject to substantial errors of interpolation (as we have seen to be the case in the 1950s).

Considering the period after the First World War, and taking the unaveraged annual data, we may test the acceleration view by extending the regression model to include T^2, which on this hypothesis would have a significant negative coefficient. The results is shown in line (b) of table 6.8. This casts doubt on the acceleration hypothesis as far as the arithmetic trend in the share of the top 1 per cent is concerned, since the coefficient on T^2 is far from being significant. The impression of acceleration may arise from the once-for-all shift between 1959 and 1960. If we estimate the equation leaving out the dummy variables D_1 and D_2 (line (c) in table 6.8), then T^2 is significant but the equation gives a less satisfactory fit. In particular, the Durbin–Watson statistic suggests that it is mis-specified, and examination of the residuals bears this out: for example in the 1960s there is a systematic tendency to over-prediction in the early years and under-prediction in the latter part of the period.

A constant *arithmetic* downward trend implies an accelerating *geometric* trend, and in this sense our data may be seen as supporting the hypothesis. However even here we must exercise caution, since we have not so far taken account of the range of estimates (B2–B4) for each year, or of the possible errors introduced by interpolation. Some idea of the robustness of the results may be obtained by taking:

W_1^{max} — using B4 and the linear upper bound on the share $\left.\begin{array}{c}\\\\\\\end{array}\right\}$ of top 1 per cent

W_1^{min} — using B2 and the linear lower bound on the share

(The linear upper and lower bounds are those defined in chapter 5.) These suggest that, apart from the 1950s, the range for the share of the top 1 per cent is around 2 percentage points, which does not seem unacceptable as far as measuring the degree of concentration at a point in time is concerned. Turning to the measurement of the changes over time, the arithmetic trend between 1924–30 (averaged) and 1936 ranged from 0.24 per cent per annum (W_1^{min} to W_1^{max}) to 0.66 per cent (W_1^{max} to W_1^{min}). This may be compared with the 95 per cent confidence interval for the time trend of 0.29–0.56 per cent derived from equation (2). Finally, the measures of the *acceleration* of the downward trend are highly sensitive to the variation of the estimates — to the extent that we cannot reject the hypothesis that the geometric trend was the same over 1924–30 to 1936 as over 1960–2 to 1970–2.

The third hypothesis about the trends concerns the extent to which the declining share has been a feature of all top wealth groups. As we saw earlier, the arithmetic trend for the top 5 per cent is essentially the same as for the top 1 per cent, suggesting that the next 4 per cent have maintained their share constant. This may be tested directly by estimating equations for the share of this group, denoted by W_{5-1}. The results are shown in line (d) of table 6.8. In this equation, the trend is insignificantly different from zero. On this basis it appears that the next 4 per cent have not actually increased their share (in contrast to table 6.1), but that the redistribution away from top wealth groups has been confined to the top 1 per cent. Again, however, we have to bear in mind that this conclusion may be sensitive to the specification both of $W_{5-1,t}^{*}$ and of the error process.

6.5   Conclusions

In the course of this chapter we have emphasised certain points which have tended to be neglected in earlier studies of trends in the distribution of wealth. Most importantly, we feel that these studies have tended to understate the difficulties involved in making comparisons over time. There is a widespread belief that it is easier to measure the changes in the distribution over time than the degree of concentration in one particular year. However, this ignores, among other things, the changes in estate duty law and practice, the varying coverage of the estate data, and the difficulties in making comparable adjustments for the wealth of the excluded population or for other missing wealth. This does not mean that such estimates of the trends cannot be made – and one of the main aims of the chapter has been to produce a consistent series– but they must be treated with at least as much caution as the figures for the level of concentration.

The estimates which we have derived are, for the reasons described, far from fully satisfactory; we have however tried to apply more closely than in the past a consistent method of construction. Moreover, we have produced estimates for all available years over the period 1923–72, having argued that it is preferable to use estimates for individual years rather than several-year averages as in past studies. The main features of these estimates are:

> – a downward trend of some 0.4 per cent per annum in the share of the top 1 per cent (with a once-for-all jump between 1959 and 1960),
>
> – no apparent acceleration in the arithmetic rate of decline in the share of the top 1 per cent,
>
> – no apparent downward trend in the share of the next 4 per cent (but a jump upwards between 1938 and 1950, and a jump downwards between 1959 and 1960).

7

INVESTMENT INCOME APPROACH

The main features of the investment income method have been described in chapter 1. In essence it involves the application of a yield multiplier to the distribution of investment income to arrive at an estimate of the wealth distribution. The first section describes the method and sources in greater detail, comparing the approach adopted here with that in earlier studies. Section 7.2 examines the choice of yield multipliers, which are of critical importance. The third section presents results based on this method for 1968 and 1972, and these are contrasted with the estimates given in chapter 5. Section 7.4 then describes the main deficiencies of the investment income approach, and attempts to assess their quantitative importance. The final section summarises the conclusions to be drawn from the analysis.

7.1 Method and sources

The investment income method may be set out formally as follows. Suppose that an individual with wealth w invests an amount A_j in assets of type j, where j is an index of the asset classification ($j = 1, \ldots, J$). If the return obtained by the individual on asset type j is R_j, his total investment income is:

$$Y = \sum_{j=1}^{J} R_j A_j \tag{1}$$

The simplest case to consider is that where the proportion of wealth held in each asset type is the same at all levels of wealth ($A_j = \beta_j w$ where β_j is a constant). The wealth/investment income relationship is:

$$w = Y \bigg/ \left(\sum_{j=1}^{J} R_j \beta_j \right) \tag{2}$$

and the distribution of wealth is then a simple multiple of the investment income distribution. The yield multiplier is constant and the degree of concentration, as measured for example by the Gini coefficient or the coefficient of variation, is the same for wealth as for the distribution of investment income. However, although this case is straightforward, it is unrealistic in a number of respects, and needs to be elaborated.

The first factor which has to be taken into account is that the asset composition is likely to change with the level of wealth. In fact, we have seen in chapter 4 that there is a marked variation in the portfolio structure. There is, for example, a tendency for the proportion of wealth held in life assurance policies to fall with w and for the proportion held in ordinary shares to rise with w. The implications of this may be seen in the special case where A_j is linearly dependent on w:

$$A_j = B_j + \beta_j w, \text{ where } \sum_j B_j = 0, \sum_j \beta_j = 1 \text{ and } \beta_j \geqslant 0 \text{ all } j \tag{3}$$

(we consider a range of wealth $w \geqslant w_0$, where w_0 is such that $A_j \geqslant 0$ all j). The relationship between w and Y is then:

$$w = \frac{Y - \sum_j R_j B_j}{\sum_j R_j \beta_j} \tag{4}$$

In this case the degree of concentration of w is not in general equal to that of the investment income distribution. For example, the estimated coefficient of variation of wealth $\hat{V}_w$ is related to the coefficient of variation of investment income V_Y by the formula:

$$(\hat{V}_w)^2 = V_Y^2 \left[1 + \frac{\sum_j R_j B_j}{\sum_j R_j \beta_j \bar{w}} \right]^2 \tag{5}$$

It seems reasonable to assume that $\sum R_j \beta_j > 0$ (i.e. that investment income increases with wealth), but $\sum R_j B_j$ may take either sign. If assets with a wealth elasticity greater than unity (i.e. $B_j < 0$, which means that they form an increasing proportion of the portfolio as w rises) tend to have a high return, so $\sum R_j B_j < 0$, then the concentration of wealth is less than that of investment income. This may appear at first sight to be the empirically more likely case than that where assets with elasticities greater than unity have low returns; however, it has to be remembered throughout our discussion that the investment income data we use relate to *taxable* income. If those with high wealth, and consequently high marginal tax rates, choose assets which generate large capital gains but little taxable income, then R_j and B_j will tend to be positively correlated, and the concentration of wealth greater than that of investment income.

The second way in which the method needs to be developed is to allow for the possibility that the return to individual asset types (R_j) may depend on the level of wealth. This could come about because larger holdings attract a higher return: for example, commercial banks pay a higher rate of interest on deposit account holdings above a certain level. In such cases R_j would be an increasing function of w. A consideration working in the opposite direction is that those with high wealth and high marginal tax rates are likely to choose within a particular category of assets those which have a low taxable return. The implications of R_j varying with w may be seen most simply in the case where:

$$R_j = r_j - \rho_j/w \tag{6}$$

(again for w greater than or equal to some minimum w_0) so that the return rises with w if $\rho_j > 0$ and falls if $\rho_j < 0$. If for simplicity we take $B_j = 0$, so that there are constant asset proportions, we obtain a formula analogous to (5):

$$(\hat{V}_w)^2 = V_Y^2 \left[1 - \frac{\sum_j \beta_j \rho_j}{\sum_j r_j \beta_j \overline{w}} \right]^2 \tag{7}$$

If the overall return (Y/w) rises with w, then $\sum_j \beta_j \rho_j > 0$, and the coefficient of variation for wealth is less than that for investment income; conversely, if the overall return falls with w, then $\hat{V}_w^2$ exceeds V_Y^2.

Thirdly, we should allow for the possibility that people with the same wealth may have different attitudes to risk and differing tastes concerning the type of assets they wish to hold. Those who are risk-averse may prefer building society deposits to unit trust holdings. We should therefore expect to find, corresponding to any w, a *distribution* of investment income. The same effect is produced by the fact that the yields may vary between individuals with the same wealth. Given that individuals may have different luck in their choice of investment, people with the same *ex ante* expected yield may have different *ex post* incomes. Within the asset category 'ordinary shares' some choose a company that does well and some choose a company which passes its dividend. In terms of the simple model set out in equation (2), these considerations mean that the distribution of Y conditional on w depends on the distribution of taste variables (β_j) and *ex post* returns (R_j). The latter aspect – the variation in the rate of return – and its influence on the estimated distribution of wealth are examined further in appendix VII.

The standard investment income method applied in earlier studies takes account of the first of these factors (the varying portfolio composition with wealth) but not of the second or third; and the same practice is followed here. The reason for this is that we lack the data necessary to make adequate allowance for the variation in the rate of return or for differences in attitudes towards risk. At the same time, we have extended the previous analysis in section 7.4, where we attempt to make some estimate of the likely magnitude of the bias arising from variation in the rates of return, making use of the formulae given above and derived in appendix VII.

The data which we were able to employ relate to investment income (Y), to the yields (R_j) and to the asset composition (A_j). In the remainder of this section, we describe the main features of the data and draw attention to the way in which our treatment differs from that in earlier work by Barna (1945) and Stark (1972).

(a) *Classification of assets.* The classification of assets is restricted by the form in which data are made available by the Inland Revenue. Barna (1945) in his study for 1937 took 12 categories of asset; Stark (1972) took 15 categories. We felt it desirable to use as fine a classification as possible and therefore employ 28 categories of asset and liabilities as distinguished in the relevant Inland Revenue data. These categories are listed in table 7.1 and are described in more detail in appendix VIII.

(b) *Investment income data.* The possible sources are the distributions of net investment income by ranges as recorded by the Inland Revenue in the surtax returns and in the Survey of Personal Incomes. The former is limited in scope and covers only those liable to surtax (as it then was); the latter is an annual sample survey of incomes and covers a large part of the population. The two sources give slightly different results (for ranges where they overlap) because the Survey is a sample and because the surtax returns are based on more up-to-date information.[1] The latter feature is one reason for preferring to use the surtax returns. In addition, it is thought that the Survey is significantly incomplete in lower ranges, since below the surtax (higher rate) threshold investment income is not necessarily reported where tax has already been paid. In view of these considerations, we have used the surtax returns, even though their coverage is limited to the upper income ranges. It should be emphasised that the investment income data relate to tax units, rather than to individuals, which raises problems of comparability with the estate method estimates. The incomes of husbands and wives are aggregated as one unit, and this is not affected by provisions for separate assessment or taxation. In the relevant years (1968–9 and 1972–3) the income of minors was not aggregated, unless it was investment income from a deed of covenant provided by the parent (aggregated with that of the parents where the minor

1 In the 1968–9 Survey, estimates are based on figures available at the end of that year (*Inland Revenue Statistics* 1971:69), whereas the surtax estimates are based on assessments before 30 June 1971 (15 months after the end of the year of assessment). The surtax data were kindly made available by the Inland Revenue; the published data (*Inland Revenue Statistics* 1971: table 4.7) refer to assessments before 30 June 1970. The year of assessment for surtax was the year *following*, i.e. 1969–70 for 1968–9.

was unmarried — see Stark 1977). The income of adult dependent relatives and permanent housekeepers is not included.

(c) *Yields.* The sources for the yields are described in the next section. As pointed out above, the definition of income is that applied for tax purposes, which means that non-taxable income (such as interest on national savings certificates) is excluded, as are capital gains (although not, of course, the corresponding wealth).

(d) *Asset composition.* Ideally we should like to use data on the asset composition derived from the income side. Thus, if the investment income data were classified by type (Y_j), the yield multiplier applicable to investment income $Y, R(Y)$, could be calculated as

$$\frac{1}{R(Y)} = \sum_{j=1}^{J} \frac{Y_j}{Y} \frac{1}{R_j} \tag{8}$$

However, the income data available to us were only tabulated according to very broad categories[2] and were not suitable for this purpose. For this reason, following earlier studies, we had to use the asset composition data estimated by the estate duty method as described in earlier chapters. The implications of this are examined in section 7.4. It should be noted that the asset composition figures, in contrast to those used, for example, by Barna (1945), are based on *wealth-holdings* rather than *estates.* This avoids the bias arising from the over-representation in the estate data of the assets held dispro-portionately by the elderly. As has been shown by Revell (1962) this bias may be quite serious as far as the composition is concerned, assets such as unquoted shares, insurance policies and household goods being under-stated, and assets such as government securities and building society deposits being over-stated.

The steps involved in the investment income method as used here, and the relationship with the estate duty approach, are summarised in figure 7.1.

7.2 Construction of the yield multipliers

This stage involves the calculation of yields for different categories of asset. We are concerned with that part of the return which is taxable as investment income, and income in such forms as capital gains or imputed rent on owner-occupied houses is not relevant. Earlier investigators made

2 For example, the *Survey of Personal Incomes* 1969–70 gives (i) dividends, interest, etc. taxed at source, (ii) Schedule D (Case VIII) and Schedule B, (iii) other government interest, income from abroad, occasional profits and short-term capital gains, and interest from building societies, and (iv) deductions from investment income.

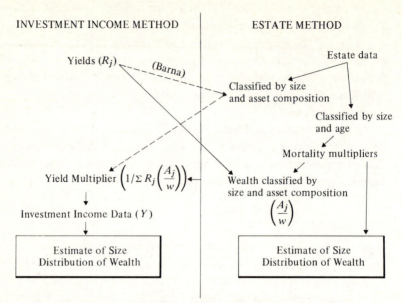

INVESTMENT INCOME METHOD

ESTATE METHOD

Figure 7.1 Investment income and estate methods

use of a variety of sources. Barna (1945), for example, took the sources shown below.

Asset	Source
British government securities Other government securities Shares	Averages of actual yields from issuing source
Insurance policies, household goods and trade assets	Zero return (income from trade assets in personal ownership is treated as earned income)
Cash and bank deposits Money lent on bonds, bills, etc. Other personalty	Assumed rates of return
Five categories of real property	Based on average number of year's purchase published by Inland Revenue

(The last of the sources is no longer available in the form used by Barna.)

The study by Stark (1972) for 1954–63 relied on averages of actual yields from issuing sources and, in the case of land and buildings, on data

from the Inland Revenue income surveys. In estimating the yields used here
for 1968–9 and 1972–3, we have followed methods similar to those of
Stark, although these have been modified in a number of respects. In
particular, we have used a finer classification of assets, with 28 categories
rather than 15, and have made a number of modifications and corrections to
Stark's analysis.[3]

The asset categories are set out in table 7.1, together with the yields for
1968–9 and 1972–3. The methods employed in deriving the yields are
described in detail in appendix VIII. In broad terms, they may be characterised as follows (the letters refer to the key in table 7.1):

> *Yield intrinsically zero (in terms of taxable investment income)*
> a, p, q, t, u
>
> *Yield available from issuing sources*
> b, o, r, s
>
> *Based on representative yields available from issuing sources*
> $c, d, e, f, g, h, i, n, \alpha, \beta$
>
> *Based on yield indices*
> j, k, l, m
>
> *Assumed yield*
> v, w
>
> *Based on income tax data*
> $x, y, z.$

These different methods are subject to varying degrees of error and the
estimates are of varying reliability. They range from those about which we
can be certain (e.g. the yield on cash), through those which are fairly firmly
based (e.g. government securities), to those which involve a substantial
element of guesswork (e.g. other personalty). To give some rough indication of
their relative accuracy, we have classified the categories in table 7.1 according
to the following scale:

> –   zero by definition
> *   relatively accurate (likely spread of yield multiplier ± 5 per
>   cent)
> **   moderately accurate (likely spread of yield multiplier ± 10
>   per cent)
> ***   less reliable (likely spread of yield multiplier ± 15 per cent)
> ****   relatively unreliable (likely spread of yield multiplier ± 25
>   per cent).

The term 'likely spread' applies to the *mean* return to that asset class, not
to the range of returns to individual wealth-holders; and the percentage
relates to the yield multiplier, so that the range for category (b) in 1968–9 is

---

3 For example, Stark included the interest on national savings certificates, which
   is not subject to tax and does not appear in the investment income statistics.
   The appropriate rate is therefore zero.

22.2 ± 1.1 (22.2 being the reciprocal of 4.5 per cent). It is founded in some cases on rather tentative judgements and the basis for the classification is discussed further in appendix VIII.

The importance of inaccuracies in the multipliers depends on how large a role is played by the particular asset category in wealth portfolios. If we consider the composition of wealth-holdings of £50,000 and over — the group with whom we are mainly concerned in subsequent analysis — this shows that

Table 7.1 Yields on different assets 1968—9 and 1972—3

Key		Asset	Classification	Yield % 1968—9	1972—3
a		National savings certificates and premium bonds (1)	—	0	0
b		Defence, development and savings bonds; tax reserve certificates (2)	*	4.5	5.9
c		Government securities maturing in less than 5 years (3)	**	5.2	5.6
d		Government securities maturing in 5 to 14 years (4)	**	6.6	8.4
e		Government securities maturing in 15 years or more (5)	**	7.8	9.5
f		2½% consols and undated government securities (6)	**	7.9	9.6
g		Northern Ireland and municipal securities (7,8)	**	8.0	7.9
h	[Stark]	Commonwealth government securities (9)	***	5.9	6.4
i	[Stark]	Other foreign government securities (10)	***	5.4	4.6
j	[Stark]	British unquoted ordinary shares (11)	****	3.5	3.4
k	[Stark]	British quoted ordinary shares (13,14)	***	3.5	3.4
l	[Stark]	British preference shares and debentures (12,15)	***	7.6	9.7
m	[Stark]	Overseas company shares (16—18)	***	3.2	3.1
n		Unit trusts (19)	**	2.8	2.7
o		Building society shares and deposits (21)	*	7.4	8.0
p		Household goods, etc. (25)	—	0	0
q		Policies of insurance (26)	—	0	0
r		Post Office and Trustee Savings Bank accounts (28)	*	3.8	5.2
s	[Stark]	Commercial bank deposit accounts (29)	*	5.4	5.3
t		Commercial bank current accounts (30), cash in the house (27)	—	0	0
u		Trade, business and professional assets (31—37)	—	0	0
v		Money on mortgage, bonds, etc. (20,22,23,38)	****	5.6	6.7
w		Other personalty (24,39—41) see note (ii)	****	3.0	3.1
x		Land (49,50,55,57)	****	1.3	0.9
y		Buildings residential (51,53)	****	1.1	0.7
z		Buildings other (52,54)	****	1.3	0.9

Table 7.1 (cont.)

Key	Liabilities	Classification	Yield % 1968–9	1972–3
α	Debts owing to residents in Great Britain and other deductions (43,46)	***	9.3	9.5
β	Mortgages and other deductions (59,60)	**	7.5	8.3

Notes: (i) The numbers in brackets refer to the Inland Revenue's classification numbers for categories of wealth as used in, for example *Inland Revenue Statistics* 1971: table 115.

(ii) For 1972–3, there are two minor differences in the classification of 'other personalty' (*w*) which includes item 38 and cash gifts.

(iii) No account has been taken of short-term capital gains subject to income tax. This biases the estimated yields downwards but the overall effect must be rather small. In addition, no account has been taken of the fact that in certain cases the income refers to that in the previous year; this is, however, likely to be of limited quantitative importance.

(iv) [Stark] indicates that we employed the same method as in Stark (1972).

(v) In certain cases the yields for 1968–9 represent a revision of those published in Atkinson and Harrison (1974: 134).

two crucial elements are the return to ordinary shares, quoted and unquoted, and the return to land and buildings. In 1972, shares accounted for 39 per cent of total net wealth in the range £50,000 – £100,000, and land and buildings for 25 per cent (*Inland Revenue Statistics* 1974: table 106). In the top wealth range (£200,000 and above), the proportions were 60 per cent and 23 per cent, respectively. These two types of asset, which in all the ranges considered accounted for over half of total wealth, are singled out for especial attention when we consider the sensitivity of the results in section 7.4.

Combining the asset composition data with the yields from table 7.1 gives the overall yield multiplier for each of the wealth ranges, and hence the 'yield curve' linking *w* and *Y*. Before this, however, one needs to determine which wealth ranges are relevant, working back from the available income data. As explained earlier, we have used the surtax returns. In 1968–9, liability to surtax commenced at £2,000 of 'assessed' taxable income: i.e. income in excess of certain personal allowances. These allowances were £120 for a married man, £465 for a married man with 3 children (under 11), and so on. A person with investment income of at least £3,000 would therefore typically be included in the statistics. At lower levels of investment income, however, the coverage becomes progressively less complete. In view of this we have confined our attention to investment income of £3,000 and over. In 1972–3, surtax commenced at £3,000 and for the same reason we have taken investment income ranges of £4,000 and over.

The restricted nature of the investment income data means, however, that we are only able to make use of the uppermost ranges in the estate estimates. Taking for the purposes of illustration a yield of 3 per cent, we can see that £3,000 investment income corresponds to wealth of £100,000. The asset composition data, on the other hand, do not provide a very extensive breakdown by wealth ranges. Even if we go down to £50,000 we can only make use of the following ranges:

1968–9: £50,000–,   £60,000–, £100,000–, £200,000– (4 ranges)
1972–3: £50,000–,   £100,000–, £200,000–   (3 ranges)

Calculating the yield multipliers, and applying them to the mean wealth in each class, gives the central yields curves plotted in figures 7.2a and 7.2b. From this it is obvious that a considerable amount of interpolation and extrapolation is involved. The procedure adopted in drawing the lines was to (i) interpolate linearly and (ii) extrapolate using the last two observed points. This procedure is far from being fully satisfactory. It would be preferable, for example, to use fitted asset portfolio equations; however, the data were not available in a suitable form. At the same time, we have sought to reduce the error of extrapolation by combining all income units above £15,000 into a single group (with average investment income of approximately £27,000).[4]

The yield curves shown by the solid lines in figure 7.2 are those employed to produce the 'central' estimates given in the next section. It may however be helpful to show the effect on the yield curve of the possible errors in the individual yields. Suppose that for each of the assets the yield multiplier $(1/R_j)$ is increased by the maximum amount indicated in the classification in table 7.1: e.g. the yield multiplier for unit trusts is raised by 10 per cent. This generates the yield curve shown by the upper dashed lines in figure 7.2, and a corresponding calculation taking the minimum yield multiplier generates the lower dashed lines. These curves give some indication of the range of variation in the overall multiplier.[5] This range is quite substantial, with the wealth corresponding to a given investment income ranging by ± 20 per cent in 1968–9 and rather more in 1972–3, which limits the conclusions which can be drawn.

---

4 It should also be noted that the largest estate range in 1972 appears to have an unusually high proportion of liabilities (see table 4.3). This may be a reflection of the estate sample in that particular year and may cause the yield to be biased downwards – see below.

5 In these calculations, and in table 7.2, the interest payable on liabilities (a,β) was held at its central value.

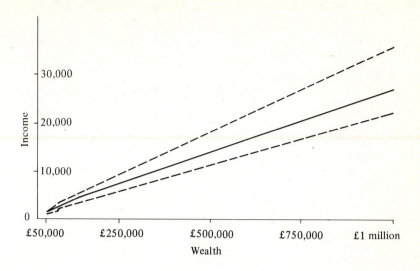

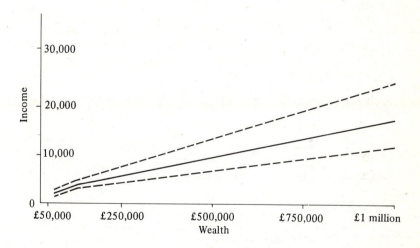

Figure 7.2 Yield curves 1968—9 and 1972—3

A more detailed analysis of the sensitivity of the yield curve is provided by table 7.2, which shows the contribution of individual asset categories to the variation in the yield curve in 1968—9. This reflects both the likely spread of yields and the importance of particular asset categories. Again this bears out

Table 7.2 Sensitivity of yield curve to individual asset yields 1968–9

Change in overall percentage yield as a result of increasing/decreasing multiplier by extent of likely spread.
(Excluding assets where zero yield or where change less than 0.01 in all cases)

Asset type		£50,000–	£60,000–	£100,000–	£200,000–
c Short-term	+	0.01	0.01	0.01	0.01
government	–	–	0.01	0.01	0.01
d Medium-term	+	0.01	0.01	0.01	0.01
government	–	0.01	0.01	0.01	0.01
e Long-term	+	0.01	0.01	0.01	–
government	–	0.01	0.01	0.01	–
f Consols and	+	0.01	0.01	0.01	–
undated	–	0.01	0.01	0.01	–
g Northern Ireland	+	0.01	0.01	0.01	–
and municipal	–	0.01	0.01	0.01	–
j British unquoted	+	0.08	0.07	0.09	0.34
shares	–	0.05	0.04	0.05	0.21
k British quoted	+	0.21	0.25	0.27	0.18
shares	–	0.15	0.19	0.20	0.13
l British preference	+	0.06	0.05	0.04	0.02
shares	–	0.04	0.03	0.03	0.02
m Overseas shares	+	0.02	0.02	0.03	0.02
	–	0.01	0.02	0.02	0.02
o Building society	+	0.02	0.02	0.01	–
	–	0.02	0.01	0.01	–
s Commercial bank	+	0.01	0.01	0.01	0.01
deposits	–	0.01	0.01	0.01	0.01
v Money on mortgage	+	0.09	0.10	0.09	0.05
etc.	–	0.06	0.06	0.05	0.03
w Other personalty	+	0.05	0.05	0.04	0.09
	–	0.03	0.03	0.03	0.05
x Land	+	0.03	0.02	0.03	0.03
	–	0.02	0.01	0.02	0.02
y Residential buildings	+	0.04	0.03	0.02	0.03
	–	0.03	0.02	0.01	0.02
z Other buildings	+	0.01	0.01	–	–
	–	–	–	–	–

Note: The figures have been rounded to the nearest 0.01%. A dash denotes a change less than 0.01% in absolute magnitude. The figures measure the change in the *percentage* yield, so that a figure of 0.1 would mean that the return rose (say) from 5% to 5.1%.

the key role played by ordinary shares and land and buildings, although there are certain other categories, such as money on mortgage and other personalty, which may be important because of their **** rating (it must be remembered that our ranking convention is the reverse of that in the *Guide Michelin*). To help put the results in perspective, we may note that a reduction of 0.10 in table 7.2, starting from a base yield of 3 per cent, would raise the estimated wealth corresponding to a given investment income by some $3\frac{1}{2}$ per cent. This may be compared with a difference in the overall total wealth of $13\frac{3}{4}$ per cent arising from the use of A4 (life office) rather than A1 (Inland Revenue) multipliers – see table 3.4.

7.3   Results and comparison with estate estimates

In this section we describe the results obtained using the investment income method, and compare them with those derived from the estate approach. The differences between the results from the two methods have been examined by writers dealing with *total* personal wealth, and this was indeed a major concern of early investigators (see, for example, Mallet and Strutt (1915) and the subsequent discussion). There has, however, been little effort made to see how far the estimates of the *size distribution* from the two sources may be reconciled. This is rather surprising, since the figures necessary for such a comparison were compiled in studies by Barna (1945) and others.

The number of tax units, and average investment income in each range of investment income, are shown in the first 3 columns of tables 7.3a and 7.3b. They are taken from the surtax returns and by definition relate only to the upper income ranges. (As noted earlier, the Surveys of Personal Income provide information covering the whole income range, but there are a number of ways in which this is less satisfactory for our purpose.) This means that the data for 1968–9, for example, cover only some 116,000 tax units, or around $\frac{1}{2}$ per cent of the total. These top wealth-holders are, however, of particular interest, and it is estimates for this group which may be most affected by estate duty avoidance. For these reasons the results given below, although limited in coverage, are still of considerable value.

The conversion from investment income to net worth is made using the central multiplier in figure 7.2. The resulting wealth ranges and average levels of wealth are shown in columns 4 and 5 of tables 7.3a and 7.3b, and the cumulative numbers and total wealth in columns 6 and 7.

In comparing these estimates (referred to as the II estimates) with those obtained from the estate method (referred to as the ED estimates), the following points need to be taken into account:

(a) *Date*

The ED estimates relate to the calendar year, the II estimates to the tax year. In order to make approximate allowance for the possible bias caused by asset values rising over time, we have taken an average of the ED estimates for 1968 and 1969 with weights of three quarters and one quarter respectively (corresponding to the assumption about the delay with which estates appear in the statistics). In the case of 1972, we did not at the time have access to comparable data for 1973, so that this adjustment is not made.

Table 7.3a Investment income and derived holdings of wealth – United Kingdom 1968–9

1. Investment income (lower limit of range) £	2. Number of income units	3. Average investment income £	4. Derived wealth range (lower limit) £	5. Derived average wealth £	6. Cumulative total (Numbers)	7. Cumulative total (Wealth) £ million
3,000	43,349	3,447	98,000	112,000	116,100	25,170
4,000	23,595	4,458	129,200	145,400	72,800	20,310
5,000	14,013	5,462	165,600	182,800	49,200	16,880
6,000	15,117	6,874	202,900	235,500	35,200	14,320
8,000	7,284	8,902	277,600	311,200	20,000	10,760
10,000	4,010	10,910	352,200	386,200	12,800	8,490
12,000	3,380	13,326	426,900	476,400	8,700	6,940
15,000	5,364	27,199	538,900	994,200	5,400	5,330

Source: The data given in columns 1–3 were supplied by the Inland Revenue, and are a more up-to-date version of table 47 in *Inland Revenue Statistics* 1971.

Note: Columns 4 and 5 are rounded to the nearest £100; column 6 is rounded to the nearest 100, and column 7 to the nearest £10 million.

Table 7.3b Investment income and derived holdings of wealth – United Kingdom 1972–3

1. Investment income (lower limit of range) £	2. Number of income units	3. Average investment income £	4. Derived wealth range (lower limit) £	5. Derived average wealth £	6. Cumulative total (Numbers)	7. Cumulative total (Wealth) £ million
4,000	30,544	4,460	130,660	160,300	92,900	35,550
5,000	18,206	5,470	195,200	225,500	62,400	30,650
6,000	19,025	6,866	259,700	315,600	44,200	26,550
8,000	9,313	8,910	388,700	447,400	25,200	20,550
10,000	5,145	10,911	517,700	576,500	15,800	16,380
12,000	4,184	13,346	646,800	733,600	10,700	13,410
15,000	6,500	26,564	840,300	1,586,400	6,500	10,340

Source: Data in columns 1–3 from a more detailed version of table 23 in *Inland Revenue Statistics* 1975, supplied by the Inland Revenue.
Note: Columns 4 and 5 are rounded to the nearest £100; column 6 is rounded to the nearest 100, and column 7 to the nearest £10 million.

(*b*) *Country*

The ED estimates relate to Great Britain but the II estimates to the United Kingdom. An approximate adjustment is made to the ED estimates by increasing all figures proportionately (the numbers in relation to the total population aged 15 and over, and total wealth in relation to Revell's figures for 1961 (1967:147)).

(*c*) *Tax unit*

The ED estimates relate to individuals, whereas the II estimates relate to income units, which aggregate the income of husbands and wives. If only one partner in a marriage owns assets, this would make no difference, but where both wives and husbands possess wealth, the number of income units with wealth above £*w* is higher than the number of individuals above £*w*. The problem of 'marrying-up' individuals in the ED estimates is discussed in chapter 9. Here we make use of the two extreme assumptions described there:

(i) rich married to poor – where it is assumed that those in the upper wealth ranges are married to spouses with no wealth. The total number (total wealth) of tax units with wealth above £*w* would then be the sum of the number (wealth) of males and females shown above £*w* in the estate estimates. (This was the procedure followed in Atkinson and Harrison 1974).

(ii) rich married to rich – where it is assumed that the wealthiest married males are married to the wealthiest married females.[6] This involves combining the wealth of two individuals to form a single unit, which in itself reduces the total numbers above £*w* but not the total wealth, and introducing new tax units where the individual wealth was below £*w* but whose combined total is greater, which increases both the total numbers and the total wealth above £*w*.

(*d*) *Adjustment for wealth missing or incorrectly valued*

The asset composition information used to make the investment income estimates was obtained following the Inland Revenue approach, and therefore no adjustment has been made for missing wealth (e.g. certain settled property) or for the differences in methods of valuation described in chapter 4. For purposes of comparison, we take therefore the 'first stage' ED estimates of chapter 5 (constructed on A3/B3 assumptions).

6 It is assumed that the proportion married is independent of the level of wealth and no restriction is placed on the ages of the hypothetical marriages – see chapter 9.

The results of the investment income method are graphed in figures 7.3a and 7.3b, together with the ED estimates. The latter are on a tax-year (for 1968–9), UK basis as described, and have been converted to tax units on the first of the two assumptions set out above ('rich married to poor'). The range of wealth covered is broadly £100,000–£500,000. As we have seen, the investment income data do not provide adequate coverage below £3,000 in 1968–9 (£4,000 in 1972–3), which corresponds to a wealth of £98,000 (£130,660 in 1972–3). At levels of investment income above £15,000 (corresponding to wealth of £538,900 in 1968–9), use of the yield curve involves extrapolation well outside the observed points; and the estate estimates are increasingly subject to sampling error.

In considering the results, it should be borne in mind that the scale used is logarithmic. Considering first the total numbers in excess of £w, we can see that the typical difference is around 80 per cent, although there is a tendency for the gap to narrow (in 1968–9) or widen (in 1972–3). (The dashed lines for 1968–9 are discussed later.) The numbers as estimated on the II basis are, therefore, some 80 per cent higher than on the ED basis. The discrepancy for total wealth in excess of £w is somewhat smaller – of the order of 60 per cent. But despite this rather smaller discrepancy, it is still the case that at a specified total number of tax units, estimated total wealth is higher under the II method. Thus, in 1968–9 the top 20,000 owned, on the II basis, £10.8 billion, whereas according to the ED estimates they owned £9.5 billion. If the estimated total wealth were the same, then the Lorenz curve for the II method would at this point be outside that for the ED method – the estimated share would be larger.

It appears that the cumulative frequency and cumulative total wealth curves have a broadly similar shape in the two cases (II and ED) – and indeed both appear to the eye to be close to the linearity predicted by the Pareto distribution – but that the differences in levels are quite substantial. These may in part be explained by the assumption in constructing the ED estimates that those in the upper ranges were married to spouses with no wealth. The effect of the alternative 'rich married to rich' assumption in 1968–9 may be seen from the figures below (all rounded to the nearest thousand). In moving

	Numbers in excess of £100,000
1. ED 'rich married to poor'	63,000
2. ED 'rich married to rich'	86,000
3. II	112,000

from line 1 to line 2, the numbers are first reduced as we 'marry up' the estimated 19,000 couples each with £100,000 or more. The numbers are then

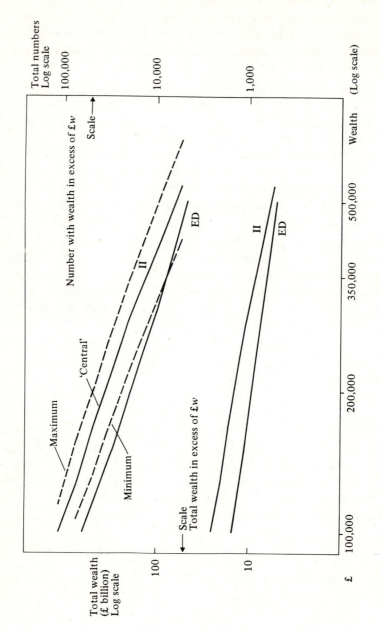

Figure 7.3a Comparison of estate and investment income estimates 1968–9

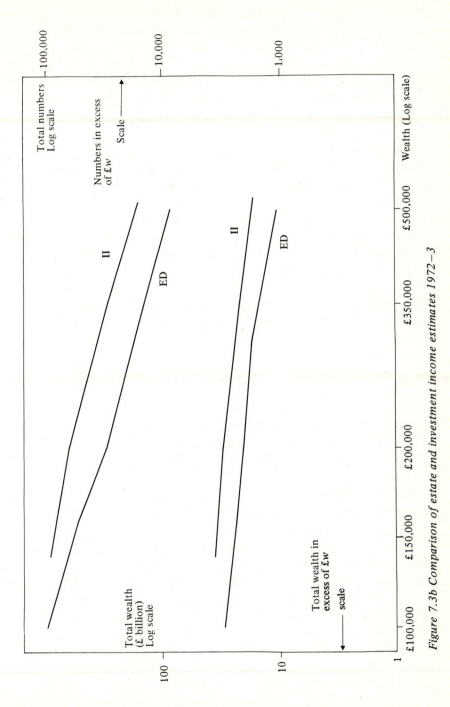

Figure 7.3b Comparison of estate and investment income estimates 1972–3

increased as we add in 42,000 couples who individually own less than £100,000 but whose combined wealth takes them above this amount. The net effect is to move the ED estimate towards the II figure — indeed to go more or less half way towards closing the gap. The 'rich married to rich' assumption is an extreme one but may be more realistic than that of 'rich married to poor'. (This is discussed further in chapter 9.)

The criterion applied above when comparing the estimates is that of the differences in the cumulative frequencies and in the cumulative total wealth. In earlier chapters we have tended to attach more weight to the effect on the estimated *shares* — the position of the Lorenz curve. Since the II estimates do not cover the whole population, we have not attempted this comparison here. It is however worth noting that some of the variations considered earlier gave rise to quite large changes in the cumulative frequencies. Thus different mortality multipliers led to a range of estimates for the numbers of individuals with wealth in excess of £100,000 in 1970 of some 50,000 (general multiplier) to 70,000 (life office multipliers). Seen in this light, the 26,000 difference between the ED 'rich married to rich' and the II estimates appears less perturbing; and to the extent that the II method leads to corresponding increases in both numbers and wealth, the effect on the Lorenz curve is less substantial than the difference in absolute numbers suggests.

The sensitivity of the yield curve was discussed in the previous section. It may be useful to show the effect of variation in the yields on the size distribution of wealth, and the dashed lines in figure 7.3a illustrate for the cumulative frequency distribution in 1968—9 the effect of taking the maximum and minimum yield multipliers described earlier. The range is initially some 60 per cent, but widens at higher wealth levels, to reach some 130 per cent. Even at the £200,000 level the range is of the order of 100 per cent, which is considerably larger than the differences found, for example, with the use of different mortality multipliers. This supports the view that the results may indeed be highly sensitive to the choice of yields — although again it is possible that the effect on the Lorenz curve is less marked. It may be noted that the ED estimates lie between the dashed lines above £350,000, and that if we were to make the alternative assumption about marrying up then the inter-section would come sooner. Given the wide range of the II estimates, it is difficult to reject the hypothesis that they are consistent with those produced via the estate method — at least at higher wealth ranges.

The results presented above concern relatively recent years. We have not attempted to make estimates using the investment income method for earlier periods but it may be of interest to consider briefly the study by Barna (1945), since he had all the ingredients necessary to make a comparison of the two methods. In table 7.4 we have brought together his results for the United Kingdom. The estate method estimates are on a 'rich married to poor' assumption, and are comparable with those given for 1968–9 and 1972. On the other hand, the investment income data used are grouped according to size of *total* income rather than investment income. If, as seems likely, wealth is less than perfectly correlated with total income, the use of these data means that the extent of concentration of wealth is under-stated by the II method (see Friedman 1939:131–9). This may be illustrated by the fact that applying a similar method to the data for 1968–9 yields an estimate of the number with investment income in excess of £3,000 (and hence wealth above £98,000) of some 70,000 compared with the correct figure of 116,100. We should not, therefore, expect the results to be fully in line with those given for 1968–9 and 1972–3, although, as Barna (1945:268) points out, the estimates for total numbers and total wealth are more accurate than those for the wealth *ranges*.

Bearing these points in mind, the results for 1937 appear to be consistent, both internally and with the pattern for more recent years. The II estimates for total numbers seem to be similar to, or greater than, the ED estimates; and the estimates for total wealth are definitely higher on the II basis. Thus the top 40,000 on the II basis owned £5.9 billion compared with the top 42,000 owning £5.5 billion according to the ED estimates. Barna went further than we have done and estimated on the II basis that the total capital was £20.4 billion. If the total number of income units is taken as 24 million (see Lydall 1959) then his results show that:

> 166,000 units (representing 0.69 per cent) owned 46.9 per cent of total capital
> 287,000 units (representing 1.2 per cent) owned 54.6 per cent of total capital

Interpolating, the investment income method indicates that the share of the top 1 per cent of income units was some 50 per cent — a figure not very different from that for individual wealth-holdings obtained using the estate method (the estimate given for 1938 in table 6.5 is 55 per cent).

7.4 Deficiencies of the investment income method

In this section we examine some of the main deficiencies of the investment income approach, grouped under the following headings:

(a) Use of estate data for asset composition,

(b) Deficiencies of investment income data,

(c) Sensitivity to individual yields,

(d) Bias of standard investment income method.

Table 7.4 Comparison of estate and investment income results 1937

Investment income method (II)			Estate method (ED)		
Lower end of wealth range	Cumulative numbers	Cumulative wealth (£ million)	Lower end of wealth range	Cumulative numbers	Cumulative wealth (£ million)
£			£		
912,000	500	879	1,000,000	300	510
264,000	4,000	2,284	250,000	3,700	1,930
123,000	12,600	3,737	100,000	14,700	3,610
57,000	39,500	5,901	50,000	41,700	5,470
24,000	109,900	8,444	25,000	104,700	7,700

Source: Barna (1945), tables 13, 71 and 76.
Note: We have replaced Barna's estimates of the ranges, which appeared rather broad approximations, by our own interpolations using the evidence on yields and unearned income.

(a) Use of estate data for asset composition

As pointed out earlier, we have to rely on asset composition data derived using the estate method. This means that the results are not fully independent and that some of the deficiencies of the estate method are incorporated. In certain respects, these deficiencies are less important in the present application. For example, the mortality multipliers are only important in relation to the differentials between age/sex groups; and the overall level of the multipliers, which is the main possible source of error, is not relevant to the investment income method. It is of course still possible that inaccuracies in the mortality differences, or the sampling errors embodied in the estate method, may lead to the asset proportions being in error. One indication of the possible magnitude of the bias due to the multipliers is provided by Revell's comparison of the estimates made by him for 1960 based on assured lives multipliers (A4) with those made by the Inland Revenue (A1). Despite the substantial difference in the estimate of total wealth ($12\frac{1}{2}$ per cent), the asset proportions were relatively similar: building society deposits constituted 5.6 per cent under A1 and 5.9 per cent under A4, quoted shares were 14.7 per cent and 15.6 per cent respectively, and dwellings were 18.1 per cent in both cases (Revell 1967: table 5.6). Since part of the difference can probably be attributed to the differing estimates of the numbers in the various wealth ranges, this provides some grounds for believing that this source of error is of limited importance. Against this, however, must be set the greater sampling errors which are likely to arise with asset composition data, particularly when considering higher wealth ranges. This may be illustrated by the fact that in 1972 there appeared to be an 'unusually' high proportion of liabilities in the highest wealth range (see table 4.3). The effect of this on the yield may be seen by replacing liabilities of 17.6 per cent of net worth by 7.6 per cent (reducing all assets proportionately to give the same net worth). The net yield rises from 1.93 to 2.63 per cent. This illustrates the possibility of substantial error being introduced, and cautions us against placing too much reliance on the estimates.

One class of problems with the asset composition data which should be discussed is that arising from property which is missing or incorrectly valued. The asset composition data are obtained following the Inland Revenue approach, and to make estimates on a par with the 'final' figures in chapter 5, further adjustments would be necessary. These adjustments, covering items such as life assurance policies and settled property, would follow the same pattern as in chapter 4 (although the adjustments could possibly be refined in certain cases where the investment income data are more complete). Seen in this way, the problems of valuation or exclusion of wealth are no different from those discussed in earlier chapters — as far as the asset composition is concerned. Further difficulties are however introduced where the coverage of the investment income data is different, and to this we now turn.

(b) Deficiencies of investment income data

The information on incomes published by the Inland Revenue has been the subject of considerable criticism, notably by Titmuss (1962). Our purpose here is not to provide a full review of these issues but rather to concentrate on those relevant to our particular use of the data.

The first set of problems is that arising from the differences in scope of the sources used for investment income and for asset composition. Thus it is possible that wealth could be missing from the estate returns but the corresponding income included in the surtax data. Conversely, the income may be excluded from the investment income data but the asset included in the estate returns. Where this applies to the whole of a particular category of income, for example National Savings certificates, the value of R_j can be set to zero and this procedure was followed in the construction of the yield multipliers. Difficulties arise where only part of the income is excluded: for example, where items are set against investment income (e.g. covenants) or there may be simple evasion. These cause the investment income, and hence the estimated wealth, to be under-stated.

Secondly, if we accept the definition of investment income which underlies the investment income data, it remains the case that the coverage is incomplete. The Inland Revenue has recognised for a number of years that the figures show a deficiency of investment income, as revealed by comparison with independent totals. Such comparisons can only be approximate but the Inland Revenue estimated in the 1964–5 Survey of Personal Incomes that the deficiency was £60 million, or slightly over 4 per cent of total investment income (Inland Revenue, 109th Report: 93). A more recent estimate is that in Stark (1977), which refers to the rather higher figure of 12 per cent.

Two main reasons have been advanced for the deficiency: (i) where investment income is taxed at source, the net income rather than the gross may be reported (for basic rate taxpayers this would not affect the tax paid), and (ii) the previous year's figures are sometimes reported if no up-to-date ones are available. It should be noted that the second of these could, in certain circumstances, lead to an over-statement, but for the years in question it seems likely to have led to a deficiency. The Inland Revenue have estimated that the two causes are responsible for about 60 per cent and 40 per cent respectively of the deficiency (109th Report: 94). There are some reasons for expecting the surtax data to be more complete (for the ranges covered). They are compiled at a later date, so that the second of the causes is less likely to apply; and since reporting of net of tax income would lead to tax being under-assessed it is more likely that it will be checked by the Inland Revenue. Even, therefore, if we take the figure in Stark (1977) as the starting point, it is possible that the deficiency for the surtax data is 10 per cent or less. In terms of figure 7.3a, this would be equivalent to around one tenth of the difference between 'minimum' and 'maximum' estimates.

Income may also be missing where it is set against interest paid. The data we have used relate to *net* investment income. This would not itself necessarily lead to error since the yield multipliers are calculated net of interest paid.[7,8] However, the estate data almost certainly under-state mortgage liabilities: Revell pointed out that in 1960 the estate estimate of house mortgages was less than a third of the total known from the issuing sources (1967:173). Some guide to the approximate effect of such an understatement can be obtained by increasing the mortgage liability by a factor of 3 and adding this amount to the asset side in the form of life policies (or other assets with $R_j = 0$). The resulting changes in the yield multiplier are rather small, and tend to increase the estimated wealth corresponding to a given level of investment income by 0–3 per cent (Atkinson and Harrison 1974: table 7). This factor does not therefore seem to be especially important.

In considering the categories of income covered by the investment income data, it may be noted that in certain circumstances the investigator may have a choice. If adequate data exist on the investment income from a sub-class of assets, $j = 1, \ldots, K$ then the yield multiplier may be employed, setting $R_j = 0$ for $j = K + 1, \ldots, J$. Thus Lehmann (1937) in the United States used evidence on dividend income, taking a yield multiplier based only on the dividend return (weighted by the proportion of wealth held in this form). Where yield information on other assets is difficult to obtain, this method may have considerable advantages but, for our purposes, it cannot really be used because the investment income categories at present published are too broad.[9]

7 A further difficulty is that people with positive net worth may have zero or negative investment income and hence not be adequately represented in the statistics. As noted earlier, this is one reason for concentrating on the upper income group.

8 There have been a number of changes in the tax treatment of interest charges. Prior to 1969–70, most interest charges were deductible. The 1970 Budget restricted allowable deductions but by 1972–3 this was relaxed subject to disallowance of the first £35 paid in the year (except for house purchase or improvement or business use).

9 Separate figures for dividend income alone are to be published in the 1973–4 Survey of Personal Incomes, and it would be interesting to compare the results obtained applying the Lehmann method with those given here.

Table 7.5 Investment income estimates of size distribution 1968–9 – different assumptions

Investment income (lower limit of range) £	Number of income units	Average income £	Derived average wealth £	Alternatives (derived average wealth £)			
				I	II	III	IV
5,000	14,013	5,462	182,800	223,000	189,000	177,000	174,000
6,000	15,117	6,874	235,500	289,000	244,000	228,000	225,000
8,000	7,284	8,902	311,200	384,000	322,000	301,000	297,000
10,000	4,010	10,910	386,200	477,000	400,000	374,000	368,000
12,000	3,380	13,326	476,400	590,000	493,000	461,000	454,000
15,000	5,364	27,199	994,200	1,238,000	1,028,000	962,000	948,000

Alternatives   I   Yield on ordinary shares reduced by a quarter.

II   (III) Return to real property decreased (increased) by a half.

IV   Return to residential buildings raised to 3 per cent.

(c) Sensitivity to individual yields

The earlier analysis identified two classes of asset where the yield estimates are likely to be especially important, and these are considered in turn. Our concern here is with the mean return for a given level of wealth; the implications of variation in individual returns are the subject of the next sub-section.

The first class of assets is that of ordinary shares (and unit trusts). In the foregoing analysis we used the FT/Actuaries (500 industrial) dividend index, but even viewed as an overall figure for all wealth-holdings this is open to challenge. Personal holdings account for under half of total quoted shares, and even the total personal portfolio may not correspond to that represented by the FT/Actuaries industrial index. Some indication of the range of variation in the dividend yield is provided by the fact that in January 1972, when that index was 3.4 per cent, the FT/Actuaries financial index was 2.6 per cent, and the de Zoete index (on 1 January) was 3.6 per cent. When we consider the yield appropriate for large wealth-holdings, further problems emerge. In one direction, one would expect wealthier holders to obtain a higher return on account of better advice and lower transaction costs; on the other hand, tax reasons provide a strong incentive for this group to hold assets with a low taxable return. This latter point may be illustrated with reference to yields on unit trusts: for example in 1968, the Save and Prosper 'Capital' Trust gave a yield of only 1.6 per cent compared with 4.3 per cent on the Save and Prosper 'High Yield' Trust.

In view of these problems it is difficult to suggest an appropriate alternative, and all that we can do is to provide an indication of the effect on the results of different assumptions. Alternative I in table 7.5 shows the effect of variation in the yield on ordinary shares, reducing it by a quarter (from an initial value of 3.5 per cent to 2.625 per cent). With this reduction, which broadly corresponds to the range in the FT/Actuaries indices, the effect is to increase the derived average wealth by some 20–25 per cent.

The second class of assets of critical importance is 'land and buildings', and the method of calculating the yield for this item is highly approximate. Alternatives II and III in table 7.5 show the effect of variation in the yield by a half in either direction. The effect, which is of the order of 3–4 per cent, is less dramatic than in the case of shares although still noticeable. A rather different variation is that shown under alternative IV, which allows for the fact that the residential property owned by those in the upper wealth ranges is less likely to be owner-occupied, raising the return to 3 per cent, which corresponds to two thirds being rented (see appendix VIII). The results show a slightly larger effect – of the order of 5 per cent – but again this appears not to be as significant as that caused by the change in the yield on shares.

(d) Bias in the standard investment income method

All the analysis to date has been based on the standard investment income method; yet we saw in section 7.1 that the method ignored a number of factors which may lead to the results being biased. In particular we need to take account of the yield varying with the level of wealth, differing attitudes towards risk, and variation between individuals in the rate of return.

In order to explore in a preliminary way the bias which may be introduced by the first and third of these factors, let us divide the different asset categories into three broad groups:

$j = 1$ assets with zero return (categories a, p, q, t and u in table 7.1),
$\quad = 2$ company shares (categories j–n in table 7.1),
$\quad = 3$ remainder.

In broad terms these made up 25 per cent, 20 per cent and 55 per cent of total personal wealth in 1972; and the averaged yields in 1972–3 were zero, 3.7 per cent and 1.5 per cent, respectively.

First, we may use this simple model to measure the bias in the coefficient of variation as given by formula (7) on page 173, where the rate of return varies with w according to:

$$R_j = r_j - \rho_j/w \tag{6}$$

and there are assumed to be constant asset proportions (β_j). Taking the values of β_j set out at the end of the last paragraph, and varying ρ_j (while determining r_j such that it generates the appropriate average yield), we obtain the results below for the percentage bias in V_w (i.e. the square bracket in (7)).

	$(\rho_2/\overline{w}) = -\frac{1}{2}\%$	0	$\frac{1}{2}\%$
$(\rho_3/\overline{w}) = -\frac{1}{2}\%$	1.11	1.08	1.05
0	1.03	1.00	0.97
$\frac{1}{2}\%$	0.94	0.91	0.87

It may be noted that $(\rho_2/\overline{w}) = \frac{1}{2}$ per cent means that the return varies from 3.2 per cent on holdings half the average to 4.2 per cent as a limiting upper value (as w tends to infinity). For $(\rho_3/\overline{w}) = \frac{1}{2}$ per cent, the corresponding figures are 1 per cent and 2 per cent. The results indicate that the bias (up or down) is of the order of 10 per cent. In view of the highly simplified nature of the calculations, one must clearly be cautious in drawing conclusions. However, they suggest that, although the bias should be taken into account, it may not be too substantial.

In order to illustrate the effect of other sources of bias, we take the case of variation in the rates of return and draw on the more detailed discussion in appendix VII. For this purpose we take the case of linear asset equations and the following parameters (estimated from the portfolios of those above and below £10,000 in 1972 — a crude procedure but one which seemed adequate for these illustrative calculations):

$$B_1 = 284 \qquad \beta_1 = 0.17$$
$$B_2 = -461 \qquad \beta_2 = 0.33$$
$$B_3 = 177 \qquad \beta_3 = 0.50$$

From these we can calculate $\bar{Y}_j$, ϵ_j, $\bar{Y}$ and ϵ (see appendix VII). This leaves the coefficient of variation for R_j — i.e. the degree of dispersion in the rates of return. Concentrating on the case of shares ($j = 2$), some evidence is provided by Singh and Whittington (1968). Although not directly applicable, their data on the dividend yield of quoted UK companies indicate a value of around two thirds. The variation for unquoted companies is probably greater than that for quoted; at the same time other data for quoted companies, such as those of Morgan and Taylor (1957) suggest lower values. If we work with a coefficient of variation of 0.7, then application of formula (10) in appendix VII gives an upward bias in the estimated coefficient of variation of some 10 per cent (for values of the coefficient in the range 4.0–8.0 — see chapter 5, table 5.5). Again this suggests that the bias on account of variation in returns for this one asset type is large enough to be taken seriously but not sufficient to discredit totally the investment income method.

Conclusions
This examination of the various deficiencies of the method bears out the earlier suggestion that the assumptions about yields, particularly that on ordinary shares, are of crucial importance. Closely related to this are the possible sampling errors associated with the asset composition data, and the problems of extrapolating the yield curve. Probably of lesser quantitative significance are the deficiencies of the basic investment income data and the bias in the standard method, although both require further investigation.

7.5   Summary
This chapter has had two main objectives. The first has been to subject the investment income method to closer scrutiny than it has typically received in the past. This has shown that there are major difficulties with the method. The most important are the restricted coverage of the estimates and the sensitivity of the yield multipliers to the assumptions about particular assets (notably shares). The former arises because the underlying investment

income data relate only to higher incomes, combined with the limited information on asset composition, which means that the yield curves have to be
extrapolated over a wide range. Other shortcomings include the deficiencies
of the investment income data, the bias arising from variation in the rates of
return, and reliance on asset composition data derived using the estate
method (with attendant sampling and other errors). For these reasons, we do
not feel that the investment income method in its present form is likely to
replace the estate multiplier as the principal source of evidence about the top
wealth-holders.

At the same time, we consider that the investment income approach is
worth further development, since it provides a largely independent check on
the estate method. The second purpose of this chapter has been to see how
far the results are consistent. The comparison is not straightforward in view
of the differences in definition and the fact that the investment income
method estimates cover only the upper tail of the distribution. In broad
terms, it appears that the investment income approach gives higher estimates
of both numbers and total wealth, but that − given the range of estimates
corresponding to different assumptions about yields and about different ways
of 'marrying up' the estate estimates − it is difficult at this stage to reject the
hypothesis that the distributions are the same.

8

THEORIES OF THE DISTRIBUTION OF WEALTH*

Our primary concern to this point has been with the assembly of evidence about the distribution of wealth. In the last part of the book we turn to the analysis and interpretation of the data presented in earlier chapters. This is a broad subject, and we make no attempt to be comprehensive. Our purpose is simply to illustrate some of the uses to which the estimates may be put.

The analysis of the evidence involves both theoretical and empirical considerations and — as in other areas of economics — there have been few attempts to integrate these two aspects of the subject. Empirical studies have tended to ignore insights provided by models of the size distribution; and, although theoretical contributions have often taken as a starting point perceived regularities in the data (such as the Pareto Law), they have typically paid little attention to empirical testing. With certain notable exceptions, there are effectively two separate literatures: one concerned with theoretical models of the size distribution, and one with the development of empirical estimates. Yet a theoretical framework is essential in order to interpret the estimates and, conversely, in order to discriminate between alternative models we must confront them with the observed distribution.

It is clearly over-optimistic to hope for complete integration of theory and empirical evidence. The estimates of the size distribution are, as we have seen in earlier chapters, limited in their scope and subject to qualification. The theories of wealth-holding are, as will emerge in this chapter, based on strong qualifying assumptions and not as yet sufficiently developed to encompass the full range of factors likely to influence the distribution. Nonetheless, it seemed to us worthwhile to explore the relationship between the two branches of the literature. To this end, we have in this chapter surveyed some of the

---

* This chapter is more technical than the rest of the book. The main conclusions are summarised briefly in section 8.4 on pages 226–8, and the reader can go straight to that section without loss of continuity.

theories which have been put forward to explain the size distribution of wealth.[1]

In seeking to understand the distribution of wealth, there are two rather different approaches which could be adopted. We could, on the one hand, attempt to derive relationships governing individual wealth-holding and then aggregate these to obtain the overall distribution. On the other hand, we could formulate the problem directly in terms of the size distribution, and not seek to trace each individual life-history. This distinction between *individual* and *distributional* models is reflected in the organisation of the survey:[2] in the first two sections (8.1 and 8.2) we deal with the former, and in section 8.3 with the latter. In section 8.1 we describe models which emphasise the accumulation of wealth and try to identify the forces underlying the dynamics of individual wealth-holdings. In section 8.2 we introduce the transmission of wealth. Particular attention is paid to the mechanisms of inheritance and marriage, and to their interaction with the accumulation process. In section 8.3 we consider the same forces – the accumulation and transmission of wealth–but in the context of models designed to explain the evolution of the distribution rather than individual wealth-holdings.

Within the scope of this survey, it is not possible to review the whole range of theories of wealth-holding, and the coverage is necessarily selective. We have chosen to concentrate on two main aspects: (i) the predicted shape of the size distribution, and (ii) the forces making for increased or decreased concentration over time. These have been selected because they are frequently the subject of debate and because they are among the most obvious points of contact between theory and evidence. In the former case, there are, for example, a number of theories predicting that the upper tail of the distribution is approximately Pareto in form, and that the Pareto exponent bears a certain relationship to identifiable economic factors. The fitting of this functional form to the data for Britain provides a test of such predictions. Conversely, if it can be established that the distribution may be adequately described by a particular functional form, this is of considerable assistance in using the empirical data: for example, in the problem of interpolation discussed in chapter 5. Similarly, the predictions of theoretical models may throw light on the causal factors influencing the wealth distribution, and provide valuable

1 An earlier version of this chapter was presented to the Royal Economic Society Conference on the Personal Distribution of Incomes at Lancaster in July 1974.

2 There is a close parallel with recent work in general equilibrium theory and indeed with the Marshallian theory of value. In the context of wealth distributions there is a good discussion of this distinction in Vaughan (1975). This chapter owes a great deal to the work of both Vaughan and Shorrocks (1973).

aid in interpreting the evidence. Where, as is typically the case, the actual observations do not correspond to the concept of wealth with which we are concerned, theoretical results may allow us to link the two. Thus, for example, if we wish to draw conclusions about family wealth from data on individuals, then analytical considerations may suggest ways of putting upper and lower bounds on the results obtained (as we have already seen in chapter 7).

8.1   Accumulation of wealth

In building a bridge between theory and evidence, it has to be recognised that they often relate to different concepts of wealth-holding, and we need at the outset to clarify some of the definitional problems.

The first concerns the distinction between *current wealth*, which is the concept typically employed in empirical studies, and measures of *lifetime wealth,* which often appear in models of the development of wealth-holding.[3] This may be set out formally with the aid of some simplifying demographic assumptions (which will be retained throughout this section):

(i)   each person has a fixed (and known) lifetime, and the units of time are chosen such that this is one period,

(ii)   each person is replaced at death by one heir, who receives the entire estate at that time and there is no other transmission of wealth,

(iii)   the number of people born at each instant t is constant, so that the total population is constant (equal to P).

The second assumption means that we can trace the development of wealth-holding in terms of dynasties; and we use a superscript i to denote dynasty i. If we write $A^i(u)$ for the current wealth-holding of the present incumbent, and K_t^i for the amount inherited by dynasty i at time t, then

$$A^i(u) = K_t^i + \int_t^u S^i(v)\,dv \qquad (1a)$$

$$\text{for} \quad t \leqslant u \leqslant t+1$$

$$K_{t+1}^i = A^i(t+1) \qquad (1b)$$

where S^i denotes the net saving by person i at time v. We can therefore distinguish between the distribution of current wealth $A^i(u)$ among all those alive at u, and the distribution of lifetime wealth K_t^i among those in the generation born at time t. Although it is possible in theory to go from one to the other, if we know the savings relationship $S^i(v)$, this is not necessarily a straightforward process, even with the simplifying assumptions made here.

The second distinction is that between wealth-holding by *individuals* and that by *families*. Thus we may observe the distribution of individual

---

3   There are, of course, intermediate concepts, such as that of 'permanent' wealth.

holdings $A^i(u)$, or we may — as in the case of the investment income estimates — observe the combined wealth of husband and wife. Again, in theory we can 'marry up' the individual holdings if we know sufficient about the pattern of marriage, although in practice this is not likely to be easy.

Thirdly, the definition of *wealth* itself needs to be borne in mind. The theoretical models tend to consider a comprehensive measure of wealth-holding, whereas the estimates typically fall short of complete coverage. This means that one must be careful in the interpretation. For example, the accumulation of wealth for life-cycle purposes may in part take the form of pension rights, which are not included in the estimated size distribution when wealth is valued on a realisation basis. In matching theory against evidence, one needs to make sure that comparable concepts are being employed. More generally, the concept of wealth may be broadened to include 'human capital', and theoretical models have treated the acquisition of both human and non-human wealth (for a recent review, see Beach and Flatters 1976). As explained in chapter 1, our concern here is with non-human capital, but it should be remembered that this may give only a partial picture.

With these distinctions in mind we may consider the process of individual accumulation with the demographic assumptions (i)—(iii) made earlier. A natural starting point is the brief, but suggestive, discussion in Meade (1964) which stimulated a great deal of the interest in this area (he has recently returned to this subject in Meade 1975). He begins with a model in which savings are related to wealth and to income, which he assumes to consist of earnings E_t and capital income r_t per unit of wealth. Although Meade appears to be primarily concerned with current wealth-holding, we shall begin by interpreting the model as an inter-generational process, linking the amounts inherited in the $t + 1$st generation (K^i_{t+1}) to that inherited by the immediately preceding generation (K^i_t):

$$K^i_{t+1} = K^i_t + S^i(E^i_t + r_tK^i_t) - \theta K^i_t \tag{2}$$

where E_t and r_t now relate to the time period of one generation. In this simple accumulation process, referred to below as the 'Meade process', there are two offsetting forces for change: the accumulation out of income represented by the second term, and the last term representing the assumption that 'the proportion of income saved out of any given income falls the larger is the property owned' (Meade 1964: 45).

Meade uses this framework to examine some of the forces making for equality or inequality, and in particular the influence of earnings, differential rates of return and differences in propensities to save. In each case we may distinguish between a functional dependence on the level of wealth and the existence of intrinsic differences between individuals. The former refers to a

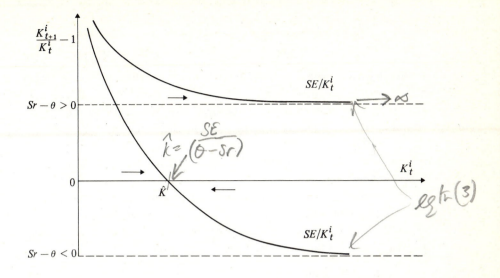

Figure 8.1 Two outcomes of the 'Meade process' depending on the 'internal rate of accumulation'

situation where, for example, the rate of return depends on the level of wealth (as in the previous chapter, where we assumed that $R_j = r_j - \rho_j/w$). The latter refers to a situation where there are differences unrelated to wealth: for example, if dynasty i has higher earnings than j, so that $E^i > E^j$.

(a) A simple model

To begin with, we take the simplest possible case where there are no intrinsic differences between individuals, the second term in (2) is proportional to income (S^i is a constant, as is θ), and neither E^i_t nor r^i_t are functionally dependent on K^i_t. The evolution of wealth-holdings from generation to generation is then determined by:

$$g = \frac{K^i_{t+1}}{K^i_t} - 1 = \frac{SE_t}{K^i_t} + (Sr_t - \theta) = 0$$

(3)

If E_t and r_t were constant over time (the conditions under which this is true are discussed in the next paragraph), then the path of individual wealth K^i_t would be as shown in figure 8.1. If $Sr - \theta > 0$, then K^i_t increases without limit, since the right-hand side of equation (3) is then strictly positive (and tends to $(Sr - \theta)$ as K^i_t tends to infinity). If, on the other hand $Sr - \theta < 0$, then there is a value $\hat{K}^i$ such that the right-hand side of equation (3) is zero, given by

$$\frac{SE_t}{\hat{K}_t} = -(Sr - \theta) \quad \text{or} \quad \hat{K} = \frac{SE}{(\theta - Sr)}$$

$$\hat{K} = \frac{SE}{\theta - Sr} \tag{4}$$

As may be seen from figure 8.1, this equilibrium wealth level is unique, and all wealth-holdings converge to $\hat{K}$. In the long-run therefore we would observe a completely equal distribution of lifetime wealth; moreover, at any date the relative distance between any two wealth-holdings would be narrowing.[4] The expression $(Sr - \theta)$, which plays a crucial role here, and later, may be seen as the 'internal' rate of accumulation: i.e. the rate at which capital grows on its own accord. The higher the internal rate of accumulation, the more likely it is that wealth-holdings diverge.

The constancy of E_t and r_t depends on the general equilibrium behaviour of the economy. In order to analyse this, we make the simplest possible assumptions about the production side of the model: that output per person (y) is a function of the total capital stock per person (k):

$$k_t = \sum_i K_t^i/P \tag{5}$$

$$y_t = g(k_t) \quad \text{where } g' > 0, g'' < 0$$
$$\text{and } g'(0) = \infty, g'(\infty) = 0 \tag{6}$$

This production function is assumed to exhibit constant returns to scale and be unchanging over time (technical progress could readily be introduced). From (2), we can see that the change in the total capital stock is given by:

$$P(k_{t+1} - k_t) = \sum_i S^i E_t^i + \sum_i S^i r_t K_t^i - \theta \sum_i K_t^i \tag{7a}$$

which in the present case reduces to (since $S^i = S$ and $E_t^i = E_t$ all i):

$$= SP(E_t + r_t k_t) - \theta P k_t$$
$$= SPy_t - \theta P k_t \tag{7b}$$

In other words, the aggregate behaviour is independent of the distribution of wealth, a property demonstrated in a more general model by Stiglitz (1969). (It may be noted that it does not depend on the assumption of perfect competition made by Stiglitz; the behaviour of k_t is independent of the division of national income between labour and capital so long as we assume that all individuals have the same marginal propensity to save.) From (7b) and the assumptions about $g(k)$ it may be seen (figure 8.2) that k_t converges to a stable equilibrium with $Sy = \theta k$, and that at this equilibrium

$$Srk < Sy = \theta k \tag{8}$$

4 That is $(K_{t+1}^i/K_{t+1}^j) < (K_t^i/K_t^j)$ if and only if $K_t^i > K_t^j$.

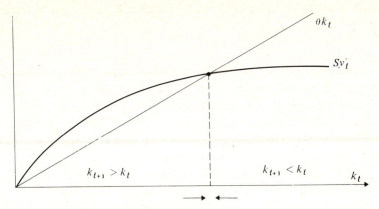

Figure 8.2 Aggregate equilibrium

i.e. the internal rate of accumulation is negative. This means that, even if initially $Sr > \theta$, the economy ultimately approaches a steady state where $Sr < \theta$, and hence a distribution of wealth which is completely equal.[5] Moreover along the approach to equilibrium, the degree of concentration as measured by the Lorenz curve is declining. If we rank individuals according to their wealth in increasing order $i = 1, \ldots, n$ (this ranking is preserved for all t), then the Lorenz curve is defined by

$$F^i \equiv i/P \quad \text{all } t$$

$$L^i_t \equiv \sum_{j=1}^{i} (K^j_t/Pk_t)$$

(9)

The Lorenz curve moves inward (i.e. towards less concentration) over time,[6] as we should expect from the earlier observation that relative distances were narrowing.[7]

5 The global stability of the steady state does not carry over to more general cases. For example, Stiglitz sets (in our notation) $k_{t+1} - k_t = Sy_t - A - \theta k_t$, which leads to two equilibria. In this case $Sr < \theta$ is the condition for *local* stability.

6 This is the case since (using equations (2) and (7))

$$L^i_{t+1} - L^i_t = \frac{SE}{k_{t+1}} [F^i - L^i_t] > 0$$

which is clearly satisfied since $F^i > L^i$ by the definition of the Lorenz curve.

7 This may appear to be in conflict with the argument by Tsuji that 'the comparison of rates of growth of wealth . . . does not reveal the direction of change of any particular measure of inequality' (1972: 947). He reached this conclusion by comparing – in the Stiglitz model – the timepaths of the Gini coefficient and the variance. The latter is not a measure of *relative* inequality, and if he had taken the coefficient of variation he would have found it to be decreasing over time. There also appears to be an error in his definition of the Gini coefficient.

The analysis of this first model has shown that where the inter-generational saving process is of the form in equation (2) with S^i and θ constant and identical for all, where all individuals receive identical wages and rates of return, and where the production function satisfies the conditions in equation (6), *then* the long-run equilibrium has a completely equal distribution of income and wealth, and the Lorenz curve moves monotonically over time in the direction of reduced concentration. It is, of course, difficult to relate this finding, concerned as it is with the distribution of *lifetime* wealth, to the measured distribution. If, however, one were to observe concentration of lifetime wealth, then this could be explained in two different ways. On the one hand, we could accept the model described above as providing a reasonable approximation to the underlying process, and attribute the observed concentration to the fact that convergence is slow and that we may be a considerable distance from the long-run equilibrium. On the other hand, we may feel that the model is over-simplified and that important features of reality need to be incorporated. It is the latter approach which we consider first, and indeed it is this which has dominated the literature. We return later to the question of convergence and the relevance of studying steady state equilibria.

(b) More elaborate accumulation models

The first variation is to allow for a non-linear accumulation relationship, resulting from the functional dependence of S, E, r and θ on K. This dependence may arise for a number of reasons. First, it may be that E is a function of K. A person with substantial inherited wealth may in addition have improved earnings opportunities; conversely he may take life rather easily. Secondly, Meade argues that r is likely to rise with K, at least as 'between the really small properties and the large range of big properties' (1964: 44). This may not apply to certain types of property (for example, owner-occupied houses), but in general seems likely to be true when we consider the total return, including capital gains. Thirdly, bequests may be a luxury good, so that S is an increasing function of K (or θ a declining function). For example, it is possible that below a certain level of income there is no saving for bequests, and that the positive accumulation is restricted to a small number at the top of the distribution.

The implications for individual wealth-holding of a non-linear accumulation relationship may be seen if we write:

$$\frac{K_{t+1}^i}{K_t^i} - 1 = S(K_t^i)\left[\frac{E(K_t^i)}{K_t^i} + r(K_t^i)\right] - \theta(K_t^i) \tag{10}$$

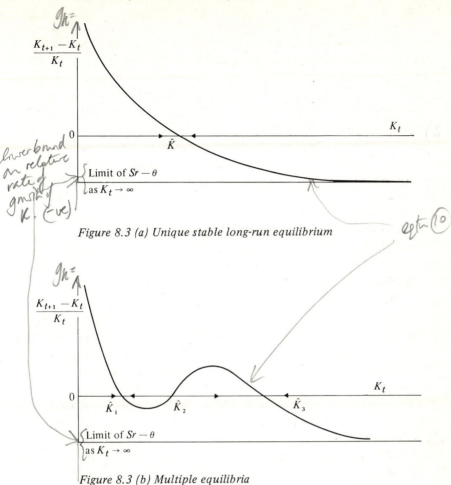

Figure 8.3 (a) Unique stable long-run equilibrium

Figure 8.3 (b) Multiple equilibria

and assume, for the moment, that $S(K_t^i) > 0$ all K_t^i. Two possible forms of the right-hand side are shown in figures 8.3a and 8.3b. As has been pointed out by Meade (1964), it is reasonable to suppose that a person can earn even though he has no capital, so that $E(0) > 0$. This implies that the right-hand side of equation (10) tends to infinity as K_t^i tends to zero, as shown in the diagrams. Conversely, as K_t^i tends to infinity, earnings are likely to rise less rapidly and E/K to tend to zero: 'in the case of our multi-multi-millionaire, E will be negligible relative to K' (Meade 1964: 43, our symbols). If the limiting value of Sr as K tends to infinity is less than θ, then the right-hand side is negative, again as shown in the diagrams. This in turn means that there must be at least one equilibrium ($K_{t+1}^i = K_t^i$). There may, however, be more than one. This may happen where the right-hand side of equation (10) is an increasing function of K_t^i for some part of the range: for example, because S, E or r increase with K_t^i or θ decreases with K_t^i. In figure 8.3b, we show the case where there are three equilibria, two locally stable, one unstable, and in this situation the ultimate equilibrium depends on the initial distribution. All those starting to the left of $\hat{K}_2$ converge to $\hat{K}_1$, and all those starting to the right of $\hat{K}_2$ converge to the higher equilibrium $\hat{K}_3$. We have therefore a two-class steady state resulting from differences in initial endowments not from any intrinsic differences. If we relax the assumption that $S^i > 0$, and allow for the possibility that below a certain income there is no saving for bequests, then zero lifetime wealth may be a further equilibrium of the process. The link between wealth and earnings, or between wealth and savings, or between wealth and the rate of return, may therefore lead to enduring differences in wealth-holding; even where it does not, the stronger the link the slower the speed of convergence to the egalitarian steady state.

The second variation on the Meade process is to allow for intrinsic differences between individuals. These can, once again, arise in a number of different ways. One example is provided by the Cambridge savings theory. In the version articulated by Pasinetti (1962), the capitalist class (superscript c) has zero wage income and saves a fraction S^c of its capital income; the working class saves a fraction S^w of its income (from both wages and capital) where $S^w < S^c$. If the production function satisfies the conditions in equation (6), the rate of return is a declining function of k, and in each case savings are reduced by a factor θK^c (respectively θK^w) as in equation (2),[8] then the equilibrium may take one of two forms. In the first (a sufficient condition for which is $S^w = 0$), there is an equilibrium with $S^c r = \theta$, with equality of per capita wealth-holding among the working class (zero if $S^w = 0$) but inequality among the capitalist class. In the second case, the share in total wealth of the capitalist class tends asymptotically to zero and wealth is held (equally) by the working class. The empirical relevance of the two cases has been the subject of debate between Kaldor (1966) and Samuelson and Modigliani (1966). To the extent that the first case applies, the class savings model can explain the persistence of concentration, although it is an unsatisfactory feature of the model that no explanation is given of the origins of the capitalist class or of the distribution of wealth within the class. It should also be noted that there is no reason why per capita wealth should be higher in the capitalist class than in the working class (where $S^w > 0$).

Both of the variations described so far involve multiple equilibria for

8 In the Pasinetti (1962) formulation, θ corresponds to the effect of population growth.

individual wealth-holdings. These mean that in the long-run we would observe a discontinuous frequency distribution with people clustered at a finite set of equilibria (possibly only two, as in figure 8.3b or in the Cambridge model). There would in the long-run remain concentration of wealth, depending on the initial conditions, but it would be concentration of a rather special sort. This outcome may in fact be contrasted with that where the long-run inequality of wealth is associated with a distribution of intrinsic characteristics. Thus there may, for example, be a distribution of earned incomes, E^i. If we assume that these persist across generations,[9] then with the assumptions made earlier in the simple Meade process, individual wealth-holdings converge to:

$$\hat{K}^i = \frac{SE^i}{\theta - Sr} \tag{11}$$

It follows that the long-run distribution mirrors the distribution of earnings, and that the degree of concentration is the same as that in earned income. This suggests in turn two observations. First, in fitting size distributions, the range of possible candidates could include all those proposed for the distribution of earned incomes and in particular the lognormal. Secondly, when considering the degree of concentration of wealth-holding, there is an argument for focussing attention on the difference between the distribution of wealth and the distribution of earned incomes. On this view, the source of the long-run inequality of wealth in this model is the 'exogenous' distribution of wages, and it is concentration in excess of that in E^i which may be attributed to the wealth accumulation process. Such inferences become, of course, more difficult to draw when we allow for the influence of life-cycle saving.

8.2 Transmission of wealth

The simple transmission process assumed in the previous section does not do justice to the range of possible influences on the distribution of wealth, and in this section we examine in more detail the role of inheritance, family size, and marriage.

(a) Division of estates

The first step in this analysis is to incorporate population growth. Each person is assumed to produce (at present unaided — marriage is introduced later) $1 + n$ children, who are 1 period younger than their parent. If we now interpret K_t as the wealth inherited *per person* by generation t and define

---

9 A more realistic model would allow for regression towards the mean.

K_t^* as the total wealth passed on by the person at death, we have the following:

the accumulation process (K_t becomes K_t^*)

the transmission process (K_t^* is divided to give K_{t+1})

In the second process, the fact that each person has more than one child introduces the possibility of the *division of estates*. Leaving on one side the transfer of wealth to persons other than children, the testator has the choice between:

equal division $K_{t+1} = K_t^*/(1+n)$

primogeniture $K_{t+1} = K_t^*$ for 1 child

$= 0$ for remainder

and a whole variety of intermediate patterns.

If we begin with the case of equal division, we can readily see that the analysis of section 8.1 applies with a reinterpretation of the parameters of the model. With the accumulation relationship (2), constant E and r:

$$K_{t+1} = \frac{K_t^*}{1+n} = \frac{K_t + S(E + rK_t) - \theta K_t}{1+n}$$

or

$$\frac{K_{t+1}}{K_t} - 1 = \frac{S(E/K_t) - (n + \theta - Sr)}{1+n} \tag{3'}$$

stability $n + \theta > Sr$

Writing $S' = S/(1+n)$ and $\theta' = (n+\theta)/(1+n)$, this gives the same relationship as equation (3). We can therefore interpret the accumulation process of the previous section as one where individuals die and pass their wealth on equally to the next generation. The parameter θ' corresponds to the effect of the rate of population growth (n), and, as we should expect, a rapid rate of growth is an equalising factor. The stability condition for individual holdings ($S'r < \theta'$) is then satisfied where the rate of growth of population (n) exceeds the 'internal' rate of growth of the capital stock from saving out of capital income ($Sr - \theta$).

[margin note: Eg: gtr rt of pop growth (n) equalizing]

The sensitivity of the results to the assumption about the division of estates is illustrated by the same model if we turn to the opposite case of primogeniture. Suppose that generation t leaves all its wealth to the eldest child. In generation $t + 1$, there are a proportion $(1/1 + n)$ of elder children with wealth (setting $\theta = 0$ for simplicity):

$$K_t + S(E_t + rK_t)$$

and a proportion $(n/1 + n)$ of younger children with no inherited wealth. The equilibrium distribution under this assumption can be derived from an extension of the analysis of Stiglitz (1969). If the economy has been in permanent steady state growth, with constant r and E, the same for all individuals, there will be the distribution of wealth shown below.

Proportion		Inherited Wealth
$n(1 + n)$	Younger children	zero
$n/(1 + n)^2$	First generation older children	$SE (= K_1)$
$n/(1 + n)^3$	Second generation older children	$SE + (1 + Sr)SE (= K_2)$
$n/(1 + n)^{i+1}$	ith generation older children	$\frac{E}{r}[(1 + Sr)^i - 1] (= K_i)$

Sol.

The proportion of the population with wealth greater than or equal to K_i is therefore

$$1 - F(K_i) = \frac{n}{1 + n} \sum_{j=1}^{\infty} \frac{1}{(1 + n)^j} = (1 + n)^{-i}$$

or

$$1 - F(K_i) = \left[\frac{K_i + E/r}{E/r} \right]^{\frac{-\log(1+n)}{\log(1+Sr)}} \tag{12}$$

holding mean constant inc in absol. whe of pareto coefft ⟹ red. inequality

where use has been made of the stability condition $n > Sr$ (where $\theta = 0$). We have then the Pareto type II distribution (see appendix IX). The Pareto exponent is given by $\alpha = \log(1 + n)/\log(1 + Sr)$. With $S = 10$ per cent, $r = 3.5$ and $n = 0.6$ (it has to be borne in mind that the unit of time is the generation so that the return is over 30 years or so), this gives a value of α of 1.56.

inc n ⟹ less inequality (same as equal ÷)

We have therefore a sharp contrast between equal division, which leads in the long-run to equality, and primogeniture which generates a distributional equilibrium with persistent concentration. The mechanism by which the latter operates is that the absolute number of people above any K_t increases over time, but it is counter-balanced by the inflow of younger offspring with no wealth, so that the *proportions* remain unchanged.

but not increasing

Various intermediate cases between primogeniture and equal division may be considered — and may indeed be more realistic. Blinder (1973) has suggested that wealth may be divided, but not necessarily equally, with the eldest child receiving a disproportionate share. Another possible pattern is that there is equal division up to a certain level and that all further wealth is then divided unequally: for example, people often talk of making 'adequate provision' for all children and then settling the rest of the estate on one child. There may also be a link between family size and the pattern of inheritance; for example, it may be more likely that primogeniture is practised if there are a large number of children.

(b) Marriage

To this point no account has been taken of the influence of marriage on the process of wealth transmission. If all wealth were held by men alone, or all wealth by women alone, then the earlier analysis would remain valid; however, where both partners to a marriage may own property, we have to consider how far marriage tends to increase or reduce the concentration of inherited fortunes.

The effect of marriage on the distribution of wealth has been analysed by Blinder (1973). He assumes that each couple has two children – one boy and one girl – and that the boy receives a proportion Ω of the parental wealth, so that if we denote by K_t^* the total left by the parents in generation t, the boy receives ΩK_t^* and the girl $(1 - \Omega)K_t^*$. The children are all assumed to marry, and the distribution of their combined wealth (K_{t+1}) depends on the pattern of marriage. If $p(X_2 \mid X_1)$ denotes the probability that a man of wealth X_1 marries a woman of wealth X_2, then the frequency function for the combined wealth is given by:

$$f_{t+1}(K_{t+1}) = \int_0^{K_{t+1}} f_t^*\left(\frac{X}{\Omega}\right) p(K_{t+1} - X \mid X) d\left(\frac{X}{\Omega}\right) \tag{13}$$

where f_t^* is the frequency function for total wealth left by the tth generation (K_t^*). Equation (13) represents the transmission process; if we combine it with the accumulation relationship linking K_t to K_t^*, then we can relate the distribution of wealth inherited by the present generation (K_t) to that of the wealth inherited by the next (K_{t+1}).

Blinder in effect makes the simplest possible assumption about accumulation – that there is no net saving – so that $K_t^* = K_t$. With this assumption, the ratio of the coefficient of variation in generation $t + 1$ to that in the previous generation is given by (Blinder 1973: equation 12):

$$\frac{V_{t+1}}{V_t} = \sqrt{[1 - 2\Omega(1 - \Omega)(1 - \rho)]} \tag{14}$$

where ρ is the correlation between husbands' and wives' inheritances. From this we can see at once there are three cases where there is no reduction in inequality over time as a result of marriage: $\Omega = 1$ (all wealth accrues to sons), $\Omega = 0$ (all wealth accrues to daughters), and $\rho = 1$ (class marriage). The fact that these three are equivalent should not be surprising, since class marriage is in this context equivalent to everyone marrying their own sister/brother. It is also clear that the rate of equalisation will be higher, the closer Ω to a half, and the smaller ρ. In the case of zero correlation ('random' marriage),

Table 8.1. Wealth transmission under alternative assumptions

[handwritten annotation: Still +ve job sons who are heirs marry daughters: heiresses ⟹ come]

	Primogeniture – eldest child	Primogeniture – eldest son	Equal division among sons	Equal division among all children
		Marriage irrelevant		
Each Family has 2 Children (1M/1F) Marriage 'random' (ρ = 0)	Tendency towards inequality	Stable distribution *[handwritten: pareto]*	Stable distribution (same as primogeniture – eldest son)	Tendency to equalisation
Class marriage (ρ = 1)				Same as equal division among sons
Each Family has more than 2 Children Marriage 'random' (ρ = 0)	Tendency towards inequality	Tendency towards inequality	Stable distribution	Tendency to equalisation
Class marriage (ρ = 1)				Same as equal division among sons

Note: 'Son' could be replaced by 'daughter' throughout the table.

equation (13) reduces to the convolution of the two densities.[10] As Blinder notes, the division of the estate may be governed by law or custom, or it may be an expression of parental preferences. A recent treatment of family values in a utility-maximising context is provided by Ishikawa (1975), who also integrates decisions about human and non-human wealth. A theory of the economic determinants of ρ has been advanced by Becker (1973).

The work of Blinder illustrates the interaction between the pattern of marriage and the division of estates, but his analysis is limited by the fact that he considers only a static population. As a result, he fails to bring out certain important factors: for example, that where each family has only one son, there is no difference between primogeniture (in terms of the wealth going to the eldest son), and equal division among sons. This is shown in table 8.1 where it is again assumed that $K_t^* = K_t$ (there is no net saving) and that each family has an equal number of girls and boys. Where each family has two children, five of the eight possibilities shown lead to a stable distribution (no change in inequality over time). In the case of equal division among all children/random marriage (more generally $0 < \Omega < 1$ and $\rho < 1$) there is a tendency to equalisation; and in the case of primogeniture – eldest child, not considered earlier, there is a tendency towards increased inequality (since some of the eldest children marry other eldest children). Where each family has more than two children, it is still true that class marriage combined with equal division is equivalent to equal division among all sons (or all daughters), but it is no longer the same as primogeniture. Where there is primogeniture in terms of wealth going to the eldest son, the wealth remains in the hands of the same absolute number of people but they form a decreasing proportion of the population, so that inequality tends to increase.

(c) Simulation models

The difficulty of obtaining analytical results in more complicated models of individual accumulation and transmission has led some authors to explore the alternative of simulation methods. The attractions of this approach have been well described by Pryor as follows: 'either we model these factors mathematically, which requires some drastic simplifications . . . or we take more factors into account by simulating their impact. While the latter procedure does not lead to a completely general solution it does permit us to investigate certain features of economic systems using parameters of particular interest' (1973: 50). At the same time, there are obvious drawbacks. First,

10 As Blinder (1973) points out, it is known that for certain types of distribution (e.g. the normal), that if X_1 and X_2 follow the same probability law, then their convolution also has that form. The class of such 'stable' distributions is, however, very restricted (see Mandelbrot 1960 and Feller 1968).

the approach may provide little insight into the reasons why the results emerge in the way they do. According to Pryor, 'summarising the results . . . is extremely difficult for a number of counteracting factors influenced the results . . . the results feature a number of small puzzles which are difficult to explain' (1973: 62). Secondly, there may be problems of ensuring that all equilibria have been located and that the process has converged, and Pryor refers to the 'difficulties in determining the exact equilibrium distribution of income' (1973: 53).

These points are in fact well illustrated by Pryor's work (1973). On the one hand, he has succeeded in constructing a model of considerable richness, which includes not only inheritance and marriage rules of the kind discussed above, but also a distribution of earned incomes E^i, net saving and an aggregate production function. On the other hand, a number of the results could have been obtained analytically and such a derivation provides a much clearer picture of the underlying processes. This may be seen from some of his results reproduced in table 8.2 for the Gini coefficient of the long-run distribution of income.[11] The first set relates to the case of no net savings, as considered earlier, and the results can in fact be deduced from table 8.1.[12] With equal division and 'equal choice' marriage ($\rho = 0$), the distribution of wealth in the long-run approaches equality; and the distribution of income is determined by the labour incomes E^i, which are assumed to be normally distributed. It follows that we can approximate the expected value of the Gini coefficient by:[13]

$$\hat{G} = \frac{\delta \sigma}{\sqrt{\pi}}$$

where δ is the share of labour in total income and σ is the coefficient of variation of earnings. With the values used by Pryor ($\delta = 0.75$, $\sigma = 0.15$), the estimated Gini coefficient is 0.06, which corresponds to the result in the table. (The same applies to the 'limited choice' assumption about marriage.) In the case of equal division and 'no choice' we would expect the distribution to remain unchanged; however, Pryor assumes that people marry the person next to them on the *income* scale, in which case overlap

11 The results relate to the case where each family has two children. However, with the forms of primogeniture and equal division considered this makes little qualitative difference (see table 8.1).

12 Pryor gives some of these analytical results (1973: table 1) but does not make use of them in the numerical sections.

13 This uses the formula for the mean difference of a normal population (Kendall and Stuart 1969: 241), dividing by the sample mean. The latter introduces a bias, and for this reason the formula is only approximate; however it is unlikely to be substantial (Glasser 1962: 652).

Table 8.2. Simulation results of Pryor—Gini coefficients for the distribution of income

Inheritance rule	Marriage rules[*]		
	No choice	Limited choice	Equal choice
No net saving $K_t^* = K_t$			
Primogeniture (eldest child)	0.307	0.308	0.297
Equal division (among all children)	(see text)	0.064	0.060
Net saving $K_t^* = S[E + rK_t]$			
$S = 2.0$			
Primogeniture (eldest child)	0.167	0.169	0.162
Equal divison (among all children)	0.066	0.066	0.063
$S = 2.5$			
Primogeniture (eldest child)	0.165	0.170	0.164
Equal division (among all children)	0.065	0.063	0.062
Net saving $K_t^* = S[E + rK_t - Y_0], K_t^* \geqslant 0$			
$S = 2.0$			
Primogeniture (eldest child)	0.306	0.301	0.300
Equal division (among all children)	0.293	0.266	0.206
$S = 2.5$			
Primogeniture (eldest child)	0.308	0.309	0.306
Equal division (among all children)	0.296	0.260	0.199

Source: Pryor (1973), tables 2 and 4.
Note[*] No choice = marry next person on income scale; Equal choice = random marriage; Limited choice = chance of marriage greater, the closer two people are on income scale.

in the distributions of wage and property income leads to an equalisation of wealth. Turning to the case of primogeniture, the assumption that all wealth passes to the eldest *child* means that the distribution of wealth converges to a situation where all the wealth is in the hands of one person. The income distribution is then formed by the normally distributed wage income, with one person receiving all capital income and the effect on the expected value of G may be approximated[14] by adding $(1 - \delta)$. This explains values of the order of 0.31 which appear in table 8.2.

The argument of the previous paragraph is related to the no net savings case, and as the model becomes more complicated, it clearly becomes more difficult to derive results analytically. However, where it can be obtained, the analytic solution provides a good deal more understanding as to what is going on. In particular, the value $G = 0.06$, which occurs (subject to sampling error) in all Pryor's tables of numerical results, has the straightforward interpretation that it is the degree of income inequality when there is equality in the distribution of wealth. This means, for example, that there is no point in this

14 This is the limiting result as the sample size tends to infinity, and may be obtained by considering the area under the Lorenz curve when this is scaled down by a factor δ.

case in examining, as Pryor does, the effect of the redistribution of wealth; one can predict without any simulation calculations that G is the same under equal division for all levels of capital redistribution (Pryor 1973: table 3).

Simulation models are likely to play an important role in this area (a recent interesting example is the work by Wolfson (1977)), but they must be developed side by side with analytical methods. At the same time, the latter do become increasingly intractable as we attempt to enrich the models considered. For this reason we turn now to the class of distributional models, which do not seek to explain individual wealth but are concerned with the distribution as a whole.

8.3 Distributional models

As described in the introduction to this chapter, there is a distinction between models based on individual wealth-holding and those which take the size distribution as the basic unit of analysis. In the models discussed in the preceding two sections it was possible to trace the development of an individual's holding K^i; in this section we now consider models where it is the development of the distribution $f(K^i)$ which is the focus of the analysis, and where the assumptions may be consistent with a variety of specifications of individual behaviour.

(a) Nature of distributional models

In the previous sections we considered the long-run development of wealth-holding in relation to the equilibrium of individual wealth-holding. The distributional approach, however, leads us to extend the notion of equilibrium in an important way. It is quite possible that individual holdings may not approach a steady state level but that there is still an equilibrium of the distribution as a whole. There may be an equilibrium for $f(K^i)$ but not for K^i. This is, of course, parallel to the famous Marshallian conception of industry equilibrium: 'we may read a lesson from the young trees of the forest as they struggle upwards through the benumbing shade of their older rivals . . . at last in their turn they tower above their neighbours, and seem as though they would go on for ever, and for ever become stronger as they grow. But they do not . . . one after another they give place to others' (Marshall 1920: 316). The forest is in long-run equilibrium, even though individual trees are growing or dying. Since Marshall wrote, this extended concept of equilibrium has tended to be neglected by economists (at least until recently – see Hahn 1973), although statisticians and others have continued to draw attention to its significance. Thus in 1950, Kendall referred to: 'Laws of a peculiar kind in mass action which permit of the prediction of the behaviour of an aggregate when it is quite impossible to frame laws concerning the individual . . . we can derive quite definite laws which are obeyed by aggregates of such individuals' (Kendall 1950: 131).

The relevance of the concept of distributional equilibrium to the study of wealth should be apparent. We could indeed translate the Marshallian trees directly into wealth-holdings, by introducing a propensity to decay (with a certain fraction losing their fortune each generation). In this case the simple Meade process could lead to a distributional equilibrium even where $Sr > \theta$, so that individual holdings continue to grow until they are struck down. More generally, if we interpret distributional equilibrium in terms of the proportions of a growing population, then an example is provided by the primogeniture model of section 8.2. In that model, individual wealth could increase without limit, yet there existed an equilibrium for the form of the distribution as a whole. The eldest son of a dynasty founded ten generations ago would have greater wealth than his father, but as a proportion of the population he and his peers would have yielded place to those founded nine generations before.

The distributional approach is typically seen as being concerned with stochastic models. Kendall, for example, referred explicitly to the 'certain aggregates called random or stochastic, the members of which not only do not conform to law in the older sense of nineteenth-century determinism but actually happen by chance' (1950: 131). It is however misleading to regard the two – distributional and stochastic – as synonymous.

The stochastic approach typically begins with the individual accumulation relationship, adding to it a random component, which means that the outcome of the wealth-holding process is no longer deterministic but is specified in terms of a probability distribution over a range of values. This may be illustrated by the 'queuing' model recently put forward by Shorrocks (1975). Suppose that the accumulation process is such that in the time interval $(t, t + \Delta t)$ an individual with K units of capital has

probability $(a + bK)\Delta t$ of receiving one additional unit

and probability $(dK)\Delta t$ of losing one unit

where there is a negligible probability of obtaining or losing more than one unit, and terms which tend to zero faster than Δt have been ignored. (Wealth is now measured in discrete units.) This could be seen as a stochastic generalisation of the Meade process ($a + bK$ corresponding to $SE + SrK$ and dK to θK) but should be interpreted as relating to current rather than lifetime wealth. If we denote by $f_K(t)$ the probability that an individual has wealth K at time t, then it is possible to solve for the behaviour of $f_K(t)$. The probabilities must satisfy (see Shorrocks 1975) equations such as

$$\frac{df_K}{dt} = -[a + (b + d)K]f_K + [a + b(K-1)]f_{K-1} + d(K+1)f_{K+1}$$

$$\text{for } K \geqslant 1 \tag{15}$$

Under the 'stability' condition that $d > b$ (there is an analogy with $\theta > Sr$), the probability distribution converges to an equilibrium. For large K, this may be approximated by the discrete form of the Gamma (Pearson Type III) distribution (Shorrocks 1975: 634).

How should these results be interpreted? Strictly, all that has been done is to describe the long-run probability distribution for individual wealth-holdings. In itself, this tells us nothing about the size distribution *among* individuals. This depends, *inter alia*, on the independence or otherwise of the individual processes. If the events which determine for individual i whether his wealth increases or decreases (for example, good or bad harvests) are the same for all individuals, then—if everyone starts off equally — the size distribution exhibits perfect equality. The equilibrium distribution f_K simply tells us the probability that the common value of wealth is K. We should not, in such a case, observe a distribution of wealth at a particular date which approximated the Gamma distribution.

The stochastic model as formulated is not, therefore, a distributional model. In order to convert it into such a model — that is to reinterpret the probabilities f_K as frequencies — there are two possible routes we can take. First, assuming independence of the accumulation process across individuals, it is possible to justify this as 'the most probable macro-configuration' (Vaughan 1975: 57). However, as Vaughan has pointed out, there are a number of difficulties with this approach — for example, the problem of reconciling the independence assumption with a deterministic aggregate wealth. Secondly, the model can be reformulated as a *deterministic* one explaining the distribution f_K. The differential/difference equation (15) is then the fundamental element of the analysis. Underlying the distribution f_K there may be a stochastic process governing individual behaviour, but we are no longer concerned with tracing each life history. Moreover the process has ceased to be in a strict sense stochastic, and a number of authors (for example, Newman and Wolfe) have instead used the term 'quasi-stochastic' (1961: 55).

(b) Accumulation

Adopting this interpretation, we now consider some of the distributional models which have been put forward, drawing particularly on the work of

Vaughan (1975).[15] As our starting point we take the following 'diffusion' equation for the behaviour of the frequency function $f(K, t)$:

$$\frac{\partial f}{\partial t} = -\frac{\partial}{\partial K}(\mu_s f) + \frac{1}{2}\frac{\partial^2}{\partial K^2}(\sigma_s^2 f) \tag{16}$$

This represents an accumulation process, where μ_s denotes the mean level of savings and σ_s^2 the variance of savings.[16] The basic case considered by Vaughan is that where it is assumed that μ_s is a linear function of income and capital and that the standard deviation is proportional to income:

$$\mu_s = S(E + rK) - A - \theta K \equiv b_0 + b_1 K \tag{17a}$$

$$\sigma_s^2 = \gamma^2(E + rK)^2 \equiv a_0 + a_1 K + a_2 K^2 \tag{17b}$$

This reduces to the simple deterministic Meade process where $\gamma = A = 0$.

Vaughan analyses in detail the out-of-equilibrium behaviour, but initially we concentrate on the steady state equilibrium, which he shows to be stable under the assumption that there is a lower bound on wealth K_L where:

$$K_L \leqslant 0 \leqslant E + rK_L \tag{18}$$

and an appropriate upper boundary condition. Setting $df/dt = 0$, we can then integrate (16) to see that the equilibrium frequency distribution must satisfy (using the boundary condition):

$$\frac{1}{2}\frac{\partial}{\partial K}(\sigma_s^2 f) = \mu_s f \qquad \text{for } K \geqslant K_L \tag{19}$$

Substituting from (17a) and (17b), we have

$$[a_0 + a_1 K + a_2 K^2]\frac{df}{dK} = [2(b_0 + b_1 K) - a_1 - 2a_2 K]f \tag{20}$$

which is identical to the differential equation generating the Pearson system (see Kendall and Stuart 1969: 148, and Ord 1972: 2). In the particular case considered by Vaughan, where $\sigma_s^2 = \gamma^2(E + rK)^2$, the distribution is of the Pearson Type V (see appendix IX). As Vaughan (1975) shows, we may write

$$f = C(E + rK)^{-\alpha-1} e^{\delta^*/(E+rK)} \qquad \text{for } K \geqslant K_L \tag{21}$$

---

15 In his thesis, Vaughan presents a variety of models, and those described here are only representative.

16 For the derivation of this equation, referred to in the physics literature as the Fokker–Planck equation, see, for example, Prabhu (1965: 92). Vaughan takes as his starting point a more general equation, from which (16) is derived as a special case. There is an interesting, and suggestive, discussion of diffusion models in an unpublished paper by Sargan (1958) presented at the Chicago Meeting of the Econometric Society in 1958.

where C is a constant, and

$$\alpha = 1 + 2(\theta - Sr)/(\gamma^2 r^2), \quad \delta^* = 2(Ar - \theta E)/(\gamma^2 r^2) \tag{22}$$

For large K, the distribution is approximately Pareto in form, with exponent α. We may also note the special case where $\delta^* = 0$ (arising where, for example, $A = \theta = 0$) which is the Pareto Type II distribution referred to earlier.

(c) Transmission of wealth

The model just described assumes in effect that each person is succeeded by a single heir, as in section 8.1. Vaughan (1975) goes on to modify this by introducing more realistic assumptions about family size and the division of estates. In order to obtain analytical solutions it is often necessary to simplify the assumptions about the savings process. In order to consider the effect of primogeniture we first set $A = \theta = 0$, so that the comparison is with the Pareto Type II distribution with exponent $\alpha = 1 - 2S/\gamma^2 r$. This does not have a finite mean, and in terms of the deterministic process, it is equivalent to the 'explosive' case $Sr > \theta$ in figure 8.1. To introduce primogeniture, it is assumed that a constant proportion γ of the population die at any instant, each being replaced by $(1 + n/\lambda)$ children. Of the children, one inherits and the others commence with zero wealth (which is assumed to be the lower boundary). Vaughan (1975) shows that the equilibrium distribution is again of the Pareto Type II, where the exponent satisfies the quadratic:

$$\alpha^2 - \alpha\left[1 - \frac{2S}{\gamma^2 r}\right] - \frac{2n}{\gamma^2 r^2} = 0 \tag{23}$$

Solving for the positive root,

$$\alpha = \frac{u_1 + \sqrt{[(2 - u_1)^2 + 4(1 - u_1)(u_2 - 1)]}}{2} \tag{24}$$

where

$$u_1 = \left(1 - \frac{2S}{\gamma^2 r}\right) < 1 \quad \text{and} \quad u_2 = n/Sr.$$

From this we may see that primogeniture and a growing population tend to increase the Pareto exponent, and that if $n > Sr$, then $\alpha > 1$ so that there is a finite mean. There is a clear parallel with the deterministic model (see p. 213). We may in fact identify u_1 as the exponent which would emerge from the pure accumulation process and u_2 as that from the transmission process with zero variance of savings ($\gamma = 0$).

The introduction of primogeniture only involves an inflow of people at the boundary; if estates are divided, the diffusion equation must be modified.

Vaughan (1975) does this by writing:

$$\frac{\partial f}{\partial t} = \frac{1}{2}\frac{\partial^2}{\partial K^2}(\sigma_s^2 f) - \frac{\partial}{\partial K}(\mu_s f) - \lambda f + \lambda h^2 f(hK) \qquad (25)$$

where the last two terms on the right-hand side represent the effects of mortality (λf) and the division of estates. The parameter h reflects the extent of division of estates: $h = 1$ would mean primogeniture and the last two terms would then cancel, leaving the diffusion equation unchanged. Where $h > 1$, the wealth is assumed to be divided equally, and $h = (1 + n/\lambda)$ is the case of equal division among all children. Vaughan was unable to provide an analytical solution but goes on to show that if we assume that there is no saving out of wage income, then the Pareto Type I distribution satisfies the equilibrium conditions. The corresponding special case of the pure accumulation model is also the Pareto Type I form (obtained by setting $E = 0$ and $\delta = 0$ in equation (21)), and the difference lies in the exponent. In the pure accumulation model $\alpha = 1 - 2S/\gamma r^2$, whereas in the present case we obtain:[17]

$$\alpha^2 - \alpha \left(1 - \frac{2S}{\gamma^2 r}\right) - 2[(\lambda + n) - \lambda h^{1-\alpha}]/\gamma^2 r^2 = 0 \qquad (26)$$

This reduces to equation (23) when $h = 1$ (primogeniture), and where $n > Sr$ the effect of increasing h is to raise the Pareto exponent. In this sense, the division of wealth tends to reduce concentration. As Vaughan notes, where h is sufficiently large for $h^{1-\alpha}$ to be disregarded, the effect of division of estates is to raise the exponent associated with the transmission process from n/Sr to $(\lambda + n)/Sr$.

In the model formulated above, there is a difficulty with the lower boundary. With the Pareto Type I distribution, this cannot be zero; at the same time a lower boundary $K_L > 0$ raises problems where the estate to be divided is less than hK_L. This may however be dealt with along the lines proposed by Wold and Whittle (1957). Their solution was to distinguish a pool of 'propertyless' workers (with less than K_L), some of whom leave to join the propertied but whose numbers are increased by the heirs receiving less than K_L. An appropriate rate of inflow from this pool ensures a balance in the distribution among the propertied class. In the model examined by Wold and Whittle, they set $\gamma = 0$, so that the saving process is deterministic.

---

17 This may be seen by substituting $f = AK^{-\alpha-1}$ into equation (25), where the condition for equilibrium is that $\partial f/\partial t = nf$ and, by the assumptions made,

$$\mu_s = SrK$$
$$\sigma_s^2 = \gamma^2 r^2 K^2.$$

This leads to the special case of (26):

$$\alpha = (\lambda + n - \lambda h^{1-\alpha})/Sr \qquad (27)$$

and where $h = 1$ (primogeniture) this reduces again to $\alpha = n/Sr$.[18] A rather different treatment of the Wold–Whittle model has been given by Steindl (1972) in terms of branching processes.

The model may also be seen as a special case of that proposed by Sargan (1957), which allowed for the effects of gifts and marriage, as well as for more general specification of the pattern of inheritance. In its most general form, however, the Sargan model is not particularly illuminating: 'the solution is so general and vague that it does not reveal anything of the nature of the behaviour of the distribution function over time, and it is necessary to specialise the model before useful results can be obtained' (Sargan 1957: 575). He then considers what he refers to as the 'homogeneous case', and argues that the distribution will ultimately approach the lognormal form, with a variance that is an increasing function of time. For further discussion of this model, the reader is referred to Vaughan (1975).

(d) Out-of-equilibrium behaviour

To this point we have concentrated on the steady state equilibrium, but the relevance of this is clearly open to question. It is quite possible that convergence to the steady state may be a slow process. This has been emphasised by Shorrocks (1975) in the case of wealth distributions and by Champernowne (1973) for income. The latter reports the results of a simulation exercise based on an observed year-to-year transition matrix. These show that convergence may be 'very slow' (Champernowne 1973: 195). If, for example, the Pareto exponent is taken as summarising the shape of the upper part of the distribution, then commencing from a value of 2.51 the convergence to the equilibrium value of 3.01 is as follows: after 10 years, 2.44–2.58, after 20 years, 2.49–2.79, after 50 years, 2.75–3.05 (where the range of values corresponds to different levels of income from £10,000 up – Champernowne 1973: 200). Convergence may therefore be slow, and not necessarily monotonic. This has also been demonstrated by the work of Shorrocks (1975), who has analysed the dynamic behaviour of the queuing model in terms of the summary statistics, mean and variance. From this he concludes that the half life for the mean (the time required to cover half the distance to the equilibrium value) is likely to be large. Moreover, the convergence of the variance is not necessarily monotonic. Just as with

18 As pointed out by Vaughan, there is an error on page 591 of Wold and Whittle (1957), where the right-hand side of the equation for α has been inverted by mistake.

Champernowne's example, the degree of concentration may cycle around the equilibrium value. In particular, it may be falling even though it will ultimately approach a long-run equilibrium at a higher level. In such a situation, extrapolating past trends would lead to misleading conclusions.

Slow convergence also has the implication that it is much less plausible to suppose that the parameters of the wealth process are time-invariant – a point which has been stressed by Shorrocks (1975). The influence of economic forces is likely to vary over time, and may indeed respond to changes in the distribution of wealth. Thus in the queuing model we may expect a, b and d to depend on – among other things – the rate of return, and hence mean wealth. In effect this requires us to embed the distributional model within a general equilibrium framework – just as in earlier sections. With the quasi-stochastic approach, where the distribution is governed by a deterministic equation, this can be done – at the cost of added complexity. An interesting illustration of a time-dependent model is provided by Shorrocks (1975), who shows how asset-holding will evolve over the lifespan with time-varying earnings and consumption patterns.

Although the steady state equilibrium of the distribution has received most attention in the literature – for reasons that should be apparent – it is clear that study of disequilibrium behaviour is of great importance. This has to be borne very much in mind when considering the relationship between theory and evidence – a qualification which applies equally to the models discussed in the preceding sections.

8.4 Implications for the interpretation of the evidence

At the beginning of this chapter we said that our survey of the theoretical literature would concentrate on two main topics: (i) the predicted shape of the size distribution, and (ii) the forces making for increased or decreased concentration. In this section we summarise some of the main implications under these headings.

As emphasised at the outset, it is difficult to build an adequate bridge between theory and evidence, since they often relate to different concepts. Thus, much of the survey has been concerned with the determinants of lifetime wealth, whereas the estimates presented in earlier chapters are of current wealth-holding. Furthermore, an important problem which has emerged in the course of the survey is that a great deal of the literature concentrates on the equilibrium, or steady state, distribution, whereas we may be observing a disequilibrium situation.

In the face of these difficulties, we can only draw conclusions by abstracting from some central features of the problem. We may, for example, feel that it is essential to consider out-of-equilibrium behaviour and be willing to leave on one side refinements of the basic model. To this end, we could take the simple Meade process, ignoring the variation in the return to saving, and interpret it as applying to current wealth-holding (which was probably the interpretation Meade (1964) intended). On this basis, we can say little about the *shape* of the distribution,[19] but we can identify some of the *forces* making for equality or inequality. First, saving out of wage income tends to be an equalising factor, at least at the ends of the wealth scale, since it allows those with no capital to make a 'start' and is of negligible importance for those with large wealth. (Differences in earned income, either intrinsic or related to wealth, may qualify this.) Second, the 'internal' rate of accumulation ($Sr - \theta$) is a force for increased concentration, being the rate at which capital tends to reproduce itself. Third, increased population growth/ family size (n) tends to reduce concentration. This works in the case of primogeniture through the fact that the owners of growing fortunes represent a declining proportion of the population and in the case of equal division through the splitting of estates. Fourth, the pattern of inheritance affects the development of the distribution, with equal division being a force for equality. Finally, the pattern of marriage interacts with that of inheritance, and may be an equalising force where estates are divided and the wealth of husbands and wives is less than perfectly correlated.

On the other hand, we may wish to refine the model and be willing to accept the steady state distribution as a reasonable approximation to that observed. As we have seen, different assumptions about the sources of inequality lead to a range of predicted *shapes* for the distribution, including the Pareto Types I and II, the lognormal (Sargan model and that arising from intrinsic differences in earnings), the Gamma (Shorrocks 'queuing' model) and the Pearson Type V (Vaughan model). However, the three arising from the main models discussed in the chapter have in common a Pareto upper tail: i.e. at large wealth-holdings the distribution approximates the Pareto Type I. In this context, the various forces making for greater or less concentration may conveniently be summarised in terms of their effect on the Pareto exponent (as given, for example, in equation (26)). Certain of the influences described above are not included (for example, the model does not allow for marriage); however, many of the same considerations are relevant. The Pareto exponent increases, indicating less concentration (see appendix IX), with the rate of population growth (n), and with the wider

---

19 It should be noted that Vaughan (1975) is able to characterise the out-of-equilibrium behaviour for certain cases and shows how it depends on the initial distribution.

division of estates (h), but decreases with the internal rate of accumulation (in this case Sr). Moreover, the model incorporates two further factors. The variance of savings (γ) tends to reduce the Pareto exponent, representing as it does a further source of inequality. The rate of mortality λ (inverse of the life expectancy) increases the exponent where estates are divided ($h > 1$).

The factors described above are all relevant to the empirical analysis in the next chapter. Before leaving the subject we should however refer to the effect of government intervention, which has not so far been discussed. Most important are taxes on the ownership or transfer of wealth. The wealth tax may be seen as affecting the net rate of return, and hence the internal rate of accumulation. To the extent that r is reduced, the Pareto exponent will increase. A tax on capital income may affect r, and, depending on the loss offset provisions, the variance of savings. Again the effect may be seen from the earlier analysis. The impact of an inheritance tax is more complex, but it operates in some respects in a similar way to an increase in h, hence raising the Pareto exponent.[20]

20 As is shown in Wold and Whittle (1959) and Vaughan (1975), the last term in the partial differential equation (25) becomes

$$\lambda h^2 f(hK/(1 - \tau))/(1 - \tau)$$

where τ is the (proportional) rate of inheritance tax. The effect on the Pareto exponent may be seen by substituting $f = AK^{-\alpha-1}$ into this equation – see footnote 17 above. The square bracket in the last term of equation (26) becomes $[(\lambda + n) - \lambda h^{1-\alpha}(1 - \tau)^{\alpha}]$, so that the effect of τ is similar to that of h.

9

INTERPRETATION OF THE EVIDENCE

In previous chapters we have emphasised that the evidence about wealth-holding needs careful interpretation. In this chapter we discuss some of the problems which arise in trying to assess the meaning of the estimates whose construction has been described in earlier chapters. We have seen that the share of the top 1 per cent in total private wealth in the early 1970s was of the order of one third and that it appeared to have been declining over the previous 50 years at an annual rate of some 0.4 per cent. How can these observations be interpreted? What are the forces underlying the downward trend? How can we relate current wealth-holding by individuals to the life-time wealth of families, which may be more relevant for some purposes?

In seeking to answer these questions, we adopt two different lines of attack. The first takes the estimated shares and tries to relate these to the economic and social forces influencing the distribution. This approach is followed in the first two sections of the chapter, where we analyse the determinants of the share of the top 1 per cent. Section 9.1 draws on the theoretical literature surveyed in the previous chapter to derive the specification for the regression analysis presented in section 9.2, where we examine the role of factors such as changing asset prices and taxation. The second approach is to try to refine the estimates. In sections 9.3 and 9.4, we disaggregate the results, and consider the distribution between men and women and among age groups. By this means, we hope to throw light on the effect of moving to a family rather than an individual basis and on the role of life-cycle factors. Here again we draw on the theory described in chapter 8, in this case to make inferences about aspects of the distribution which we cannot observe.

9.1 Determinants of the share of the top 1 per cent

Throughout this book we have concentrated on top wealth-holdings, and in this (and the next) section we restrict our attention still further to the share of the top 1 per cent. This group consists of a small number of people (some 400,000 in 1970) but it is a group of especial interest since it appears to hold a substantial fraction of total personal wealth. According to the estimates presented in chapter 5, these people were worth at least £30,000 in 1970, and their share of total personal wealth was 33 per cent (on a realisation basis) and 29 per cent (on a going concern basis). We are particularly interested in the changes in their share over time. Between 1923 and 1972, the share of the top 1 per cent in England and Wales fell, according to the estimates in chapter 6, from 61 per cent to 32 per cent. In absolute terms, the amount owned rose from £9.4 billion to £43.9 billion, representing a three-fold increase on a per capita basis, although this was less than the rise in retail prices.

Our aim in this section, and in the econometric analysis of section 9.2, is to illuminate the forces underlying these changes in the position of the top 1 per cent. The reasons why this is of interest should be clear. It would, for example, make a great deal of difference to our thinking about the distribution of wealth if it could be shown that the observed decline was associated with particular economic or social changes, rather than reflecting an inexorable downward trend. It would be of value if we could estimate the contribution made to the decline by estate duty and if we could predict how the share would respond to changing stock market prices. In what follows we do not pretend to have provided definitive answers to these questions, but hope to give some indication of the lines along which the analysis should proceed.

(a) Explanatory variables

In the final section of the preceding chapter, we summarised some of the main forces influencing the distribution, and we now consider in turn how each is likely to affect the share of the top 1 per cent.

Saving out of earned income. For those in the bottom 99 per cent, and especially for those in the bottom 90 per cent (£7,000 and below in 1970), saving out of earned income is likely to be a primary source of capital. Moreover, there are good reasons for expecting that this would have grown substantially over the period 1923–72, reflecting increased owner-occupation, the spread of pension schemes, and the acquisition of consumer durables. The first of these is undoubtedly important. Between the 1920s and the 1970s the proportion of homes which were owner-occupied rose from less than 20 per cent to more than 50 per cent. This does not necessarily imply a corresponding increase in net worth, since mortgage liabilities have also risen, but it is likely to be associated with a growth in saving out of wages. The spread of pension schemes, on the other hand, is probably less relevant, since the resulting wealth is not adequately captured in the estimates (see the discussion in chapter 6). For this reason, we have left this aspect on one side. Finally, the quantitative importance of consumer durables may be less than that of the other factors, but they should obviously be taken into account. In what follows, we take the growth in the value of owner-occupied houses plus the value of consumer durables as representing the expansion of 'popular' wealth.

'Internal' rate of accumulation. The internal rate of accumulation ($Sr - \theta$ in the notation of the previous chapter) depends on the savings behaviour of the 'upper class' and on the rate of return. In the latter case, the relevant return is that to assets which feature prominently in the portfolio of the top 1 per cent, and we therefore focus particularly on the return to shares. In the case of the savings propensities, S and θ, there is little evidence relating to the top 1 per cent which can be brought to bear. It is possible that savings may react differently to capital gains, included in the rate of return in the theoretical models, and this is discussed further below.

Variance of savings. Evidence on the variance of the savings process is hard to come by, and the derivation of any explanatory variables is likely to be highly speculative. This factor may be seen as related to the extent of 'entrepreneurial' profits, and one approach might be to take as an index the growth of new industries or sectors of the economy (such as property development). An alternative, followed here, is to take the level of the share price index, relative to its long-run trend.

Demographic factors, marriage and inheritance. The influence of demographic factors, such as the size of families and life expectancy, is likely to be relatively slow-moving. For this reason, their effect is treated as part of a general trend over the period. The same applies to marriage and the pattern of inheritance, except that here customs may have changed discretely over the Second World War, a possibility which is allowed for in the equations estimated.

Taxation. The two elements of taxation of greatest significance are that on investment income and that on estates. In the former case, it is the combination of the income tax rate on unearned income and the capital gains tax rate (depending on the mix of income) which is relevant; in the latter case, it is estate duty (and legacy and succession duties prior to 1949).

(b) Specification

The explanatory variables described above may be incorporated in a variety of ways into a regression equation explaining the share of the top 1 per cent. The basic equation which we estimate in the next section treats the 'true' *[handwritten: × (gap in data 1939-49]*

value of the share, denoted by W_1^*, as being determined by:

$$\log W_1^* = a_0 + a_1 T + a_2 D1 + a_4 \Pi \text{ (or } \log \Pi) + a_5 PW \tag{1}$$

with variations where the terms $a_6 RR$ and $a_7 ED$ are added. The variables are T(time trend), $D1$ (dummy variable 0 until 1938, 1 from 1950), Π (index of share prices), PW ('popular' wealth as a percentage of the remainder of personal wealth), RR (dividend yield after tax and inflation), and ED (estate duty paid by top 1 per cent as proportion of capital).

This specification was derived from the simple 'Meade' accumulation process described in the previous chapter, with certain additional assumptions. The derivation is explained in the next sub-section. The reader who is willing to take this on trust may note that the equation embodies a number of the factors outlined above. Saving by the bulk of the population is represented by the term for 'popular' wealth (PW). The internal rate of accumulation of the wealthy is related to capital gains via Π and to dividend income via RR. The influence of 'entrepreneurial' profits is reflected, probably inadequately, in Π; the time trend (T) may measure the slow-moving changes in the patterns of marriage and inheritance; and a shift in wealth-holding associated with the Second World War may be captured in the dummy variable ($D1$). Finally, taxation is represented implicitly by RR and directly by ED.

The equation may also be seen as incorporating a number of the factors referred to by earlier authors. Thus, Revell saw the growth of owner-occupation and 'the great rise in the price of land and other real property in recent years' as tending to lessen concentration (here incorporated in PW). He went on to say that 'as a short term effect changes in the relative prices of fixed interest securities and ordinary shares can also make noticeable differences in the degree of concentration from one year to another' (1965: 381); this is represented here by Π. In the same way, Smith and Franklin observe that for 1945–69 in the United States 'periods when the actual wealth share was above (below) the trend were generally preceded by periods of market increases (declines)' (1974: 164). Finally, Sargan drew attention to the fact that 'during normal periods it is possible that average saving in any wealth group is approximately proportional to wealth ... During wars, however, forced saving raises the savings of the poor and increased income and profits taxes affect the saving of the wealthy' (1957: 589). This may be reflected in the coefficient of $D1$.

* (c) Derivation of equation (1)

The starting point for the derivation is the simple 'Meade' process, which may

* This, more technical, passage may be omitted without loss of continuity.

be written for convenience in continuous time:

$$\dot{K} = SE + (Sr - \theta)K \tag{2}$$

(equation (3) in chapter 8), where for the present we treat the internal rate of accumulation $(Sr - \theta)$ as a constant. We assume that this process applies both to total wealth (denoted by K) and, with different parameters, to the wealth of the top 1 per cent (denoted by K_1). (Since the composition of the top 1 per cent changes over time, this should be viewed as a 'distributional' rather than an 'individual' model, in the terminology of chapter 8.)

We begin with total wealth. Integrating equation (2), we obtain:

$$K(t) = K(0)e^{(Sr-\theta)t}\left[1 + \frac{\int_0^t SE\,e^{-(Sr-\theta)(u-t)}du}{K(0)e^{(Sr-\theta)t}}\right] \tag{3}$$

The second term in the square brackets reflects the saving out of earned income, and we assume that it can be represented by $a_5 PW$, where PW is the ratio of popular assets to other wealth (the coefficient a_5 takes account of the fact that it is only a proxy for this form of saving).

For the top 1 per cent, we assume that saving out of earned income is relatively unimportant.[1] The main driving forces are taken to be the internal rate of accumulation and the 'entrepreneurial profits' referred to above. In the former case, we felt it desirable to treat saving out of capital gains as a separate component. Where Π denotes the index of capital values, the formulation:

$$\dot{K}_1 = (S_1 r - \theta_1)K_1 + S_2(\dot{\Pi}/\Pi)K_1 \tag{4}$$

allows for a differential rate of response of K_1 (the capital of the top 1 per cent) to different types of income. If $S_2 > S_1$, then consumption adjusts more slowly to capital gains than to dividend and interest income (r) – see Feldstein (1973) – and this seems a reasonable assumption to make. Integrating equation (4), we derive:

$$K_1(t) = K_1(0)e^{(S_1 r - \theta_1)t}\Pi^{S_2} \tag{5}$$

where $\Pi(0) = 1$. Saving out of 'random' entrepreneurial profits cannot be represented directly in this deterministic model; however, we can envisage them as a source of 'new' wealth in the same way as saving out of earned income (SE). The modification to the equation for $K_1(t)$ may be seen by analogy with equation (3), and we assume that the effect can be represented by a term $(1 + a_4\Pi)$. In other words the accumulated capital gains are taken

---

1 To the extent that this is incorrect, it will be reflected in a lower value of a_5 (see below).

as a proxy for this form of saving. In both this formulation, and that in equation (5), we take capital gains on shares, as the most important class of assets owned by the top 1 per cent.[2]

Combining equations (3) and (5), we obtain the share of the top 1 per cent (K_1/K).[3] Denoting its true, as opposed to its observed, value by W_1^*, and taking logarithms (to base e), we have:

$$\log(W_1^*) = a_0 + a_1 T + a_4 \log \Pi + \log(1 + a_5 PW) \tag{6}$$

where $a_1 = (S_1 r - \theta_1) - (Sr - \theta)$, i.e. the difference between the internal rates of accumulation, and $a_4 = S_2$. In order to estimate a_5 without recourse to a non-linear procedure, we approximated the last term by $a_5 PW$ (the accuracy of this is discussed below). The formulation described above is based on equation (5); if instead we had taken account of saving out of 'entre-preneurial profits', then $a_4 \log \Pi$ would have been replaced by $\log(1 + a_4 \Pi)$ which is again approximated by $a_4 \Pi$. This is the alternative form of equation (1).

To this point we have assumed that the internal rates of accumulation are constant over time. The first modification to this which should be considered is that there may have been a shift as a result of the Second World War. This may affect savings behaviour, as suggested by Sargan (1957), or it may affect the way in which estates are divided (the term θ) – see Fijalkowski-Bereday (1950). It is for this reason that the dummy variable $D1$ is included in equation (1). The second modification is to allow for variation in the rate of return, and for taxation. Where Sr varies over time, and is subject to income tax, the appropriate term in the equation for $\log(W_1^*)$ is:

$$\int_0^t [S_1 r(1 - I_1) - Sr(1 - I)] du \tag{7}$$

where I_1 is the rate of income tax for the top 1 per cent and I for the population as a whole. In the absence of suitable evidence on S_1 and S, it is difficult to decide on an appropriate specification. As one variation on equation (1) we have included RR (real net dividend yield), although this is not a fully satisfactory procedure. The treatment of transfer taxes is more straightforward. The equation for $\log(W_1^*)$ is modified by the term

$$a_7 \int_0^t (\tau_1 - \tau) du \tag{8}$$

2 No account is taken of Capital Gains Tax, which was introduced towards the end of the period considered. The estimates of wealth-holding do not include any explicit allowance for contingent Capital Gains Tax liabilities.

3 An alternative approach would be to treat K as the wealth of the bottom 99 per cent. This leads to rather similar results.

where a_7 is the fraction of the tax paid out of reduced saving, τ_1 is the tax rate (as a percentage of capital) for the top 1 per cent and τ is the average tax rate on all capital. This variable is referred to as *ED*.

9.2 Empirical estimates

The model described in the previous section is now applied to the estimates of the share of the top 1 per cent constructed for the period 1923–72 in chapter 6. In that chapter, we presented a limited set of regression results, being concerned only with the measurement of the time trend and the effect of discontinuities in the data. We pointed out that the incomplete specification of the equation may have led to misleading conclusions.

The basic equation in which we are interested is that labelled (1) earlier. This however relates to W_1^*, and in order to relate this to the observed values W_1, we need to allow for discontinuities in the data (chapter 6) and for the error process (chapter 5). In both cases, we take over the assumptions of earlier chapters, although in the present case they apply to the logarithm of W_1 (the assumption that the errors and shift effects are proportional rather than absolute may indeed be more reasonable). This leads to the following equation to be estimated:

$$\log W_1 = a_0 + a_1 T + a_2 D1 + a_3 D2 + a_4 \Pi \text{ (or } \log \Pi) + a_5 PW + \epsilon_t$$

$$(9)$$

where ϵ_t is a normally and independently distributed random variable with zero mean and constant variance (the question of serial correlation is taken up below). The dummy variable $D2$ is zero until 1959, one from 1960.

In order to relate the results obtained with equation (9) to those in chapter 6, we begin with a logarithmic form of the main equation discussed there. This is equation A in table 9.1. The results are similar to those in the linear form (which is given for reference at the top of the table). The time trend, for example, is 1 per cent per annum, or 0.43 percentage points at the mean value (compared with 0.42); the shift between 1959 and 1960 (dummy variable $D2$) is 7.5 percentage points (compared with 6.9); and the variable $D1$ is not significant.

The results obtained with equation (9) are shown in lines B and C of table 9.1, the former relating to the specification with Π and the latter to that with $\log \Pi$. Equation B appears to be superior: the $\bar{R}^2$ is higher and the standard error of the regression is smaller. Our discussion relates therefore to this equation.

Comparing equations A and B, we can see that the latter provides a better fit, with the standard error of the regression being reduced from 0.038 to 0.034. The coefficients of the variables added (Π and PW) are of the expected

Table 9.1. Regression equations for the share of the top 1 per cent

Equation	Constant	Dummy variables		Time	Share price		'Popular' wealth	Net return	Estate duty	$\bar{R}^2$	S.E.	D.W. (four gaps)
		$D1$	$D2$	T	Π	$\log \Pi$	PW	RR	ED			
Chapter 6	60.6	-2.91 (1.6)	-6.90 (7.1)	-0.42 (6.5)	—	—	—	—	—	0.983	1.42	2.26
A	4.12	-0.022 (0.5)	-0.201 (7.7)	-0.0097 (5.6)	—	—	—	—	—	0.977	0.0381	2.23
B	4.10	-0.017 (0.3)	-0.235 (5.4)	-0.0089 (4.2)	0.0014 (2.6)	—	-0.151 (2.8)	—	—	0.982	0.0344	2.19
C	4.12	-0.035 (0.6)	-0.223 (6.4)	-0.0097 (3.5)	—	0.057 (1.1)	-0.066 (1.6)	—	—	0.978	0.0377	2.22
D	4.10	-0.017 (0.3)	-0.237 (8.0)	-0.0088 (4.0)	0.0014 (2.6)	—	-0.149 (2.7)	0.042 (0.2)	—	0.981	0.0350	2.18
E	4.08	-0.025 (0.5)	-0.200 (5.1)	-0.0022 (0.4)	0.0016 (2.9)	—	0.064 (0.7)	—	-0.024 (1.3)	0.982	0.0339	2.13
F	4.07	-0.034 (6.8)	-0.192 (6.1)	—	0.0016 (3.0)	—	0.041 (0.7)	—	-0.030 (4.5)	0.983	0.0334	2.09

Note: The dependent variable is $\log_e W_1$, except in the equation from chapter 6 where it is W_1. The figures in brackets are t-statistics.

Source of variables:
    See over

Notes to Table 9.1

Source of variables:

Dependent variable: log (to base e) of share of top 1 per cent as shown in table 6.5, but to 2 decimal places.

Dummy variables: $D1$ is zero up to and including 1938, one thereafter. $D2$ is zero up to and including 1959, one thereafter.

Time: T is 1 in 1923 and 50 in 1972.

Share price: Π is the price index for industrial ordinary shares published in *Key Statistics 1900–1970* by the London and Cambridge Economic Service (table M), extended to 1972.

Popular wealth: PW is estimated from national balance sheet data as described in appendices II and VI, from information on owner-occupation and the number of dwellings derived from *Housing Statistics*, Censuses of Population and a variety of other sources, and the house price index published in *Key Statistics* (table I), again extended to 1972.

Net return: RR is dividend yield based on index published by de Zoete and Bevan (*Equity and Fixed Interest Investment*, annual), less the standard rate of income tax on investment income and the rate of inflation (increase in retail prices).

Estate duty: ED is revenue from death duties (from annual reports of the Inland Revenue) expressed as a percentage of total capital, multiplied by $(X_1/W_1 - 1)$ where X_1 is the share of duties paid by the top 1 per cent (estimated from information in the Inland Revenue annual reports about net receipts by ranges), and cumulated from 1923.

sign, and are significant at the 5 per cent and 1 per cent levels, respectively. A rise in the share price index of 20 points from its 1972 level of 211 would lead to an increase in the share of the top 1 per cent of nearly 1 percentage point (in 1972). The coefficient of *PW* means that a rise in the value of owner-occupied houses and consumer durables from 40 per cent to 50 per cent of other wealth would reduce the share of the top group by about $\frac{1}{2}$ percentage point (in 1972). (It may also be noted that the terms $a_4 \Pi$ and $a_5 PW$ both have mean values of around 0.09; this suggests that the approximation $\log(1 + ax) \simeq ax$ may not be unreasonable, since the terms in $(ax)^2$ and higher powers are likely to be small.)

The dummy variable for the impact of the Second World War is not significant; this does not however necessarily mean that there is no such effect. This depends on the interpretation of the discontinuities in the data. As we saw in chapter 6, it is conceivable that to some extent (up to half) the data shift applies only during the 1950s, reflecting the much reduced coverage in that period and the possibility that we may have under-stated the wealth of the excluded population.[4] If this is so, then the data discontinuities would cause an apparent upward jump between 1938 and 1950, and the insignificance of *D*1 may result from this cancelling with a genuine downward shift as a result of the War. The existence of such an effect would be consistent with the evidence about the trend in the distribution of income, although it is difficult to reach any firmer conclusion. This clearly warrants further consideration.

The model is extended to include the rate of return (*RR*) and estate duty variables (*ED*) in equations *D–F*. The rate of return is the dividend yield after allowing for tax at the standard rate and for the effect of inflation. From equation *D* it may be seen that the coefficient is nowhere near being significant. This may reflect the wrong choice of variable or be interpreted as saying that the rate of return does not contribute to the explanation of the *differential* rate of accumulation. In the case of estate duty we should expect the differential impact to be greater. In equations *E* and *F*, we have taken the difference between the death duties estimated to have been paid by the top 1 per cent as a percentage of their capital and the average rate of death duties on all capital. The amount is cumulated from 1923 onwards. The results in equation *E* are rather mixed. The overall fit is (marginally) improved but none of the explanatory variables apart from *D*2 and the share price index is significant. The remaining variables, particularly *T*, *PW* and

---

4 This argument was suggested to us by Michael Parsonage of the Royal Commission.

ED, are highly collinear; moreover, it is possible that the time trend in earlier equations has been standing as a proxy for other factors, including the progressive impact of estate duty. In view of this, we have omitted T from the final equation. The fit appears more satisfactory (the standard error of the regression is the smallest of all six equations), although the coefficient of *PW* is not significantly different from zero. The coefficients of Π and *ED* are significant at the 1 per cent level, and the latter implies that if the top 1 per cent pay $2\frac{1}{2}$ times their 'share' of death duties and the revenue is 0.3 per cent of total wealth, then the share of the top 1 per cent would be reduced by 4 percentage points in 10 years.

In our discussion of the error process in chapter 5, we suggested that the errors ϵ_t might be negatively serially correlated, with a 'bunching' of estates in one year being associated with an error in the opposite direction in the next. It is interesting that all the equations have Durbin–Watson statistics in excess of 2.0, which is consistent with this view. However, the critical value for five explanatory variables, apart from the constant, at the $2\frac{1}{2}$ per cent level is 2.26, so that the results do not lead us to reject the hypothesis of zero serial correlation.[5] As noted earlier, it is possible that alternative assumptions about the error process may be more appropriate; the study of these is, however, limited by gaps in the data, and this is a subject we leave to a later occasion. In the same way it would be interesting to extend the analysis to the share of groups below the top 1 per cent (e.g. the next 4 per cent), where the explanatory variables are likely to be rather different,[6] and to make use of the fact that the error terms are likely to be correlated across equations (applying the technique of seemingly unrelated regressions).[7]

To summarise, we have two equations which provide a reasonable fit to the data, but which embody rather different explanations of the decline in the share of the top 1 per cent. According to equation B, the decline has been associated with the spread of 'popular' wealth, coupled with an exogenous downward trend (possibly reflecting differential rates of accumulation or changes in marriage and inheritance customs), with the upward movement in share prices working in the opposite direction. In equation F there is no exogenous downward trend, and the effect of popular wealth is insignificant. According to this, the main motive forces have been estate duty, either

5 This is for a one-tailed test against the alternative of negative serial correlation; for a two-tailed test the significance level is 5 per cent.

6 A preliminary analysis is given in Harrison (1976). The data have however been extensively revised since then, and the specification is rather different.

7 We are grateful to Charles Beach for valuable suggestions on this and other points.

directly through transferring money to the Treasury or indirectly via family rearrangements of wealth, and – in the opposite direction – the rise in share prices. In both cases, there may or may not have been a shift between 1938 and 1950 reflecting the impact of social changes in the war-time period; this depends on the way in which the discontinuities in the data are interpreted.

The results are not, therefore, conclusive. They do nonetheless provide some insight into the processes at work. This may be illustrated by the 1973–4 fall in share prices. Some commentators suggested that this had led to a dramatic decline in the share of the top 1 per cent. According to Day (*Observer*, 22 September 1974), 'the squeeze on wealthy individuals . . . is already taking place with a vengeance because of the Stock Market collapse', and he estimated that the top 1 per cent had lost between a quarter and a third of their wealth between 1973 and 1974. The estimates of the Royal Commission were less extreme, indicating a fall in the share of the top 1 per cent from 27.6 to 23.9 per cent (Series B 1975, table 49). Our own analysis does not allow for assets other than shares (except via the effect of house prices on PW), but these were the major element in the decline, and it is interesting to see the predicted change. Between mid 1973 and mid 1974 share prices fell by about 40 per cent, equivalent to a fall of some 85 points in the index Π. Both equations B and F have similar coefficients for this variable (around 0.0015) and these imply a fall of 12 per cent in the share of the top 1 per cent, or from 27.6 to 24.3 per cent. This appears quite consistent with the results reported by the Royal Commission. Moreover, it shows that the wealth share is indeed sensitive to the behaviour of the stock market but that the effects should not be exaggerated.[8]

In this, and the preceding section we have used the simple Meade model as a framework within which we can interpret the data and develop econometric estimates. It should be clear that a full-scale testing of different models requires further developments in terms both of theory and of the econometric methods applied. The models, and the restrictions they embody, need to be cast in a form such that we can relate them to the observed evidence. The econometric treatment, particularly that of lags and the error structure, needs to be refined. We hope however that we have shown that this rather neglected subject – the time series analysis of distributional data – would repay further attention. (For a useful review of similar work on income distribution, see Beach and Flatters (1976)).

8 It has also to be remembered that there are indirect effects via the holdings of institutions.

9.3 Wealth-holding and the family

In the second half of this chapter, we consider the refinement of the estimates which is made possible by disaggregation. First, by examining the wealth-holding of men and women (this section), we may throw light on *family* holdings; secondly, the disaggregation by age groups (section 9.4) may help in the understanding of the role of *life-cycle* factors.

The reasons why family holdings are of interest should be clear. As was pointed out by Daniels and Campion, 'it would be obviously misleading to place the wives and children of persons with £50,000 in the same category as paupers' (1936:55). They go on to say that 'the inequality of the distribution of capital will be exaggerated in our estimates in so far as it is general practice for the whole or the main part of the capital of a family to be legally vested in one of the parents' (1936:55). More recently, this point has been stressed by Polanyi and Wood, who argue that 'if every person included in the top 10 per cent had only one unrecorded dependant, the formula would be reduced to 20 per cent [rather than 10 per cent] of the people owning 40 per cent of the wealth' (1974:40). Similarly, the measurement of the *trends* may be affected: for example, Horsman recently suggested that the trend towards reduced concentration

> which they seem to reveal could be misleading; all that has in fact been taking place may have been a transfer of wealth by gift, under the incentive of the high rates of estate duty, from parents to their children, or from husbands to their wives. The concentration of personal wealth within *families* may be just as great as ever [1975: 524].

In the United States, Lampman concluded that 'the decline in inequality shown on the basis of individuals tends to overstate the decline which would be found on a family basis' (1962:206—7).

It is essential to clarify at the outset what we mean by 'family wealth', since different authors seem to be concerned with rather different concepts. One interpretation is the wealth of those who currently form a *nuclear family* (husband, wife and dependent children), which is what Polanyi and Wood (1974), for example, appear to have in mind. Alternatively, we might consider the wealth of a *dynasty*, which would mean combining the holdings of parents, children, grand-children, great-grand-children, and other issue alive at the point in time. This interpretation would take account of the transfers referred to by Horsman (1975), since transfers from parents to children before death would have no effect on dynastic wealth. In what follows, we concentrate on the former concept — the distribution among nuclear families — but we feel that dynastic holdings should be further studied. Indeed some of the techniques used in estimating the wealth of the nuclear family may be applicable to this further refinement of the data.

Since our estimates of wealth-holding relate to the adult population, the estimation of the holdings of nuclear families reduces to the problem of 'marrying up' the wealth of husbands and wives. In considering this, the analysis in chapter 8 (pages 214–16) provides a valuable starting point. We saw there that the relationship between individual wealth and that of married couples depends on two important factors. The first is the relative wealth-holdings of men and women. From the estate data we can derive the distribution disaggregated in this way, and the results for 1970 on assumptions A2/B3 (comparable with chapter 6) are shown in table 9.2. In constructing these estimates we have assumed that the per capita wealth of the excluded population is the same for both groups; to the extent that per capita wealth is lower for women, the estimated shares of the top 1 per cent etc. will be higher. As may be seen, women are out-numbered in the top wealth ranges, but not by a large margin. They account, in fact, for 40 per cent of those above £100,000, and their estimated share in total wealth in 1970 is also 40 per cent. It is interesting to note that the distribution among women appears to exhibit greater concentration, and this would be even more marked if the per capita wealth among the excluded population were lower for women and correspondingly higher for men.

The second factor is the pattern of marriage. In the analysis of Blinder (1973), concerned with the transmission of wealth, the relevant consideration was whether rich men married rich women. In the present context, the question is whether rich men tend to have rich wives.[9] Rich men may marry Eliza Doolittles but subsequently transfer wealth to them; conversely they may marry heiresses who make over their wealth to their husbands. There is rather limited evidence about this question, and the analysis is based on a range of assumptions about the degree of correlation. From chapter 8, we can deduce that the cases $\rho = 1$ (rich men have rich wives) and $\rho = -1$ (rich men have poor wives) give upper and lower bounds on the degree of concentration of family wealth. This approach has been employed by Lyons (1974) and by the Royal Commission (1975:95–6).

Before considering the empirical results, we should take account of two further factors: the proportion married and the weighting for family size. Lyons makes 'the important assumption [that] wealth was shared between married and single persons in proportion to their relative numbers in the sex/ age group as a whole' (1974:195). As Lyons observes, this assumption may well be wrong, but the direction of the error is not clear. The evidence of

---

9 We are grateful to Michael Parsonage of the Royal Commission for drawing our attention to the importance of this distinction.

Table 9.2. Distribution of wealth among men and women — England and Wales 1970

Wealth range (£)	Men Number (thousands)	Women Number (thousands)
1,000 −	3,745	2,819
5,000 −	1,715	873
10,000 −	409	238
15,000 −	302	183
25,000 −	166	122
50,000 −	74	51
100,000 −	21	15
200,000 −-	10	6

	Share of top x% of men in total wealth owned by men	Share of top x% of women in total wealth owned by women
Top 1%	27.7	32.1
5%	50.0	58.1
10%	63.9	72.9

Note: Estimated on assumptions A2/B3/C0/D1/E0.

Lampman (1962) and Smith (1974) for the United States provides some support for the view that married men may be over-represented and married women under-represented among top wealth-holders. Lampman (1962:table 51) showed that in 1953, 2.3 per cent of married men were in his class of top wealth-holders, compared with 1.2 per cent of single, divorced or widowed men; whereas for women the corresponding percentages were 0.7 per cent and 1.1 per cent. Smith reports a similar finding for 1969 and notes that 'these differences reflect, to some extent, the fact that women tend to outlive their husbands and thus add to their own wealth the assets of their deceased spouses' (1974:148).[10] We have therefore presented a range of estimates with different assumptions about the proportions of men and women in the top 1 per cent who are married (these proportions are denoted by Ψ_m and Ψ_f respectively). To this extent our analysis is a development of that of Lyons,

10   The Royal Commission have shown us some interesting calculations based on the investment income data which suggest that women's wealth is heavily concentrated among single women. This evidence needs however to be interpreted in the light of the differences in average yields — see below.

although our calculations are less refined in that we do not allow Ψ to vary with age.

Finally, there is the weighting for family size. Suppose that the total wealth of a family is w, and the number of (equivalent) family members is $(1 + n)$. We could then imagine a number of different procedures, including:

(i) count the family as one unit with wealth w (no allowance for family size),

(ii) count the family as one unit with wealth $w/(1 + n)$,

(iii) count the family as $(1 + n)$ units with wealth $w/(1 + n)$ per capita.

The procedures are frequently confused. Thus Polanyi and Wood (1974) use (i) on p. 35 and (iii) on p. 40 without apparently recognising that they are different. In what follows, we take (i) and (iii) to illustrate the consequences of different definitions, and in the latter case we set $n = 1$ (most equivalence scales calculated in the literature in fact treat a couple as less than 2 equivalent adults, but these are not necessarily appropriate in the present context).

It will be clear that the estimates of family wealth-holding presented below are conditional on the assumptions made about the pattern of marriage (ρ), the proportions married (Ψ) and the definition of the unit. Before turning to the empirical results, it may therefore be helpful to consider some of the implications in the 'Pareto' model set out in earlier chapters. If we further simplify by assuming that the excluded population has zero wealth, then the proportion of individuals with wealth in excess of w is given by $w^{-\alpha}$ (normalising such that $\underline{w} = 1$), and the share in total wealth by:

$$1 - L(w) = w^{-(\alpha - 1)} \tag{10}$$

Let us first examine the case where $\Psi_m = \Psi_f = 0$ (i.e. all of the top 1 per cent are single). This means that the absolute frequency distribution of top holdings is unchanged; the implications for the proportions depend however on the weighting for family size of married couples (who by assumption are in the bottom 99 per cent). Suppose that the fraction of the population married is denoted by 2β. Under assumption (iii) about the definition of the unit, this does not affect the total number of units (we count a couple as two); however, under assumption (i) the number of units is reduced to $(1 - \beta)$. As a result, the top 1 per cent of total *units* is now a smaller number of people (they are all single) and the share is reduced by a factor:[11]

---

11 The number of individuals in the top 1 per cent is now $(1 - \beta)$ times its previous value, and the wealth level required to be in the top 1 per cent rises from w^0 to w^1, where:

$$(w^1/w^0) = (1 - \beta)^{-1/\alpha}$$

Substituting in equation (10) gives the adjustment factor in the text.

$$[1 - \beta]^{(\alpha - 1)/\alpha} \tag{11}$$

So that with $\alpha = 1.5$ and $\beta = 0.35$, this means that the share of the top 1 per cent would be reduced to 0.87 of its value on an individual basis.

Suppose now that we go to the other extreme, and assume that all the top 1 per cent are married. Moreover, to begin with let us assume that their spouses have zero wealth ($\rho = -1$). Under assumption (i) about the definition of the unit, the ranking of units at the top is unaffected, and the adjustment is simply that for the total number of units described above. With these assumptions about ρ and the definition of the unit, therefore, we should not expect the proportion married to be critical to the calculations. On the other hand, with assumption (iii), treating a couple as 2 units with wealth $w/2$, the top 1 per cent (of individuals) are counted as twice that number, and their share is reduced by a factor:[12]

$$\left(\frac{1}{2}\right)^{(\alpha - 1)/\alpha} \tag{12}$$

With $\alpha = 1.5$, this means that the share of the top 1 per cent is reduced to 0.79 of its value on an individual basis.

Finally, there is the case where the top 1 per cent are all married, with the richest man being married to the richest woman, and so on down the wealth scale. If the distribution of wealth among men and women were identical, then the top 1 per cent would marry each other, and on assumption (iii) they would constitute the top 1 per cent of units. Their share would be the same as on an individual basis. On assumption (i) the position is more complicated. The top 1 per cent of individuals are now treated as half that number of units (on the assumption that they marry each other); on the other hand, the total number of units is reduced. The share is now adjusted by a factor:[13]

$$[2(1 - \beta)]^{(\alpha - 1)/\alpha} \tag{13}$$

With the values used earlier ($\alpha = 1.5, \beta = 0.35$), the share is increased by a

12 This assumes that the richest single person has less than half the wealth necessary to be in the top 1 per cent. The wealth required to be in the top 1 per cent of units rises to w^1 where:

$$(w^1/w^0) = 2^{1/\alpha}$$

13 The number above w is reduced by a factor of 2; on the other hand, the total number of units is reduced to $(1 - \beta)$ of its previous level.

factor 1.09. The way in which this works may be seen as follows. Suppose that the total number of individuals is 40 million. If 70 per cent (2β) are married, then families (counting couples as 1) number 26 million. The top 1 per cent of individuals (400,000 people) marry each other and constitute 200,000 families, which is less than 1 per cent of all families. In order to arrive at the share of the top 1 per cent of *units*, we need to add families and hence the share increases. These conclusions depend on the assumption that the distribution of wealth is the same, which we have not seen to be the case; however, the way in which they need to be modified should be apparent.[14]

With this background, we may examine the actual results obtained for Great Britain in 1970. Table 9.3 shows the estimated share of the top 1 per cent under different assumptions. If we begin with the case where none of the top wealth-holders is married, and we take the definition (iii) of the unit (couple = 2), then the results are the same as for the distribution among individuals: the share is 30.8 per cent. Retaining this definition of the unit, we can see that where the rich are married to the rich there is little change in the share, as predicted above (the slight decline being attributable to the lower average wealth of women). If the rich are married to those with little wealth, then the share is reduced: by some 6 percentage points in the case where the proportion married is the same as for the population as a whole.

The adoption of the alternative definition of the unit (couple = 1), which appears to be that used by the Royal Commission (1975), leads to a fall in the shares where none of the top 1 per cent is married, but to higher shares with the other assumptions. Where the proportions are those of the population average, the share is 5.3 percentage points lower on a rich married to poor basis than with the individual distribution but 0.6 percentage points *higher* on a rich married to rich basis. These figures are close to those given by the Royal Commission for 1972, which are 4.9 and 0.2 percentage points respectively (1975:96). (The Royal Commission also give results for the case where the wealthiest men are married to the wealthiest women within the relevant age group, which turn out to give a share identical to that for individuals for the top 1 per cent (1975:96)).

It is sometimes argued that Ψ_f is likely to be less than Ψ_m in the higher wealth ranges, or that wealthy women are more likely to be single than

14   The possibility that the Lorenz curve will shift outward may be illustrated by the position of the richest person. Supposing that he (or she) is married, then his share in both wealth and total population increases under definition (i) of the unit. The former will outweigh the latter, and the Lorenz curve shift outwards, if the wife's share of their joint wealth is greater than β. This suggests how (13) may be generalised.

wealthy men. The explanations offered for this include the fact that many wealthy women are widows, a consequence of greater female longevity. However, the evidence used to support the claim tends, we feel, to over-state the difference,[15] and it is unlikely that the effects of, say, halving Ψ_f would be very significant.

In summarising their results, the Royal Commission observed that 'the limited range of the quantile shares . . . is noteworthy' (1975:96) and concluded that 'the distribution of wealth among single person and husband and wife units is not greatly different from that among individuals' (1975:126). The Commission did not consider the way in which the estimates varied with the definition of the unit or with the assumptions about the proportion married, and one of our purposes has been to draw attention to the assumptions which are implicit in many discussions of this question. As a result, we have obtained a wider range of estimates: from 23 to 34 per cent. Nevertheless, we feel on the basis of both the hypothetical calculations using the Pareto model (equations (11)–(13)) and the results of table 9.3, which are in close agreement, that for likely values of the parameters the Commission's conclusions are probably correct. The lowest of our figures (23 per cent) is based on an extreme assumption about the wealth-holding of husbands and wives which is very unlikely to be realistic, and the figure only applies to one definition of the unit. In general, it seems probable that the reduction in the share of the top 1 per cent would not exceed 5 percentage points, and may well be considerably smaller.

To this juncture, we have concentrated on the estimates of concentration in one particular year (1970); we turn now briefly to the ways in which the estimates on a family basis may reveal a different trend over time. It would clearly be possible to replicate the calculations made in table 9.3 for earlier years. However, the range of estimates for a single year mean that it would be difficult to draw any definite conclusions about the changes over time. A

15 As noted earlier, the Royal Commission have used the division of investment income between single persons and married couples to estimate that the proportion of women's wealth held by single women is around two thirds (for men the proportion is around a quarter). The argument is, in essence, that – given the relatively large investment income accruing to single women – the share of married women in the investment income of married couples must be small, if the figures are to be consistent with the overall share of women in total wealth. This however assumes that the yield is identical for wealth owned by men and women. Our own calculations using the yield data in chapter 7 suggest that the yield is considerably higher for the wealth-holdings of women, and that their share in investment income is larger than their share in total wealth. To this extent, the division of wealth may be closer to the proportions in the population than the Royal Commission's figures indicate.

Table 9.3. Family distribution of wealth — share of top 1 per cent under different assumptions — Great Britain 1970

	None of top 1 per cent married ($\Psi_m = \Psi_f = 0$)	All top 1 per cent married ($\Psi_m = \Psi_f = 1$)	Proportion of top 1 per cent married = population average ($\Psi_m = \Psi_f = 0.7$)
Couple = 1 unit (Assumption (i))			
Rich married to rich ($\rho = 1$)		33.5	31.4
Rich married to poor ($\rho = -1$)	26.5	25.6	25.6
Couple = 2 units (Assumption (iii))			
Rich married to rich ($\rho = 1$)		30.5	30.5
Rich married to poor ($\rho = -1$)	30.8	23.1	25.1

Note: Calculated on the basis of assumptions A2/B3/C0/D1/E0 and assuming equal per capita wealth among the excluded population.

range of 5 per cent, for example, is equivalent to a trend of 0.4 percentage points operating for $12\frac{1}{2}$ years.

In view of this, we limit our attention to some of the forces which may have influenced the relative estimates on an individual and a family basis. Of these, one of the most important is the share of wealth owned by women. As it is described by the Royal Commission:

> the treatment of wealth on an individual basis may also affect apparent trends in the distribution over time. For example, the share of total wealth owned by women has been rising over the years, according to the estate multiplier estimates, but this may simply represent increased wealth sharing within the family, partly as a response to changing tax provisions. To this extent, the distribution of wealth on a family basis is unchanged, despite an apparent trend towards greater equality in the distribution of wealth among individuals [1975:95].

The belief that the share of women in total personal wealth has been increasing steadily over the years is widely held. It appears to be based on the estimates of Revell (1965) who showed the share as having risen from 33.1

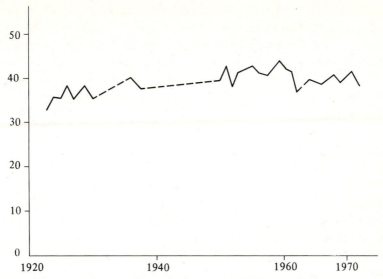

Note: Calculated on the basis of assumptions A2/B3/C0/D1/E0.

Figure 9.1 Share of wealth owned by women – England and Wales 1923–72

per cent in 1927 to 42.1 per cent in 1960, which means that their wealth *relative* to that of men has increased from 49 per cent to 73 per cent. These figures are quoted by the Royal Commission but they proceed to show that since 1960 the trend has reversed (1975 : 103–5).

Our own estimates, given in figure 9.1, confirm the view held by the Royal Commission. These figures show the share of women in total personal wealth-holding in England and Wales over the period 1923–72. The assumptions are the same as those made in chapter 6. We have allocated men and women in the excluded population identical per capita holdings, but the alternative assumption that per capita holdings are in the same proportion as in the included population gives a similar trend. It should be noted that the estimates exhibit considerable year-to-year variation. This may be due to sampling fluctuations or to the effect of short-run asset price changes (since the types of asset held by men and women are rather different). It should be noted that no adjustment has been made for missing wealth. This is especially important in the case of the exemption for property settled on a surviving spouse, which leads to an under-statement of the wealth owned by widows.

The general impression from the figure is of a rise in the share of women's wealth between the 1920s and the 1950s, although somewhat less marked than Revell's figures indicated. (The reason for the difference probably lies in the choice of social class multipliers and the allowance for the wealth of the excluded population.) Moreover, there has been a decline between the late 1950s and the early 1970s. This is illustrated by the (four-year) averaged figures shown below.

	Share (%)	Ratio to men's wealth (%)
1925–8	36	57
1950–3	40	66
1958–61	42	74
1969–72	39	65

These changes may indeed affect the interpretation of the trends over time. The matter is, however, more complex than indicated in the passage from the Royal Commission's *Initial Report* quoted above, since the fall in recent years has to be explained (and, of course, other factors taken into account). This complexity reinforces the warnings given in chapter 6 about the difficulty in drawing conclusions concerning the trends in concentration over time.

9.4   Wealth-holding, age and the life-cycle

In the recent literature, there has been considerable discussion of the need to interpret evidence on current wealth-holding in the light of the systematic variation with age, reflecting life-cycle factors. Adapting the notation of chapter 8, we can write the current wealth at time 0 of a person i aged a as:

$$w_{ai} = K_0^i - K_T^i + \int_{-a}^{0} S(v)dv \qquad (14)$$

Inherited wealth received · Inherited wealth passed on · Net saving

All of these factors may be influenced by age. If we define K_0^i as the present value of receipts, then it is likely to increase with a (as is K_T^i); cumulated net saving may follow a hump-shaped pattern as people save for retirement and then dissave. A number of studies have therefore disaggregated the estate estimates by age groups, seeking in this way to abstract from those age differences which are common to all. In effect this procedure involves looking at the distribution of $w_{ai}/\bar{w}_a$ among those aged a, where $\bar{w}_a$ is the mean wealth for that age group. Such an analysis has been presented in Atkinson (1971), which estimated the shares of top wealth groups in 1963–7 and suggested that these were not substantially different from the shares in the overall distribution, and in Astin (1975), which demonstrated that there was a similar picture in 1972.

The analysis of life-cycle factors via the disaggregated distribution within age groups has been criticised in the Royal Commission's *Initial Report*:

> the distribution of wealth within age groups may be as unequal, and possibly under certain circumstances even more unequal, than in the population as a whole, and yet be consistent with a very strong life-cycle effect . . . a more revealing test of the lifecycle theory is given by an examination of the absolute average level of wealth-holding within age groups [1975:114–15].

The Commission proceeds to examine how far the life-cycle theory does in fact explain savings behaviour.

In our view this discussion by the Royal Commission confounds two separate issues. The first is the extent to which individual wealth-holdings are governed by life-cycle or age factors; the second is the extent to which the current distribution is influenced by variations in average wealth across age groups. The first is essentially a time series question, and what is required is a cohort analysis. (This issue, and the difficulties involved, are discussed by Shorrocks (1975a).) We need to examine the wealth-holding of the same people at different dates in order to have a fully satisfactory test of the life-cycle theory of savings behaviour. The second question, however, is simply concerned with cross-section data – the contribution of differences *between* cohorts to the overall dispersion of wealth-holdings. The Royal Commission tends to discuss these questions as though they were the same. For the second purpose, an analysis of average wealth-holding by age is necessary, but it is not an alternative to the study of within-age group concentration.

What is undoubtedly true is that the results need careful interpretation. They cannot, for example, be regarded as isolating the pure effect of inheritance. Net saving is likely to reflect not simply age but also the distribution of earned income, so that we should expect to find concentration of $w_{ai}/\bar{w}_a$ arising from differences in wages (as noted in chapter 8). Even if net saving were the same for all people of the same age, the distribution would be translated by a constant term.[16] Even if there were no saving out of wages, the differences in the timing of the receipt of inheritance and the timing of gifts might cause concentration of inheritance to be over-stated (see Atkinson 1971). Nor can it be assumed that all age differences have been eliminated, since the time path of saving may differ from one person to the next. All that has been taken into account is the common age difference as reflected

---

16 This would be likely to vary with a, since the changes in mean wealth reflect (in terms of equation (14)) variation in K_0 and K_T as well as in net savings.

in the mean wealth.

The conclusions which can be drawn from the disaggregated data are therefore strictly limited. Moreover, the estimates themselves need to be qualified in three important respects. First, there is at present no satisfactory means of allocating the wealth of the excluded population by age groups. We have in table 9.4 allocated an equal per capita amount. This is likely to cause the age factor to be under-stated, but does at least allow for the varying proportion in the excluded category in different age groups. Secondly, the estimates are not corrected for valuation or wealth missing from the estate returns (they are on an A2/B3/C0/D1/E0 basis as in chapter 6). Again this is because we lacked the data necessary to make adjustments, but it may well lead to biased results. Of particular significance is the adjustment for the valuation of life assurance policies. As the Royal Commission has recently shown (1976:54) these feature much more importantly in the net worth of younger age groups, and the failure to adjust these may seriously distort the age profile. Finally, when considering the distribution disaggregated by age, sampling errors are likely to be more important, especially for the youngest age groups.

Bearing these qualifications in mind, with regard both to interpretation and to the possible bias, we may examine the results shown in table 9.4. As found in earlier studies, the shares within particular age groups are not greatly different from the figures for all ages combined (the bottom row shows the shares for all men and all women respectively). In the case of men, the share of the top 5 per cent is *higher* for four of the age groups, and the same is true for the share of the top 10 per cent. It is in the main the older age groups for which the shares are higher. For women, in contrast, it is the younger age groups where the shares are highest. As noted by Astin (1975), the average wealth profile has become much less hump-shaped; and our data disaggregated by sex (he combined men and women) show that this is due to the substantial average wealth of the younger male age groups (see also figure 9.2). This may well be attributable to the life policy effect referred to above. The age group 35–44 were estimated to hold 28.6 per cent of their net worth in this form in 1973 (Royal Commission 1976:54). If we reduce the value from that of sums assured to the cash surrender value, then net worth would be reduced by a factor of some 0.877, so that mean wealth becomes £3,110; the corresponding adjustment to those aged 55–64 would make their mean wealth £3,600.

We turn now to the trends over time and their relation to the age distribution. A number of authors have noted a shift in the age composition of wealth over the past fifty years. Revell drew attention to the fact that 'while

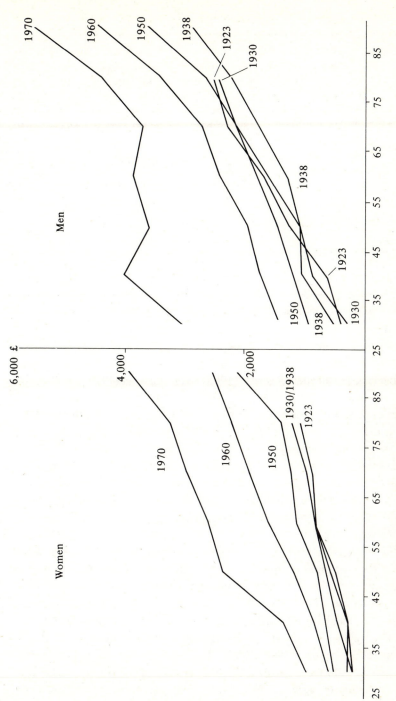

Figure 9.2 Age profiles of wealth-holding 1923–70

Table 9.4. Distribution by age groups — England and Wales 1970

Age	Men				Women			
	Share of top			Mean wealth £	Share of top			Mean wealth £
	1%	5%	10%		1%	5%	10%	
25–34	26.7	44.8	58.7	3,037	31.0	54.8	66.6	930
35–44	27.8	46.5	59.3	4,042	32.4	58.9	72.9	1,309
45–54	24.3	48.5	63.0	3,612	36.2	60.8	73.1	2,321
55–64	27.2	51.6	64.8	3,851	27.7	54.0	68.9	2,591
65–74	25.8	51.2	65.5	3,771	24.3	49.2	64.6	3,026
75–84	26.9	53.1	67.5	4,412	24.8	51.1	65.8	3,268
85 and over	27.9	54.7	68.6	5,774	25.7	53.4	67.6	3,891
Total population	27.7	50.0	63.9	3,348	32.1	58.1	72.9	1,980

Note: Calculated on the basis of assumptions A2/B3/C0/D1/E0.

the age distribution of the male population over 15 years of age has shifted towards the older age groups, the age distribution of personal wealth owned by men has remained unchanged' (1965:381). Horsman (1975) has recently given figures showing that men below the age of 45 acquired an increasing share of total wealth owned by men between 1954 and 1971, although this needs to be qualified in the light of the problems discussed above.

Any levelling of the age profile which has taken place would tend to reduce the overall degree of concentration. It is therefore interesting to consider how the distribution within age groups has changed over the period. Table 9.5 shows the distributions for a representative selection of years (at approximately ten-year intervals), constructed on the same basis as the estimates in table 9.4.

From this table, we can make two interesting comparisons. The first is to follow the changes in the distribution for a given age group — and to compare these with the changes in the distribution as a whole. Suppose, for example, we consider the share of the top 1 per cent among men aged 55–64, a group where sampling error is less important than at younger ages and which is less affected by the over-valuation of life assurance. In 1923, the share for this group was 3.9 per cent below that for the population as a whole (table 6.5). The gap tended first to narrow, then widen (reaching 9.0 per cent in 1950), and finally narrow again (in 1970 it was 2.5 per cent). Even, therefore, if the overall rate of decline is similar, the experience of individual age groups has been rather different within sub-periods: for example, there is a smaller fall in the share between 1950 and 1970. The differences for women are even more marked. In 1923, the distribution among women was in each case less concentrated than among men of the same age; in 1970 this was true of only two out of six age groups (the oldest). Taking the age group 55–64, the share of the top 1 per cent fell by 8.0 between 1923 and 1950, compared with an overall fall of 13.7, and between 1950 and 1970 it fell by 13.4 per cent, compared with 17.5 per cent.

The second aspect of table 9.5 which is of interest is the experience of particular cohorts. As has been noted by Shorrocks (1975a), the estate data allow one to follow a cohort by making observations at ten-year intervals. If we take, for example, those born within five years of 1890, then they will appear in the cohort 35–44 in 1930, 55–64 in 1950, 65–74 in 1960 and 75–84 in 1970. We may also take 25–34 in 1923 and 45–54 in 1938 as reasonable approximations. For this 'cohort' the share of the top 5 per cent changed as shown below.

	Men	Women	Overall distribution (chapter 6)
1923	78.3	67.6	82.0
1930	80.5	70.0	79.2
1938	75.5	70.1	76.9
1950	66.7	69.6	74.3
1960	59.5	55.6	59.4
1970	53.1	51.1	53.6

(We have taken the top 5 per cent, rather than the top 1 per cent, since the sampling errors are likely to be smaller, which is an important consideration for the younger age groups.)

The evidence from a cohort of this kind needs to be interpreted with care. The degree of concentration reflects, for example, both life-cycle and secular changes. There are reasons why one might expect concentration to vary systematically with age. Thus the 'queuing' model of Shorrocks (1975) suggests that concentration will decline over the working life and then rise during retirement. In order to draw any conclusions about secular changes one would have therefore to abstract from this effect. This illustrates once again the need for further work to build closer links between theory and evidence.

There is however one issue which we can address with the tools developed

Table 9.5. Distribution by age groups — England and Wales 1923—70

	Men			Women		
Share of top	1%	5%	10%	1%	5%	10%
1923						
Age						
25—34	66.6	78.3	84.2	46.2	67.6	74.9
35—44	55.1	77.0	85.7	50.0	72.4	80.8
45—54	59.1	80.8	89.2	46.3	73.3	83.6
55—64	57.0	80.9	88.7	49.1	74.9	86.3
65—74	57.6	82.5	89.8	47.5	75.5	87.5
75—84	56.8	84.0	91.5	47.8	78.3	90.1
All ages	63.3	83.0	90.1	53.1	78.3	86.2
1930						
25—34	42.6	61.3	70.8	48.7	67.8	75.7
35—44	64.9	80.5	86.7	47.7	70.0	78.2
45—54	55.2	76.3	85.5	49.7	73.9	82.5
55—64	55.2	79.0	87.2	42.2	69.6	82.2
65—74	56.1	81.1	88.9	43.4	72.0	84.1
75—84	54.2	81.7	89.8	41.2	73.0	85.0
All ages	60.7	80.7	88.0	50.5	76.0	83.6
1938						
25—34	61.8	76.4	82.2	44.2	59.5	66.9
35—44	65.4	79.6	85.9	55.9	73.3	80.4
45—54	53.1	75.5	85.3	46.0	70.1	80.2
55—64	45.7	72.3	82.5	40.2	66.3	79.5
65—74	48.4	74.8	84.4	40.5	67.8	80.1
75—84	49.6	77.2	86.6	39.2	70.5	82.3
All ages	57.3	78.3	86.6	49.3	73.7	89.9

Table 9.5. continued

Share of top	Men			Women		
	1%	5%	10%	1%	5%	10%
1950						
Age						
25–34	71.7	–	–	44.4	–	–
35–44	49.4	72.5	86.2	45.7	70.5	–
45–54	36.4	66.3	80.4	42.6	72.8	–
55–64	38.2	66.7	80.7	41.1	69.6	84.6
65–74	40.2	70.0	83.7	35.4	66.9	82.4
75–84	42.5	72.5	85.4	37.0	68.6	83.7
All ages	48.6	74.8	87.1	44.2	72.4	81.7
1960						
25–34	24.6	42.0	54.2	32.9	53.7	63.7
35–44	29.5	52.0	62.0	40.0	59.4	70.4
45–54	30.9	58.6	72.8	34.5	61.4	73.2
55–64	32.2	59.8	72.8	30.7	57.0	72.9
65–74	32.5	59.5	73.1	30.4	55.6	69.5
75–84	34.9	61.4	74.5	29.2	55.2	68.7
All ages	32.9	57.4	69.8	34.5	61.0	73.2
1970						
25–34	26.7	44.8	58.7	31.0	54.8	66.6
35–44	27.8	46.5	59.3	32.4	58.9	72.9
45–54	24.3	48.5	63.0	36.2	60.8	73.1
55–64	27.2	51.6	64.8	27.7	54.0	68.9
65–74	25.8	51.2	65.5	24.3	49.2	64.6
75–84	26.9	53.1	67.5	24.8	51.1	65.8
All ages	27.7	50.0	63.9	32.1	58.1	72.9

Note: (i) Constructed on assumptions A2/B3/C0/D1/E0.
     (ii) – denotes outside the range of the estate statistics.
     (iii) The figures for 'all ages' refer to the population 25 and over.

here. As Shorrocks (1975a) has pointed out when examining changes in average wealth, differential survival rates by wealth classes mean that those alive at a particular date are unrepresentative of the original cohort (with which we are presumably concerned). Using the life office multipliers, he calculates the relative survival ratios for the wealthy as being over 50 per cent higher at age 75–84. In order to get back to the same composition as the original cohort we need in effect to apply a social class differential of $\frac{2}{3}$ (i.e. $1/(1.5)$) or smaller. From the results of earlier chapters we can see that this change could raise the share for that age group by some 4 percentage points, which would make a noticeable difference to the trend indicated by the figures above.[17]

9.5 Summary

In this chapter, we have examined some of the ways in which the estimates of the distribution of wealth may be used to throw light on the underlying processes, and the difficulties which arise in the interpretation of the evidence.

In the first two sections, we investigated the changes in the share of the top 1 per cent over the period 1923–72 and how they can be related to the models of wealth-holding described in chapter 8. From the simple 'Meade' model of accumulation, we derived an equation to be estimated, which incorporated several of the factors which have been thought to explain the trends over time. The results were not conclusive, but provided some insight into the forces at work. In particular, we explored the effect of share prices, of increased 'popular' wealth, and of estate duty.

The third and fourth sections have been concerned with the disaggregation of the estate estimates. Section 9.3 examined the relationship between individual and family wealth, and this showed that the 'marrying up' of the wealth of husbands and wives would probably lead to a decrease in the estimated share (although on certain assumptions it might increase), but that the effect is less dramatic than has sometimes been suggested. Finally, in section 9.4 we presented estimates of the distribution by age groups for a representative selection of years and showed how one could trace the history of a particular 'cohort'. There are however a number of difficulties in drawing inferences from such evidence, particularly about the way in which the distribution has changed over time.

17 This may be seen from the results in chapter 3 on the simple 'Pareto' model. Applying equation (10) from chapter 2, and taking $\alpha = 1.5$, $\sigma^* = 0.09$, a third reduction in λ which leads E to rise from 0.4 to 0.6 causes the estimated share to rise by a factor of 1.07. The share of 53.1% would therefore rise to nearly 57%.

10

SUMMARY AND DIRECTIONS OF FUTURE RESEARCH

10.1 Summary of main findings

The aim of this study has been to throw light on methods of estimating the distribution of wealth, on the evidence about top wealth-holdings in Britain, and on the ways in which the observed distribution and the trends over time may be interpreted. The principal findings under each of these three headings are described below:

Methodology

The book has concentrated on the estate approach, which has a long history and has been used by the Inland Revenue since 1960 to prepare official estimates of the distribution of wealth. Some authors, for example Titmuss (1962) and Polanyi and Wood (1974), have argued that these figures are highly sensitive to the assumptions underlying the estate method and have little value as indicators of the extent of concentration. The conclusion we have reached in our work is that this extreme view is unwarranted, and that there is little convincing evidence that the share of the top 1 per cent in total private wealth in a particular year would be drastically modified by changes in the method. Thus, it has been claimed that the estimates are highly sensitive to the assumptions made about mortality rates, but this is not borne out by our investigation in chapter 3 of the choice of mortality multipliers: the share of the top 1 per cent in 1968 ranged with different multipliers from 34 per cent to 37 per cent (page 78). In the same way, a great deal has been made of the upward bias in the share of the top wealth groups caused by the fact that the official estimates are on an individual rather than a family basis, but our analysis in chapter 9 shows that the share of the top 1 per cent would probably be reduced by some 5 per cent or less and might actually increase. The effect on the shares of the top wealth groups of converting to a family basis is less dramatic than critics of the Inland Revenue estimates have suggested.

In our view, therefore, the estate method provides a valuable foundation for estimating the distribution of wealth. At the same time, the Inland Revenue estimates suffer from a number of deficiencies and are in need of further development. Inevitably, the work of the Revenue is linked to the administration of capital taxation, and no attempt is made to cover the entire distribution or to adjust for all elements of missing wealth. The main difficulties with the official estimates were reviewed in chapter 2, and for a summary of these the reader is referred to table 2.2 on pages 46–47.

One of the primary ways in which the estimates may be refined is through the use of balance sheet information on the totals of holdings of different assets by the personal sector; we may know, for example from the issuing source, the total amount of a particular type of wealth owned by individuals. In chapter 4 we have tried to show how this information can be used to allow for the wealth of those missing from the estate returns and for the understatement of holdings covered by the statistics, both of which represent important shortcomings of the official estimates. This can only be done by making assumptions about the allocation of missing wealth by size of holding, and the results are presented in the form of ranges. Since we first published estimates on this basis (Atkinson 1975), the Royal Commission has taken up the use of this kind of data. We naturally welcome this development but feel that the Commission has been too uncritical in its use of the balance sheet totals to replace the estate totals. In certain cases, the balance sheet data for the personal sector are derived as residuals, and the divergence from the estate estimates may simply reflect errors in the estimates for other sectors. In our view, therefore, the Commission are wrong to conclude that the differences can entirely 'be attributed to the errors introduced by the various deficiencies in coverage and valuation of the estate multiplier approach' (1975:85). What we have done instead is to base our adjustments on the following principles: (a) that corrections should only be made where there is an *a priori* reason to expect that wealth is missing from the estate statistics (these reasons have been described in chapter 2), (b) that account should be taken of the assessment made by Revell (1967) of the reliability of the balance sheet totals, and as far as possible only totals employed where they are rated as 'very reliable' or 'fairly reliable'.

A second way in which we have tried to refine the estate method is in the presentation and use of the estimates. In chapter 5, we have explored a number of problems. These include the interpolation of the data to estimate the proportion of wealth held by groups such as the top 1 per cent, where these do not coincide with the available wealth ranges. It is possible to put upper and lower bounds on the interpolated figures, and with the full set of ranges in the present-day estate data the margin of error is extremely small.

However, where there are only broad ranges, as in the case of earlier years, there is room for error which may be significant in relation to the magnitude of changes over time. Moreover, the commonly used log–linear, or 'Pareto', interpolation procedure may lead to results inconsistent with these bounds; it should therefore be employed with caution. Sampling error is a further reason for qualifying the results, and it is a problem which has received too little attention. In chapter 5, we have looked at several different ways of assessing its implications. It was suggested that the results for the level of concentration may not be seriously affected, but that sampling fluctuations may be more significant when measuring changes over time. We have also argued that it was preferable in the latter context to consider the full set of annual observations, rather than averaging data over a number of years as in past studies, such as Lydall and Tipping (1961). Finally, we have investigated the use of summary measures of concentration and concluded that they were of rather limited value in the present context.

As a check on the validity of the estate approach, we have considered in chapter 7 the results of applying the investment income method to data on upper incomes. Our discussion of this alternative approach showed that there are major difficulties, the most important being the restricted coverage of the estimates and their sensitivity to the assumptions about the yields of assets such as ordinary shares. In view of this, we do not believe that the investment income method is likely to replace the estate method as the primary source of evidence about the distribution of wealth. At the same time, because of its value as a largely independent check, we feel that it is worth further study. The comparison with the estate estimates is not straightforward, but it appears from the results in chapter 7 that the investment income method tends to give higher figures for both numbers and total wealth. However, the range of estimates is such that it would be difficult at present to reject the hypothesis that the two methods lead to the same results, and further work is needed.

Evidence

In the course of our work, we have prepared a revised set of estimates for the distribution of wealth in the years 1966–72 (the 'final stage' estimates of chapter 5). In broad terms, these indicate that at the beginning of the 1970s the shares of the top wealth groups in the adult (18 and over) population in total private wealth were as shown below.

		Realisation/going concern basis for valuation
Top	1%	33/30
	5%	57/53
	10%	69/66

By varying the choice of assumptions, and by restricting attention to those aged 25 and over, it would be possible to reduce the going concern figures by 5 percentage points (7 points) in the case of the top 1 per cent (5 per cent), but within the framework of our analysis these assumptions are extreme and unlikely to be realistic. At the other extreme, and with the population aged 15 and over, the shares on a realisation basis would be increased by 4 percentage points, and 6 percentage points, respectively. The estimated shares would be lower on a family rather than an individual basis, but again only an extreme assumption about the pattern of marriage would lead to any very substantial difference.

The central figures given above are not materially different from those derived from the official estimates. This reflects the fact that a number of the adjustments turned out to be relatively small and they tended in certain cases to work in opposite directions. Thus the allowance for the wealth of those not covered by the estate returns makes a noticeable difference to their position (the share of the bottom two thirds of the population is increased markedly), but as far as the shares of the top 1 and 5 per cent are concerned, the effect is largely offset by the allowance for wealth 'missing' from the estate returns.

In chapter 6, we have presented a revised series of estimates for the fifty-year period 1923–72. Although it is commonly argued that changes over time are more reliably measured by the estate statistics than is the level of concentration, in our view this is not necessarily the case. Changes in estate duty law and practice, variations in the extent of coverage of the estate returns, differences in the adjustments made to the data, and – more broadly – the impact of social and demographic changes on the nature of wealth-holding, all mean that estimates at different dates may not be comparable. Moreover, when considering trends over time, and even more the acceleration or deceleration of trends, differences of 1 or 2 percentage points may be of much more significance than when measuring concentration in one year. In chapter 6 we have tried to construct a series which is closer to being consistent than those typically discussed in the past. Nonetheless, there are still breaks in the series which need to be taken into account in analysing the trends over time. When this is done, there appears to be an annual downward trend of some 0.4 per cent in the share of the top 1 per cent, but no apparent trend in the share of the next 4 per cent.

The qualifications surrounding the estimates summarised above are discussed in the relevant chapters, and the reader is urged to bear these in mind when making use of the figures. We should however stress once again that our concern has been with *top* wealth-holders (the shares of the top 1 and 5 per cent), and we have not studied the distribution as a whole. The distribution within the bottom 90 per cent, and the way it has changed over time, is an interesting subject but one which we have only touched on in passing. We should also emphasise that the estimates relate to the distribution of current wealth at a particular date. They do not follow the life history of individuals nor relate directly to the distribution of *inherited* wealth which may be thought more relevant for certain questions of economic justice. The estimates are limited to *private* wealth, and do not include elements of social or corporate property which could be attributed to individuals.

Interpretation

In the course of the book we have argued that the interpretation of the evidence requires, on the one hand, consideration of different theories of wealth-holding and, on the other, further analysis of the empirical observations.

In chapter 8 we have surveyed some of the theories put forward to explain the size distribution of wealth. The simplest model of accumulation implied that in the long-run there would be an egalitarian equilibrium with no concentration of wealth, or no more than that arising from differences in earned incomes. This conclusion was however modified by alternative assumptions about the transmission of wealth between generations, and by incorporating a 'random' savings process. In these cases, the long-run equilibrium of the distribution could be characterised by enduring concentration of wealth, and we showed that the distribution might take a variety of functional forms, with the parameters having particular economic interpretations. This equilibrium, like the egalitarian equilibrium, only represents the long-run outcome. Convergence to this may well be slow, and the process itself may be changing over time. It is therefore difficult to draw inferences from the observed shares of top wealth-holders about the likely long-run development: for example, the degree of concentration may be declining for some time even though eventually it will approach a long-run equilibrium at a higher level.

This survey of different theories points to the need for caution, but at the same time it offers some insight into the interpretation of the evidence. In particular, it casts light on the forces making for change over time in the degree of concentration, and on the factors influencing the shape of the distribution. These are summarised in section 4 of chapter 8 on pages 226–8. In the first part of chapter 9 we have then drawn on this theoretical analysis when deriving the specification of the equations estimated to explain the changes over time in the share of the top 1 per cent. There we examine the hypothesis that the share responded positively to the rate of return, and in particular to rising share prices, negatively to increased estate duty, and negatively to the spread of owner-occupation (and increased ownership of consumer durables) among the bulk of the population. The results are brought together on pages 239—40.

The second part of chapter 9 considers how far the disaggregation of the estimates, by sex and by age, may assist the interpretation of the evidence. By examining the distribution between men and women, and different assumptions about the pattern of marriage, we try to explore the effect of moving from an individual to a family basis. In the course of this, we investigate the share of total wealth owned by women. We find that there has not been the steady upward trend sometimes suggested and that it appears to have declined over the 1960s. Finally, the decomposition by age groups gives some indication of the role played by life-cycle factors in leading to the observed concentration.

10.2 Suggestions for future research

At many points in the text we have stressed the need for further research, and emphasised that, until it has been carried out, the results must be qualified in a number of respects. Indeed the final product of our study reads more like an extended research proposal than the completed monograph we had originally planned. Although we have been able to draw on valuable work by earlier authors, we have discovered that there are major areas — such as the construction of a consistent time series, the assessment of sampling error, or the investigation of the reliability of the investment income method — where a great deal remains to be done; and some questions which we thought were settled — such as techniques of interpolation — have turned out to need reinvestigation. In this section we collect together the main suggestions made in earlier chapters.

These recommendations for future research raise the issue of the division of labour between official researchers and academics. The record of official statisticians in this area has been outstanding, as is exemplified by the work of pioneers such as Sir Robert Giffen and Sir Bernard Mallet. (In this connection it is interesting that the former before entering the Civil Service made it a condition that he be allowed to continue to write on current economic matters.) In the last fifteen years, the Inland Revenue has introduced the official estimates of the distribution of wealth and has considerably extended the range of statistics available. It has also begun to present its own analysis of the data: for example the work of Astin (1975). Recently, the Royal Commission has acted as a stimulus to work in this area and has published some interesting material. At the same time, outside researchers clearly have a role to play. They can take initiatives and experiment with new techniques in a way that would be difficult for the Inland Revenue today. Thus, for example, Lyons (1974) pioneered the marriage adjustment to the estimates which was later taken up by the Royal Commission. In view of this, our suggestions are divided into two categories: those which represent a natural development of official statistics, and those raising wider issues which may be more appropriate for research in universities or research institutes.

Development of official statistics

Recommendation 1. The Inland Revenue should use balance sheet data to estimate the wealth of the excluded population and other missing wealth, and they should publish estimates on a basis similar to that of the 'final stage' estimates of chapter 5. A precondition for this is that the personal balance sheet data be compiled and published regularly by the Central Statistical Office, a development which was regarded by the Royal Commission as having 'special priority'. In using the balance sheet information, the methods should be more refined than those employed so far by the Royal Commission. In particular, the possibility of errors in the balance sheet totals should be taken into account; the range of possible variation should be further examined; and a consistent basis of valuation should be adopted throughout.

Recommendation 2. The Inland Revenue should publish estimates of family wealth-holding based on different assumptions about the pattern of wealth-holding by husbands and wives, about the proportions married, and about the definition of the unit. The estimates should be refined by making use of the information about marital status contained on estate returns and from the investment income data.

Recommendation 3. The Royal Commission should in future use a series of estimates over time which is closer to being on a consistent basis than that published in their *Initial Report* (1975). They should carry out a detailed study of the comparability of the figures for different years. The Inland Revenue should be asked to publish a guide to the most important changes in estate duty legislation and practice, and in the methods of collecting statistics, which have affected the comparability of the series over time, indicating where possible their likely quantitative significance.

Recommendation 4. The work of the Inland Revenue on the pattern of wealth-holding by age should be continued, and extended, using balance sheet data. Drawing on the information available to the Revenue on the composition of estates by age, it would be possible to allocate, under a range of assumptions, missing wealth by age groups and to correct for problems such as the over-valuation of life policies.

Wider issues

The scope of this study has been circumscribed in a number of respects, and the limitations point to important areas where further research is necessary.

We have concentrated almost exclusively on the top wealth groups, in particular the top 1 per cent and 5 per cent, and have not in general considered the rest of the distribution. It is nonetheless valuable to know what has happened *within* the bottom ranges. The redistribution associated with the spread of owner-occupation, for example, may have been largely confined to those in the top half. The estate method is not, of course, well suited for answering this kind of question, and it would be necessary to make use of sample survey or other data.

Recommendation 5. The distribution of wealth within the bottom ranges should be examined further, with the estate data being linked to sample survey or other information.

The definition of wealth in this study has been in terms of *private* wealth, and has excluded social or corporate property which may be attributable to individuals. A number of people, including one of the present authors (Atkinson 1971), have made estimates of the value of state pension rights, and social property of this type warrants further investigation. In doing this, it needs to be borne in mind that the results may be highly sensitive to the assumptions made. In Atkinson (1971), the estimates are presented with the qualification that the value 'is a very approximate one', and they depend crucially on the rate at which future income streams are discounted. In chapter 1, we drew attention to the positive net worth of the company sector and suggested that this 'corporate property' might be allocated to shareholders on a going concern basis. Again the effect on the estimates of such an adjustment may depend critically on the assumptions made.

Recommendation 6. The role of social and corporate property should be further investigated, with particular attention being paid to the sensitivity of the results to the assumptions made and to the implications of imperfections in the capital market.

The distribution of wealth has been considered here largely independently of the distribution of income. The joint distribution of the two variables is however of considerable interest and policy significance (for example, when examining the impact of a wealth tax). The techniques discussed in chapter 7 provide a natural approach to this question, and should be further explored from this point of view.

Recommendation 7. It would be valuable to have estimates of the joint distribution of income and wealth, and ways in which the two can be linked, particularly via the investment income data, should be investigated.

Finally, there is the *composition* of wealth-holdings, which has played a key role at certain points, but which has not been discussed extensively in its own right. The way in which portfolios vary with wealth, with rates of return, with taxation, and other variables is a subject which would repay attention.

Recommendation 8. The asset composition data now being made available by the Inland Revenue should be used to examine portfolio behaviour and the relationship between *types* of wealth-holding and the overall distribution.

Some of the topics listed above are ones which we plan ourselves to investigate further, but we hope that other researchers, both inside and outside the government service, will be stimulated to take up these important — and interesting — questions.

APPENDIX I

SAMPLE SURVEY EVIDENCE

The best known sample surveys covering wealth-holding in Britain are those carried out in the early 1950s by the Oxford Institute of Statistics, the results of which were used by Lydall and Tipping (1961) to estimate the lower tail of the distribution. While the Oxford surveys have not been repeated, a national survey of household income and wealth was carried out in 1968–9 by Abel-Smith and Townsend (the LSE–Essex Poverty Survey, see Townsend 1977); and there have been a number of surveys by market research organisations, including the recent Economists Advisory Group study (Morgan 1975). Taking the Oxford and Economists Advisory Group surveys to illustrate this approach to the estimation of wealth-holding, we examine the problems which arise and their implications for the accuracy of the results which are obtained.

I.1 Features of surveys
Oxford savings surveys
The aims of the Oxford surveys were 'to build up a complete picture of the financial position and behaviour of individual persons or families' (Hill 1955 : 129). Their main focus was on incomes and saving, but the 1953 and 1954 surveys also collected information about net worth. The unit of analysis was defined as the 'income unit', being the closest approximation to the ideal 'group of persons who could be expected to pool their income and their assets' (Lydall 1955:197). The surveys covered Great Britain, and were restricted to income units living in private households (i.e. excluding those living in institutions).

The 1953 survey was based on a two-stage sample design. At the first stage, the rating authorities of Great Britain were divided into groups, and from each one authority was selected at random. Within each rating area, a further stratification into two groups was made: an upper stratum with dwellings having a rateable value (taken as an approximate indicator of economic status) of at least £30 (£40 in London) and a lower stratum with a rateable value below this level. The sampling fractions for the two sub-strata were in the ratio 8:1. The final total of completed questionnaires was 2,104, representing a response rate of 66 per cent. The response achieved in the lower sub-stratum (69 per cent) was considerably higher than that in the upper sub-stratum (47 per cent) — see Hill (1955:160). The 1954 survey was also a two-stage sample, although of a rather different design. The final total was 2,463 successful interviews with income units. The overall response rate (67 per cent) was very little higher than in 1953, but there was much less difference between the upper and lower strata.

The main results of the 1953 and 1954 Oxford surveys are described in Hill (1955) and Straw (1955). The former presents estimates of mean net worth per income unit, and the average holding of different types of asset, in 1953 and 1954. He also gives tables for the distribution by ranges of net worth, and of the following components: total liquid assets, total National Savings, real property, and mortgage debt outstanding. Straw's article concentrates on the data for 1953, providing a more detailed analysis of the distribution of net worth by age and sex, occupation, housing status, and income, as well as of the distribution of individual assets.

Lydall and Tipping (1961) made use of the results of the 1954 Oxford survey, which was regarded as the more reliable of the two (see Hill 1955), to establish the likely distribution of wealth below the exemption limit. They did this by extrapolating on a double-logarithmic scale the cumulative frequency distribution obtained for those above the estate duty exemption level to pass through the point corresponding to the total population and an assumed minimum level of wealth. This yielded estimates of the frequencies for the wealth classes below the exemption level corresponding to those in the savings survey. Multiplication of the frequency by the mean value of net worth in each class yielded an estimate, when the class totals were added together, of total wealth owned by the excluded population. This total was checked by adopting a similar approach for each main class of asset, where the control amounts of total wealth held in each asset were also derived from the surveys.

Economists Advisory Group (EAG) Survey
This survey, carried out in 1974, is representative of a number of surveys undertaken by market research organisations (earlier studies include, for example, that by the British Market Research Bureau in 1965—6 — see Morgan 1975). The survey was particularly directed at the ownership of stock exchange securities and other financial assets, and the author recognised it to be very different from the Oxford surveys 'both in objectives and methods'

(Morgan 1975:2). The fieldwork was carried out in 1974 by NOP Market Research, and involved the following three samples:

(i) Sample 1 with 3705 respondents was asked questions covering ownership of financial assets, household composition, housing tenure, income and other personal characteristics,

(ii) Sample 2 with 9388 respondents was interviewed using a shorter questionnaire with less detail on personal characteristics,

(iii) Sample 3 consisted of a more detailed interview with the subsample of 534 respondents from Sample 2 who stated that they owned any of the following assets: unit trusts, property bonds, other bonds, investment trusts, stocks and shares, government or local authority securities.

The response rates reported (excluding those who had died or moved away) were 70 per cent for Sample 1 and 66 per cent for Sample 2.

I.2   Problems with the use of sample survey data

Sample survey data have a number of obvious attractions for estimating the distribution of wealth. There is no problem of mortality multipliers; the data are not related to tax returns with their attendant hazards; the questions can be framed to suit the purpose at hand. However, there are also a number of drawbacks, and the importance of these is investigated below.

(a) Non-response

The relatively low response rate was referred to above and this is a problem inherent in any sample survey. The Oxford Institute made a number of external checks on representativeness, and used, for example, evidence from the Census of Population. In their discussion of the 1953 Survey, Hill, Klein and Straw (1955) devoted considerable attention to the problem of non-response. First, it is interesting to note that of all failures to achieve a satisfactory response, two thirds were direct refusals, and only a third resulted from non-contact or rejection at the editing stage. Secondly, there appeared to be systematic differences in the response rate: 'the response is lowest from the self-employed (businessmen, farmers, etc.). There is also a relatively low response from the professional, technical and executive classes, and from the retired and unoccupied — especially, it seems, the more wealthy retired people' (Hill, Klein and Straw: 100). There are, therefore, strong reasons to expect the upper wealth groups to be under-represented in the results from the survey.

(b) Incomplete information

Even where an interview is successfully completed, there remains the possibility that the information provided may have been incomplete. The respondent may have under-stated the value of his assets or omitted to tell the interviewer of certain possessions. This may reflect deliberate dishonesty, but probably more important are the problems of remembering all items of wealth and of making an accurate valuation. As Hill points out, 'the valuations given by informants can only be rough and ready in many cases . . . This problem is of course most acute in the case of shares in private companies, and several informants frankly admitted that the values they placed on such shares were hypothetical' (Hill 1955:151). In the EAG survey, the author similarly recognised that 'respondents may be either unable or unwilling to give answers that disclose "the truth, the whole truth and nothing but the truth"' (Morgan 1975:3). They may find it difficult to recall everything they own, and may simply forget to mention holdings. They may fear that their answers would be divulged to the tax authorities and under-state the value of their holdings. For these reasons 'there is little doubt that some underestimation does occur' (Morgan 1975:3).

(c) Incomplete coverage in survey design

The third problem is that savings surveys typically cover only certain types of asset, and the resulting definition of net worth is not comprehensive. The components of net worth in the Oxford surveys are described below.

Assets	*Liabilities*
Liquid financial assets	Overdrafts
Stocks, shares and other securities	Hire purchase debt
Land, property and unincorporated businesses	Mortgage debt
Cars	Other debt
Loans	

(Source: Hill 1955:146).

Among the items *not* taken into account were: life, industrial and endowment (except in conjunction with mortgages) insurance policies, pension rights, furniture, household goods, jewellery, holdings of notes and coin, and settled property. The EAG survey did cover life assurance, but on the other hand was primarily concerned with financial assets and did not include questions on the value of real property.

(d) Sampling error

The sampling errors associated with the Oxford savings surveys are discussed by Lydall (1955) and Klein and Vandome (1957), the latter presenting estimates of the sampling error for the 1953 and 1954 surveys. The general conclusion reached by Lydall for the 1952 survey was that 'it is a fair guess that more serious errors are caused by reporting and processing errors than by sampling fluctuations' (1955:240). At the same time, the EAG survey drew attention to the fact that 'a special case that is important in this context is the very rich . . . Millionaires are so few that even a large sample is unlikely to include one at all' (Morgan 1975:2). (In this connection, it is interesting to note that the Inland Revenue estate data included 25 millionaires in the year 1973–4.)

The quantitative importance of the first two of the problems described above may be illustrated by comparing the totals obtained by 'blowing-up' the sample means with those known from external sources. This was discussed by Hill, Klein and Straw (1955) in relation to the liquid asset holdings indicated by the 1953 Survey, and their findings are shown in table I.1 (where we have made an approximate adjustment for non-personal holdings included in their control totals). They concluded that 'there seems little doubt that in all eight types of assets the Survey estimates are too low' (1955:118), and that 'the most probable explanation for the Survey's low liquid assets figures seems to be that those persons with the largest asset holdings were the least co-operative and more inclined to understate their wealth' (1955:118). This is supported by the fact that under-statement was less for the assets which were more widely held: for example, the number of cars appeared to be fairly accurately measured by the Survey (Hill, Klein and Straw 1955:121).

In the case of the EAG survey, it is less easy to make such comparisons. Most of the results are presented in terms of the total number of *holders* rather than total holdings. This raises difficulties in that individuals may have more than one holding and in that joint holdings were excluded from the survey. Nonetheless, there is clear evidence of holdings not being disclosed. For example, only 35 per cent of those with National Savings Bank investment accounts disclosed an ordinary account even though depositors on investment account are required to have an ordinary account balance of at least £50 (Morgan 1975:21). The reason why the results are mainly in terms of the *number* of holders is that only very limited information was obtained on the *value* of holdings. The response to the question on the value of holdings was not very satisfactory, as the figures below show.

Table I.1. Comparison of sample survey results with external sources 1953

Type of asset	(1) Survey estimate £m	(2) External total £m	(3) Percentage personally held (1957) %	(4) Survey estimate as % adjusted total[†]
Post Office Savings Bank Deposits	920	1,802	} 99	52
Trustee Savings Bank Deposits	440	949		47
National Savings Certificates	880	1,749	100	50
Defence Bonds	480	820	54	62
Building society shares and deposits	330	1,401	97	24
Co-operative Society shares and deposits	110	230	67	71
Joint stock bank personal deposits	920	2,100	–	–

Sources: Columns (1) and (2) from Hill, Klein and Straw (1955: table XXII), column (3) from Revell (1967:446–52).
Note [†] : Column (1) divided by the product of column (2) and the proportion personally held (column (3)).

	Percentage giving size of holding (of those with holdings)
Bank savings/deposit account	59.5
NSB ordinary account	73.7
NSB investment account	68.7
National giro account	53.1
Premium bonds	79.7
Building society	63.0
SAYE	54.3

Source: Morgan (1975:18).

For at least some asset types there was evidence that the non-response to this question was concentrated at the upper end. For example, in the case of NSB investment accounts, Morgan concluded 'that there has been a substantial understatement in replies to our questionnaire' (Morgan 1975:23).

The problems of non-response have been studied in the United States in two interesting investigations by Ferber et al. of shareholdings (1969a) and savings accounts (1969). These compared household interview data on the number and size of holdings with institutional records. In effect they began with data on known holdings by individuals and then interviewed the holders to see what they reported. Although the results need to be qualified in certain respects, they indicated that 'substantial nonsampling errors exist in the reporting of savings account information by consumers, that the principal sources of these errors are nonreporting by respondents and the much larger holdings of the refusals, and that methods are badly needed to supplement the usual survey methods to correct for this bias' (1969 : 444). For common stock, the conclusions were virtually the same. The error in the average holdings as estimated from the respondents was an under-statement of 46 per cent for the mean balance in savings accounts and 35 per cent for the average number of shares. The breakdown of the error between different sources, shown below, is similar for the two types of asset.

	Percentage of error in estimated mean	
	Number of shares	Mean balance in savings accounts
Errors in average holdings reported	−0.2	−1.7
Errors in estimation of holding where existence but not amount reported	1.0	1.9
Non-reporting of holdings	61.2	59.7
Non-respondents:		
Refusals	21.7	29.8
Other	16.3	10.3
Total	100.0	100.0

Sources: Ferber, Forsythe, Guthrie and Maynes 1969a: Table 7; and 1969: table 4.

Over half the errors are caused by the non-reporting of holdings, and the rest arise mainly because the holdings of non-respondents on average exceed those of respondents.

I.3   Use of sample survey evidence – conclusions

The experience to date suggests that sample surveys are unlikely by themselves to provide a fully satisfactory source of information about the size distribution of wealth as a whole. Neither of the surveys described above was designed to cover all types of wealth-holding and there are evident difficulties in extending the coverage. There is the problem of a relatively low response rate and the systematic under-representation of the upper wealth groups.

Even where interviews are carried out, the non-reporting of holdings appears to be a major problem. Sample surveys may be a valuable supplement to the estate data, throwing light on wealth not covered by the estate returns; they may also provide useful information about the holdings of certain types of asset (e.g. consumer durables). But in our view they cannot provide an alternative to the estate method as a source of evidence about wealth-holding at the top of the scale.

APPENDIX II

BALANCE SHEET TOTALS 1966–72

This appendix describes the method of estimating the balance sheet totals used in constructing the adjusted distributions in chapters 4 and 5. In general, the approach is similar to that of Revell (1967) and Roe (1971), the only major exception being the treatment of household goods. Their work does not cover all the years in question,[1] and we have extrapolated the estimates using as far as possible the same methods. (In what follows, the short-hand expression 'extrapolation' should be taken to mean 'employing the same methods as described in Revell (1967)'.) The figures do however differ from those of Revell and Roe in that our estimates relate to Great Britain and are a weighted average for the year rather than year-end figures. (The assumptions involved are described in chapter 4.)

In what follows we describe the source of the balance sheet totals set out in table II.1 for eight of the ten categories of asset and liability considered. The categories not shown are settled property (item 6), which is discussed in the main text, and company shares (item 7) for which no adjustment is made. For convenience of cross-reference, we give in each case the category number IRx corresponding to that used in *Inland Revenue Statistics* 1971, table 115.

(1) *Unquoted UK government securities (IR 1 and 2) and savings bank deposits (IR 28)*

The totals in issue are known from official statistics and are published regularly in *Financial Statistics*. The breakdown between personal and non-personal holdings is an extrapolation of that by Revell (1967). The only case in which there seems any risk of sizeable error is that of tax reserve certificates and the amounts involved here are small. Even if the estimate of personal holdings of this item were reduced by a half, it would only reduce the total for the group as a whole by some 1 per cent. The figures shown in

---

1 Mr A. Roe kindly made available certain unpublished estimates. Those for 1969 and 1970 are published in Revell and Tomkins (1974), table 3.1.

Table II.1 Balance sheet totals 1966—72 — Great Britain £ million

	1966	1967	1968	1969	1970	1971	1972
1. UK government securities and savings bank deposits	8,160	8,200	8,330	8,360	8,320	8,660	9,430
2. Cash and bank deposits	7,420	7,890	8,610	9,120	9,670	10,550	11,920
3. Building society deposits	5,350	6,200	7,120	7,950	9,030	10,700	12,830
4. Household goods	8,200	8,620	9,290	10,160	11,000	12,130	13,660
5. Trade assets	4,880	5,040	5,170	5,270	5,250	5,410	5,590
8. Life funds							
(i) life policies	6,300	6,950	7,700	8,500	9,250	10,000	11,200
(ii) funded pensions	7,500	8,200	8,850	9,800	10,400	11,450	12,300
(iii) unfunded pensions	5,500	5,850	6,200	6,600	6,950	7,350	8,750
9. Land and buildings	37,400	39,900	42,700	45,700	49,200	55,000	77,700
10. Liabilities	6,820	7,020	7,290	7,560	7,930	8,770	10,170

Note: All figures rounded to nearest £10 million (except item 8 which is rounded to nearest £50 million, and item 9 which is rounded to nearest £100 million).

table II.1 are weighted averages of the June and December figures with the weights set out in chapter 4.

(2) *Cash and bank deposits (IR 27, 29 and 30)*
The total for bank deposits is taken from *Financial Statistics*, and personal holdings are estimated by subtracting an allowance for non-profit bodies (Revell's figures suggest that the 2½ per cent taken by the Royal Commission (1975) is not unreasonable). The personal holdings of cash are estimated, following Revell (1967:150), as 15 per cent of the average in circulation in December but this is clearly not a very reliable figure. The overall total is a weighted average of the December figures.

(3) *Building society deposits (IR 21)*
Total shares and deposits are taken from *Financial Statistics*, and non-personal holdings are taken as 1 per cent. The figures given in table II.1 are weighted averages of the June and December totals.

(4) *Household goods (IR 25)*
The balance sheet totals given by Revell and Roe are based on a perpetual inventory method, and the same approach is adopted here. Their estimates related, however, only to cars and consumer durables, and did not include

other household capital items. The Royal Commission (1975), on the other hand, calculated the value of stocks for seven types of goods, as shown below.

	Annual depreciation rate
(i) clothing	0.8
(ii) motor cars and cycles	
(iii) household durables	
(iv) other household goods	0.25
(v) books	
(vi) recreational goods	0.5
(vii) miscellaneous goods	0.33

The procedure of Revell and Roe is equivalent to taking only (ii) and (iii) which in 1972 accounted for some 60 per cent of the Royal Commission's total.

Although in earlier work (Atkinson 1975) we followed Revell and Roe, we have been persuaded that the wider definition adopted by the Royal Commission is more appropriate, and in the results presented in this book, the balance sheet totals cover all of items (i)–(vii). The only major way in which we have departed from their procedure is in taking (vii) to be only half of the Blue Book category 'other miscellaneous goods'.[2] In each case the figures shown are weighted averages of those for December.

(5) *Trade assets (IR 31–37)*

This item includes the assets of unincorporated businesses apart from land and buildings, i.e. plant and equipment, stocks and trade debtors. The balance sheet estimates of these items, derived from perpetual inventory and other calculations, exceed the estate duty estimates, even allowing for the fact that the latter include the items 'goodwill' and 'unallocated share of partnership', and this reflects the differences in method of valuation. Table II.1 shows the figures used, which are averages of the December figures given by Revell and Roe (extrapolated).

(8) *Life policies and pension rights (IR 26)*

The balance sheet total for this item was considered under three sub-

---

2 This category includes (among other items) stationery and writing equipment, paper goods, and smokers' requisites (Maurice 1968:172) so that it does not seem reasonable to regard it entirely as consisting of durable items.

headings: (i) life assurance policies, (ii) funded pension rights, and (iii) rights
in unfunded pension schemes (of which civil service pensions are an important component). The estimates are in each case based on those of Revell and
Roe, projected where necessary. In 1969, for example, the year-end figures
given for the three categories by Revell and Tomkins (1974:64–5) were (for
the UK) as shown.

	£ billion
(i) life policies (L_I)	9.1
(ii) funded pensions ($L_P + O_P$)	10.1
(iii) unfunded pensions	6.9

where L_P denotes the pension element of life office business, and O_P denotes
independent pension funds. The division into these components for these
years was obtained as follows. Firstly the total of life business ($L_I + L_P$) was
estimated using data on funds given in *Life Assurance in the United Kingdom*
(published by the life offices' associations) with adjustment for overseas
business. The split between L_I and L_P was then taken to be the same percentage as in 1969. Finally, O_P was determined as a residual from the sum
($L_I + L_P + O_P$) based on the Revell/Roe estimates. The figures given in
table II.1 are averages for December (and relate to Great Britain). It may be
noted that the figure for the total value of pension rights (funded plus
unfunded) in 1972 is close to the £20,000 million taken by the Royal
Commission (1975:89).

In order to divide the amounts missing from the estate statistics between
ordinary and industrial branch assurance, we need the total sums assured and
the average per policy. The statistics used are again taken from *Life Assurance
in the United Kingdom*, and are shown in table II.2.

(9) *Land and buildings (IR 49–57)*
The balance sheet total is obtained by Revell and Roe through the capitalis-
ation of rents as reflected in rateable values, and the figures given in table
II.1 are an extrapolation on the same basis (weighted average of December
figures). The method allows dwellings to be isolated as a sub-category, and
this is used when allocating missing wealth (see appendix III).

(10) *Liabilities (IR 43, 46, 59, 60)*
There are two major items under the general heading of 'liabilities'. The first
is house mortgages, for which Revell's totals are very considerably higher than
the estate estimates, which he attributes to netting out at death against life

Table II.2. Life assurance: sums assured in the UK

Sums assured: (£ million)	1966	1967	1968	1969	1970	1971	1972
Life branch	20,940	23,690	26,690	30,570	34,470	40,240	47,020
Industrial branch	5,330	5,580	5,820	6,080	6,320	6,580	6,900
Average per policy: £							
Life branch	1,300	1,410	1,530	1,670	1,760	1,950	2,190
Industrial branch	50	50	55	60	60	65	70

Sources: *Life Assurance in the United Kingdom* 1962–6, 1966–70 and 1969–73.
Note: The figures are the averages of those for December. The life branch covers both ordinary life assurance (including linked life assurance from 1969) and the life offices' pension business. All figures have been rounded.

policies. As explained in the text, we have made no adjustment for this item. The second consists of other liabilities such as hire purchase, taxes, bank advances, etc., and it is to these that this category refers. Revell's estimates for this item are described as 'a mixture of reliable estimates for bank advances and hire purchase [from known totals outstanding] and frank guesses at most of the remaining items' (Revell 1967:158). The figures given in table II.1 are from Roe (1971), extrapolated where necessary, and are weighted averages of the December figures.

APPENDIX III

TREATMENT OF LAND AND BUILDINGS

In chapter 4 we drew attention to the substantial difference between the estate method and balance sheet estimates for this item, and described the assumptions $E1$ and $E2$ made in allocating the excess. In this appendix we discuss in more detail the rationale for these assumptions, focusing on dwellings (which are the main component). For this purpose it is convenient to make use of the following notation:

V_B = balance sheet total (adjusted for settled property)
V_E = estate estimate of total
N_E = number of cases with property in estate estimates
h = number of houses per case
V_X = value of property owned by excluded population
p = average price of house

These denote, with the exception of h and V_X, variables which we can observe; they may however be measured with error. The true values are denoted therefore by an $*$. Our purpose is to estimate

$$V_X^* \quad \text{and} \quad V_E^*/V_E$$

respectively the amount to be allocated to the excluded population and the adjustment factor to be applied to the estate estimates, where

$$V_X^* + V_E^* = V_B^*.$$

In his discussion of the difference, Revell argues that 'the shortfall of the estate duty estimates is mostly a question of valuation' (1967:148);[1] in other words, houses are unlikely to be owned by the excluded population 'except in very rare cases of joint ownership when the deceased had no other assets for which a grant was needed' (Revell 1967:169). On this basis, the adjustment, which we refer to as assumption $E1$, involves:

$$V_X^* = 0 \quad \text{and} \quad V_E^*/V_E = 1 + a\left(\frac{V_B}{V_E} - 1\right)$$

1 Revell also refers to 'a technical fault in the drawing of the Inland Revenue samples' (1967:148), but this is not relevant to the period considered here.

where *a* is a factor reflecting the degree of confidence in the balance sheet estimate; $a = 1$ means that the figure is taken as correct, $a = 0$ that no adjustment is made. Revell himself notes that 'the personal sector element of the (balance sheet) series which we have used is far from reliable' (1967:148). In applying $E1$, we have taken $a = 1$, but the sensitivity to *a* may be assessed by comparing the results with those obtained on the no adjustment assumption $E0$ (which is equivalent to $a = 0$).[2]

This adjustment assumes that no cases of house ownership are missing from the estate estimates. The assumption made by the Royal Commission on the other hand[3] attributes to the excluded population part of the discrepancy. The adjustment made in the *Initial Report* is not given any justification but can be rationalised as follows. If one assumes that *p* equals the average price of existing dwellings (as published in *Housing and Construction Statistics*), and that $h = 1$ (i.e. that there are no cases of multiple ownership in the estate statistics), then one can calculate the discrepancy between the total number of dwellings (V_B/p) implied by the balance sheet figures and the number covered by the estate estimates (N_E). Assumption $E2$ then allocates half the missing dwellings to the excluded population:

$$V_X^* = p(V_B/p - N_E)/2$$

and the remaining part to the included population (to allow for multiple holdings, incomplete coverage, etc.):

$$V_E^* = p(V_B/p - N_E)/2 + V_E \left(\frac{p}{V_E/N_E} \right)$$

i.e. the remaining half of the missing dwellings (first term) plus a revaluation of the estate data (second term), using the explicit price *p* rather than that implicit (with $h = 1$) in the estate estimates (V_E/N_E).

Although the Royal Commission method avoids the extreme assumption that none of the discrepancy is allocatable to the excluded population, it is open to the following objections:

   (i)   the balance sheet figure may not be fully reliable,
   (ii) the price series *p* may not be appropriate,
   (iii) the assumption $h = 1$ has no foundation (in other words, one

2 One reason for not allocating all the difference is that the balance sheet figure does not allow for any future capital gains tax liability for houses which are not owner-occupied.

3 This section has been extensively revised in the light of the *Initial Report* (Royal Commission 1975); our earlier work was based on the Revell $E1$ adjustment.

cannot calculate a 'price' per house simply by dividing the total estate estimate for value by the number of cases).

The first of these has already been discussed and applies equally to $E1$. In the case of the second, there are a variety of price series (for a discussion of some of the differences in the case of new house prices, see Evans 1975). Comparison of the implied total of dwellings ($V_B/p = 8.7$ million in 1972) with independent information on house ownership suggests that the figure may be too low. The third objection is partly one of presentation, since one would get the same result if one assumed that

$$h = 1 + \tfrac{1}{2}(V_B/pN_E - 1)$$

and allocated all the excess to the excluded population. This is, however, no more or less arbitrary.

In the case of land and buildings other than dwellings, we assume that the shortfall is due to differences in valuation and allocate it to the included population. This assumption is also made by the Royal Commission.

APPENDIX IV

SUMMARY MEASURES OF CONCENTRATION

IV.1 Properties of summary measures in the simple 'Pareto' model

The 'Pareto' model considered here is essentially that described in chapter 2 and discussed at a number of points in the text. It is however in one respect more general and for this reason we begin by restating the assumptions:

(i) the wealth-holdings covered by the data are distributed over the range $\underline{w} \leqslant w \leqslant w_u$ according to the density (expressed as a proportion of the total population)

$$f(w) = B\alpha w^{-\alpha-1} \underline{w}^{\alpha} \tag{1}$$

(where $\alpha > 1$),
and hence the cumulative distribution is

$$1 - F(w) = B\underline{w}^{\alpha}[w^{-\alpha} - w_u^{-\alpha}] \tag{2}$$

(ii) the excluded population (as a proportion of the total population) is therefore

$$E = 1 - B(1 - \xi^{-\alpha}) \tag{3}$$

(where $\xi = w_u/\underline{w}$)
and it is assumed that their average wealth is $\sigma\underline{w}$, where $0 \leqslant \sigma \leqslant 1$.
This model is identical with that in chapter 2 except that we have allowed for a finite upper limit w_u (and have subsumed the multiplier process in equation (1)).

From this we can obtain the mean wealth

$$\bar{w} = \underline{w}\left[E\sigma + \frac{B\alpha}{\alpha - 1}(1 - \xi^{-(\alpha-1)})\right] \tag{4}$$

and the variance

$$= E\sigma^2\underline{w}^2 + \frac{B\alpha}{2 - \alpha}[\xi^{2-\alpha} - 1]\underline{w}^2 - \bar{w}^2 \tag{5}$$

From this we can calculate that the coefficient of variation V is given by:

$$1 + V^2 = \left(\frac{w}{\bar{w}}\right)^2 \left[E\sigma^2 + \frac{B\alpha}{2-\alpha}(\xi^{2-\alpha} - 1)\right] \tag{6}$$

This expression clearly depends crucially on whether $\alpha \gtreqless 2$. For the distributions with which we are concerned, it appears that in general $\alpha < 2$ and that $\alpha \simeq 1.5$ would be a reasonable approximation. Taking realistic values for ξ, which is likely to be 10,000 or larger, this means that we can in effect ignore terms in $\xi^{-\alpha}$ and $\xi^{-(\alpha-1)}$, but not that in $\xi^{2-\alpha}$. This leads (using (3) and (4)) to the following approximation for the coefficient of variation

$$1 + V^2 = \left[E\sigma^2 + \frac{(1-E)\alpha}{2-\alpha}(\xi^{2-\alpha} - 1)\right] \bigg/ \left[E\sigma + \frac{(1-E)\alpha}{\alpha-1}\right]^2 \tag{7}$$

In table IV.1 we have tabulated V for a range of possible parameter values. The choice of parameters is clearly a matter of judgement, but it should give some indication of the sensitivity to different aspects of the distribution. As the form of equation (7) suggests, it is dominated by changes in ξ and α. Within the range of variation of the parameters considered here, the coefficient more than doubles. It should also be noted that V *increases* with α, a point discussed further below. There is relatively less response to changes in σ and E, so that it is not particularly sensitive to the size of excluded population or their estimated wealth. For example, $\sigma = 0.15$ represents a quite substantial allocation of wealth to the excluded population, but the effect on V is less than one tenth of that of a move from $\alpha = 1.5$ to $\alpha = 1.75$.

If we now turn to the other measures, they do not depend sensitively on the extreme values (with realistic values of ξ); and for convenience we take the limit as ξ tends to infinity. (In other words we return now to the case described in chapter 2.) The relative mean deviation is defined by (for a general distribution)

$$D = \int_{-\infty}^{\infty} [w/\bar{w} - 1] \, dF = 2 \int_{\bar{w}}^{\infty} (w/\bar{w} - 1) dF \tag{8}$$

($D/2$ is sometimes referred to as the Pietra ratio, see Gastwirth (1974).) In the present case we may calculate that:

$$D = \frac{2(1-E)}{\alpha-1}\left[E\sigma + (1-E)\frac{\alpha}{\alpha-1}\right]^{-\alpha} \tag{9}$$

The Gini coefficient may be defined as (for a general distribution)

$$G = \frac{1}{2}\int_{-\infty}^{\infty}\int_{-\infty}^{\infty} |x-y|/\bar{w} dF(x) dF(y) \tag{10}$$

or half the relative mean difference. Geometrically it is the ratio of the area

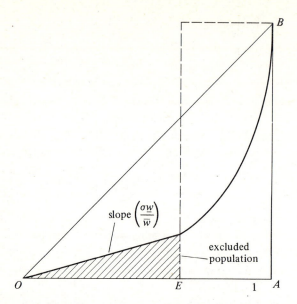

Figure IV.1 Lorenz curve and Gini coefficient

between the diagonal and the Lorenz curve to the whole triangle OAB. This is illustrated in figure IV.1, which also shows how the value of the coefficient may be obtained for the special case considered here by calculating the appropriate areas. This gives an expression

$$1 - G = \frac{E^2 \sigma}{\left(E\sigma + (1 - E)\dfrac{\alpha}{\alpha - 1} \right)} + 2(1 - E)\left(\frac{\alpha - 1}{2\alpha - 1} \right) \qquad (11)$$

where the first term on the right hand side corresponds to the shaded 'excluded population' triangle. Rearranged, this gives equation (1) in chapter 5.

The second and third lines in table IV.1 show the values of D and G for different parameter values. The first point to be noted is that both fall as α rises, in contrast to the coefficient of variation. Taking the case where $\sigma = 0$, we can see that where $\xi \to \infty$, a rise in α shifts the Lorenz curve towards the diagonal (see chapter 2 and Chipman (1974)). The movement of D and G is therefore in the expected direction. Where, however, there is a finite upper wealth level w_u, the Lorenz curve shifts outward at the top (since $\bar{w}$ falls and hence the slope at $B(= w_u/\bar{w})$ rises). With the values of α considered, the coefficient of variation attaches such weight to this outward movement at the top that it registers overall an increase in concentration. The second point is that both D and G are relatively sensitive to changes in E, and that the

Table IV.1 Simulation of measures of concentration

	$E = 40\%$			$E = 60\%$		
	$\sigma = 0.0$	0.15	0.30	$\sigma = 0.0$	0.15	0.30
$\alpha = 1.5$						
1. Coefficient of variation (V)						
$\xi =$ 2,500	5.12	4.95	4.79	6.31	5.86	5.47
10,000	7.35	7.11	6.88	9.03	8.39	7.84
40,000	10.47	10.13	9.81	12.84	11.94	11.15
2. Relative mean deviation (D)	0.994	0.946	0.902	1.217	1.092	0.987
3. Gini coefficient (G)	0.700	0.687	0.675	0.800	0.758	0.722
$\alpha = 1.75$						
1. Coefficient of variation (V)						
$\xi =$ 2,500	10.20	9.77	9.39	12.51	11.41	10.48
10,000	14.53	13.93	13.39	17.81	16.24	14.93
40,000	20.63	19.77	19.01	25.29	23.05	21.18
2. Relative mean deviation (D)	0.888	0.825	0.769	1.205	1.026	0.885
3. Gini coefficient (G)	0.640	0.624	0.608	0.760	0.707	0.663

response to changes in σ increases noticeably as we move from the case $E = 40\%$ to $E = 60\%$. Where $E = 40\%$, a quite substantial change in σ (from 0 to 0.15) reduces the Gini coefficient by only $1-1\frac{1}{2}$ percentage points and D by some 0.05, whereas with $E = 60\%$ the corresponding changes are 4−5 percentage points and some 0.15.

IV.2   Behaviour of Inland Revenue Gini coefficients 1960−73

The results for the simplified Pareto model suggest that the Gini coefficient is likely to reflect movements in E, α and σ. In this section we consider briefly whether this is borne out by the actual behaviour of the Gini coefficients estimated by the Inland Revenue over the period 1960−73.

The Series B Gini coefficients are shown in column 1 of table IV.2. The series is that covering the entire adult population (which is defined by the Inland Revenue as aged 15 and over) and makes no allowance for the wealth of the excluded population, so that $\sigma = 0$. For simplicity, we decided to take the share of the top 1 per cent (W_1) as a proxy for α, and estimated the following equation (the values of the independent variables are shown in columns 2 and 3):

Table IV.2. Inland Revenue Series B Gini coefficients and
explanatory variables

	(1) G	(2) E	(3) W_1
1960	0.874	0.541	0.382
1961	0.872	0.537	0.371
1962	0.867	0.539	0.360
1963	0.874	0.540	0.357
1964	0.864	0.519	0.344
1965	0.864	0.544	0.330
1966	0.856	0.561	0.318
1967	0.861	0.577	0.321
1968	0.867	0.579	0.327
1969	0.847	0.559	0.290
1970	0.853	0.586	0.290
1971	0.840	0.540	0.276
1972	0.860	0.588	0.299
1973	0.840	0.538	0.276

Sources: (1) *Inland Revenue Statistics* 1972:157; and 1975:161.
(2) *Social Trends* 1975:106; 1974:114; 1973:111;
1972:86; 1971:81; and calculated from *Inland
Revenue Statistics* 1970 and *Annual Abstract of
Statistics* (various years).
(3) Royal Commission (1975), table 45.

$$G = 0.659 + 0.163E + 0.343 W_1 \qquad R^2 = 0.93$$
$$\quad (3.8) \qquad (12.9) \qquad D.W. = 1.82$$

where the figures in brackets are *t*-statistics. This equation seems to provide a
good fit to the observations and means that from knowledge just of E and W_1
we can predict the value of G with a 95% confidence interval of ± 0.006. The
extra information contained in G appears on this basis to be rather limited. It
is also interesting to note that if a time trend is introduced into the equation,
the coefficient is insignificant at the 10% level.

The equation was estimated using time series information, and one test of
its predictive power is to apply it to the cross-section estimates of the distribution within age groups in 1972 given by Astin (1975). The actual and
predicted Gini coefficients are as shown below.

	actual	predicted		actual	predicted
age under 25	0.96	0.95	age 25—34	0.84	0.87
age 35—44	0.82	0.82	age 45—54	0.83	0.84
age 55—64	0.84	0.84	age 65—74	0.83	0.83
age 75—84	0.83	0.83	age 85—	0.83	0.82

Source: actual coefficients from Astin: table 1; predicted coefficients calculated from values of E and W_1 given by Astin.

Within the degree of precision with which Gini coefficients are typically quoted (two decimal places), the predicted values are close to those actually reported. Again, therefore, there appears to be little information conveyed by the Gini coefficient over and above that contained in W_1 and E.

APPENDIX V

METHODS OF INTERPOLATION

At a number of points in the text, it has proved convenient to interpolate between observations on the Lorenz curve. For this purpose a variety of methods have been suggested, and this appendix examines some of these in more detail (for discussion in the text, see chapter 5, section 3).

The basic problem may be stated as follows. It is assumed that we have the following observations:

(a) the share of the bottom $(i-1)$ groups, who constitute a proportion F_{i-1} of the population, is given by L_{i-1},

(b) the ith group consist of a proportion f_i of the population, whose wealth lies in the range $w_i \leqslant w < w_{i+1}$, and whose average wealth is $\bar{w}_i$.

The overall mean is denoted by $\bar{w}$. We wish to obtain by interpolation the value L^* of the share of the bottom F^* as a proportion of the population, where

$$F_{i-1} < F^* < F_{i-1} + f_i = F_i$$

The situation is summarised in terms of figure V.1 where P_{i-1} is the point on the Lorenz curve corresponding to the bottom $(i-1)$ groups and P_i that corresponding to the bottom i groups. It is assumed that we are concerned with a closed interval (as was the case in the text); the problem of extrapolating in the open-ended upper range needs to be treated in a somewhat different manner.

V.1 Linear upper and lower bounds

The most straightforward procedure is to draw a straight line between P_{i-1} and P_i, and this assumption is implicit in formulae often used, for example, to calculate the Gini coefficient. It is clear, however, that this causes the share of the top wealth groups to be under-stated. This method gives a *lower bound* on the degree of concentration.

In effect this lower bound is based on all those in the ith group holding an equal amount ($\bar{w}_i$). The opposite extreme case is that where members are

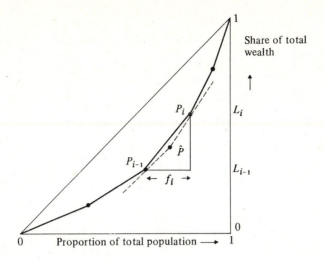

Figure V.1 Linear bounds on Lorenz curve

located at the ends of the range, a proportion η with w_i and $(1 - \eta)$ with w_{i+1}, where

$$\eta = \frac{\bar{w}_i - w_i}{w_{i+1} - w_i}$$

ensures that mean wealth equals $\bar{w}_i$. This gives a Lorenz curve, again piece-wise linear, of the form $P_{i-1}\,\hat{P}\,P_i$, where the slope of $P_{i-1}\,\hat{P}$ is given by $w_i/\bar{w}$, and that of $\hat{P}\,P_i$ by $(w_{i+1}/\bar{w})$. The resulting estimate is an upper bound on the shares of the top x per cent.

V.2   Bounds for distributions with non-increasing frequency

The adoption of the bounds described involves no assumption about the nature of the distribution of wealth within the ith group: the Lorenz curve cannot lie outside the range $P_{i-1}\,\hat{P}\,P_i$ whatever form the distribution takes. If it is possible to restrict the class of distributions under consideration, then these bounds may be refined.

One important type of restriction is that explored by Gastwirth (1972) where the distribution $F(w)$ is concave (i.e. $F'' = f' \leqslant 0$). This case of a non-increasing frequency function is one which applies to the data considered in the text, and is of wide applicability when considering the upper ranges of the distribution.

Both the extreme cases considered in the previous section (all the weight in the middle, and all the weight at the extremes) are ruled out by the

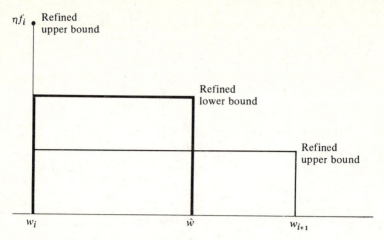

Figure V.2 Assumed densities with refined bounds

requirement that frequencies be non-increasing. Gastwirth shows that refined upper and lower bounds are given by (1972: theorem 5):

lower bound a uniform distribution over the range $[w_i, \hat{w}]$ where $\hat{w} \leqslant w_{i+1}$. It may be noted that the density is given by $f_i/(\hat{w} - w_i)$ and that $\hat{w}$ is equal to $(2\bar{w}_i - w_i)$. The fact that f is a non-increasing function ensures that

$$\bar{w}_i \leqslant \frac{w_i + w_{i+1}}{2}$$

and hence that $\hat{w} \leqslant w_{i+1}$.

upper bound a fraction η of the group have wealth w_i, and the remainder distributed uniformly on $[w_i, w_{i+1}]$. The fraction η is given by

$$\eta = \frac{w_i + w_{i+1} - 2\bar{w}_i}{w_{i+1} - w_i}$$

(Again the fact that the frequency is non-decreasing implies that $\eta \geqslant 0$.) The assumed densities in the two cases are shown in Figure V.2.

From these results we can calculate the refined upper and lower bound Lorenz curves. It may be noted that both Lorenz curves have slopes equal to w_i at P_{i-1}, but that the lower bound has slope $\hat{w}$ rather than w_{i+1} at P_i (the upper bound has slope w_{i+1}). The resulting interpolation formulae are respectively quadratic, and piece-wise linear/quadratic, as may be seen from the following formula for the lower bound on $1 - L^*$:

$$1 - L_{i-1} - \frac{(F^* - F_{i-1})}{\bar{w}} \left[w_i + \frac{(F^* - F_{i-1})}{(F_i - F_{i-1})} (\bar{w}_i - w_i) \right]$$

and for the upper bound:

$$= \min \left[1 - L_1^*, 1 - L_2^* \right]$$

where

$$L_1^* = L_{i-1} + \frac{w_i}{\bar{w}} (F^* - F_{i-1}) \qquad \text{(i.e. linear)}$$

$$L_2^* = L_i - \frac{(F_i - F^*)}{\bar{w}} \left[w_{i+1} - \frac{(F_i - F^*)(w_{i+1} - w_i)^2}{4(F_i - F_{i-1})(\bar{w}_i - w_i)} \right]$$

(i.e. quadratic)

V.3   Interpolation formulae

A number of interpolation formulae have been used in the literature. These typically satisfy some but not all of the following conditions:

(a) pass through the points P_{i-1} and P_i,

(b) slope at P_{i-1} equal to $w_i/\bar{w}$,

(c) slope at P_i equal to $w_{i+1}/\bar{w}$,

(d) lie between the linear upper and lower bounds,

(e) lie for concave F between the refined upper and lower bounds.

Graphical interpolation

One method employed by a number of writers (e.g. Lampman 1962) is that of fitting a Lorenz curve by eye. This can be done quickly and it is fairly straightforward to ensure that the gross upper and lower bounds are satisfied. It is, however, impossible for other researchers to reproduce this method of interpolation, and this renders it unsatisfactory for most purposes.

Log–linear interpolation

The most widely used method apart from the graphical technique is probably that of log–linear or Pareto interpolation. In the context of the Lorenz curves, this involves the assumption that

$$\left(\frac{1-L}{1-L_i} \right) = \left(\frac{1-F}{1-F_i} \right)^{\gamma} \quad \text{where} \quad 0 < \gamma < 1 \tag{1}$$

where γ is determined by the requirement that the curves pass through P_{i-1},

$$\gamma = \frac{\log(1 - L_{i-1}) - \log(1 - L_i)}{\log(1 - F_{i-1}) - \log(1 - F_i)} \tag{2}$$

This satisfies requirement (a); it does not however necessarily satisfy (b) and (c); this depends on the form of the underlying distribution. If the distribution is Pareto in form, then equations (1) and (2) give a precise interpolation with the correct slope. If the distribution deviates from the Pareto form, this is no longer true, and difficulties may arise.

The problems with the log–linear interpolation may be seen if we look at the implied upper and lower limits to the range. The interpolation procedure makes no use of w_i and w_{i+1} but the implicit values (denoted by $\hat{w}_i$) may be obtained by differentiating the Lorenz curve

$$\frac{w}{\bar{w}} \equiv \frac{dL}{dF} = \gamma_i \left(\frac{1 - L_i}{1 - F_i}\right) \left(\frac{1 - F}{1 - F_i}\right)^{\gamma_i - 1} \tag{3}$$

Hence

$$\frac{\hat{w}_i}{\bar{w}} = \gamma_i \left(\frac{1 - L_{i-1}}{1 - F_{i-1}}\right) \quad \text{and} \quad \frac{\hat{w}_{i+1}}{\bar{w}} = \gamma_i \left(\frac{1 - L_i}{1 - F_i}\right) \tag{4}$$

where the subscript i indicates that γ_i is the value estimated for that range. From this it is clear that if the distribution is not strictly Pareto in form, and γ_i varies with i, then the implied ranges will not coincide with the actual ranges. In particular, if γ_i were to fall as we move to higher wealth ranges, the interpolated Lorenz curve would be non-convex. Moreover, if $\hat{w}_i < w_i$, then the interpolated shares will be greater than the linear upper bound. These features of the log–linear interpolation cast serious doubt on its usefulness.

Cubic interpolation

An alternative method of interpolation proposed by a number of authors is that of fitting a cubic polynomial. The following function satisfies the requirements that the slope at the end points equals $w_i/\bar{w}$ and $w_{i+1}/\bar{w}$ respectively:

$$L^*(Z) = L_{i-1} + Z\left(\frac{w_i f_i}{\bar{w}}\right) + Z^2\left[L_i - L_{i-1} - \frac{w_i f_i}{\bar{w}}\right]$$
$$+ 2Z^2(1 - Z)\left[L_i - L_{i-1} - f_i \frac{(w_i + w_{i+1})}{2\bar{w}}\right] \tag{5}$$

where $Z = [(F^* - F_{i-1})/f_i]$ and hence $0 \leqslant Z \leqslant 1$. The fact that the slope at the end points is equal to $(w_i/\bar{w})$ and $(w_{i+1}/\bar{w})$ respectively may be seen by evaluating

$$\frac{dL^*}{dF^*} = \frac{1}{f_i}\frac{dL^*}{dZ}$$

$$= \frac{w_i}{\bar{w}} + 2Z\left[\frac{L_i - L_{i-1}}{f_i} - \frac{w_i}{\bar{w}}\right] \tag{6}$$

$$+ 2Z(2 - 3Z)\left[\frac{L_i - L_{i-1}}{f_i} - \frac{w_i + w_{i+1}}{2\bar{w}}\right]$$

at $Z = 0$ and $Z = 1$. Taking the second derivative, we obtain [replacing $(L_i - L_{i-1})/f_i$ by $\bar{w}_i$]

$$\frac{1}{6f_i}\frac{d^2L}{dZ^2} = \left[\bar{w}_i - \frac{(2w_i + w_{i+1})}{3\bar{w}}\right] - 2Z\left[\bar{w}_i - \frac{w_i + w_{i+1}}{2\bar{w}}\right] \tag{7}$$

Evaluating at first $Z = 0$ and then $Z = 1$ this is positive where

$$\tfrac{2}{3}w_i + \tfrac{1}{3}w_{i+1} < \bar{w}_i < \tfrac{1}{3}w_i + \tfrac{2}{3}w_{i+1} \tag{8}$$

Since it is possible to construct distributions such that this does not hold, we cannot rule out the possibility that the interpolated Lorenz curve is non-convex. Further, the non-convexity at P_{i-1} implies that the interpolated Lorenz curve lies outside the linear upper bound. (The slope is equal to that of $P_{i-1}\hat{P}$ in figure V.1; if $d^2L/dZ^2 < 0$ the slope is decreasing, so that the interpolation takes us below the line $P_{i-1}\hat{P}$.) Again, therefore, the method does not necessarily satisfy requirement (d), and on this account is not very satisfactory.

V.4   Relationship to fitted distributions

Any interpolation formula embodies assumptions about the form of the density function within the interval. The log–linear method, for example, is based on the assumption that the distribution is piece-wise Pareto in form. A different approach to the question, therefore, is through fitting distribution functions to the whole range of available data. This does not lead to an interpolation which satisfies the requirements listed above, since it will not provide an exact fit to the observed points on the Lorenz curve. At the same time, it may have the advantage that the underlying density function is considered more reasonable on *a priori* grounds.

It is important to distinguish these two approaches since they are intended to serve different functions. The interpolation methods described in this appendix are designed to solve a mechanical problem in a way which can be reproduced and which meets certain requirements. The fitted distributions place less weight on the actual observations, in that they treat the relationship as stochastic, but bring to bear some prior conceptions about the form of the distribution. In some cases, attempts have been made to combine elements of both approaches, as in the log–linear interpolation based on the Pareto distribution, but this runs the risk of being unsatisfactory on both scores.

DATA FOR CHAPTER 6

This appendix describes the data sources for the new estimates for the period 1923–72 presented in chapter 6. They are set out under the following headings:

    (i) population figures
    (ii) mortality figures
    (iii) social class mortality differentials
    (iv) estate data
    (v) adjustment for funeral expenses
    (vi) wealth of excluded population

(i) Population figures

The population figures are those obtained in the decennial censuses and the intervening mid year estimates by the Registrar General. The mid year estimates are an extrapolation of the most recent census, with allowance for births, deaths, and migration into and out of the country, and are typically revised in the light of the subsequent census. The effect of such revision on the wealth estimates was discussed by Daniels and Campion (1936: 10–11). They compared the extrapolated mid year estimate for 1931 with that based on the 1931 Census returns, and adjusted the published mid year figures for 1924–30, interpolating the difference between the 1931 estimated and the 1931 Census figures. Since they wrote, the Registrar General for England and Wales has produced a new mid year population series for the period, making use of the final results of the 1931 Census. These estimates, published in the Decennial Supplement, Part II (Registrar General for England and Wales 1950: table I), have been used in our estimates.

For the more recent years, we have in each case used the latest available version of the mid year estimates of the population. Thus for England and Wales we have used figures for 1936 and 1938 revised by the Registrar General in the light of the National Register in 1939, for 1950–60 revised by him in the light of the 1961 Census and a study of the age and sex of migrants, and for 1961–71 revised in the light of the 1971 Census.

It should be noted that for 1950 onwards the population figures are those
for *home* population rather than *total* population.[1] In some ways the latter
might be more appropriate for our purposes, but we have used the home
population to secure comparability with the Census figures, and hence with
the population estimates for the years 1923—38.

(ii) Mortality

The mortality figures refer to deaths in the calendar year, and are taken from
the annual statistics published by the Registrar General: for example, those
for 1924 are taken from the *Statistical Review of the Registrar-General for
England and Wales 1924,* Part I Medical, table 15.

(iii) Social class mortality differentials

The sources of the adjustments to the Census data are described briefly below
for individual years.

1921. The differentials are obtained from the 1921 Decennial Supplement
on the same basis as assumption A2. They are expressed relative to the total
occupied and retired (for those 65 and over — see text), adjusted for errors in
occupational statements, averaged over social classes I and II, and graduated
at age 65 and above in the light of data for later years.

1931. The treatment for men followed that for 1921. The differentials for
women are an average of those for married and single women. They are not
adjusted for errors in occupational statements, but are otherwise the same as
those for men.

1951. The differentials are obtained from the 1951 Decennial Supplement
and are identical with those used by Lydall and Tipping (1961) (except for the
graduation at age 75 and above). The figures for Scotland are given below.

1961. The differentials are derived from the 1961 Decennial Supplement
following the procedure described in chapter 3 (the figures for England and
Wales are those given in table 3.1, column 2). The figures for Scotland are
given below.

Social class differentials for Scotland

	1951		1961	
	Male	Female	Male	Female
20—24	1.14	1.64	0.89	0.81
25—34	1.31	1.36	1.27	1.25
35—44	1.23	1.08	1.29	1.34
45—54	1.25	1.13	1.25	1.27
55—64	1.17	1.05	1.22	1.20
65—74	1.05	1.00	1.12	1.15
75—84	1.05	1.04	1.06	1.10
85—	1.04	1.04	1.03	1.03

1   The difference is essentially that the former excludes armed forces and seamen
    abroad (while including foreign forces in Britain), whereas the latter includes
    forces abroad (and excludes foreign forces in Britain).

In applying the differentials to individual years, the basic procedure was to interpolate linearly, with the following exceptions:
  (a) for women, the 1931 differentials were applied for all years prior to 1931,
  (b) for 1938, the differentials applied in the case of Scotland were those relating to 1951,
  (c) for 1961–72 the differentials used were those for 1961.
The linear interpolation is clearly arbitrary but it avoids the sudden jumps introduced by the Inland Revenue's practice of discontinuously changing the differentials when new occupational mortality data become available.

(iv) Estate data

The estate data for 1923–62 are taken from the annual reports of the Inland Revenue and relate to the net capital value of estates in the financial year (assumed to correspond to the previous calendar year). They include fixed duty estates, those where the age is not stated, and a proportion of those under 25 years (see text). The multiplier for the age-not-stated group is taken as a weighted average of that for those whose age is recorded as 45 and above. The multiplier for those aged under 21 is based on that for the age group 15–24. The estate data for 1964–72 are based on unpublished tabulations provided by the Inland Revenue, giving greater detail of estates by ranges and by country.

(v) Adjustment for funeral expenses

Following Daniels and Campion, we have made an adjustment to the published estate data for funeral expenses.[2] This involved adding back a sum which varied with the size of the estate. For the period 1923–38 the sum was taken as fixed in cash terms, and ranged from £6 for the smallest estates (£100) to £45 for the largest. For 1950 onwards, the amount was adjusted for inflation. In 1959, for example, it ranged from £56 for estates of £5,000 to £131 for the largest estates.

(vi) Wealth of excluded population

The basic method followed is that described in chapter 4. It involves the use of balance sheet totals, viewed in relation to the estimated totals derived from the estate data, and with some proportion of the excess being allocated to the excluded population. It gives rise to a range of estimates which in

---

2   From 1965 it is also necessary to adjust where capital gains tax liability has been incurred as a result of death, although for the relevant periods we had access to the unpublished IR data which had already been corrected in this respect (and for funeral expenses).

terms of the wealth of the excluded population may be described as below.

B2 – 'upper estimate ⎫
B3 – 'central' estimate ⎬   for total excluded wealth
B4 – 'lower' estimate ⎭

The estimates are on a realisation basis, and cover the following items (see table 4.5):

1. Unquoted UK government securities and savings bank deposits,
2. Cash and bank deposits,
3. Building society deposits,
4. Households goods,
8. Life policies,
9. Land and buildings,
10. Liabilities.

(The numbering follows that employed in chapter 4.) In the case of asset categories 5 (trade assets), 6 (settled property) and 7 (shares) no adjustment is made in chapter 4 for the excluded population for reasons given there.

As is explained in the text, the limited availability of the basic data means that we cannot follow the procedure of chapter 4 precisely for the entire period 1923–72, and the estimates for earlier years are probably less reliable. In view of this we describe below the main additional assumptions necessary for each sub-period, working back from the most recent period 1966–72, for which we have used the estimates described in chapter 5 on assumptions A2/B2-B4/CO/D1/E2 (excluded population only).

1960–5. For these years we have the Revell/Roe balance sheet totals which form a firm foundation for the estimates. On the other hand we do not have asset composition data by wealth ranges, and for the estate estimate totals we used the unadjusted Inland Revenue figures (from Inland Revenue Statistics 1970, table 120). The assumptions B2–B4 followed those set out in table 4.5; and the land and buildings figure for the excluded population was based on assumption E2 described in chapter 4. In the case of household goods, the allowance was related to the average in lower wealth-holdings covered by the estate estimates (as in chapter 4), but with a correction for the changing coverage of the estate returns, particularly as a consequence of the Administration of Estates (Small Payments) Act 1965.

1950–9. The basic data for this period are less satisfactory. The Revell/Roe balance sheet totals do not go back before 1957, and have to be extended in a rather approximate fashion. For each of the items we have chosen a series to use for this extrapolation. In some cases the series is close to the required aggregate: for example, we have calculated the value of stocks of household goods following the same procedure as described in appendix II.

In other cases, the series can only be described as 'representative' of the items making up the total.

The next step was to estimate how much of these balance sheet totals should be allocated to the excluded population. For the 1950s this is particularly tricky in view of the fact that the estate data only cover holdings above the exemption level, and that the exemption level was increased from £2,000 to £3,000 in 1954. As a result the excluded population was more than 90 per cent of the total in 1959 compared with about 50 per cent in 1960. The procedure followed was to take 1960 as a base and to estimate, using asset composition data for a recent year, the effect on the total of each asset type of increasing the excluded population to this extent. Thus it was estimated that if the coverage of the estate data in 1960 had been restricted to the same as that in 1959 then the total for items 1 and 2 owned by the excluded population would have been some 3 times larger. These adjustment factors, with due allowance for the change in the exemption level in 1954, were applied to give estimates for each of the years 1950–9.

The construction of estimates in this way, and especially the use of a 1960 benchmark for estimates as far back as 1950, is clearly prone to error. Fortunately, we may compare our estimates for 1954 with those made by Lydall and Tipping (1961). They made use of the results of the 1954 Oxford Savings Survey and the comparison provides therefore an independent check on our methods. Their asset categories are not the same as ours, but broadly it seems that our estimates are higher for household goods (item 4) and life policies (item 8) and lower for government unquoted securities (item 1), cash and bank deposits (item 2), and land and buildings (item 9). From consideration of Lydall and Tipping's overall totals for these items, and comparison with those of Morgan (1960) for 1955 and Revell (1967) for 1957, it does appear that they may have over-stated the totals for items 1 and 2, and under-stated those for items 4 and 8. The reason for this appears to be that Lydall and Tipping used – for want of better information – data on the asset composition of estates rather than wealth-holdings. As they noted, this assumed that the asset composition was independent of the age and sex of the owner, and in later work Revell showed that 'the assumption is far from correct, and that the method gave a distorted picture of the asset composition of personal wealth' (1962: 363). The correction factors suggested by Revell are in fact (rounded) 0.8 for items 1 and 2, 1.1 for item 4 and 2.7 for item 8.[3] The adjustment factor for land and buildings is 0.9 (1962: table IV). To

3   The implications for the wealth of the excluded population depend on the method of allocation of the balance sheet total. From the description by Lydall and Tipping it appears that the 1954 Oxford survey was used to give a proportional division of each asset total between individuals above and below £2,000. This would cause the wealth of the excluded population to be proportionately over- or under-stated

some extent, therefore, the difference between our estimates and those of Lydall and Tipping may be explicable. Nonetheless, it should be emphasised that the estimates for the 1950s are less reliable than those for the 1960s, and that it is quite possible that they are too low. In the text, to illustrate this possibility, we have taken the Lydall and Tipping figure of £9,150 million for 1954, which is rather less than our B2 estimate.

1923–38. Applying the same method to the even earlier period before the Second World War clearly involves even greater difficulties and in a number of respects the estimates must be regarded as more tentative still. At the same time, we can draw on the work of Clay (1925), Daniels and Campion (1936), and Langley (1951), and on studies of savings at that time such as those by Bray (1940) and Radice (1939).

The balance sheet totals were obtained by methods similar to those for the 1950s, that is by extrapolating using an appropriate series. These totals may be related to the corresponding asset categories used by Clay (1925) in his estimate of 'working class' savings for 1921:

Category 1. Clay's savings bank deposits + savings bank stock held for depositors + co-operative societies' share and loan capital + savings certificates.

Category 2. Clay makes no allowance.

Category 3. Clay's building societies' shares and deposits.

Category 4. See below.

Category 8. Clay's industrial life insurance fund.

Category 9. Clay makes no allowance.

Category 10. Clay makes no allowance.

It may be noted that Clay included a number of items which only have value on a going concern basis and are therefore not taken into account here. Among these are friendly society funds and trade union funds, as well as items such as the National Health Insurance Fund which represent 'social' rather than 'private' property. In the case of household goods, our estimate follows the procedure of chapter 4 and is based on the average holding in the lowest estate range.

The extent to which this property should be allocated to the excluded population has been the subject of considerable debate. Clay in effect deducted some 20 per cent from the total of items 1, 3 and 8. His procedure was criticised by Daniels and Campion (1936) who felt that his total for the excluded population was too high. The subject is discussed at some length by Radice (1939) who quotes the estimates below.

	Held by 'wage-earners'
1. Post Office and Trustee deposits	$\frac{2}{3}$
Post Office and Trustee government stock held for depositors	$\frac{1}{3}$
National Savings Certificates	$\frac{1}{4}$
2. Building societies shares and deposits	$\frac{1}{3}$

Radice also makes the point that the proportions are likely to have varied over the years, and that 'in particular it is probable that the fall in the rate of interest after 1931 raised the proportionate share in these types of savings of persons with incomes over £250, owing to the comparative rigidity of rates of interest paid on them [relative to other assets]' (1939: 50–1).

In view of this we have made the assumptions listed below concerning the proportions allocated to the excluded population.

	B2	B3	B4
Item 1	$\frac{3}{5}$ $(+\frac{1}{5})$	$\frac{1}{2}$ $(+\frac{1}{5}$ post 1930)	$\frac{1}{3}$ $(+\frac{1}{5})$
Item 3	$\frac{1}{2}$ $(+\frac{1}{8})$	$\frac{1}{3}$ $(+\frac{1}{8}$ post 1930)	$\frac{1}{4}$ $(+\frac{1}{8})$
Item 8	1	$\frac{5}{6}$	$\frac{3}{4}$

In order to take account of the point made by Radice concerning the changing proportions in the 1930s, we have allocated a smaller fraction of the increase after 1930; these proportions are shown in brackets.

In the case of item 4, the figures for B2 and B4 are assumed to be $1\frac{1}{4}$ and $\frac{3}{4}$ times the central B3 figure, respectively. This leaves items 2, 9 and 10. In the case of land and buildings we follow Clay in making no allowance, it being assumed that at this time all owner-occupiers would be covered by the estate returns. For both item 2 and item 10, however, we should clearly make some allowance. In the former case, we have simply taken an arbitrary figure of around £2 per head for cash and money in the bank (with a range of £1–£4). In the latter case we have allowed for liabilities of 5 per cent in 1923–30 and 10 per cent in 1936–8. These percentages were based on evidence about the composition of small estates (from the Inland Revenue reports) and on figures for more recent years.

The resulting estimates (see table VI.1) may be compared with those of Daniels and Campion (1936), and of Langley (1951). The former take a range of £500–£900 million for the period 1924–30, which may be compared with our range (averaging over those years) of £590–£1,035 million.[4] As we have argued in the text, there are reasons to believe that the Daniels and Campion figure for the 1920s is too low, so that the estimates given here do not seem unreasonable. (These authors do not explain in detail the basis of their estimates, so that we cannot compare individual asset categories.)

If we turn to 1936–8, Langley (1951) took a central total of £911 million

---

4   The Daniels and Campion estimates relate to the population aged 25 and over; but this is unlikely to make a substantial difference.

in 1936–8 for the population aged 25 and over. She also suggested that the
average capital of those aged 15–24 was £20, which would give a total for
our economically independent population of some £960 million, with a
range of £720 – £1,200 million.[5] Our own central figure, £1,070 million, lies
well within this range, and – given that Langley seems to have used a simple
average – does not appear unreasonable. Both our estimates, and those of
Langley, are however high in relation to those of Campion (1939), who takes
the figures below (for the population aged 25 and over).

	£ million
1926–8	500–900
1936	450–950

These figures show in effect no increase over the period, but the reason
given for this – that the number of people with small estates was larger – is
not particularly convincing since there was a similar increase in the numbers
below £100. In our view, the estimates given here and by Langley are more
reasonable, in light of the following considerations. Firstly, the period saw a
substantial expansion in the industrial life insurance business (Ginsburg
1943). Secondly, although the spread of domestic appliances and other
consumer durables may have to some extent been offset by a decline in their
price, it does not seem reasonable to suppose that their average value per
person would have fallen between the mid 1920s and the late 1930s. Thirdly,
total deposits in the Post Office Savings Bank and Trustee Savings Bank went
up by 60 per cent between 1920 and 1935, and although this should not all
be regarded as 'working class' savings (see the discussion above) it provides
ground for believing that there was some expansion over the period.

Summary

The resulting estimates for the total wealth of the excluded population are
shown in table VI.1. For the period 1923–38 these relate to England and
Wales, for 1950–72 to Great Britain. In allocating wealth between the
countries (e.g. to obtain England and Wales totals for the postwar period), it
is assumed that per capita wealth-holdings of the excluded population are
the same in the two countries, although the estimated shares are not
particularly sensitive to this assumption.

---

5   The range is based on Langley's figures of £35–£60 applied to those aged 25
    and over plus £50 million for those aged under 25.

Table VI.1 Estimated wealth of the excluded population (£ million)

	B2	B3	B4	
1923	929	732	528	
1924	957	752	543	
1925	986	776	562	
1926	1,003	789	573	
1927	1,028	806	588	England and Wales
1928	1,065	829	608	
1929	1,083	845	620	
1930	1,123	875	643	
1936	1,300	1,039	797	
1938	1,365	1,099	854	
1950	8,805	5,755	3,648	
1951	9,318	6,090	3,860	
1952	9,578	6,260	3,968	
1953	9,922	6,485	4,110	
1954	10,442	6,825	4,326	
1955	14,550	9,510	6,028	
1956	15,774	10,310	6,535	
1957	16,992	11,060	7,010	
1958	17,901	11,700	7,416	
1959	19,033	12,440	7,885	
1960	5,215	3,400	2,155	
1961	6,195	4,250	2,890	Great Britain
1962	7,180	5,145	3,665	
1963	8,805	6,355	4,545	
1964	7,020	4,525	2,815	
1965	7,205	4,455	2,550	
1966	7,970	5,294	3,486	
1967	8,761	5,636	3,676	
1968	10,178	6,178	3,535	
1969	9,043	5,314	2,704	
1970	10,938	6,025	3,075	
1971	9,567	5,106	2,484	
1972	15,705	8,430	4,174	

APPENDIX VII

BIAS IN THE INVESTMENT INCOME METHOD

This appendix examines the implications of differences in rates of return, independent of w, for the investment income method.

For this purpose we use the following highly simplified model:

(i) asset-holdings are linear in w

$$A_j = B_j + \beta_j w \quad (j = 1, \ldots, J) \text{ where } \sum B_j = 0, \; \sum \beta_j = 1.$$

(ii) wealth-holdings are distributed over a range $w \geqslant w_0$, where w_0 is such that $A_j \geqslant 0$ all j.

(iii) concentration is measured by the coefficient of variation.

These assumptions are restrictive but should suffice to give some indication of the possible bias.

We further suppose that the return to an individual's holding of asset type j, R_j, is randomly distributed and is independent both of w and of R_k $(k \neq j)$. Since

$$Y = \sum_{j=1}^{J} (B_j + \beta_j w) R_j \tag{1}$$

we may write the variance of Y as:

$$\mathrm{Var}(Y) = \sum_j \mathrm{Var}\,[R_j(B_j + \beta_j w)]$$
$$+ \sum_j \sum_{k \neq j} \mathrm{cov}[R_j(B_j + \beta_j w), R_k(B_k + \beta_k w)] \tag{2}$$

Making use of the independence assumptions, and of the formula for the variance of a product (Goodman 1960), this simplifies to:

$$\mathrm{Var}(Y) = \left(\sum_j \bar{R}_j \beta_j \right)^2 \mathrm{Var}(w)$$
$$+ \sum_j [\beta_j^2 \, \mathrm{Var}(w) \, \mathrm{Var}(R_j) + (B_j + \beta_j \bar{w})^2 \, \mathrm{Var}(R_j)] \tag{3}$$

Now if we apply the standard investment income method, w is estimated from:

$$\left(\sum_j \bar{R}_j \beta_j \right) w = Y - \sum_j \bar{R}_j B_j \tag{4}$$

and the estimated variance is:

$$\widehat{\text{Var}(w)} = \text{Var}(Y) \Big/ \Big(\sum_j \bar{R}_j \beta_j \Big)^2 \tag{5}$$

This may be compared with the true variance, which may be calculated from (3):

$$\text{Var}(w) = \frac{\text{Var}(Y) - \sum_j (B_j + \beta_j \bar{w})^2 \; \text{Var}(R_j)}{\left[\Big(\sum_j \bar{R}_j \beta_j \Big)^2 + \sum_j \beta_j^2 \; \text{Var}(R_j) \right]} \tag{6}$$

Where $\text{Var}(R_j) > 0$, this leads to the variance of w being over-stated by the investment income method. As we should expect, the distribution of returns, independently of w, leads to greater variance in incomes than allowed for in the standard method.

In order to examine the extent of the bias more closely, it is convenient to write $V(x)$ as the coefficient of variation of x and define

$$\bar{Y}_j = \bar{R}_j (B_j + \beta_j \bar{w}) \tag{7}$$

the mean income from asset type j,

$$\epsilon_j = \frac{\bar{R}_j \beta_j \bar{w}}{\bar{Y}_j} \tag{8}$$

the elasticity of A_j with respect to w, evaluated at $\bar{w}$, and

$$\epsilon = \sum_j \bar{R}_j \beta_j \bar{w} / \bar{Y} \tag{9}$$

where $\bar{Y}$ is overall mean income given by $\sum_j \bar{Y}_j$, and it may be noted that ϵ is the elasticity of $\bar{Y}$ with respect to w. With this notation, we may rewrite (6) as

$$V^2(w) = \frac{\hat{V}^2(w) - \dfrac{1}{\epsilon^2} \left[\sum_j (\bar{Y}_j/\bar{Y})^2 \; V^2(R_j) \right]}{1 + \dfrac{1}{\epsilon^2} \left[\sum_j \left\{ \dfrac{\epsilon_j \bar{Y}_j}{\bar{Y}} \right\}^2 V^2(R_j) \right]} \tag{10}$$

From this it may be seen that the bias in the standard investment income method appears to be larger:

the greater the variation in the individual returns $V^2(R_j)$,

where large variations are associated with important assets, measured according to their contribution to total income (Y_j/Y),

(iii) where large variations are associated with assets with a high wealth elasticity (ϵ_j),

(iv) where the elasticity of mean income with respect to mean wealth (ϵ) is low.

ESTIMATED YIELDS FOR INVESTMENT INCOME METHOD (chapter 7)

This appendix describes the assumptions underlying the calculation of the taxable investment income yielded by different assets. As noted in the text we took as a starting point the techniques employed by Stark (1972: appendix 4), and where our procedure is identical with his we have indicated this by [Stark]. The data source, unless otherwise indicated, is *Financial Statistics* (referred to as FS). The fact that, when calculating weighted average yields, the weights relate to different dates in the relevant year reflects the availability of data on particular asset holdings.

(a) National savings certificates and premium bonds
As pointed out in the text, these provide no taxable income and the appropriate yield is therefore zero.

(b) Defence, development and savings bonds, and tax reserve certificates
The interest rates, net of bonuses, on defence bonds, national development bonds and British savings bonds were weighted by the respective amounts invested in each category (published in the Consolidated Fund National Loans Fund Account for 1968/9 and 1972/3) to give an average yield for these items. Tax reserve certificates are free of all tax so that the appropriate yield is zero. These yields were weighted by the total invested in bonds and the total personal holdings of tax reserve certificates (taken from balance sheet data – see chapter 4). *Accuracy:* the information on yields is largely derived from the issuing source and it therefore seemed reasonable to allocate this asset class to the category subject to the smallest degree of error (classification* in table 7.1).

(c), (d) and (e) Government securities
The government securities used to calculate the yields on these assets were the ten dated securities listed in FS, April 1969 and April 1973. They were divided into three categories as follows (maturity year in brackets):

1968/9 (c) maturing in less than 5 years: 6% Exchequer loan (1970), 3% Savings bonds (1960–70), 5% Conversion stock (1971), $6\frac{1}{4}$% Exchequer loan (1972);

        (d) maturing in 5 to 14 years: $6\frac{1}{2}$% Treasury loan (1976), 5% Exchequer loan (1976–8), $5\frac{1}{4}$% Funding loan (1978–80);

        (e) maturing in 15 years or more: $6\frac{1}{2}$% Funding loan (1985–7), $6\frac{3}{4}$% Treasury loan (1995–8), $5\frac{1}{2}$% Treasury stock (2008–12).

1972/3 (c) maturing in less than 5 years: $5\frac{1}{4}$% Treasury stock (1973), $6\frac{3}{4}$% Treasury stock (1974), 3% Savings bonds (1965–75), $6\frac{1}{2}$% Treasury loan (1976), $6\frac{1}{4}$% Treasury stock (1977);

        (d) maturing in 5 to 14 years: $8\frac{1}{2}$% Treasury stock (1980–2), $6\frac{1}{2}$% Funding loan (1985–7);

        (e) maturing in 15 years or more: 9% Treasury loan (1994), 8% Treasury stock (2002–6), $7\frac{3}{4}$% Treasury stock (2012–5).

For each security we computed the monthly flat yield and derived an average over the year. These yields were then weighted by the value of the amounts outstanding in the securities in December of each year to give three average yields corresponding to the categories of maturity. *Accuracy:* see (f).

(f) $2\frac{1}{2}$% Consols and undated securities
The mean of the monthly gross flat yields of $2\frac{1}{2}$% consols and $3\frac{1}{2}$% War Loan (taken as a reasonable proxy for undated securities) for 1968/9 and 1972/3 were weighted by the actual outstanding value of the two assets in December of each year (the nominal amount multiplied by the ratio of the net price to the nominal price). *Accuracy:* Since the information used for items (c)–(f) is based only on representative yields available from source, there is clearly a greater margin of possible error than in the case of, say, item (b) and the yields were therefore allocated to the moderately accurate category** in table 7.1.

(g) Northern Ireland and municipal securities
Since the size of the stock of Northern Ireland government securities is small, the yield on 3 month deposits with local authorities averaged over the twelve months was taken as a suitable proxy for this item. *Accuracy:* the reliability rating was the same as that used for British government securities.

(h) Commonwealth government securities [Stark]
As a proxy for this category we took an average of the means of the four quarterly yields (e.g. 1968 II – 1969 I) of the government securities of Australia, Canada and New Zealand, published in *IMF International Financial Statistics. Accuracy:* see (i)

(i) Other foreign government securities [Stark]

The yield on US Treasury bills was taken as representative for this item (source as (h)). *Accuracy:* both (h) and (i) are broad asset groups based on fairly narrowly defined representative sources, and the accuracy of these yields is likely to be less than that for British government securities. We therefore allocated them to the category below that used for British government securities (*** in table 7.1).

(j) British unquoted company shares [Stark]

The yield on item (k), British quoted shares, was used as a proxy for this asset, although it could be argued that unquoted companies would be better represented by an index of the yield on the shares of small quoted companies. *Accuracy:* we therefore felt it necessary to regard the yield multiplier as relatively unreliable, the poorest of our four categories****.

(k) British quoted company shares [Stark]

Following Stark we took the average of the twelve monthly dividend yields of the Financial Times/Actuaries share index of 500 industrial ordinary shares from April to March (FS, April 1969 and April 1973). This index is not wholly appropriate, and a case could be made for using the wider index of 651 shares including financial companies. This would tend to reduce the yield; on the other hand, there are some reasons for believing that the index may be on the low side, when compared for instance with the de Zoete index. The yield for this item and its accuracy is discussed further in the text.

(l) British preference shares and debentures [Stark]

Since there were no figures available for weighting preference shares and debentures, and since the former probably account for the bulk of the total, we followed Stark and took the average of the twelve monthly yield averages of the Financial Times/Actuaries share index of preference stocks (FS, April 1969 and April 1973). *Accuracy:* the yield taken is only representative of part of the category and therefore is classified as *** in table 7.1.

(m) Overseas company shares [Stark]

In the absence of any better information, the yield on this item was proxied by the annual average of the composite yield of US shares for 1968 and 1972, published in *Moody's Bank and Finance Manual. Accuracy:* the proxy nature of this yield led us to rate it in the 'less reliable' category***.

(n) Unit trusts

For a composite yield on this item, the yields at 31 December on all the unit trusts listed in the *Unit Trust Yearbook* (1969 edition for December 1968, and 1973 edition for December 1972) were weighted by the amounts invested in the trusts, also given in the *Yearbook. Accuracy:* the mean yield was regarded as more reliable than that on British quoted shares given the amount of information available, and the allocated rating was therefore**.

(o) Building society shares and deposits
The net of tax yields on shares and deposits (FS, August 1969 and September 1973) were grossed up at the standard rate of income tax, and these yields were then weighted by the totals outstanding in shares and deposits in December (taken from the Report of the Chief Registrar of Friendly Societies). *Accuracy:* the information is all available from source and the mean yield was therefore regarded as relatively accurate*.

(p) and (q) Household goods, insurance policies
Neither of these items yields any taxable investment income.

(r) National (Post Office) and Trustee Savings Banks
The average yields on ordinary and investment accounts with the NSB and the TSB were estimated (weighted by the number of months an individual rate prevailed), and the overall yield was then derived using as weights the balances remaining invested in each type of account at the end of March. It should be noted that the first £15 interest (the first £21 in 1972/3) on ordinary accounts with both the NSB and the TSB was liable to surtax in 1968/9 grossed up at the standard rate of income tax to take account of its exemption from income tax. Thus the appropriate yield for ordinary accounts should be a weighted average of the grossed up yield and the flat yield. The information required for this purpose was not, however, available, so that the flat yield was used with the result that the overall yield for this item in table 7.1 is likely to be slightly under-stated. *Accuracy:* the effect of the £15/£21 exemption is likely to be small, and overall it seemed reasonable to use the relatively accurate rating* since all the information is available from source.

(s) and (t) Commercial bank accounts [s = Stark]
Current accounts bear no interest so that, like cash in the house, zero is the appropriate yield. The yield on commercial bank deposit accounts was estimated as the average of the twelve monthly rates paid on deposits between April and March. *Accuracy:* the data are from the issuing source and should be relatively accurate*.

(u) Trade, business and professional assets
These yield no taxable investment income. (Any income generated is returned under schedule D.)

(v) Money on mortgage etc.

This item includes money on mortgage of real estate, money on municipal bonds, personal loans to other individuals, deposits with co-operative and friendly societies and cessers of annuities. In the absence of any firm information about the precise composition, or about the yields on a number of these assets, the return was taken as the average of that for items (m) and (p), and the lowest accuracy rating was allocated****.

(w) Other personalty

In the absence of any information on this item, the yield was estimated as the average of all assets (a)–(v) weighted according to their importance in all wealth-holdings (i.e. the weights do not vary with the size of the individual holding). As with (v), the result was regarded as 'relatively unreliable'.

(x), (y) and (z) Land and buildings

The amounts of wealth held in the three categories of land, residential buildings and other buildings were taken from the estimates made by the Inland Revenue and published in *Inland Revenue Statistics* 1970: table 121 (for 1968); and *Inland Revenue Statistics* 1974: table 103 (for 1972). This gave a breakdown of 3:23:1 in 1968 and 5:49:1 in 1972 (£ billion rounded). The total investment income from this source *(Inland Revenue Statistics* 1971: table 60; and 1975: table 47) was then expressed as a percentage of gross landed property, the total of these three categories, with an adjustment for those not covered by the income statistics and for the rents from furnished lettings. The overall return is extremely low reflecting the large component of owner-occupied property with no taxable income.

The procedure of Stark was simply to take this total return for all assets (x), (y) and (z). We felt that this was unsatisfactory since it made no allowance for the extent of owner-occupation or for any possible difference in return between residential property (y) and the other categories (x) and (z). We have therefore treated (x) and (z) as one category (with subscript 1) and (y) as another (subscript 2), and estimated the yields from the relationship.

$$rW = r_1(1 - h_1)W_1 + r_2(1 - h_2)W_2$$

where $W_i(W)$ denotes wealth in category i (total wealth)

$r_i(r)$ denotes landlord's return to category i (total yield)

h_i denotes proportion corresponding to owner-occupied in category i.

On the basis of the rent figures used in the Annual Review and Determination of Guarantees and other evidence about the return to investment in agriculture (see Bosanquet 1968) we took $r_1 = 2\%$ in 1968/9 and $1\frac{1}{2}\%$ in 1972/3. For h_1 we took 50% in 1968/9 and 57% in 1972/3, reflecting the tendency for an increase in owner-occupation and the extension of institutional ownership. (It should be noted that h is the ratio of occupied property to the total in *personal* ownership, so property owned by institutions is excluded.) For h_2 we assumed that one half of private rented accommodation was owned by individuals which gave $h_2 = 0.86$ in 1968/9 and 0.88 in 1972/3. Solving the equation for r_2 gave 4.5% in 1968/9 and 3.1% in 1972/3. Comparing these with the imputed rent assumed by the CSO on owner-occupied houses (*National Income and Expenditure* 1973, table 26) suggests that these figures are not unreasonable. In applying the yields r_1 and r_2 we had to make certain assumptions about the proportion owner-occupied. It seems reasonable to suppose that for the ranges of investment income considered this lies between zero and the average for all holdings: i.e. multipliers based on $r_i(1 - h_i)$ and r_i. For the central case we took the midpoint of these multipliers $(1/r)$. This gave the results shown.

1968−9				1972−3			
(x) and (z) Multiplier (Yield)		(y) Multiplier (Yield)		(x) and (z) Multiplier (Yield)		(y) Multiplier (Yield)	
75	(1.3%)	88	(1.1%)	111	(0.9%)	151	(0.7%)

(α) Debts owing

For this item we took as a reasonable proxy the commercial banks lending rate to individuals. There owever no definite figure for this. In 1968 it was quoted as not less than 1 ove Bank Rate while in 1972 it ranged between 1% and $4\frac{1}{2}\%$ above the c rcial banks' base rate. In general the rate charged depended on th s of the individual customer and the selection of a particular rate is unavoidably arbitrary. Since however we were advised that banks rarely went above 3% over Bank Rate in 1968 we took the figure of 2% plus Bank Rate for that year. For 1972 we again selected a point roughly midway between the upper and lower limits, and chose 3% above base rate. *Accuracy:* because of the range of rates described above, we allocated this item to the 'relatively unreliable' category[***].

(β) Mortgages

The average interest rate charged on building society mortgages between February and January was used for this item. This time period is the closest to that actually required which is available. It is unlikely however that the effect of this is very large, so that overall this yield was regarded as moderately accurate[**].

SPECIFIC DISTRIBUTION FUNCTIONS

This appendix describes some of the features of the main distribution functions to which reference has been made in the text.

IX.1 Introduction

The distribution of wealth is described by a density function $f(w)dw$ and a cumulative distribution function $F(w)$, where these are expressed as proportions of the total population. The proportion with wealth in excess of w^* is therefore

$$1 - F^* = \int_{w^*}^{\infty} f \, dw = \int_{w^*}^{\infty} dF \qquad (1)$$

Their share of total wealth is given by

$$1 - L^* = \int_{w^*}^{\infty} w/\bar{w} \, f \, dw \qquad (2)$$

where $\bar{w}$ is the mean wealth. The Lorenz curve is defined by $L(F)$, that is by eliminating w^* from equations (1) and (2). It has the following properties:

$$dL/dF = w/\bar{w} \quad d^2L/dF^2 = 1/(\bar{w}f) \geqslant 0 \qquad (3)$$

IX.2 Pareto Type I distribution (see also appendix IV)

The Pareto distribution is given by

$$1 - F(w) = \left(\frac{w}{\underline{w}}\right)^{-\alpha} \quad w \geqslant \underline{w} > 0 \qquad (4)$$

where $\underline{w}$ is the lowest level of wealth. The frequency is everywhere decreasing, see figure IX.1. The mean wealth is given by $[\alpha/(\alpha - 1)] \, \underline{w}$, and the Lorenz curve by

$$1 - L = (1 - F)^{\gamma} \qquad (5)$$

where
$$\gamma = 1 - 1/\alpha.$$

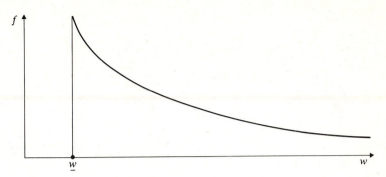

Figure IX.1 Pareto distribution

The exponent α was taken by Pareto as an index of inequality, and this has been followed by many subsequent writers. There has, however, been some confusion about the interpretation. As Chipman (1974) has pointed out, the effect of increasing α depends on whether one is holding constant mean wealth $(\bar{w})$ or the lower boundary $(\underline{w})$. The former interpretation is the one adopted here, and concentration then declines as α increases, as may be seen from the Lorenz curve (equation (5)), since a higher α moves the Lorenz curve closer to the diagonal. The summary measures bear this out, since they are declining functions of α:

$$G = 1/(2\alpha - 1) \qquad \text{so that } \alpha = 1.5 \text{ implies } G = 0.5$$

$$D = 2(1 - F(\bar{w}))/(\alpha - 1) \quad \text{so that } \alpha = 1.5 \text{ implies } D = 0.77$$

$$V^2 = 1/(\alpha(\alpha - 2)) \qquad \text{so that the coefficient of variation is only finite for } \alpha > 2.$$

IX.3   More general Pareto distributions

Pareto himself suggested the more general form (see Chipman 1974 and Creedy 1974):

$$1 - F = A(w + b)^{-\alpha}e^{-cw} \tag{6}$$

This has the obvious merit in the present context of allowing for negative wealth. Where $c = 0$, the distribution is referred to as the Pareto Type II distribution. As w tends to infinity, this approximates the Pareto Type I distribution.

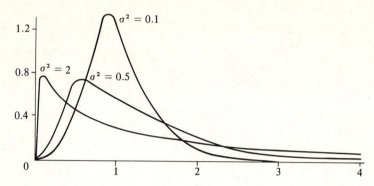

Figure IX.2 Lognormal distribution for different values of σ

IX.4   Lognormal distribution

Writing $y = \log_e w$, then y is normally distributed with mean and variance σ^2. The distribution is hump-shaped and positively skew, as indicated by the relative position of

$$\text{Mode } (e^{m-\sigma^2}) \quad \text{Median } (e^m) \quad \text{Mean } (e^{m+\frac{1}{2}\sigma^2})$$

The shape of the distribution is illustrated in figure IX.2, which is taken from Aitchison and Brown (1957), the standard reference on this subject. The value of σ is a measure of the degree of concentration, as is illustrated by the summary measures:

$$V^2 = e^{\sigma^2} - 1 \text{ and } G = 2N(\sigma/\sqrt{2}) - 1 \tag{7}$$

where N denotes the cumulative normal distribution with zero mean and unit variance. The relationship between σ and G is illustrated below:

$$\sigma = 0.1 \qquad G = 0.06$$
$$0.5 \qquad\qquad 0.28$$
$$1.0 \qquad\qquad 0.52$$
$$1.5 \qquad\qquad 0.71$$
$$2.0 \qquad\qquad 0.84$$

IX.5   Pearson family of distributions

The Pearson family is generated by the differential equation given in the text (chapter 8, equation 20):

$$\left[a_0 + a_1 K + a_2 K^2 \right] \frac{df}{dK} = \left[2(b_0 + b_1 K) - a_1 - 2a_2 K \right] f \tag{8}$$

The form of the distribution may be classified in terms of the characteristic

$$\kappa = \frac{a_1^2}{4a_0 a_2} \tag{9}$$

(see Ord 1972: 4; Elderton and Johnson 1969: 41; and Kendall and Stuart 1969: 151). Among the distributions (apart from the normal which emerges as a special case) are:

Type I (Beta distribution)   if $\kappa < 0$,

Type IV   if $0 < \kappa < 1$ (unimodal with unlimited range in both directions),

Type V   if $\kappa = 1$ (infinite range in one direction),

Type VI   if $\kappa > 1$ (infinite range in one direction, transformation $Z = c/w$ reduces it to Beta distribution),

Type III (Gamma distribution)   if $a_2 = 0$ ($\kappa \to \infty$).

The two referred to in the text (chapter 8) are described in more detail below.

IX.6   Pearson Type V distribution

This distribution is given by

$$f = C(w + a)^{-\alpha-1} e^{-\beta/(w+a)} \text{ for } w \geqslant -a \tag{10}$$

The mean wealth is $\beta/(\alpha - 1) - a$, and the mode $\beta/\alpha + 1$. For large w, it approaches the Pareto Type I. The coefficient of variation is given by:

$$V = \frac{\beta}{\beta - a(\alpha - 1)} (\alpha - 2)^{-\frac{1}{2}} \tag{11}$$

and is only finite for $\alpha > 2$.

IX.7   Gamma distribution

The distribution is given by

$$f = Cw^{\alpha-1} e^{-\beta w} \quad w \geqslant 0, \alpha > 0 \tag{12}$$

The mean wealth is α/β and the mode $(\alpha - 1)/\beta$. The distribution is J-shaped when $\alpha \leqslant 1$ and hump-shaped when $\alpha > 1$. The degree of concentration depends only on α and not on β, which is simply a scale parameter. This is illustrated by the coefficient of variation, which is given by $1/\sqrt{\alpha}$ (see Salem and Mount 1974).

REFERENCES

Aitchison, J. and Brown, J.A.C. (1957). *The lognormal distribution,* Cambridge University Press.

Astin, J.A. (1975). 'The distribution of wealth and the relevance of age', *Statistical News.*

Atkinson, A.B. (1971). 'The distribution of wealth and the individual life-cycle', *Oxford Economic Papers.*

(1972). *Unequal shares,* Allen Lane and Penguin.

(1974). 'A model of the distribution of wealth', Massachusetts Institute of Technology discussion paper.

(1975). 'The distribution of wealth in Britain in the 1960s – the estate duty method re-examined', in *Personal distribution of income and wealth* (ed. J.D. Smith), National Bureau of Economic Research, New York.

(1975a). *The economics of inequality,* Oxford University Press.

Atkinson, A.B. and Harrison A.J. (1974). 'Wealth distribution and investment income in Britain', *Review of Income and Wealth.*

(1975). 'Mortality multipliers and the estate duty method', *Bulletin of the Oxford Institute of Economics and Statistics.*

(1977). 'The distributic   ...ɔnal wealth', in *Sources and nature of the statistics of the UK* (ed. W.F. Maunder), Heinemann.

Bailey, A.H. (1908). Discussion of Mallet (1908).

Barna, T. (1945). *Redistribution of incomes 1937,* Oxford University Press.

Baxter, R.D. (1869). *The taxation of the United Kingdom,* Macmillan.

Beach, C.M. and Flatters, F. (1976). 'The size distribution of income: a theoretical survey', unpublished manuscript, Queen's University, Canada.

Becker, G.S. (1973). 'A theory of marriage: part I', *Journal of Political Economy.*

Bedford, N.M. and McKeown, J.C. (1972). 'Comparative analysis of net realisable value and replacement costing', *The Accounting Review.*

Blinder, A. (1973). 'A model of inherited wealth', *Quarterly Journal of Economics.*

Bosanquet, C.F.C (1968). 'Investment in agriculture', *Journal of Agricultural Economics.*

Bray, J.F.L. (1940). 'Small savings', *Economic Journal.*

Buse, A. (1976). 'Aggregation with the estate multiplier method', Research Paper 35, Department of Economics, University of Alberta.

Campion, H. (1939). *Public and private property in Great Britain,* Oxford University Press.

Cartter, A.M. (1953). 'A new method of relating British capital ownership and estate duty liability to income groups', *Economica.*

Champernowne, D.G. (1973). *The distribution of income between persons,* Cambridge University Press.

(1974). 'A comparison of measures of inequality of income distribution', *Economic Journal.*

Chesher, A.D. and McMahon, P.C. (1976). 'The distribution of personal wealth in Ireland – the evidence re-examined', *Economic and Social Review.*

318

Chipman, J.S. (1974). 'The welfare ranking of Pareto distributions', *Journal of Economic Theory.*

Clay, H. (1925). 'The distribution of capital in England and Wales', *Transactions of Manchester Statistical Society.*

Colwyn Committee on National Debt and Taxation (1927). *Report,* HMSO, London.

Committee to Review National Savings (1973). *Report,* HMSO, London.

Creedy, J. (1974). 'Páreto and his équation générale de la courbe des revenus', University of Reading Department of Economics Discussion Paper 66.

Crothers, C. (1975). 'Trends in the distribution of private wealth in New Zealand', unpublished paper, Department of Sociology and Social Work, Victoria University of Wellington.

Daniels, G.W. and Campion, H. (1936). *The distribution of national capital,* Manchester University Press.

Day, A. (1974). *Observer,* 22 September.

Easton, B. (1974). 'Personal wealth in New Zealand', unpublished manuscript.

Economist (1966). 'The indefensible status quo', 15 January.

Elderton, W.P. and Johnson, N.L. (1969). *Systems of frequency curves,* Cambridge University Press.

Emmerson, F.W. (1974). Appendix to Poduluk (1974).

Evans, A.W. (1975). *The five per cent sample of building society mortgages,* HMSO, London.

Feldstein, M.S. (1973). 'Tax incentives, corporate saving and capital accumulation in the United States', *Journal of Public Economics.*

Feller, W. (1968). *An introduction to probability theory and its applications,* volume 1, Wiley.

Ferber, R., Forsythe, J., Guthrie, H.W. and Maynes, E.S. (1969). 'Validation of a national survey of consumer financial characteristics: savings accounts', *Review of Economics and Statistics.*

(1969a). 'Validation of consumer financial characteristics: common stock', *Journal of the American Statistical Association.*

Fijalkowski-Bereday, G.Z. (1950). 'The equalizing effects of the death duties', *Oxford Economic Papers.*

Friedman, M. (1939). Discussion of Stewart (1939).

Gastwirth, J.L. (1972). 'The estimation of the Lorenz curve and Gini index', *Review of Economics and Statistics.*

(1974). 'Large sample theory of some measures of income inequality', *Econometrica.*

Giffen, Sir Robert (1913). *Statistics,* Macmillan.

Ginsburg, L. (1943). 'Industrial life assurance', in *Social Security* (ed. W.A. Robson), Allen and Unwin.

Glasser, G.J. (1962). 'Variance formulas for the mean difference and coefficient of concentration', *Journal of the American Statistical Association.*

Goodman, L.A. (1960). 'On the exact variance of products', *Journal of the American Statistical Association.*

Government Actuary (see Major data sources at end).

Hahn, F.H. (1973). *On the notion of equilibrium in economics,* Cambridge University Press.

Harris, W.J. and Lake, K.A. (1906). 'Estimates of the realisable wealth of the United Kingdom', *Journal of the Royal Statistical Society.*

Harrison, A.J. (1975). *The distribution of personal wealth in Scotland,* Fraser of Allander Institute Research Monograph No. 1.

(1976). 'Trends over time in the distribution of wealth', in *Economics and Equality* (ed. A. Jones), Philip Allan.

Harrison, M.J. (1976a). 'Comment', *Economic and Social Review.*

Harrison, M.J. and Nolan, S. (1975). 'The distribution of personal wealth in Ireland',
   Economic and Social Review.

Hill, T.P. (1955). 'Incomes, savings and net worth: the savings survey of 1952–1954',
   Bulletin of the Oxford University Institute of Statistics.

Hill, T.P., Klein, L.R. and Straw, K.H. (1955). 'The savings survey 1953: response rates
   and reliability of data', *Bulletin of the Oxford University Institute of Statistics.*

Hollingsworth, T.H. (1957). 'A demographic study of the British ducal families',
   Population Studies.

Horsman, E.G. (1975). 'The avoidance of estate duty by gifts *inter vivos:* some
   quantitative evidence', *Economic Journal.*

Ishikawa, T. (1975). 'Family structures and family values in the theory of income
   distribution', *Journal of Political Economy.*

Kaldor, N. (1966). 'Marginal productivity and the macro-economic theories of
   distribution', *Review of Economic Studies.*

Kendall, M.G. (1950). 'The statistical approach', *Economica.*

Kendall, M.G. and Stuart, A. (1969). *The advanced theory of statistics,* volume I, Griffin,
   London.

Klebba, A.J. (1970). 'Mortality from selected causes by marital status', *Vital and Health
   Statistics.*

Klein, L.R. and Vandome, P. (1957). 'Sampling errors in the savings surveys', *Bulletin of
   the Oxford Institute of Statistics.*

Lampman, R.J. (1962). *The share of top wealth-holders in national wealth, 1922–1956.*
   Princeton University Press.

Langley, K.M. (1950, 1951). 'The distribution of capital in private hands in 1936–1938
   and 1946–1947', *Bulletin of the Oxford University Institute of Statistics,* volumes
   12 and 13 (article in two parts).

   (1954). 'The distribution of private capital, 1950–1951', *Bulletin of the Oxford
   University Institute of Statistics.*

Lehmann, F. (1937). 'The distribution of wealth', in *Political and Economic Democracy*
   (ed. M. Ascoli and F. Lehmann), Norton.

Lydall, H.F. (1955). *British incomes and savings,* Basil Blackwell.

   (1959). 'The long-term trend in the size distribution of income', *Journal of the Royal
   Statistical Society.*

Lydall, H.F. and Lansing, J.B. (1959). 'A comparison of the distribution of personal
   income and wealth in the United States and Great Britain', *American Economic
   Review.*

Lydall, H.F. and Tipping, D.G. (1961). 'The distribution of personal wealth in Britain',
   Bulletin of Oxford University Institute of Economics and Statistics.

Lyons, P.M. (1972). 'The distribution of personal wealth in Northern Ireland', *Economic
   and Social Review.*

   (1974). 'The size distribution of personal wealth in the Republic of Ireland', *Review
   of Income and Wealth.*

   (1975). 'Estate duty wealth estimates and the mortality multiplier', *Economic and
   Social Review.*

Mallet, B. (1908). 'A method of estimating capital wealth from the estate duty statistics',
   Journal of the Royal Statistical Society.

Mallet, B. and Strutt, H.C. (1915). 'The multiplier and capital wealth', *Journal of the
   Royal Statistical Society.*

Mandelbrot, B. (1960). 'The Pareto–Lévy law and the distribution of income',
   International Economic Review.

Marshall, A. (1920). *Principles of Economics,* Macmillan.

Maurice, R. (1968). *National accounts, statistics, sources and methods,* HMSO, London.

Meacher, M. (1972). 'Wealth: Labour's Achilles Heel', in *Labour and Inequality* (ed. P. Townsend and N. Bosanquet), Fabian, London.

Meade, J.E. (1964). *Efficiency, equality and the ownership of property,* Allen and Unwin.

(1975). *The just economy,* Allen and Unwin.

Mendershausen, H. (1956). 'The pattern of estate tax wealth' in *A study of saving in the United States* (ed. R.W. Goldsmith), volume 3, Princeton University Press.

Merwin, C.L. (1939). 'American studies of the distribution of wealth and income', in *Studies in Income and Wealth,* volume 3, NBER, New York.

Morgan, E.V. (1960). *The structure of property ownership in Great Britain,* Oxford University Press.

(1975). *Personal savings and wealth in Britain,* Financial Times, London.

Morgan, E.V. and Taylor, C. (1957). 'The relationship between the size of joint stock companies and the yield of their shares', *Economica.*

Newman, P. and Wolfe, J.N. (1961). 'A model for the long-run theory of value', *Review of Economic Studies.*

Ord, J.K. (1972). *Families of frequency distributions,* Griffin.

Page Report (1973). See Committee to Review National Savings (1973).

Pasinetti, L.L. (1962). 'Rate of profit and income distribution in relation to the rate of economic growth', *Review of Economic Studies.*

Podder, N. and Kakwani, N.C. (1976). 'Distribution of wealth in Australia', *Review of Income and Wealth.*

Poduluk, J.R. (1974). 'Size distribution of personal wealth in Canada', *Review of Income and Wealth.*

Polanyi, G. and Wood, J.B. (1974). *How much inequality?,* Institute of Economic Affairs, London.

Prabhu, N.U. (1965). *Stochastic processes: basic theory and its applications,* Macmillan, New York.

Projector, D.S. and Weiss, G.S. (1966). *Survey of financial characteristics of consumers,* Board of Governors of the Federal Reserve System, USA.

Pryor, F.L. (1973). 'Simulation of the impact of social and economic institutions on the size distribution of income and wealth', *American Economic Review.*

Radice, E.A. (1939). *Savings in Great Britain,* Oxford Universtiy Press.

Registrar General for England and Wales (see Major data sources at end).

Revell, J.R.S. (1962). 'Assets and age', *Bulletin of the Oxford University Institute of Statistics.*

(1965). 'Changes in the social distribution of property in Britain during the twentieth century', *Actes du Troisième Congrès International d'Histoire Economique,* Munich.

(1967). *The wealth of the nation,* Cambridge University Press.

Revell, J.R.S. and Roe, A.R. (1971). 'National balance sheets and national accounting − a progress report', *Economic Trends.*

Revell, J.R.S. and Tomkins, C. (1974). *Personal Wealth and Finance in Wales,* Welsh Council.

Roe, A.R. (1971). *The financial interdependence of the economy, 1957−1966,* Chapman and Hall.

Royal Commission on the Distribution of Income and Wealth (1975), *Initial report on the standing reference,* HMSO, London.

(1975a), *Income from companies and its distribution,* Report No. 2, HMSO, London.

(1976), *Second report on the standing reference,* Report No. 4, HMSO, London.

Salem, A.B.Z. and Mount, T.D. (1974). 'A convenient descriptive model of income distribution: the gamma density', *Econometrica.*

Samuelson, P.A. (1973). *Economics,* McGraw-Hill, ninth edition.

Samuelson, P.A. and Modigliani, F. (1966). 'The Pasinetti paradox in neo-classical and more general models', *Review of Economic Studies.*

Sargan, J.D. (1957). 'The distribution of wealth', *Econometrica.*
  (1958). Unpublished paper presented at the Chicago Meeting of the Econometric Society.

Select Committee on Wealth Tax (1975). *Report and Memoranda of Evidence,* volumes I–III, HMSO, London.

Shorrocks, A.F. (1973). Thesis presented to the University of London.
  (1975). 'On stochastic models of size distributions', *Review of Economic Studies.*
  (1975a). 'The age-wealth relationship: a cross-section and cohort analysis', *Review of Economics and Statistics.*

Simons, H.C. (1938). *Personal income taxation,* University of Chicago Press.

Singh, A. and Whittington, G. (1968). *Growth, profitability and valuation,* Cambridge University Press.

Smith, J.D. (1974). 'The concentration of personal wealth in America 1969', *Review of Income and Wealth.*

Smith, J.D. and Franklin, S.D. (1974). 'The concentration of personal wealth, 1922–1969', *American Economic Review.*

Soltow, L. (1975). 'The wealth, income and social class of men in large northern cities of the United States in 1860', in *The personal distribution of income and wealth* (ed. J.D. Smith), NBER, New York.

Stamp, Lord (1916). *British incomes and property,* P.S. King and Sons, London.

Stark, T. (1972). *The distribution of personal income in the United Kingdom, 1949–1963,* Cambridge University Press.
  (1977). 'A survey of personal income statistics', in *Sources and Nature of the Statistics of the UK* (ed. W.F. Maunder) Heinemann.

Steindl, J. (1972). 'The distribution of wealth after a model of Wold and Whittle', *Review of Economic Studies.*

Stewart, C. (1939). 'Income capitalization as a method of estimating the distribution of wealth by size groups', in *Studies in income and wealth,* volume 3, NBER, New York.

Stiglitz, J.E. (1969). 'Distribution of income and wealth among individuals', *Econometrica.*

Straw, K.H. (1955). 'Consumers' net worth – the 1953 savings survey', *Bulletin of the Oxford University Institute of Statistics.*

Taussig, M.K. (1976). 'Wealth inequality in the United States', unpublished manuscript, Rutgers College.

Titmuss, R.M. (1962). *Income distribution and social change,* Allen and Unwin.

Townsend, P. (1977). *Poverty in the United Kingdom,* Allen Lane.

Tristram, T.H. and Coote, H. (1970). *Probate practice,* Butterworth.

Tsuji, M. (1972). 'A note on Professor Stiglitz' "distribution of income and wealth"', *Econometrica.*

Vaughan, R.N. (1975). Thesis presented to the University of Cambridge.

Wedgwood, J.C. (1929). *The economics of inheritance,* Routledge.

Whalley, J. (1974). 'Official estimates of the size distribution of wealth in Great Britain: some reservations', unpublished paper, LSE.

Wheatcroft, G.S.A. (1972). *Guide to the estate duty statutes,* Sweet and Maxwell.

Wold, H.O.A. and Whittle, P. (1957). 'A model explaining the Pareto law of wealth distribution', *Econometrica.*

Wolfson, M. (1977). Thesis presented to the University of Cambridge.

Wright, L.C. (1968). 'Personal wealth in Scotland and Great Britain', *Three Banks Review.*

MAJOR DATA SOURCES[1]

Official statistics (HMSO, London).
Central Statistical Office, *Annual Abstract of Statistics,* annual.
Central Statistical Office, *Financial Statistics,* monthly.
Central Statistical Office, *National Income and Expenditure,* annual.
Central Statistical Office, *Social Trends,* annual since 1970.
Department of Environment, *Housing and Construction Statistics,* quarterly.
Government Actuary, *Occupational Pension Schemes,* occasional.
Inland Revenue, *Annual Report of the Commissioners,* annual.
Inland Revenue, *Estimated Wealth of Individuals in Great Britain,* annual since 1973.
Inland Revenue, *Inland Revenue Statistics,* annual since 1970.
Inland Revenue, *Survey of Personal Incomes,* occasional.
Registrar General for England and Wales, *Decennial Supplement: Occupational Mortality,*
    appears (sometimes in several volumes) with delay after Census of Population.

Other sources
Fundex, *Unit Trust Yearbook,* annual.
Life Offices' Association, *Life Assurance in the United Kingdom,* annual.
London and Cambridge Economic Service, *Key Statistics,* occasional.
de Zoete and Bevan, *Equity and Fixed Interest Investment,* annual.

[1] Statistical sources are described in greater detail in Atkinson and Harrison (1977).

INDEX OF NAMES

SUBJECT INDEX

acceleration in trend in distribution,
141–2, 167–9
accumulating trusts, 93, 162
accumulation of wealth, 203–11, 221–3,
227
adjustments to estate data. *See* excluded
population, missing people,
missing wealth, valuation
administration of estates (small payments)
act 1965, *see also* estate duty,
36–7, 80, 90
adult population, definition of, 20, 126,
153–4
age and wealth-holding, 250–8
agricultural property, 39n
allocation of excess wealth, 85–9
asset composition, 83–5, 87, 115, 172,
175, 178–80
use of estate data in investment income
method, 193–4
asset prices, 122, 232, 238–40
asset valuation. *See* valuation
Australia, distribution of wealth, 15
averaging of estimates, 130
avoidance of estate duty. *See* estate duty
avoidance

balance sheet, national. *See* national
balance sheet
balance sheet, totals. *See* national balance
sheet totals
bank deposits, 91
bias in investment income method, 172–4,
198–9, Appendix VII
building society deposits, 91–2
buildings, *see also* houses, 99, 105, 112,
197
business assets, 43

Cambridge savings theory, 210–11
Canada, distribution of wealth, 14
capital gains, 175, 233–4
capital gains tax, 4, 32n, 114, 234n

capital holdings and income ranges, 12
capital transfer tax, *see also* estate duty, 7
capitalist class, 210–11
cash, 91
census of population, 27, 61–4, 125–6,
297
children, wealth of, 90, 92
coefficient of variation, 122–4, 172–3,
284–7
cohorts, distribution of wealth by, 255–8
committee to review national savings. *See*
Page Committee to Review National
Savings
company sector, 3, 266
company shares, *see also* share prices, 4, 95
yield on, 179, 182, 197
composition of net wealth holdings. *See*
asset composition
concentration, measures of, 122–4, 128,
Appendix IV
concentration ratio. *See* Gini coefficient
consumer durables, *see also* household
goods, 43, 158, 238
valuation of, for estate duty, 43
continuous mortality investigation, 69–70
control over the economy, 4
convergence to equilibrium, 207–8, 211,
217, 225–6
corrective adjustments to estate data, 33–4

debts. *See* liabilities
decennial supplement on occupational
mortality. *See* Registrar General's
Decennial Supplement on
Occupational Mortality
deficiencies in pre-1914 data. *See* pre-1914
data, deficiencies in
deficiency of investment income, 194
definition of wealth. *See* Wealth
diffusion equations, 222–4
discretionary trusts, 39–40, 93–4, 162
disequilibrium, behaviour of wealth models,
225–6